Rethinking Islamic Studies

Studies in Comparative Religion
Frederick M. Denny, Series Editor

Rethinking Islamic Studies

From Orientalism to Cosmopolitanism

Edited by

Carl W. Ernst and
Richard C. Martin

The University of South Carolina Press

Published by the University of South Carolina Press
Columbia, South Carolina 29208

www.sc.edu/uscpress

Manufactured in the United States of America

19 18 17 16 15 14 13 12 11 10
10 9 8 7 6 5 4 3 2 1

Library of Congress Cataloging-in-Publication Data
Rethinking Islamic studies : from orientalism to cosmopolitanism /
edited by Carl W. Ernst and Richard C. Martin.
      p. cm. — (Studies in comparative religion)
  Includes bibliographical references and index.
  ISBN 978-1-57003-892-1 (cloth : alk. paper) — ISBN 978-1-57003-893-8
(pbk : alk. paper)
  1. Islam—Study and teaching. 2. Orientalism. I. Ernst, Carl W.,
1950– II. Martin, Richard C.
  BP42.R48 2010
  297.09—dc22
                                        2009051152

Contents

Series Editor's Preface

Over the past four decades the rethinking of Islamic studies has encouraged the energetic cooperation and the engaged collaborative attention of scholars of Islam and religious studies in exciting and productive new ways. During that period the study of Islam and of Muslim peoples has increasingly merged with theory and method in religious studies, which itself has increasingly developed its discourses in interdisciplinary relation with the humanities and social sciences. *Rethinking Islamic Studies* is indeed, as editors Carl W. Ernst and Richard C. Martin assert, a collection of essays "envisaged as a generational sequel and advance upon" 1985's innovative and influential *Approaches to Islam in Religious Studies*, which was also edited by Martin.

The Studies in Comparative Religion series also published its first work in 1985. Nothing could be finer for the twenty-fifth anniversary of this scholarly series than a fresh array of essays on Islam and Muslims focusing on Islamic perspectives for rethinking modernity, on social scientific and humanistic perspectives for rethinking religion, and on Asian perspectives for rethinking the whole subject, as this book does. The collection ends with a stimulating and responsive essay by Bruce B. Lawrence, one of the most influential scholars in the rethinking of Islamic religious studies to date.

FREDERICK M. DENNY

Preface and Acknowledgments

The papers in this volume are part of a long-ranging project in the field of religious studies, with special reference to the study of Islam. We as editors look back on the last three decades as a period of extraordinary growth and creativity in this area. This period has been a liberating experience for us as scholars initially trained in narrowly textual "Orientalist" approaches, as we have been forced by circumstance to address many issues of contemporary political and social relevance, not to mention the numerous theoretical developments that have taken place in the humanities in recent years. While we still deeply appreciate the discipline of the philological study of medieval Islamic texts, we have also welcomed the opportunity to engage with interdisciplinary research, new social-scientific methodologies, and transregional approaches to Islamic studies in the contemporary world. This volume harks back to previous benchmarks in Islamic studies, going back to essays by Charles Adams from the late 1960s and early 1970s, and at the same time it charts new courses for future research.

In particular we recall the pathbreaking collection of papers edited by Richard C. Martin, *Approaches to Islam in Religious Studies* (Tucson: University of Arizona Press, 1985). That volume, based on a 1980 conference, signaled a major transition from unself-conscious forms of Oriental studies to a more reflexive application of religious studies approaches. The essays in the current volume are envisaged as a generational sequel and advance upon that earlier effort, taking full account of the critical developments in the understanding of Islam in recent years.

Earlier versions of these papers were presented in a symposium, "Islam in Theory and Practice," held at Duke University in January 2006. We would like to express our thanks to Emory University, Duke University, and the University of North Carolina at Chapel Hill for their support of our efforts. In particular it is a pleasure to thank Emory graduate students Abbas Barzegar and Anthony R. Byrd for their many valuable contributions to editing the papers in this volume in 2009. We are also grateful for the support of series editor Frederick Denny, acquisitions editor Jim Denton, and other staff at the University of South Carolina Press for their visionary support of this project. Finally we commend the efforts of all the contributors to this volume, which we hope will serve as a benchmark for the future development of Islamic studies.

The editors would like to dedicate their work on this volume to Bruce Lawrence and miriam cooke, for their continuing collegial inspiration, and to Charles Adams and Edward Said, for opening our eyes to the possibility of new directions in the study of Islam.

Carl W. Ernst and Richard C. Martin

✢

Introduction

Toward a Post-Orientalist Approach to Islamic Religious Studies

CARL W. ERNST AND
RICHARD C. MARTIN

The Immediate Context

Public interest in Islam has increased dramatically in the first decade of the twenty-first century. The evidence for this includes a new abundance in colleges and universities of faculty openings and curriculums that deal with the Islamic religious tradition. As a consequence Islamic studies as a field in departments of religion in North America has recently become more apparent than in the past— in the classroom, bookstores, professional societies, and conferences worldwide on Islamic topics. The reasons for this sudden surge of interest in Islam since September 11, 2001 by liberal arts deans, religious studies departments, and scholars worldwide require little explanation. As recently as the last decades of the twentieth century, however, interest in, and room for, curriculum on Islam and Muslims could be found in barely one-tenth of the approximately 1,200 academic departments of religious studies in North America. With the rapidly increasing demand for Islamic studies in the first decade of this century, when at least fifty academic positions for specialists in Islam in religious studies had been advertised annually until the collapse of the economy in 2008, there were not enough qualified candidates trained in religious studies who are also trained in Islamic studies.[1] Yet it was not so long ago that Islam did not even have a primary presence in the major professional society for faculty of religion, the American Academy of Religion (AAR). Indeed as recently as the middle of the twentieth century, Islam was included within the AAR's coverage of world religions at its annual meetings as a subunit of the "History of Christianity" section. Now "The Study of Islam" is a major program unit within the AAR, with many subsections and sessions cosponsored with other religious traditions. Was 9/11 the cause of all that?

Not entirely. While Islamic studies as a field has been powerfully affected by political events, debates within the academy have had a longer and more pervasive role in shaping, and sometimes ignoring, this area of inquiry, the trajectory of which we briefly sketch in this introduction. That trajectory over the past quarter century, we contend, has encouraged scholars to rethink how to theorize and problematize the textual and social data of Islam and how to adjust their investigations to methodologies that address the urgencies of Islamic studies in the twenty-first century.

Islam in Religious Studies Revisited

The short supply of expertise on Islam in religious studies has been observed and lamented for several decades. In an article titled "The History of Religions and the Study of Islam," Charles J. Adams concluded in 1967 that despite the ferment going on at the University of Chicago in comparative studies in the history of religions, it was difficult for him "to see a direct and fructifying relationship between the activities of Islamicists and those of historians of religion."[2] Adams further emphasized this problem in an identically titled companion article in 1974, written when he discovered that he was the only scholar to present a paper on Islam the previous year at the annual meeting of the AAR.[3] The scope of those essays was limited, but they presented a portrait of the institutional and disciplinary constraints that still result in conflicts and tensions between religious studies generally and the study of Islam as carried out by Orientalists and area studies specialists.[4] Until very recently departments of religion, including graduate programs, often looked to departments of Oriental studies and area studies programs to teach courses about Islam. Adams's paper can be seen as a kind of snapshot of that earlier time, which helps us to understand what has happened to the study of Islamic religion over the past thirty-five years.

The study of Islam has been, in effect, uneasily poised between Orientalism and area studies on the one hand and religious studies on the other. It is important to examine the implications of both area studies and religious studies, including critiques emerging within these fields, if scholars are to deal effectively with issues relating to Islam in the global public culture that is being formed today. Our contention is that a growing number of historians of religion specializing in Islam in the present critical moment are bridging and transforming these two traditions of scholarship—Orientalism and religious studies. They are pursuing Islamic studies within newer theoretical frameworks, such as critical theory and cosmopolitanism. The purpose of this volume is to demonstrate this claim and, in this introduction and in the essays that follow, to assess its implications.

Historically speaking, what we today call Islamic studies emerged from Orientalism, the erudite study of texts and ideas that became a highly developed field in the nineteenth and twentieth centuries in Europe and the United States. Albert Hourani published a thoughtful introduction to *Islam in European Thought* (1991), in which he sketched a nuanced intellectual history of European Orientalism. In the introduction Hourani stated that his purpose was to show the roots of the European tradition of Islamic studies about God, man, history, and society that lie at the heart of what we call "Orientalism." In particular he tried to show how the study of Islam, when it emerged as a separate focus of study in the nineteenth century, was given its direction by certain ideas that were current at the time: ideas about cultural history, the nature and development of religions, the ways in which sacred texts should be understood, and the relationships between languages.[5] Orientalism influenced many nineteenth-century intellectual trends, including the historical and literary criticism of the Bible.

In his usual lucid manner, Hourani was summoning academics in the emerging field of Islamic studies to reassess the achievements of scholars such as Ignaz Goldziher (1850–1921) without the polemics of the Orientalism debate. Hourani's Orientalists were academics rooted in different university, national, denominational, and theological backgrounds. His treatment of them brought out their individual achievements and failings. In Hourani's account they were shorn of the negative "Orientalist" stereotype in which they and their work tend to be lumped today. Hourani was of course responding to the highly influential work of Edward Said, another Christian Arab intellectual, whose critique of Orientalism has had far-reaching consequences in Middle Eastern area studies and Islamic studies but also in religious studies.

As Said noted in *Orientalism*,[6] Europe's earlier concept of the Orient corresponded to today's Islamic Middle East. His implicit suggestion that Orientalism should be extracted and banished from Middle Eastern studies is too well known to require extensive treatment here. Suffice it to say that it is not necessary to subscribe to all of Said's critical analyses, based in part on his reading of the postmodern writings of Michel Foucault, to acknowledge that there were issues of power and colonialism associated with the institutional aspect of Orientalist study. Often referred to as the founder of postcolonial studies and criticism, Said analyzed Orientalism not in terms of intellectual and social history, as Hourani was later to do, but rather through textual criticism of Orientalist writings. He was able to expose the false assumptions about Middle Eastern (Islamic) societies and the romanticism that was ascribed to them in Orientalist constructions. Said's was a bold and polemical project with many influences, ripples, and disturbances throughout the humanities and social sciences, especially in critical theory. It is interesting to note that after *Orientalism* was published in 1978, Said was invited by Hourani to be one of the few to present a paper on the occasion of the 1980 Levi della Vida Award, whose recipient that year was Hourani himself. Inevitably several critical ripostes to *Orientalism* have appeared since 1978. For example, *Reading Orientalism: Said and the Unsaid,* by Daniel M. Varisco (2007), is written from the point of view of what we will describe as post-Orientalist scholarship. Nonetheless Orientalism remains for most scholars the bête noire in the expanding family of Islamic studies today.

Middle East is more than a benign descriptive geographical term. It had been popularized by an American naval historian, Alfred T. Mahan, in 1902 to describe the sea lanes from Suez to Singapore as the crucial connector between the Near East and the Far East, at the high point of the British Empire. The term was later taken up as a geographical category by the Office of Strategic Services (precursor to the CIA) during World War II, having its main applicability during the cold war.[7] Both departments of Near Eastern studies[8] and Middle Eastern studies can be conveniently listed under the category of area studies rather than be construed as an academic discipline as such. Near Eastern studies departments typically include a large array of languages ranging from ancient cuneiform scripts to modern Hebrew and Arabic, with an enormous temporal range covering several discrete religions and civilizations. They do not offer a coherent intellectual program, since the specialists in these departments work on texts and languages that most of their colleagues cannot read. Departments of Middle East studies, which focus on the modern period, are supported in the United States by approximately eighteen federally funded National Resource Centers for Middle Eastern Studies (supported by the Title VI program in the U.S. Department of Education). These were created on the justification of the immediate relevance of the Middle East for security issues and policy users (during the 1960s and 1970s, study of languages such as Arabic and Persian was supported by the National Defense Foreign Language fellowship program, which sounded too suspicious for scholars to mention when doing research overseas). Most Middle East specialists are social scientists (historians, anthropologists, political scientists, sociologists) or experts in language and literature. The intellectual justification for Middle East centers and departments rests generally on the concept of an interdisciplinary approach to a given region.

The academic study of religion in Euro-America emerged over the last century, first in Protestant seminaries, then in Catholic and, eventually, in Jewish institutions. While academic departments of religious studies are frequently found in private universities with religious affiliations (some of which have divinity schools), since World War II public universities have established departments of religion as well. Religious studies has struggled to gain recognition as a humanities discipline in the face of opposition from both secularists and sectarians. This is not the place to attempt any kind of complete description of the development of religious studies. But it is important to note the expansion of departments of religious studies beyond the standard subjects of biblical studies and Protestant theology, with the inclusion of Catholic Christianity, Judaism, and the religions of Asia, Africa, and the Americas, particularly since the 1960s. The changes to religious studies have mirrored the growth of globalization.

Charles Adams had described the study of religion in his day mainly from a history of religions viewpoint, and he used the German term *Religionswissenschaft* to present its genealogy. In his view the field was primarily concerned with the phenomenology of religion as defined by Mircea Eliade (1907–1986) and other scholars at the University of Chicago. His critique of it began with the observation that departments of religion, when attempting to overcome their parochialism, generally preferred to concentrate on tribal religions or on Asian traditions such as Hinduism, Buddhism, or Far Eastern religions. He observed that there were then hardly any graduate programs in religious studies that included Islamic studies as a field. Area studies centers and departments, he maintained, generally considered religion to be a secondary subject of no major importance, which reflected the influence of secularization theory on the social sciences. In addition the publishing industry offered few books on Islam, in comparison with Eastern religions. Finally the bias toward archaic religions in the history of religions excluded historical and rational religions such as Islam. The result was a situation of impoverishment, in which the history of religions had failed seriously to engage with a major world-historical civilization. While the field of religious studies has expanded considerably in both scope and method since 1974, we feel that Adams's observations about the isolation of Islamic studies from religious studies still in part holds true, but that Islamic studies is currently in the process of change, as the papers in this volume document.

To counter the situation as he saw it, Adams proposed a stern remedy: what was needed was "old-fashioned historical, literary, and philological studies directed to the Islamic tradition, the mastery of linguistic tools, and the study of an enormous textual tradition."[9] This immersion was unavoidable, he argued, because highlighting the general and the comparative would necessarily make the study of Islam superficial. From today's perspective Adams's point of view, which now seems odd outside the context of the time in which he wrote, seemed to amount to a reassertion of some aspects of Orientalism. However, there were a number of items missing from his description of Islamic and religious studies that would definitely be needed today. For example he makes no mention of the reactions of Muslims to Euro-American scholarship (although he does in a later statement), or to their participation in it. His discussion of Islamic studies does not consider the impact of having Muslim students in the classroom. Nor is there any reflection on the scholars' own precommitments. He does not discuss the massive stereotypes of Islam relating to terrorism, violence, oppression of women, and so forth. He makes little mention of recent history, particularly European colonialism, modernity, and fundamentalism. Furthermore he does not refer at all to the role of the media and popular culture presentations in establishing the image of Islam today. And of course the more recent phenomena of post-structuralism, deconstructive literary criticism, feminist and gender studies, post-colonial discourse, and the critique of Orientalism itself were all to influence scholarship over the decades after Adams's original essays. These more recent concerns of Islamic and religious studies vibrate throughout the present work.

In what ways, and to what extent, have these interdisciplinary concerns of religious studies influenced Islamic studies? What Adams, Wilfred Cantwell Smith, William Montgomery Watt, and other Islamicist historians of religion did achieve was to lay the foundations for a bridge from Orientalism to religious studies, across which the next generation of scholars would travel with greater ease. Thus a growing interest in Islam has slowly arrived in religion departments during the past four decades (recall that this field is still represented in only slightly more than about 10 percent of all departments in North America). However, the growth of Islamic studies has demonstrated greater sensitivity to issues of modernity, politics, and gender and to newer methods and theories of investigating social and written texts, which were missing when Adams voiced his skepticism about the history of religions. How did this change come about?

Three decades prior to the publication of the present book, a pioneering attempt was made to address the problem of the absence of Islamic studies in religious studies scholarship and curricula. The year was 1980, which, significantly, coincided with the immediate aftermath of the Iranian Revolution and the taking of American hostages in Tehran, although those events were to occur after the symposium had been planned and organized; it was also two years after the publication of Said's *Orientalism.* The International Symposium on Islam and the History of Religions, funded by the National Endowment for the Humanities, was convened at Arizona State University. Fifteen scholars were invited to present papers on the application of theories and methodologies in the humanities and social sciences to the Islamic fields of data in which they conducted research. Specialists in Islamic pilgrimage, Muhammad's biography, conversion to Islam, Qur'anic and scriptural studies, and other topics in comparative religions presented their findings. The symposium invitation encouraged these specialists in Islamic studies to address their work to new contexts, where their conversation partners would increasingly be specialists in Asian, African, European, American, and other religions, along with comparativists who were specialists in hermeneutics (interpretation) theory, ritual studies, gender issues, conversion, religion and conflict, and related approaches. In 1985 several of the papers presented at the symposium were edited and published in a volume titled *Approaches to Islam in Religious Studies.*[10] In a foreword to the volume, Adams reassessed his earlier assessment and concluded: "The conventional wisdom, to which I have added my own voice in the past, has been that historians of religions have failed to advance our knowledge and understanding of Islam as religion and that Islam[ic]ists have failed to explain adequately Islamic religious phenomena. The third factor—increasing Muslim sensitivity to Islamic studies in the West—far from resolving the issue of how to approach the study of Islam as religion to the satisfaction of either religionists or Islam[ic]ists, has created still more strident divisions."[11]

We noted that some of Adams's insights, such as those just quoted, have seemingly endured. Today foundational questions in the study of Islam, such as the origin of the Qur'anic text or the development of exegetical genres, usually take place in area studies or Near or Middle East studies programs, whereas the anthropological inquiry of Islamic ritual, such as the performance of pilgrimage or the performance of religious identity, for that matter, are often also explored in religious studies departments. Graduate institutions where students can train both in Middle East studies and religious studies are still limited in number.

Nevertheless *Approaches to Islam* was just a beginning. Its twelve chapters left much of Islamic religious history, rituals and practices, theology, and textual studies for others to approach by applying current methods and theories in comparative studies. The current volume revisits the impetus behind the project begun at Arizona State University nearly thirty years ago, taking stock of the progress made since then and moving the agenda forward for the twenty-first century. To accomplish this we have assembled fourteen articles that illustrate the paradigm shift in the new Islamic studies. To provide a link with the Arizona State symposium, we have invited a response from one of the participants in that event, Bruce B. Lawrence, who comments in an afterword on recent achievements in, and future challenges to, scholarship on Islamic religion in light of the papers that appear in this work.

The participants in the Arizona State symposium included a number of senior Islamicists, such as Adams (McGill University), James Kritzeck (Notre Dame University), Jacques Waardenburg (University of the Utrecht), Muhammad Abd al-Rauf (director of the Islamic Center in Washington, D.C.), and Richard Frank (Catholic University of America). Several younger scholars, such as Lawrence, who were to build careers in the field of Islamic studies also attended and read papers, including William Graham (Harvard University), Marilyn Waldman (Ohio State University), Frederick Denny (University of Colorado), Richard Eaton (University of Arizona), and Andrew Rippen (University of Calgary). The symposium and the subsequent volume, *Approaches to Islam in Religious Studies*, marked an occasion for younger scholars eager to build a new field of study in conversation with senior colleagues who were in sympathy with the vision of a vital emerging field of Islamic studies but who had established their careers in the era of Orientalism. The essays that follow in the present volume in many ways echo the significance of *Approaches* by also bringing together senior scholars who, in this present case, began their careers in the 1980s with younger scholars now beginning to work within the new field of Islamic studies. Much that was left unsaid and undiscussed in *Approaches to Islam* finds expression in the essays in this collection, an indication that the field is growing and changing with the times.

Toward a Post-Orientalist Islamic Studies

The heirs to the 1980 symposium writing in this volume have continued the project of incorporating within the discourses of religious studies the expertise of the past three decades of Islamic studies. In so doing they continue the transformation of the subject matter of Orientalism with theories and methods more common in contemporary scholarship. In *Approaches to Islam in Religious Studies* (1985), the works of anthropologists such as Max Weber, Jack Goody, Victor Turner, and especially Clifford Geertz were particularly in evidence in the arguments and footnotes of several chapters. In the essays of the present collection, many of the approaches and presuppositions of that earlier generation of scholars have been replaced or enhanced by newer, different, and sometimes contending ideas. In these pages the reader will find frequent reference, direct and indirect, to the ideas of historians Marshall Hodgson and Peter Brown, anthropologist Talal Asad, sociologists Pierre Bourdieu and Bryan Turner, and philosophers Michel Foucault, Charles Taylor, Alasdair MacIntyre, and Kwame Anthony Appiah, among others. This intellectual trajectory exemplifies the type of engagement that is required in the contemporary context. These essays may serve as an indication of what may be called a post-Orientalist approach to Islamic studies, an approach or cluster of approaches that includes the study of foundational texts but that insists upon connecting them to the questions and debates of contemporary scholarship across disciplines and regions.

A historian who has had considerable influence on contributors to the present volume is Marshall G. S. Hodgson. His posthumously published three-volume *Venture of Islam* resituated historical analysis of the formation of the Islamic tradition from pre-Islamic Arabia to the broader historical and cultural *oikoumene* of West Asia and Africa, "from the Nile to the Oxus."[12] Hodgson contended that the significance of Islam in world history was much more than that of a distinctly new religious tradition among others in Asia, Africa, and eventually in Europe and the Americas. It was also a civilization inclusive of other religious, ethnic, and political communities, for which he coined a new term of art, *Islamicate.* He defined *Islamicate* as something that "would refer not directly to the religion, Islam, itself, but to the social and cultural complex historically associated with Islam and the Muslims, both among Muslims themselves and even when found among non-Muslims."[13] This terminological reconceptualization has induced scholars to give more focused analysis to the impact of Islamic styles of thinking, discourse, moral and social interaction, and the like within what

Garth Fowden has termed the historic evolution among Middle Eastern religions in late antiquity "from empire to commonwealth."[14] Louis A. Ruprecht Jr. and Lawrence both give explicit reference to Hodgson's world-historical approach to Islamic studies, and to religious studies more generally, over the past quarter of a century.

Another influence at work in Islamic studies today is the critical-theory approach of anthropologist Talal Asad. Asad shares with Hodgson the belief that approaches to Islamic studies by the middle to late twentieth century were still deeply Eurocentric; Asad's criticism has seeped into the criticism of the study of Islam among a growing number of scholars in religious studies more generally. The fundamental insight of his critique of Orientalist and history of religions approaches to the study of Islam is his charge that the eighteenth-century Enlightenment was the fountainhead of academic conceptualizations of religion as well as secular matters. In Asad's view religion and the secular are mutually implicated in Western post-Enlightenment scholarship on religion; each finds its raison d'être in relation to its opposition to the other.[15] This conceit of modern scholarship, Asad reasoned, did not apply equally well to the religions of Asia, especially Islam, among whom the understanding of religion was not a product of Western understandings of modernity. In constructing his anthropology of Islam,[16] he argued forcefully that Muslim societies must be understood on their own terms and not a superimposed Western model. In 1993 Asad essayed his critique of post-Enlightenment approaches to the study of religion in *Genealogies of Religion: Discipline and Reasons of Power in Christianity and Islam*.[17] The subtitle indicates his intellectual heritage, traceable to Said and, before him, Foucault.

René Girard's books and essays on the association of religion with violence have stimulated discussion among some contemporary historians of religion. Using older concepts drawn from Continental phenomenology, Girard posits that at the root of the sacred is primordial violence caused by "mimetic desire." Religion arises out of and seeks to resolve primordial social violence *ab origine*.[18] The association of violence with religion has become a major concern of contemporary scholarship, and it is reflected in the writings of several authors in this volume. Asad and other scholars of religion writing in the post-9/11 moment have located the focus of understanding Christianity and Islam in the concept of power. Asad's articulation of the importance of this conceptual centerpiece in the study of religions is found in virtually all of his books and interviews.[19] The implications of Asad's contribution to contemporary Islamic studies in his discussions of religion in relation to the state and holders of power is discussed in this volume in the essay coauthored by Richard C. Martin and Abbas Barzegar and in Bruce Lawrence's afterword.

Beyond critical theory another philosophical influence on Asad reflected in this volume, especially in the papers by Vincent Cornell and Louis Ruprecht, is the work of Alasdair MacIntyre. Appearing just a few years following Said's *Orientalism*, MacIntyre's *After Virtue: A Study of Moral Theory* (1981) mounted a critique of post-Enlightenment constructions of rationalism and ethics.[20] Tracing the failure of post-Enlightenment humanistic disciplines to the Kantian rejection of Aristotelianism, MacIntyre sought remedy in the concepts of practice and tradition. If the authority of religion in human life was dismantled by the Enlightenment, then what reason, MacIntyre asked, do modern humans have for acting humanely and morally? The answer he found in religious and social practices of the premodern world, still working, and indeed thriving, in post-Enlightenment societies. In the first essay, Cornell deploys MacIntyre's notion of an "epistemological crisis" occasioned by a tradition's failure to explain and guide contemporary society by its classical system in order to understand critical responses of Sayyid Qutb and Osama bin Laden to Western modernity.

Still another influential philosopher in contemporary religious studies is Charles Taylor, who, like Asad and MacIntyre, has wrestled with the problematic of the first section of this collection, the encounter of religious traditions with modernity. Taylor's project at first appears to be diametrically opposed to that of MacIntyre, insofar as Taylor has sought to articulate a philosophy of modernity that builds upon the liberal moral philosophies of John Stuart Mill and John Rawls; like MacIntyre, however, Taylor is amenable to the claims of religious traditions upon the consciences of modern humans, that is, he wants to find a place for such claims for those living under the conditions of modernity. In one of his shorter but nonetheless influential works, *Multiculturalism*, Taylor tackles the contemporary post-Enlightenment condition of how Western moderns should relate to cultures and traditions of reasoning beyond modern Euro-America. It is here that he addresses a central problem of particular importance for contemporary scholars in Islamic and religious studies: how to reason with Muslim and other non-Western intellectuals in the inevitable global encounter of cultural traditions—especially acute in the twenty-first century. In this sense his project goes beyond that of Asad and critical theorists more generally by imagining the conditions under which the differences among cultural (religious) identities would not keep one tradition from recognizing and appreciating others. The title of his lead essay in *Multiculturalism* is "The Politics of Recognition." His categories dwell particularly on religion, gender, sexuality, nationalism, race, and ethnicity. "A number of strands in contemporary politics," he tells us, "turn on the need, sometimes the demand, for recognition. . . . The demand comes to the fore in a number of ways in today's politics, on behalf of minority or 'subaltern' groups, in some forms of feminism, and in what is today called the politics of 'multiculturalism.'"[21]

Taylor's multicultural approach is framed, however, as we have noted, by his avowed Western, liberal, post-Enlightenment horizon of understanding. The debate about multiculturalism comes from intellectuals who have recently come to reappreciate the Stoic notion of "cosmopolitanism." In a riposte to Taylor in the third edition of *Multiculturalism*, Kwame Anthony Appiah charges that his multiculturalism places too much emphasis on broad categories of social identity (race, religion, sexuality, and so forth) and pays little attention to more personal elements of identity that account, Appiah suggests, for conflicts and social movements within those broader social identities. What constitutes who we are and our personal differences (identities) as members of a religious tradition, gender, class, or ethnic group? Those scholars in this volume who lean more toward cosmopolitanism (see the essays by Ewing and Ruprecht) find greater explanatory power in Appiah's approach, but with some reservations. As David A. Hollinger asserts, "Multiculturalism is a prodigious movement, but its limitations are increasingly apparent. It has not provided an orientation toward cultural diversity strong enough to process the current conflicts and convergences that make the problem of boundaries more acute than ever."[22] It is "the current conflicts" that occupy much of the attention of scholars in religious studies today.

One of the most profound effects on the practices of scholars in Islamic studies and other Islam experts for the past three decades has been the dramatic increase in religious groups advocating violence, often justified by explicitly stated theological warrants. The problem of religion and violence essayed by Girard and others has become "Islam and violence" and has seemed to fall in the laps of scholars of Islam to explain to a demanding, sometimes frightened, often confused, and occasionally angry public. Within the academy one approach to the explanation and interpretation of groups such al Qaeda was the claim that they operated outside the borders of normative Islam, and anyway represented only a small percentage of the global Muslim population. This approach was endorsed by no less than President George W. Bush, who, in a speech delivered on September 17, 2001, at the Islamic Center of Washington, D.C., added a new element to the "it's not really Islamic" explanation when he assured his immediate audience and the American people more generally: "The face of terror is not the true faith of Islam. That's not what Islam is all about. Islam is peace. These terrorists don't represent peace. They represent evil and war."[23] Invoking "evil" to explain the meaning of violent acts sanctioned by religious justifications finds more consanguinity within theological studies than in the social sciences. In the humanities, and in theological studies in particular, there has been a greater ambivalence about the ontological status of good and evil and about what deserves to labeled "evil."

Within religious studies Bruce Lawrence has attempted to counter the wholesale association of Islam with violence and evil.[24] Lawrence has demonstrated the compelling power of the media to bombard audiences with images of Muslims linked to violence, and he has problematized the general Western view of

Islam as a unified body of believers, ideas, and practices that lack a history of values shared with the West; what has been missing in Western understandings of Islam, in Lawrence's view, is reference to the experience of colonialism and postcolonial struggles. Another approach to understanding movements such as al Qaeda and Lashkar-e Taiba, developed in sociology and political science, is that advocated by Charles Kurzman and Ijlal Naqvi in their essay. Kurzman and others construe al Qaeda and other fundamentalist groups as social movements or social movement organizations (SMOs). Quintan Wiktorowicz, in his "The Salafi Movement: Violence and the Fragmentation of Community," writes: "SMOs are seen as viable and enduring crucibles for contention, capable of collectivizing what might otherwise remain individualized grievances and ideological orientations. They provide formal institutionalization, leadership, mobilizing structures, and a division of labor through bureaucratic organization."[25] Wiktorowicz analyzes how the Salafi Islamist movement divides into two contending movements, the jihadists who advocate violence and the reformists who do not, and how they fit the patterns of social movement organizations globally beyond Muslim societies. By combining the study of the historical background and origins of groups such as al Qaeda with theoretical analysis of social movement organizations, Islamic studies is in a position to explain and interpret violent religious social movements in Muslim societies without reference to metaphysical notions of evil and evildoers.

We now turn to highlight further the influence of one historian of religion in particular upon the new religious discourse on Islam. The writings of Bruce Lawrence have contributed significantly to the field of Islamic religious studies, but at same time he has brought the theoretical discourses of the humanities and social sciences into critical review and productive dialogue with the Islamic tradition and Muslim subject.[26] Lawrence was among those who, as a young professor from Duke University, participated in the discussions and interventions at the 1980 symposium. As much as any other person present at that conference, Lawrence has through his subsequent writing and teaching led the way in exploring further what the symposium had set out to do—to encourage the development of a new subfield that is fully integrated with religious studies. The intellectual evolution of a scholar such as Lawrence since 1980 typifies the changes that have taken place in the field in general, and we consider him here as an example that demonstrates the new perspectives that many have come to embrace. Of particular importance to the project of this volume was his 1989 theoretical demonstration that modernity and its attendant ideologies of modernism form the contexts in which religious fundamentalism—another product of modernity— must be understood as the "countertext."[27] In *Defenders of God* and increasingly in his writing on Islam since 1989, Lawrence has engaged the notable works of Hodgson, Asad, and others outside of Islamic studies—challenging, negotiating with, and using their arguments to theorize Islamic data within religious studies. It is a hallmark of his approach that an erudite understanding of Islam can also work conversely to influence theory in the humanities and social sciences. Whereas Orientalism and even area studies still today accept the languages and history of the Middle East and other religions of the Muslim world as sufficient resources for understanding Islam, Lawrence's comparative approach to understanding religious phenomena across traditions makes Islamic studies more intelligible within the discourses of religious studies.

Like most of the senior scholars active today, Lawrence was trained essentially as a medievalist, tracking the questions highlighted by scholars of the previous generation (such as his Yale mentor, Franz Rosenthal), who were comfortable describing themselves as philologists and Orientalists. We would argue that the best of post-Orientalist scholarship in Islamic studies is based on solid training in the languages, texts, and history of premodern Islam, such as Lawrence received, as a necessary basis for discourse about Islam and Muslims today. There is a distinct difference in quality and explanatory power between Lawrence's several books on fundamentalism and modern Islam on the one hand and the growing number of works by reporters, public policy specialists, and others now regarded by the general public as experts on Islam, for whom Islamic history would seem to have begun with the Iranian Revolution or even as late as September 11, 2001. This quality of bringing critical and theoretical tools to the analysis of Islam and of Muslim societies, and the data of Islamic studies to critical and theoretical tools, is once again demonstrated in Lawrence's afterword to the present collection, and it is echoed throughout the essays that precede it.

The Present Situation

Despite the evolution of post-Orientalist approaches to the study of Islam in religious studies since the 1980s, as exemplified in the work of scholars such as Lawrence, some problems remain. Although we are now moving past the 10 percent mark for representing Islam in departments of religious studies, job descriptions in vacancy announcements still tend to focus narrowly on expertise in classical languages and texts. That is, very frequently a job in Islamic studies is defined exclusively as the study of classical Arabic texts such as the Qur'an and the foundational texts of Islamic law. While such works remain in our view as very important, an exclusive focus upon them leaves out an enormous amount of premodern Islamic civilization, not to speak of the traumas of the colonial era and the dramas of the contemporary age. Would it not be strange if academic positions in the history of Christianity were still exclusively defined in terms of the study of the New Testament Greek text, ignoring the vast spectrum of Christian thought and practice from the church fathers to Aquinas, the Reformation, and popular interpretations in our own day? Yet in dealing with Islam, it is somehow convenient to gloss over the need to document and trace multiple varieties and regional variations of Islamic religiosity in later and recent history.

One consequence of continuing to define vacant and new positions in Islamic studies in terms of the structure of the field in the heyday of Orientalism is that many among the current generation of graduate students (and their mentors) seem ready to believe that the study of Arabic legal and exegetical texts from the eighth to the twelfth centuries is sufficient to define Islamic civilization in a normative sense, without feeling the need to refer to the questions of contemporary scholarship and methodology. This exclusive focus on seminal foundational texts as such, without explaining their significance in living situations of the Muslim world, may be a vestige of, and be compared to, the "great works" approach to the history of religions that characterized nineteenth-century studies of world history, as suggested by the analysis of Albert Hourani. Such an attitude would have the unfortunate effect of keeping Islamic studies in an intellectual ghetto of philological specialization that remains impenetrable to outsiders. In this sense the problematic presented to scholars at the 1980 Arizona State symposium must still be posed to younger scholars, Muslim and non-Muslim: *By what methods and theories will you explain and interpret Islamic social and textual data to other scholars in religious and in cultural studies who are not specialists in your field?* Moreover, why should the study of other historically important (if not outright dominant) Islamic discourses such as Sufism, Shiʿism, philosophy, poetry, ethics, and history be ignored or dismissed in an effort to maintain an old, some might say "Orientalist," criterion of what is authentic or normative?

Fortunately the dialogic character of academic life in North American colleges and universities does not permit narrowly trained scholars to remain in their shells forever, as they find themselves surrounded by an interdisciplinary range of scholars outside their field to challenge them to think in new and interesting ways. In addition it seems to be the case that the most progressive academic programs in Islamic studies have integrated comparative and theoretical studies of religion into their curriculums. Nevertheless we feel that those academic graduate programs that still ignore—or even worse, resist—engagement with the theoretical and comparative questions of Islamic and religious studies are doing a severe disservice to their students and to the future of the discipline.

The essays contained in this volume, in contrast, are offered to exemplify and encourage the wider approach of the new, post-Orientalist Islamic studies. The authors of these articles are scholars at different stages of their careers; they focus on different texts, methodologies, and regions. However, they share the commitment to engage knowledge of the larger Islamic tradition with the tools of modern academic discourse in order to bring Islamic studies out of the ghetto of academic isolation, relying increasingly on newer approaches to the study of religion in the twenty-first century. We hope that the result of this project will be to encourage a larger conversation in religious studies that will include partisans of all forms of scholarship on Islam.

A Glance Ahead

The essays in this volume are gathered in three separate sections, each of which addresses a critical topic that requires rethinking in order to fulfill the goals of post-Orientalist Islamic studies. The three topics revisited by our authors are Islamic perspectives on modernity, social scientific and humanistic perspectives on religion, and Asian perspectives on the Muslim subject. We have chosen these categories to highlight the contemporary significance of the Islamic tradition, the interdisciplinary approaches that are increasingly required in religious studies, and the specifically regional and local factors and histories that govern the positioning of Muslims as subjects in particular contexts. In the afterword Lawrence reviews each of the essays in light of some central themes of the volume, such as cosmopolitanism.

Modernity, addressed in part 1 and indeed throughout the entire book, is one of the most pervasive and yet widely debated topics encountered in scholarship on religion today, to which we have already made reference above. The slipperiness of its definition paradoxically clashes with its omnipresence as a marker of current temporal awareness. In terms of our subject, however, it probably goes without saying that modernity has been defined as an intrinsic characteristic of the civilization and culture of Europe and the United States; put in somewhat different terms, modernity is seen as a direct product of the Enlightenment. A corollary of this perspective is the customary expectation that Muslim societies are by definition excluded from that modernity, despite their having been on the receiving end of the Enlightenment through widespread colonization beginning in the late eighteenth century. During the colonial period, while the so-called West was assumed to be scientific, enlightened, and powerful, the Islamic Orient was backward, superstitious, and effeminate. The relics of this mentality are still present in academe and undoubtedly contribute to the dangerously reductive "clash of civilizations" narrative brought on by Samuel P. Huntington's infamous 1993 article with that title.[28]

In part 1 Cornell, drawing on MacIntyre and Rawls, reflects on the "epistemological crisis" of Muslim intellectuals who have not yet thoroughly analyzed the principles of Islamic tradition in terms relevant today; he argues for the need to attain an "overlapping consensus" on issues such as democracy and human rights, much as was done in an earlier age when Muslim thinkers internalized the language and conceptual apparatus of Greek philosophy. More optimistically Omid Safi draws attention to the vigorous reform movement in Iran, to its insistence on applying independent reasoning (*ijtihad*) to issues of fundamental religious principle, and he suggests that progressive Muslims in North America could benefit from this powerful intellectual demonstration. Katherine Pratt Ewing comments on the way in which Turkish Islamists in Germany embrace scientific perspectives as an unself-conscious part of their own modern identity. Some modern Muslim negotiations with the age of colonialism have ended up absorbing European categories and styles of thinking so thoroughly that they have become second nature. This is the case, according to Cornell, with the widespread Muslim adoption of nineteenth-century definitions of culture as an absolute, which have been neatly turned around in the form of Occidentalist stereotypes about the culture of "the West." Likewise A. Kevin Reinhart maintains that Salafi and neo-Salafi movements have a mythical view of uncontextualized scripture that owes much to the Protestantism that Arabs experienced in the form of Christian missions. Jamillah Karim points out that African American Muslim women use the concept of culture to relativize and dismiss the claims of Arab and Asian Muslim women that they represent "true" Islam. Inevitable shifts in globalizing societies mean that religion is no longer the simple practice of everyday life, but a choice and a commitment that illustrates individual belief; Reinhart makes this point with regard to the practice of reading texts, but it equally applies to choices of gender roles, as demonstrated by Ewing and Karim.

Part 2 addresses the volatile character of religious identity through different disciplines and methods. Charles Kurzman and Ijlal Naqvi present a strongly data-based social science as the method for correction of bias in the understanding of religious movements. David Gilmartin comments on social science not as a purely scholarly method, but as an authoritative framework appealed to by the organs of the state for defining national folklore and identity. Richard C. Martin and Abbas Barzegar apply the humanities discipline of religious studies in a comparative fashion as a tool for exploring the intellectual history of Islam, while Louis Ruprecht draws on intellectual history to reconsider the character of culture and identity on a global scale. Gilmartin shows how in Pakistan Sufism has been defined in one way by the Auqaf Department (ministry of charitable trusts) in terms of pietistic exemplary lives, while in contrast the Institute of Folk Heritage considers Sufism as the voice of popular culture. Martin and Barzegar propose a concept of Islamic orthodoxy defined by changing sources of power. According to Ruprecht even the discipline of comparative religion should be seen in parallel to dominant features of modernity, including the museum, national identity, and Romanticism.

Part 3 turns to the analysis of the subject from the perspective of Muslim societies in Asia. Tony K. Stewart and Scott Kugle both discuss the formation of sacred biography in South Asian Sufism. They overlap in using the example of the prominent Chishti master Nizam al-Din Awliya (d. 1325), but their different approaches illustrate widely varying possibilities in the deployment of interpretive strategies. Stewart focuses on the role of community memory and the model of piety that makes a community ideal out of an individual life story, arguing that it is the religious ideal that forms the real subject of hagiography. Kugle, in contrast, brings out the role of poetry that depicts powerful homo-erotic features in the relationship between Nizam al-Din and his poet-disciple Amir Khusro.

Ebrahim Moosa and Carl W. Ernst examine different theaters for the appli-cation of ethics in Muslim societies. Moosa introduces the prominent leader of the Deoband seminary in India, Qari Muhammad Tayyab, who philosophically reflected on the Hanafi legal tradition in search of ethical universals. Ernst in-vestigates the program of Malaysian prime minister Abdullah Badawi, who has introduced the formula of "civilizational Islam" (*Islam hadhari*) to encourage development and pluralism while fending off the Islamist opposition. Tayyab and Badawi both struggled to implement the ethical concept of "objectives of the Shari'a" and to make proper use of *ijtihad* in ways that address the distinc-tive character of the contemporary era. Both Ernst and Moosa point out the inherent problems in attempts to streamline Shari'a as policy, whether in the name of fundamentalism or the nation-state, since neither is exempt from ques-tioning on ethical grounds.

In the final chapter, Lawrence draws out several of the themes in this volume, which he introduces in relation to voices heard (Fazlur Rahman) and not heard (Marshall Hodgson) in the 1985 *Approaches to Islam in Religious Studies* and its prior symposium. Both Rahman and Hodgson, Lawrence points out, asked the question that was prescient of the postcolonial and subaltern studies that were soon to emerge: "To what extent do scholars have to declare their precommit-ments, not just religious ones but also scholarly?" One such lingering scholarly precondition, as Talal Asad has persuasively argued, is the force, often hidden and subconscious, of Judeo-Christian prejudgments. Lawrence also identifies for further discussion the problem of the contemporary relation of the orthodox to emerging popular expressions of Islam, and how Muslims are dealing with transnational communications systems that feature, and reconstruct, Islam and Muslims themselves.

Closing Word

The essays that follow in this volume overlap considerably in the topics and categories they consider to be important for the study of Islam today, although they demonstrate a healthy independence of judgment and a willingness to argue and theorize in terms of evidential examples. They demonstrate the his-torical depth and familiarity with the textual traditions of premodern Muslim thought, which are indispensable in the appreciation of contemporary Islam, and indeed are explicitly invoked in writings of modern-day Muslim thinkers. They also apply a wide range of research methodologies reflecting the multi- and interdisciplinary character of post-Orientalist Islamic studies as they probe the characteristic problems that have to be considered, particularly ideology, gender, and the nation-state. In short we believe the following pages indicate the continuing maturation of the field of Islamic studies over the past few decades, and the importance, now more than ever, of integrating it into the wider discipline of religious studies. We hope these essays will encourage debate surrounding the issues they raise and contribute to a continued process of rethinking Islamic studies in light of post-Orientalist discourses.

NOTES

1. The shortage of specialists in Islamic studies and the high demand for the subject means that frequently non-Islamicists are called upon to teach basic courses in the study of Islam. This situation was one of the reasons for the compilation of a volume of essays titled *Teaching Islam*, ed. Brannon Wheeler (Oxford: Oxford University Press, 2002), in the Teaching Religious Studies Series sponsored by the American Academy of Religion.

2. Charles J. Adams, "The History of Religions and the Study of Islam," in *The History of Religions: Essays on the Problem of Understanding*, ed. Joseph M. Kitagawa with Mircea Eliade and Charles H. Long (Chicago: University of Chicago Press, 1967), 178.

3. Charles J. Adams, "The History of Religions and the Study of Islam," *ACLS Newsletter* 25, nos. 3–4 (1974): 1–10.

4. As an example one may consider the hostile comments of Julian Baldick in "Islam and the Religions of Iran in the *Encyclopedia of Religion*," *Religious Studies* 24, no. 1 (1988): 47–56. In defense of what he calls "traditional European scholarship," Baldick accuses American Islamicists of cowardly behavior that sacrifices objectivity by coddling the sensitivities of Muslims.

5. Albert Hourani, introduction to *Islam in European Thought* (Cambridge: Cambridge University Press, 1991), 1–2.

6. Edward W. Said, *Orientalism* (New York: Pantheon, 1978).

7. Charles Kurzman, "Cross-Regional Approaches to Middle East Studies: Constructing and Deconstructing a Region," *Middle East Studies Association Bulletin* 41, no. 1 (2007): 24–29, available online with color maps at http://www.unc.edu/~kurzman/cv/Kurzman_Cross-Regional_Approaches.pdf (accessed September 2, 2009).

8. Departments of Near Eastern studies generally include the ancient Near East, while departments and centers of Middle East studies generally do not.

9. Adams, "History of Religions" (1974), 7.

10. Richard C. Martin, ed., *Approaches to Islam in Religious Studies* (Tucson: University of Arizona Press, 1985).

11. Charles J. Adams, foreword to Martin, *Approaches to Islam*, vii.

12. Marshall G. S. Hodgson, *The Venture of Islam: Conscience and History in a World Civilization*, 3 vols. (Chicago: University of Chicago Press, 1974), 1:29.

13. Hodgson, *Venture of Islam*, 1:59.

14. Garth Fowden, *Empire to Commonwealth: Consequences of Monotheism in Late Antiquity* (Princeton, N.J.: Princeton University Press, 1993).

15. This point is made in Talal Asad, *Formations of the Secular: Christianity, Islam, Modernity* (Stanford, Calif.: Stanford University Press, 2003).

16. A seminal contribution of Asad's oeuvre is his monograph *The Idea of an Anthropology of Islam*, Occasional Papers (Washington, D.C.: Center for Contemporary Arab Studies, Georgetown University, 1986).

17. Talal Asad, *Genealogies of Religion: Discipline and Reasons of Power in Christianity and Islam* (Stanford, Calif.: Stanford University Press, 1993).

18. René Girard, *Violence and the Sacred*, trans. Patrick Gregory (Baltimore: Johns Hopkins University Press, 1979).

19. See, for example, Talal Asad, "Modern Power and the Reconfiguration of Religious Traditions: Interview with Saba Mahmood," *Stanford Electronic Humanities Review* 5 (1996), http://www.stanford.edu/group/SHR/5-1/text/asad.html (accessed September 4, 2009).

20. Alasdair MacIntyre, *After Virtue: A Study in Moral Theory* (Notre Dame, Ind.: University of Notre Dame Press, 1981).

21. Charles Taylor et al., "The Politics of Recognition," in *Multiculturalism: Examining the Politics of Recognition*, ed. Amy Gutmann, 3rd ed. (Princeton, N.J.: Princeton University Press, 1994), 25.

22. David A. Hollinger, *Postethnic America: Beyond Multiculturalism* (New York: Basic, 1995), 1. Hollinger's book is discussed by Ruprecht and by Lawrence in this volume.

23. See http://www.whitehouse.gov/news/releases/2001/09/20010917-11.html (accessed November 6, 2008).

24. Bruce B. Lawrence, *Shattering the Myth: Islam beyond Violence* (Princeton, N.J.: Princeton University Press, 1998).

25. Quintan Wiktorowicz, "The Salafi Movement: Violence and the Fragmentation of Community," in *Muslim Networks from Hajj to Hip Hop*, ed. miriam cooke and Bruce B. Lawrence (Chapel Hill: University of North Carolina Press, 2005), 209.

26. Donald K. Emmerson makes the distinction between these two referents as follows: *Islam* refers to normative beliefs, doctrines, and orthodox institutions imputed to God on a vertical divine-human axis, while *Muslim* refers to the horizontal axis of human social interaction, the observable basis of empirical discourse about Islam in history. See Emmerson's "Inclusive Islamism: The Utility of Diversity," in *Islamism: Contested Perspectives on Political Islam*, ed. Richard C. Martin and Abbas Barzegar (Stanford, Calif.: Stanford University Press, 2010), 25–27.

27. Bruce B. Lawrence, *Defenders of God: The Fundamentalism Revolt against the Modern Age* (San Francisco: Harper & Row, 1989).

28. Samuel P. Huntington, "Clash of Civilizations?" *Foreign Affairs* 72, no. 3 (1993): 22–49.

Rethinking Modernity

Islamic Perspectives

Reasons Public
and Divine

Liberal Democracy, Shariʿa Fundamentalism,
and the Epistemological Crisis of Islam

VINCENT J. CORNELL

You [Americans] are the nation who, rather than ruling by the *sharia* of God in
its Constitution and Laws, choose to invent your own laws as you will and desire.
You separate religion from your policies, contradicting the pure nature that affirms
Absolute Authority to the Lord and your Creator. You flee from the embarrassing
question posed to you: How is it possible for God the Almighty to fashion His
creation, grant men power over all creatures and land, grant them all the amenities
of life, and then deny them that which they are most in need of: knowledge of the
laws which govern their lives?

Osama bin Laden

Very few words have been the subject of controversial understanding and abuse
as the word democracy. I think that only the word religion had a similar fate
throughout history. . . . Maybe because of that, it is necessary for me to give my
own opinion on the question. I believe that God created people free and equal,
that higher or lower races do not exist, and neither do good or bad nations. I
believe that people bring with themselves a certain number of inalienable rights,
that governments have no right to limit these rights, much as I do not believe in
the unrestricted rights of the majority, as tyranny of the majority is a tyranny like
all others. I believe that the measure of liberty is the relationship to minorities,
and freedom of thought is, above all, the freedom to think differently. These, in
short, constitute my understanding of democracy.

Alija Izetbegović

The late Bosnian president Alija Izetbegović might have added that in contemporary Islam as well, few concepts have been as contested as democracy. As an

early Sufi once remarked about *tasawwuf*, "Today it is a name without a reality, but formerly it was a reality without a name." The Sufi ʿAli al-Hujwiri (d. 1071 C.E.), who cites this statement in *Kashf al-Mahjub* (Unveiling the Veiled), explains it as follows: "Formerly the practice was known but the pretense was unknown, but nowadays the pretense is known and the practice unknown."[1] The pretense of democracy is indeed well known in the contemporary Islamic world. However, in most Muslim countries, the practice of democracy is another matter. As Izetbegović also said in the speech from which the above quotation was taken, "Absolute rulers rarely admitted that they were dictators, [but] called themselves democrats and asked others to consider and call them as such."[2]

As William E. Connolly states in *The Terms of Political Discourse*, democracy, like "justice" and "freedom," is a contested concept that is embedded in rival theories.[3] Even among classical political theorists, views of democracy varied widely. For Aristotle democracy (*demokratia*) meant rule by the lower classes. He saw democracy as a deviation of polity (*politeia*), rule by the many. Aristotle divided political systems into three types. In royalty one person rules in the common interest; the deviation of royalty is tyranny, where a single person rules in his private interest. Aristocracy is rule by a favored few in the interest of the many; oligarchy, the deviation of aristocracy, is rule by the rich in the interest of the rich. Polity is rule by the many in the common interest; democracy, the deviation of polity, is rule by the many in their own interest.[4]

Aristotle did not clearly favor one political system over the others. He felt that the state should be composed, as far as possible, of citizens of equal or similar means. Given the actualities of human nature, a society composed of a large middle class was the most likely to promote justice by following the mean.[5] Aristotle was worried most of all about oligarchy. Although democracy had its faults, it was less of a threat to the establishment of justice. It was the best of the three deviations of proper rule, since the desire of the poor to rule in their own interest at least gave the possibility of promoting the interests of the greatest number of people.[6]

Aristotle's definition of democracy was the basis for the notion of democracy as "rule by the people." The concept of rule by the people recalls the notion of civil society, which is central to Osama bin Laden's critique of democracy in America. Although there are several approaches to the concept of civil society, in the United States civil society is based on a democratic, pluralist view of civic organization. According to this view, in the words of Alexis de Tocqueville in *Democracy in America* (1840), "The people reign over the political world as God reigns over the universe."[7] For Tocqueville, as for most liberal theorists of democracy, popular sovereignty is exercised through self-government, which promotes the common good by expressing the will of the majority.[8] According to the democratic pragmatist John Dewey (d. 1952), the desire for self-government and concern for the common good are not inborn values but depend on education and experience. Democratic values are nurtured by a political culture of engagement that develops out of local voluntary associations in which citizens of similar social standing, education, and temperament practice the skills of self-rule. In one sense Dewey democratizes Aristotle's notion of rule by the middle classes. More directly he affirms a principle that Thomas Jefferson enunciated in 1820: "I know no safe depository of the ultimate powers of the society but the people themselves; and if we think them not enlightened enough to exercise their control with a wholesome discretion, the remedy is not to take it from them, but to inform their discretion by education."[9]

Liberal democracy has been challenged on theological grounds by a number of Islamist critics. For Islamist ideologues Tocqueville's statement that in America "the people reign over the political world as God reigns over the universe" is evidence that democracy is grounded in *shirk* (associating partners with God), which in this case would mean the usurpation of divine sovereignty by popular sovereignty. Shortly before he was killed in a shoot-out with Saudi security forces outside of Mecca in June 2003, the al Qaeda activist Yusuf al-Ayeri published an essay that portrayed liberal democracy as a grave threat to Islam. According to Ayeri the problem with democracy is that it is based on the concept of the autonomous individual, whose participation in civil society shapes the political and moral nature of society as a whole. The exercise of personal autonomy opens the door for other individualistic doctrines such as religious pluralism and moral relativism. Democratic individualism undermines God-given moral standards by basing political relations on the lowest common denominator of human values. Furthermore, by denying divine sovereignty, democracy "seductively" causes people to believe that they are the authors of their own destinies and that they can change the laws that govern them. Muslims who support democracy are thus led to ignore the commands of God, reject the Shariʻa as the expression of God's will, and "love this world, forget the next world, and abandon jihad."[10] The gendered tone of Ayeri's critique is unmistakable: Eve, in the guise of democracy, seduces the Islamic Adam into tasting the forbidden fruits of moral autonomy and free will.

Despite its extremism Ayeri's critique of democracy has a point. Liberal notions of moral autonomy and free will may indeed pose a threat to Islamic traditionalism, if not to Islam itself. Ironically some Islamist critiques of democracy seem more attuned to historically traditional Islamic worldviews than are the accommodationist positions of Muslim democrats and other apologists for modernity. When Osama bin Laden says to Americans, "You choose to invent your own laws as you will and desire. You separate religion from your policies, contradicting the pure nature that affirms Absolute Authority to the Lord and your Creator," he is not entirely wrong. John Locke (d. 1704), who was arguably the most influential forefather of the American tradition of liberal democracy, believed that God delegated the freedom of moral and political choice to human beings, who exercised this freedom through what Jeremy Waldron has called the "democratic intellect."[11] For Locke the collective wisdom of the common people was a surer guide to God's will than the efforts of religious scholars. In premodern Sunni Islam, Locke's notion of free choice would have been condemned for the heresy of Qadarism, and his democratic populism would have been seen as an incitement to anarchy. If Lockean democracy is construed as Islamic heresy, then Osama bin Laden's critique of democracy is arguably valid, at least according to certain conceptions of Islam. Even though we may despise the conclusions of extremists, we are sometimes forced to admit that their arguments highlight important issues. If it proves nothing else, bin Laden's critique of democracy shows us that one can be logically correct and morally wrong at the same time.

Shari'a Fundamentalism and the Reification of Islamic Law

The key to bin Laden's critique of democracy does not lie in its political vision, but rather in its epistemological outlook. This outlook denies the autonomy of human reason and sees ultimate truth as accessible to the human being only through divine guidance. In *Defenders of God* Bruce Lawrence proposes a definition of religious fundamentalism that helps shed light on this issue: "Fundamentalism is the affirmation of religious authority as holistic and absolute, admitting of neither criticism nor reduction; it is expressed through the collective demand that specific creedal and ethical dictates derived from scripture be publicly recognized and legally enforced."[12] Although Lawrence believes that fundamentalism depends on scripture, his definition allows the student of fundamentalism to take the concept beyond its scriptural base.[13] This definition is based on the premise that in fundamentalism, authority is dependent on a holistic (I would say totalitarian) epistemology. Because of this the authority of fundamentalism may be grounded in scripture, but its scope extends beyond scripture in its application.

Applying Lawrence's definition of fundamentalism to Osama bin Laden's critique of democracy in the United States, one observes that the epistemological aspect of bin Laden's critique is based not so much on the text of the Qur'an as on a reification of the Shari'a as the locus of divine authority. In this reification, which depends more on a covert mystical theology than on any classical legal theory, the Shari'a becomes what Mircea Eliade called a *hierophany*, a manifestation of the sacred embodied as law.[14] As a hierophany of divine authority, the Shari'a is made equivalent to revelation as a source of transcendent truth. In premodern Islamic tradition, it was believed that the divine will was expressed through the Shari'a. In classical Islamic jurisprudence, the Shari'a, and hence

God's will, was applied through the process of *fiqh*, the reasoning of juridical scholars. The association of God's will with the collective opinion of juridical scholars had the effect of obscuring the epistemological role of *zann* (uncertainty or speculation) in the practice of juridical reasoning. This led to the belief among nonspecialists that legal approaches to religious questions had only one correct answer. This is why Muslim fundamentalists are able think of the Shari'a (in Lawrence's words) as "holistic and absolute, admitting of neither criticism nor reduction."

This form of fundamentalism is distinct enough to merit its own name: *Shari'a fundamentalism*. What makes the Shari'a fundamentalism of groups such as al Qaeda different from other varieties of religious fundamentalism is that the reification of scripture and the law are interdependent. In Shari'a fundamentalism the law and not just the scripture on which it is based is conceived as a holistic construct. Taken out of the methodological context of the traditional schools of Islamic jurisprudence, the Shari'a is seen as an idealized expression of the divine will and the locus of truth for human society. Thus in Shari'a fundamentalism both law and scripture are conceived as "holistic and absolute, admitting of neither criticism nor reduction."

Like all forms of fundamentalism, Shari'a fundamentalism depends for its hermeneutical authority on a literalistic reading of scripture. Scriptural literalism artificially simplifies contested concepts by restricting the meaning of multivalent terms. When doubt is removed from the interpretive process, epistemological certainty becomes a realizable ideal. With the attainment of certainty, there is no need for the "speculation" (*zann*) of legal-school jurists who approach the Qur'an and the Hadith through inductive reasoning. Instead the logic of certainty is sought through deductive reasoning (*bayan* or *burhan*), not through the inductive casuistry of traditional jurisprudence. Deductive logic is like a mathematical formula: the terms of the equation are predetermined, and all the interpreter of a text needs to do is supply the proper values for the variables. The privileging of deductive logic over inductive logic is a major cause of both the authoritarianism and the superficiality that characterize fundamentalist hermeneutics in Islam. Shari'a fundamentalism can be observed in a wide variety of Islamic writings and is not confined to al Qaeda tracts alone. However, this view of the Shari'a is particularly common in Salafi discourse.

The Shari'a fundamentalism of Osama bin Laden comes directly out of the writings of the Muslim Brotherhood ideologue Sayyid Qutb (d. 1966). In *Signs along the Road* (*Ma'alim fi al-Tariq*), Qutb describes the Shari'a as a "universal law" (*shari'a kawniyya*). By using this term, Qutb means to say not only that the Shari'a is universally applicable. Rather his Shari'a fundamentalism is based on a notion of universal law that approximates the law of nature. "[The concept of the Shari'a] goes back to its most comprehensive root in its decisive role in all of existence, not just in human existence alone, and in its application to all of existence, not in its application to human life alone."[15] Although at first glance this argument may seem similar to natural law theory, Qutb takes a much more sectarian stance than do Western theorists of natural law, who conceive of natural law as standing over and above the legal systems of individual societies. For Qutb natural law *is* the Islamic Shariʿa. It is the fundamental expression of the *namus* (Gr. *nomos*), the divine law that governs and regulates the universe. For this reason rejection of the Shariʿa amounts to rejection not only of the historically revealed laws of Islam, but also of God's universal law, and is a denial of God's power to determine existence by saying, "Be! And it is" (Qurʾan, 16:40): "It is God who created both the human being and universal existence, and who made the human being obedient to His divine laws along with all of existence. It is God, may He be glorified, who prescribed (*sanna*) the Shariʿa to govern the human being's voluntary life, a form of order (*tanzim*) that accords with his natural existence. Thus, on this basis, the Shariʿa is part of the Universal Divine Law (*al-namus al-ilahi al-ʿamm*) that governs human nature and the universal nature of existence together. [God] has made it a single and comprehensive totality (*wa yunassiquha kulluha jumlatan wahidatan*)."[16]

Qutb explains, "The Shariʿa that God has given to the human being to order his life is a universal law in the sense that it is related to the overall law of the universe and is harmonious with it. The only way in which true harmony can be brought about between the laws (*qawanin*) that are operative in the inner life of the human being and the laws that govern his outward actions is through obedience to the Shariʿa."[17] For Qutb the human being is not capable of creating a legal system that is in harmony with both human life and the laws of the universe. Therefore the obligation to obey the Shariʿa is greater even than the obligation to believe in Islam. Any system of laws other than the Shariʿa is nothing but the indulgence of human whims (*ahwaʾ al-bashar*).[18] The epistemology of Shariʿa fundamentalism is central to Qutb's political argument in *Signs along the Road*. It is primarily on this basis that he dismisses all non-Shariʿa-based political systems as *jahili*, existentially and theologically "ignorant" manifestations of human vanity. Political systems that are not based on the Shariʿa are not condemned for their moral failings alone, but also because of their Promethean disregard for the rights of God in favor of the rights of man.

Qutb's ideology of the universal Shariʿa came rather late in his career and does not appear in his earlier works, such as *Social Justice in Islam* (*al-ʿAdala al-ijtimaʿiyya fi al-Islam*), which was first published in 1949. However, even in *Social Justice*, which was written before Qutb officially joined the Muslim Brotherhood, the "holistic and absolute" vision of the Islamic order (*al-nizam al-islami*) that frames his later Shariʿa fundamentalism is already well developed: "Islam has one universal and integrated theory which covers the universe and life and humanity, a theory in which are integrated all the different questions; in this Islam sums up all its beliefs, its laws and statutes, and its modes of worship and of work. The treatment of all these matters emanates from this one universal and comprehensive theory, so that each question is not dealt with on an individual basis, nor is every problem with its needs treated in isolation from all other problems."[19]

In contrast with Christianity, which in Qutb's view posits an opposition between the world of human society and the world of the spirit, "Islam saw one embracing unity, which took in the universe, the soul, and all human life. Its aim is to unite earth and heaven in one world; to join the present world and the world to come in one faith; to link spirit and body in one humanity; to correlate worship and work in one life."[20] Islam is unique and incomparable, and the system it represents "has never been found in any of the other systems known to the world either before or after the coming of Islam."[21] Islam, says Qutb, does not seek to imitate any other system, nor does it seek to find similarities between itself and others. Thus any attempt to reform Islam or strengthen it through comparison with other systems is a useless endeavor and a sign of inferiority.[22]

Epistemological Crisis and the Reification of Islam as Culture

The Shariʿa fundamentalism of Sayyid Qutb and Osama bin Laden is both a response to the pressures of globalization and secular liberalism and a symptom of epistemological crisis in Islam. The philosopher Alasdair MacIntyre coined the term *epistemological crisis* to describe what happens when a tradition of inquiry fails to make progress by its original standards of rationality. Former methods of inquiry become sterile, "conflicts over rival answers to key questions can no longer be settled rationally," and arguments that have worked in the past "have the effect of increasingly disclosing new inadequacies, hitherto unrecognized incoherencies, and new problems for the solution of which there seem to be insufficient or no resources within the established fabric of belief."[23] This concept accurately describes the current situation of Islamic thought, at least in the world of Sunni Islam. Shariʿa fundamentalism, as a response to the challenges posed to Islamic thought by modernity, is an important signpost (the pun is intentional) of epistemological crisis in Islam.

According to MacIntyre the "dissolution of historically founded certitudes" is the hallmark of an epistemological crisis. When a historically founded tradition confronts a new and alien tradition, it may be that some of the original tradition's claims to truth will no longer be sustained. This threatens the integrity of the tradition as a whole. A feeling of crisis may be precipitated by the challenge of a completely new epistemology, or it may occur when social and historical conditions change such that the claims of a rival tradition provide newly cogent and illuminating explanations of why one's own tradition has been unable to solve its problems or restore its original coherence. Sometimes the conceptual language of the alien tradition may become a "new and second first language" of the tradition in crisis.[24] This happened, for example, in the second and third centuries of Islam, when, because of the crisis precipitated by Christian theological polemics against Islam, Greek logic provided conceptual tools for the newly developed tradition of Islamic theology (*'ilm al-kalam*). Muslim theologians reconceptualized the logical formulations of Greek thinkers such as Aristotle and the Stoics in ways that rendered them "Islamic." A similar process occurred in Islamic philosophy, where the philosophical languages of Platonism and Aristotelianism were recast as "Islamic" discourses. In his famous 1784 essay, "Was ist Aufklärung?" (What Is Enlightenment?), Immanuel Kant proposed that the coming of the Enlightenment heralded humanity's liberation from its self-imposed immaturity, an immaturity marked by uncritical acceptance of dogmatic religious authority.[25] More than two centuries later, Kant's vision remains the key issue in the epistemological confrontation between fundamentalist or traditionalist Islam and Western modernity.

The key to resolving an epistemological crisis is to develop new resources and frameworks for the tradition under pressure. Such resources, however, cannot be created merely by grafting elements of an alien tradition onto the original. To be acceptable, what MacIntyre calls the "new and second first languages" of tradition must be seen as authentic: they must exhibit continuity with the worldview that defined the original tradition in the first place. In addition the new resources of tradition must constitute a tradition of their own. They must provide a systematic and coherent solution to problems that have so far proven intractable. Finally the revision of tradition must be critical. It must provide an explanation of what it was that rendered the original tradition, before acquiring the new resources, sterile or incoherent or both.

Although they must be perceived as authentic, these new resources do not necessarily have to be derived directly from the earlier tradition. Rather their justification lies in their ability to engage with the previous tradition and resolve contradictions that had not been resolvable before.[26] The opportunity posed by an epistemological crisis lies in the prospect of coming up with new approaches to tradition that provide innovative solutions through a critical engagement with the past. In the words of the late historian of Christianity Jaroslav Pelikan, "A 'leap of progress' is not a standing broad jump, which begins at the line of where we are now; it is a running broad jump through where we have been to where we go next."[27] The challenge for Muslim liberal democrats is to find an authentic starting point or baseline for such a running broad jump that allows modern political theory to engage the future without abandoning the past.

For Muslim fundamentalists such as Sayyid Qutb and Osama bin Laden, the epistemological crisis of Islam is seen as a clash of civilizations defined in terms of law and culture—a conflict of values between Islam and the West. In such a view, religion and culture are conflated. Islam is seen not only as a religious alternative to other faiths, but it is also cast as the cultural antithesis of the West. Similarly Christianity, Judaism, and secularism (no meaningful distinction is made among these categories) are cast as Western cultural villains. This rhetorical strategy, in which the Orientalist dichotomy of "the West versus the rest" is turned against itself, has been called "Occidentalism." Occidentalism is a critique of Western civilization that utilizes the bipolar model of Orientalism but reverses the polarity such that an idealized image of a spiritual East is valued over a critical image of a materialistic West.[28] According to the Egyptian philosopher and Islamic modernist Hassan Hanafi, who claims to have been the first to use the term *Occidentalism* in print, Occidentalism is a liberation epistemology, an "ideology for the ruled" that functions as a liberating device for the subaltern, much as liberation theology did for Latin Americans in the 1970s. Unlike liberation theology, however, Occidentalism relies on the Romantic notions of national character and national culture rather than on the Marxist concept of superstructure.[29]

The Occidentalist critique of Western civilization is also expressed as a confrontation between tradition and modernity. However, despite the portrayal of Islam as a form of "traditional" spirituality by Muslim Occidentalists, the ways in which they conceive of religion are dependent on nineteenth-century Western notions of culture and social science. Anthropologist Kevin Avruch has identified six common but theoretically "inadequate" notions of culture in contemporary political discourse that contribute to ethnic and religious conflicts. Each of these notions can be traced to nineteenth-century concepts of culture. When applied to Islam, each of these notions is also integral to the discourses of both Islamic fundamentalism and Islamic Occidentalism:

1. *Culture is homogeneous.* When applied to Islam, this notion presumes that Islam is free of internal paradoxes and contradictions, such that it provides clear and unambiguous behavioral instructions, a system (*nizam*) for how to act as individuals and as a polity. The ideal of normative homogeneity is maintained epistemologically by recourse to deductive reasoning.
2. *Culture is a thing.* Fundamentalist epistemology views Islam as a reified "thing" that can act, believe, assert, and take on an identity independent of human actors. It can even construct a definition of itself. This type of reification is a hallmark of fundamentalist discourse in all religions.
3. *Culture is uniformly distributed among members of a group.* In Islamic fundamentalist and Occidentalist discourses, this notion confers cognitive, behavioral, and affective uniformity to all members of the Muslim community (*ummah*). In other words all true Muslims are alike. "Islamic" consciousness

is the same for all Muslims. Variation within the group is deviance. This notion is a hallmark of the so-called *tawhidic* (unitarian) worldview of Islamic reformism, which conflates the theological oneness of God (*tawhid*) with the unification (*ittihad*) or unity (*wahda*) of an idealized Islamic culture or "nation." When applied to the Shariʿa, this concept leads to Qutb's notion that Islamic law is universal natural law, the norms of which can be applied to all nations and all peoples. As we have seen, this last notion is a hallmark of Shariʿa fundamentalism.

4. *An individual possesses but a single culture.* For advocates of Islamic identity politics, a Muslim is only a Muslim. One is neither Sunni nor Shiʿite, neither Sufi nor Wahhabi. Islamic identity thus becomes synonymous with a unitary group identity. For Kevin Avruch this notion results from the privileging of "tribal culture" over cultures that are connected to different groups, structures, and institutions. The difference between Avruch's view of monoculturalism and the monoculturalism of Muslim fundamentalists lies in the understanding of what he calls "tribal culture." For Avruch tribal culture is coterminous with national identity. In the politics of Islamic identity, national identity is trumped by an Islamic identity defined in ideological terms. The "tribe" is thus not the nation, but the worldwide Muslim *ummah.*

5. *Culture is custom.* According to this notion, the content of culture is structurally undifferentiated. In Avruch's terms, "What you see is what you get." In the discourse of Islamic fundamentalism, this is the same as saying that Islam is tradition. This identification of Islam with cultural norms helps explain the common recourse to the Hadith over the Qurʾan by Muslim fundamentalists. It is in the Hadith where one can find normative interpretations of cultural attitudes and behaviors that have been handed down from the early centuries of Islamic history. The prominence of Hadith in Islamic epistemology has contributed greatly to the notion that Islam is a monoculture, despite Qurʾanic verses that imply the contrary.

6. *Culture is timeless.* This is a corollary of the previous notion. Islam, as tradition, is primordial. It is changeless, and every attempt to transform the meaning of Islam is a threat to the integrity of Islam's divine origin.[30]

In the discourse of Islamic fundamentalism, the word *Islam* can be used nearly everywhere the word *culture* is used in the above examples. In the discourse of Shariʿa fundamentalism, the word *Shariʿa* can be used nearly everywhere the word *Islam* is used. For Shariʿa fundamentalists, allegiance to Islam means allegiance to Shariʿa as tradition, in which the maxims of religion and culture are combined in a "holistic and absolute" system. In Shariʿa fundamentalist discourse, Islam is conceived in juridical-cultural terms as what used to be called a *milla* (Ottoman *millet*): a self-contained and legally demarcated religious community that exists concurrently with but in separation from other *milla* communities of the same type.[31] The Islamic *milla* is a community of true believers because all of its members submit to God's authority under the Shariʿa. Traditions that come from outside the Islamic *milla* lack authenticity because they are not Shariʿa based and depend instead on the whims (*ahwaʾ*) of human judgment rather than on the wisdom of God. This epistemological principle is foundational to the concept of Shariʿa fundamentalism. Osama bin Laden was thinking along these lines when he wrote that Americans "choose to invent their own laws as they will and desire."

Millet Multiculturalism and U.S. Constitutionalism

The epistemological premises of Alasdair MacIntyre and Shariʿa fundamentalists such as Sayyid Qutb and Osama bin Laden could not be farther apart. The integrism and political separatism that for Qutb were signs of Islamic authenticity are for MacIntyre signs of an epistemological crisis. For MacIntyre it is integrism, not the epistemology of comparison, that is the greater token of inferiority. Qutb's integrism reflects a siege mentality, a circling of the wagons designed to protect the integrity of the Islamic order from outside influences. It creates a false sense of self-sufficiency that protects an idealized notion of tradition by ghettoizing Islam as a world civilization. On this view the call by al Qaeda activists to isolate the Dar al-Islam politically and culturally should not be seen as an anomalous act of extremism, but rather as a consequence of the ideas that Qutb promoted. What should be most worrisome to nonfundamentalist Muslims, however, is not that Muslim extremists accept Qutb's premises but that many Muslims who think of themselves as moderates accept them as well. As Osama bin Laden, Ayman al-Zawahiri, and other al Qaeda leaders realize, to accept the premises of Shariʿa fundamentalism while at the same time paying lip service to democratic liberalism is not only contradictory, it is dishonest. If the Shariʿa is in fact the only legitimate legal and moral order in the eyes of God, then participating in a self-governing liberal democracy is at best a cynical exercise in political accommodationism. At worst it may be viewed as a subterfuge that exposes the Muslim citizen of a democratic state to the accusation of disloyalty.

The horns of this dilemma are apparent in a recent book by Sherman A. Jackson, a noted Muslim scholar and public intellectual in the United States. In *Islam and the Blackamerican* Jackson states that the U.S. Constitution is an obstacle that complicates Muslim Americans' full acceptance of the U.S. political system. According to Jackson this is due to two factors, which are also implicit in Osama bin Laden's critique of democracy in the United States: (1) many Muslims question the legitimacy of the U.S. Constitution on theological grounds;

(2) Muslims question the propriety of embracing any constitution that insists on the separation of church and state.[32] Although Jackson argues against both of these positions, his argument is undermined by what might be termed a soft version of Shari'a fundamentalism. This view of the Shari'a can be seen in the following statement: "It is emphatically *not* my aim to vindicate the Constitution by conferring upon it the status of law (or even a source of law) that is binding on the Muslim moral/religious conscience on a par with *shari'ah* (the Sacred Law of Islam)."[33] For Jackson the Constitution may be a relatively benign obstacle to the primacy of the Shari'a, but it is an obstacle nonetheless. The only answer to this problem is to reach a modus vivendi with the Constitution. According to Jackson the Muslim American must recognize the "immovable fact" of the Constitution in U.S. politics and use it to "inform his *shari'ah*-based approach to American life. In my approach, the U.S. Constitution is no more binding on the Muslim-American moral/religious conscience than was, say, tribalism or agrarianism on that of the early Muslim-Arabian community."[34]

This is a tepid endorsement indeed. In effect Jackson is saying that U.S. constitutionalism is a product of American custom (*'urf*) that can be worked into the Muslim American conception of the Shari'a in the way that certain customs of the *Jahiliyya*, such as tribalism and agrarianism, were worked into Islamic jurisprudence. Such a comparison may be faulted on logical grounds, not to mention the ground of fairness. The product of a constitutional convention and the inherited political structures of tribalism are too different to be compared in any meaningful way. In addition Jackson's implicit characterization of the Constitution as *jahili* is as culturally insensitive as it is anachronistic. Does he really mean to agree with Islamist ideologues such as Qutb and Abu al-'Ala al-Mawdudi (d. 1979) that liberal democracy threatens the exclusive and ultimate sovereignty of God? Although Jackson disagrees with Qutb and Mawdudi that democracy constitutes *shirk*, he acknowledges part of their argument by claiming that the Constitution "was the result of an agreement among a group of *non-Muslims* about how to distribute political rights and power within a non-Muslim polity" (italics in the original).[35]

As for the problematical issue of the separation of church and state in American political culture, Jackson acknowledges that this is not an endorsement of secularism per se, but a separation of the institutional powers of church and state. Thus there is room for the American Muslim to become involved in the political process so that Shari'a-based values might be integrated into American political life. However, even here Jackson steps back from a full endorsement of the American notion of civil society. For Jackson the Shari'a, as God's law, should always take precedence for the Muslim over the Constitution, which, in the final analysis, is a secular set of laws created by non-Muslims. He thus begs an important question when he states: "American custom (*'urf*) must be recognized as a

legally valid consideration in areas where Islamic law admits reliance on cus-
tom."[36] This is fine when American laws do not contradict Shariʿa provisions.
But what if U.S. laws contradict the Shariʿa, as in the prohibition of bigamy?
Should the American Muslim ignore such laws, as Mormon fundamentalists do?
If the American Muslim is not morally bound by the Constitution, how can she
assume the right to influence a social contract that she refuses to recognize?

Jackson's understanding of civil society is based on the "complementarity
thesis"— the idea (often promoted by Christian fundamentalists) that governmental and nongovernmental institutions play complementary roles in the
pursuit of human welfare. However, as John Kelsay has pointed out, a complementarity of functions is not the same as an identity of functions.[37] A certain
tension between governmental and nongovernmental institutions is built into
the complementarity thesis. What, for example, are the limits of authority with
regard to religious institutions? What are the limits of political authority? "The
associations covered by civil society, resting as they do on loyalties more delim-
ited and more intense than those inspired by the state, pose a kind of sectarian
problem," says Kelsay.[38] The Muslim political scientist Farhad Kazemi addition-
ally points out that civil society is not just civic, but also *civil:* "Civility implies
tolerance, the willingness of individuals to accept disparate political views and
social attitudes; sometimes to accept the profoundly important idea that there is
no right answer. Civility implies not only tolerance of the other, but also attachment to the institutions that constitute civil society."[39] On Kazemi's view of civil
society, Jackson's agnostic attitude toward the moral authority of the Constitution may be criticized for not being "civil" enough.

The question of sectarianism, and hence of potentially divided loyalties, is a
major problem in Jackson's discussion of Islam and the Constitution. Although
Jackson disavows the politics of Islamic identity, by not "conferring upon [the
Constitution] the status of law (or even a source of law) that is binding on the
Muslim moral/religious conscience on a par with *shariʿah*," he depicts the American Muslim community as a de facto *milla* with its own religiously based laws.
The political philosopher Kwame Anthony Appiah has termed a politics of identity where pluralism is conceived as the equal standing of culturally defined
interest groups "millet multiculturalism."[40] While it might be argued that millet multiculturalism can be accommodated to the notion of civil society in some
democratic countries, this was not a principle on which the United States was
founded. In the U.S. legal system, fundamental rights are individual rights, not
corporate rights. However, a certain ambiguity must be acknowledged. The
equal protection of religious beliefs and practices under the Constitution is a
hybrid concept. It is an individual right, but it most often applies to the mistreatment of a person as a member of a group.[41] This is why the issue of group
entitlements has been so fraught with controversy in U.S. politics and law.

Nevertheless individual rights still tend to trump corporate rights in U.S. political culture. Thomas Jefferson was explicit in the belief that the civility of civil society rests on a notion of civic unity that does not admit the separation of society into cultural enclaves: "A character of good faith is of as much value to a nation as to an individual. A nation, as a society, forms a moral person, and every member of it is personally responsible for his society."[42]

John Locke, who was a major inspiration for Jefferson, felt the same way. Locke's notion of commonwealth, the term he uses for civil society, included Jews, Muslims, and pagans. In the *Third Letter Concerning Toleration*, he asks: "Why might not Jews, pagans, and Mahometans be admitted to the rights of the commonwealth, as far as papists, independents, and Quakers?"[43] However, Locke was not tolerant of divided loyalties within the commonwealth. Although he was more open than Jefferson to the idea that the commonwealth might include semiautonomous religious groups, he did not believe that the members of such groups had the right to combine their difference of religious opinion with allegiance to an alternative set of laws. "It is ridiculous," he wrote, "for any one who professes himself to be a *Mahumetan* only in his religion, but in everything else a faithful subject of a Christian Magistrate, whilst at the same time he acknowledges himself bound to yield blind obedience to the *Mufti of Constantinople*, who himself is entirely obedient to the Ottoman Emperor."[44] This was Locke's way of saying that preference for the laws of the Shariʿa over the laws of the commonwealth meant that one was not a loyal citizen of the commonwealth.

Thomas Paine (d. 1809) would likely have objected to Jackson's soft Shariʿa fundamentalism because it contradicts the concept of the social contract and is a poor substitute for a real constitution. For Paine governments arise either *out* of the people or *over* the people. A system that does not arise out of the people is prone to tyranny. Religious authority is just as likely to promote tyranny as to protect the people from it. A constitutional democracy arises when "the individuals themselves, each in his own personal and sovereign right, [enter] into a compact with each other to produce a government; and this is the only mode in which governments have a right to arise, and the only principle on which they have a right to exist."[45] The Shariʿa, especially in the traditional *fiqh* form advocated by Jackson, would have represented for Paine a law of "priestcraft" and hence of superstition. Furthermore the Shariʿa is not a true constitution because it does not outline a coherent system of government: "A constitution is a thing antecedent to a government, and a government is only the creature of a constitution. The constitution of a country is not the act of its government, but of the people constituting a government. It is the body of elements, to which you can refer, and quote article by article and which contains the principles on which the government shall be established, the manner in which it shall be organized, the powers it shall have, the mode of elections, the duration of parliaments, . . . the powers which the executive part of the government shall have; and in fine, every thing that relates to the compleat organization of a civil government."[46]

One could imagine Paine asking Jackson, to paraphrase a question he asked of Edmund Burke about the British "Constitution" in *Rights of Man* (1791): "Can then Mr. Jackson produce the Islamic Constitution? If he cannot, we may fairly conclude, that though it has been so much talked about, no such thing as an Islamic Constitution exists, or ever did exist, and consequently that the people have yet a constitution to form."[47]

In addition to reifying the Shari'a and setting it up in potential opposition to the Constitution, Jackson's religiously sectarian view of U.S. democracy causes him to overlook the universalistic nature of U.S. political philosophy. By claiming that the Constitution "was the result of an agreement among a group of *non-Muslims* about how to distribute political rights and power within a non-Muslim polity," he ignores the premise that U.S. constitutional democracy was intended for all citizens, Christian and non-Christian alike. Both Jefferson and Benjamin Franklin were explicit in their inclusion of Jews and "Turks" in U.S. civil society. Furthermore, as an ideological construct, the U.S. model of democratic constitutionalism was intended for the entire world. These are issues of philosophical principle, irrespective of the attitudes and actions of U.S. governments in history. Democratic evangelism was not an invention of contemporary U.S. administrations. It has been part of the American political scene from the very beginning.

For the constitutional ideologist Paine, civil rights are based on natural rights, which are bestowed on all human beings by God and are expressed in the Golden Rule: "The duty of man . . . consists but of two points. His duty to God, which every man must feel, and with respect to his neighbour, to do as he would be done by." Among the most important natural rights are those that Paine termed "intellectual rights" or "rights of the mind." Religion is one of these rights of the mind, which is why freedom of religion must be respected in a constitutional democracy. "A man, by natural right, has a right to judge in his own cause; and so far as the right of the mind is concerned, he never surrenders it."[48] Taking a stance that would be echoed two centuries later by Alija Izetbegović, Paine asserts that the rights of the mind are inalienable. However, he goes beyond most Muslims by asserting that the human being not only *possesses* the rights given to him by God, he actually *owns* them. For Paine human rights are private property, and the usurpation of a right is like the usurpation of private property, an act that is inadmissible even for God. It cannot be God's will to take such rights away, nor is it the right of society to do so either: "[Man] therefore deposits this right in the common stock of society, and takes the arm of society, of which he is a part, in preference and in addition to his own. Society *grants* him nothing. Every man is a proprietor in society, and draws on the capital as a matter of right."[49]

Jefferson agreed with Paine's theology of natural rights. However, he extended Paine's concept of the ownership of rights to a critique of tradition, in which he used the metaphor of contract law to assert that the dead have no rights over the living. "That our Creator made the earth for the use of the living and not of the dead; that those who exist not can have no use or right in it, no authority or power over it, that one generation of men cannot foreclose or burden its use to another, which come to it in its own right and by the same divine beneficence, that a preceding generation cannot bind a succeeding one by its laws or contracts. . . . These are axioms so self-evident that no explanation can make them plainer; for he is not to be reasoned with who says that nonexistence can control existence, or that nothing can move something."[50]

For Jefferson the right of self-government was as much a part of natural law as the provisions of the Shari'a were for Sayyid Qutb: "Every man, and every body of men on earth, possesses the right of self-government. They receive it with their being from the hand of nature. Individuals exercise it by their single will; collections of men by that of their majority; for the law of the majority is the natural law of every society of men."[51] Because self-government conforms to the will of God (conceived as Nature) and the right to self-government is the possession of every human being, Jefferson believed that self-government and democratic constitutionalism are universal principles, and hence may be advocated for all peoples throughout the world:

> The eyes of the virtuous all over the earth are turned with anxiety on us, as the only depositories of the sacred fire of liberty. I hope and firmly believe that the whole world will sooner or later feel benefit from the issue of our assertion of the rights of man. May the Declaration of Independence be to the world, what I believe it will be (to some parts sooner, to others later, but finally to all), the signal of arousing men to burst the chains under which monkish ignorance and superstition had persuaded them to bind themselves, and to assume the blessings and security of self-government. Cherish every measure which may foster our brotherly Union and perpetuate a constitution of government, destined to be the primitive and precious model of what is to change the condition of man over the globe.[52]

From Millet Multiculturalism to Soft Pluralism

The ideological universalism of U.S. democratic constitutionalism confronts Sherman Jackson with a dilemma far greater than he acknowledges in his book. If, as he seems to believe, the secular and non-Muslim origin of the Constitution means that it is not founded on the same principles as the Shari'a, then the

Constitution can only be seen as an ideological rival to the Shari'a, and U.S. democracy must be seen as a counterideology to Islam. If this were the case, then Osama bin Laden and his followers would be correct. One cannot square the ideological circle by superimposing competing universalistic ideologies upon one another. Shari'a fundamentalism and U.S. democratic constitutionalism cannot coexist in the same space. But is this the only way to view the democratic challenge to Islam or the constitutional challenge to the Shari'a? Fortunately this need not be the case. However, to view the matter differently means abandoning the premises of Shari'a fundamentalism.

Unlike Jackson, the American Muslim religious leader Fesial Abdul Rauf fully acknowledges the premises of U.S. political ideology. In fact he characterizes the United States metaphorically as "a religious state with a state religion that allows all religions."[53] Abdul Rauf is a liberal Muslim intellectual, the imam of a mosque in New York City, and the founder of the Cordoba Initiative, which is devoted to building bridges of understanding between Americans and Muslims. In his acclaimed book *What's Right with Islam*, he uses F. Forrester Church's concept of the "American Creed" to argue that the Establishment Clause of the First Amendment to the Constitution calls for the separation of church and state, but does not preclude a relationship between religion and state-endorsed values.[54] According to Abdul Rauf the United States is a polity whose ethics emanate from universal moral principles that are grounded in the three Abrahamic religions of Judaism, Christianity, and Islam: "Our government's moral authority derives from the Constitution, whose moral basis is God's law—another way of saying, as Thomas Jefferson did, the 'Laws of Nature and Nature's God.'"

To bolster this assertion, Abdul Rauf cites Supreme Court justice Antonin Scalia, who argued in a 2002 paper that the U.S. system of government is not secular in origin but derives its ultimate authority from God. This argument is part of a conservative critique of utilitarian notions of democracy and rights. According to Scalia it is a "mistaken tendency to believe that a democratic government [is] nothing more than the composite will of its individual citizens [and] has no more moral power or authority than [the citizens] do as individuals." In the words of a Supreme Court opinion from the 1940s, "[Americans] are a religious people whose institutions presuppose a Supreme Being."[56] According to Abdul Rauf's understanding of Scalia's argument, the United States is neither a secular state nor a Christian state. Rather it is an "Abrahamic" state, and it was founded on principles held in common by all the Abrahamic religions.[57] This understanding is in direct contradiction to the view of Osama bin Laden, who often conflates American secularism and Christianity. Abdul Rauf's view also contradicts Jackson's conception of the Constitution as a document drafted by non-Muslim men for a non-Muslim nation.

Abdul Rauf rejects the sectarian premises of Shariʿa fundamentalism and asserts that the universal rights embodied in U.S. constitutionalism make the United States a "Shariʿa-compliant" state.[58] This claim is made on both theological and legal grounds. Theologically Abdul Rauf justifies the notion of democratic constitutionalism with the following Qurʾanic verse: "Say: Oh God, Lord of Sovereignty! You invest sovereignty in whom You please and divest sovereignty from whom You please" (3:26). Paraphrasing Scalia, he contends that "the power of a community is of a vicarious kind, being held, as it were, in trust from God. A Shariah-compliant state owes its existence to the will of the people and is subject to control by them, although it derives its ultimate authority from God."[59] In this pluralistic model of sovereignty, the authority of a democratic society is based on the trusteeship that God grants to all human beings as vicegerents of God. The natural law that Paine, Jefferson, and other Enlightenment thinkers saw as the basis for freedom of expression and self-government is Islamicized by Abdul Rauf through the Qurʾanic concepts of *din al-fitra* (30:30), which he glosses as "natural religion," and *din Allah* (3:83), which he defines as "God's own religion." As universal rights embodied in the religion of Abraham, the concepts of freedom of expression and self-government are thus morally binding on all Jews, Christians, and Muslims regardless of religious differences.[60]

The legal basis for the Shariʿa compliance of American democracy is premised for Abdul Rauf on the belief that the Constitution and system of governance uphold the core principles of Islamic law. To make this argument, he uses the concept of the "Goals of the Shariʿa" (*maqasid al-Shariʿa*), which has been part of the Islamic juridical tradition for nearly a millennium. According to this model, the purpose of the Shariʿa is to preserve the rights to life (*hayat*), intellect (*ʿaql*), religion (*din*), property (*milk*), and family or lineage (*nasl*). "Any system of rule that upholds, protects, and furthers these rights," says Abdul Rauf, "is legally 'Islamic' or Shariah-compliant in its substance. Because these rights are God-given, they are inalienable and cannot be deprived of any man or woman without depriving them of their essential humanity."[61] Abdul Rauf thus universalizes the traditional Islamic concept of the Goals of the Shariʿa to uphold what Appiah calls "soft pluralism." Soft pluralism is a political ethic in which "the individual remains both the terminus a quo and the terminus ad quem: its concern for identity groups is not only motivated by but ultimately subordinated to the well-being of the individual and the bundle of rights and protections that traditional liberalism would accord her."[62]

In making his case for soft pluralism and the compatibility of Islamic and U.S. legal ethics, Abdul Rauf draws from arguments made by Muhammad Asad (d. 1992) in *The Principles of State and Government in Islam*.[63] This largely overlooked work was written by a Jewish convert to Islam who became a noted intellectual in Saudi Arabia. Asad spent the final years of his life in southern Spain and Gibraltar, where he lived in virtual exile because of his liberal and modernist views. In this work he asserts that what makes a state "Islamic" is the incorporation of the basic tenets of Islam in the constitution of a country. Abdul Rauf takes this to mean that "a state that does incorporate such sociopolitical tenets has become de facto an Islamic state even if there are no Muslims in name living there, for it expresses the ideals of the good society according to Islamic principles."[64] Going back to Jefferson's text of the Declaration of Independence, he sees the U.S. commitment to preserve the inalienable rights of life, liberty, and the pursuit of happiness as equivalent to the Islamic commitment to preserve the Shariʿa-endorsed rights of life, "mental well-being" (ʿaql), religion, property, and family.[65] For Abdul Rauf this equivalence of values makes the United States an "Islamic" country. Being authentically Islamic does not mean that a state must hold Islam "in the liturgical sense" to be the state religion. Rather the state must be religious in the sense that God is the ultimate ruler or source of the principles on which the state is founded. By this token any state that is not atheistic can potentially be included within the "Islamic" category.[66]

Public Reason and Overlapping Consensus

At first glance Abdul Rauf appears to advocate the kind of accommodationist Islam that Tariq Ramadan has criticized for advocating "the integration/assimilation of Muslims, from which they expect a complete adaptation to the Western way of life."[67] In his attempt to overcome the epistemological crisis of Islam, he seems merely to graft elements of an alien political philosophy onto Islam. However, such a view, which would likely be held by many conservative Muslims, is unfair. In political terms the main difference between Sherman Jackson and Abdul Rauf is that Jackson seeks a modus vivendi between the Shariʿa and the U.S. Constitution, whereas Abdul Rauf seeks what John Rawls called an "overlapping consensus" of political rights and values. For Rawls a political modus vivendi is comparable to a treaty between two states or nations whose aims and interests put them at odds. It becomes the solution of choice whenever social consensus is conceived in terms of "self- or group interests, or on the outcome of political bargaining."[68] This is a fair approximation of what obtains when one thinks of relations between Muslims and a non-Muslim state in terms of millet multiculturalism. In the premodern *milla* system, minority religious communities were governed under their own laws because they were seen as independent social units. A modus vivendi with non-Muslim communities was the best that could be hoped for, because premodern Muslims saw the Shariʿa as a comprehensive and universal model of justice and did not recognize the reasonableness of social pluralism. Traditional Islamic political theory could only tolerate difference; it could not incorporate a theory of difference into its conception of justice and rights.

Such traditional attitudes toward pluralism place Muslim minorities in a precarious position in Western societies. Since traditional notions of the Shariʿa could only accommodate an arm's-length toleration of non-Muslim minorities, it is difficult for Muslim minorities to demand full integration into non-Muslim societies without appearing to advocate a hypocritical double standard. On their own logic, it could be argued that it is unfair for Muslims to demand a greater social integration into non-Muslim societies than obtains, for example, in Western European countries such as France or Germany. The 2005 communal riots in France, however, have shown how unsatisfactory a modus vivendi based on group interests can be in practice. One of the problems of Shariʿa fundamentalism is that it demands adherence to premodern Shariʿa norms in a modern political context. Historical practice has shown that such norms have not been compatible with democratic pluralism. Advocating a Shariʿa-based millet multiculturalism in the American legal context would imply that one would be willing to accept a lesser guarantee of individual rights for a greater guarantee of group rights. This would be a major yet unforeseen consequence of Jackson's refusal to accept the philosophical premises of the Constitution. Is it reasonable for Muslim intellectuals or religious leaders to ask Muslims in the United States to give up the constitutional guarantees of individual rights such as free association and freedom of conscience for an idealized (and ultimately unenforceable) notion of communal identity? Most American Muslims would answer this question with a resounding "no."

One of the advantages of political liberalism is that it is philosophically committed to maintaining the right of difference in a democratic society. Rawls summarizes the problem of difference as follows: "How is it possible that there can be a stable and just society whose free and equal citizens are deeply divided by conflicting and even incommensurable religious, philosophical, and moral doctrines?"[69] The practice of tolerance alone is not enough to solve this problem. First, as we have seen above, tolerance conceived as a form of "hard pluralism" or millet multiculturalism may not provide an adequate guarantee of individual rights. As Jeffrey Stout has pointed out, communitarian politics fails to protect the interests of those who "resist conformity to type."[70] Second, tolerance often implies a sort of theological presumptuousness, in which the human being arrogates to herself the right to judge what is acceptable or unacceptable for God. This attitude was criticized severely by Paine in *Rights of Man:*

> Toleration places itself, not between man and man, nor between church and church, nor between one denomination of religion and another, but between God and man; between the being who worships and the BEING who is worshipped; and by the same act of assumed authority by which it tolerates man to pay his worship, it presumptuously and blasphemously

sets up itself to tolerate the Almighty to receive it. Were a Bill brought into any parliament, entitled "AN ACT to tolerate or grant liberty to the Almighty to receive the worship of a Jew or a Turk," or "to prohibit the Almighty from receiving it," all men would startle, and call it blasphemy. There would be an uproar. . . . Who art thou, vain dust and ashes, by whatever name thou art called, whether a king, a bishop, a church, or a state, a parliament or anything else, that obtrudest thine insignificance between the soul of man and his Maker? Mind thine own concerns. If he believes not as thou believest, it is a proof that thou believest not as he believeth, and there is no earthly power that can determine between you.[71]

The last sentence of Paine's critique of toleration recalls, perhaps intentionally, Sura 109 of the Qur'an, *al-Kafirun*, "The Unbelievers."[72] Feisal Abdul Rauf uses this sura as part of his argument for soft pluralism and to prove the Shari'a compliance of the First Amendment.[73] In doing so he seeks to establish what Rawls called "an overlapping consensus of reasonable comprehensive doctrines."[74] In an overlapping consensus, the moral doctrines that are held in common by different groups in society endorse the concept of liberal democracy, "each from its own point of view." However, in Rawls's model the groups that endorse the overlapping consensus do not do so as corporate entities but as collectivities of individuals. No representative body such as the Islamic Society of North America or some national *fiqh* council has the authority speak for the Muslim community as a whole. Rawls consistently affirms the rights of the individual over the rights of the group. The "right of exit" from the group, which is often adduced as a protection for dissent by advocates of millet multiculturalism, is not a meaningful form of protection for religious dissenters because it amounts to self-imposed excommunication.[75] Those who exit stand to lose all of the political and social advantages of group membership.

In a liberal constitutional regime, says Rawls, political power is only legitimate "when it is exercised in accordance with a constitution the essentials of which *all citizens as free and equal* may reasonably be expected to endorse in light of principles and ideals acceptable to their common human reason" (italics in the original).[76] The purpose of an overlapping consensus is to provide agreement on the basic principles of public reason in terms that are specific to and hence acceptable for citizens who follow different social and religious traditions. These principles outweigh the differences that may otherwise exist between traditions. The notion of an overlapping consensus is fundamental to Rawls's theory of political liberalism. It is also foundational for classic social-contract theories of civil society, such as those proposed by Locke, Paine, and Jefferson. Because all citizens are expected to "buy into" the social contract, it is unreasonable to expect that immigration into the society from the outside or conversion

to a minority religion from the inside provides justification for the renegotiation of the original contract.[77]

It is this desire to renegotiate the social contract that makes millet multicul-
turalist responses to democratic constitutionalism "uncivil" in the eyes of political liberals. Tariq Ramadan has criticized the notion of "the jurisprudence of
[Muslim] minorities" on precisely this point. He notes that when the juridical
scholar Yusuf al-Qaradawi introduced the concept in his book *On the Jurisprudence of Muslim Minorities* (*Fi Fiqh al-aqalliyat al-muslima*), he subtitled the work
"The Life of Muslims in Other Societies." Qaradawi called Western societies
"other societies" because he assumed that the only societies that are normative
for Muslims are Muslim-majority societies. However, in today's globalized Islam,
says Ramadan, "there is no longer a place of origin from which Muslims are
'exiled' or 'distanced.'"[78] In his book *Western Muslims and the Future of Islam*,
Ramadan refutes the premises of Shariʿa fundamentalism by stressing the hermeneutical nature of the Shariʿa and revising its sources to include the Qurʾan, the
Sunna, and the various sociopolitical contexts in which it is interpreted.[79] By
doing so he seeks to provide Muslim minorities in the West with the interpretive tools that will allow them to remain faithful to what Rawls calls their "background culture" while acting as full partners in the pluralistic and democratic
societies in which they live.[80]

Although the ideas of Feisal Abdul Rauf and Tariq Ramadan are more con-
gruent with American notions of democratic constitutionalism and civil society
than are those of Sherman Jackson, they are not without their inconsistencies.
After making a cogent argument for a theologically and legally justified model
of Islamic liberalism, Abdul Rauf undermines his thesis by lapsing into millet
multiculturalism. At the end of his essay "What's Right with America," he calls
for the establishment of "separate Muslim, Jewish, or Christian personal status
courts to render judgments for Muslim, Jewish, and Christian couples seeking
to have their cases heard under such laws and to have these decisions ratified by
the secular state courts."[81] Not only is this proposal probably unconstitutional,
it goes against the notion of an overlapping consensus. If the United States is a
Shariʿa-compliant state, as Abdul Rauf asserts, and if American courts allow
Islamic practices to be used as precedents in cases of civil litigation, as many do
already, why should there be any need for Islamic civil courts at all? Ramadan
is more successful at avoiding the lure of millet multiculturalism, but he too
remains torn between the demands of Islamic tradition and public reason. For
example he repeatedly insists that the Qurʾanic prohibition of *ribaʾ* is unequivocal and that *ribaʾ* always means "interest." Although this latter claim is a tenet of
the modern ideology of Islamic economics, it is far from certain that all scholars of *fiqh* would agree to such a conclusion. What is Ramadan trying to say by
sowing such assertions throughout his narrative? Is he suggesting that Muslims

ought to live in economic enclaves? If so, then he too is advocating a form of millet multiculturalism. Ramadan's treatment of this issue leads one to conclude that he too may be advocating a modus vivendi rather than an overlapping consensus.

Jackson, Abdul Rauf, and Ramadan should be recognized for attempting to resolve the epistemological crisis of Islam by developing new resources and frameworks for Islamic tradition. With varying degrees of success, they seek to develop what Alasdair MacIntyre calls "new and second first languages" of tradition that are Islamically authentic yet also engage with the new traditions that Muslims must deal with if they are to feel at home, as Ramadan says, in a globalized world. However, the inconsistencies of their arguments reveal that there is still some distance to go before the epistemological crisis can be resolved. Jackson's soft version of Shari'a fundamentalism, Abdul Rauf's lapse into millet multiculturalism, and Ramadan's pragmatic attempt to achieve a political modus vivendi with liberal democratic society while seeming to advocate an overlapping consensus suggest that the liberal democratic notion of public reason remains a major obstacle in this process.

Public reason is the basis of the distinction between what Rawls called "background culture" and public political culture. According to Rawls public reason is the reason of citizens, who, sharing the status of equal citizenship and acting as a collective body, "exercise final political and coercive power over one another in enacting laws and amending their constitution."[82] To do so they must reach an overlapping consensus on the fundamental political values of society. These are values that "all citizens may reasonably be expected to endorse in the light of principles and ideals acceptable to them as reasonable and rational."[83] Of the Muslim thinkers discussed above, Abdul Rauf comes closest to advocating the ideal of public reason in his attempt to reach a consensus of fundamental rights and core political values. However, even he finds it difficult to conceive of public reason without an overarching authority—be it a sacred text such as the Qur'an or the Hadith or some sort of Shari'a court—that can legitimize the consensus of public reason.

The problem of public reason for contemporary Muslims is grounded in the failure of mainstream Islamic thought to agree on a warranted notion of unsupervised reason or of a "democratic intellect" such as that proposed by John Locke. The lack of such a concept has both political and epistemological consequences. Without a warrant for unsupervised reason, the exercise of public reason must be supervised. Supervised reason may all too easily become paternalism, authoritarianism, or at worst, totalitarianism. The pervasive mistrust of public reason as the basis for a just society in Islam can be observed in many contexts: in the tracts of Osama bin Laden, in the recent victories of Islamist parties in Iraq, Egypt, and Palestine, and even in the following semiofficial statement on the coexistence of Islam and democracy from the Hashemite Kingdom of Jordan: "Worldly authority that derives solely from the human intellect is incapable of establishing perfect human justice amongst people, even when it exerts all its efforts to safeguard the people's interests and welfare. Thus, humanity is in need of a system of legislation that is based on Divine Guidance and Light; on ethics and benevolence; on upholding the truth and protecting it, and on the fulfillment of pledges and covenants. These are the principles that Islam duly affirms in its vision of government and temporal authority."[84]

It is ironic that a statement issued on behalf of a liberal constitutional monarchy such as Jordan would echo the views of Sayyid Qutb in *Signs along the Road.* Its authors seem to have been unaware that while they deny the validity of public reason in the first sentence of the statement, in the second sentence they affirm the very theology and ethics that liberal democratic thinkers such as Locke and Paine adduce to support public reason. What must Muslims do to avoid such contradictions in their political philosophy? Can they come to endorse the strong affirmation of individual rights and political liberalism, reproduced in the epigraph to this article, that Alija Izetbegović made in his speech at the American Center for Democracy in 1997? The key to political liberalism, said Izetbegović, is in the protection of minorities and especially of minority opinions: "Freedom of thought is, above all the freedom to think differently." Such freedom can only be guaranteed by an institutionalized trust in individual and public reason. This trust in the clarity of political reason, whether it be autonomous, socially influenced, or divinely guided, is one of the foundational premises of political liberalism. It is not the Promethean individualism imagined by bin Laden and other religious critics of liberalism. In the words of John Rawls: "Freedom at the deepest level calls upon the freedom of reason, both theoretical and practical, as expressed in what we say and do. Limits on freedom are at bottom limits on our reason: on its development and education, its knowledge and information, and on the scope of the actions in which it can be expressed."[85] Thus the limits placed on public reason have much to say about the limits of freedom and ultimately about the nature of the epistemological crisis in Islam.

NOTES

The first epigraph is from Osama bin Laden, "To the Americans" (October 6, 2002), in *Messages to the World: The Statements of Osama Bin Laden*, ed. Bruce B. Lawrence, trans. James Howarth (London & New York: Verso, 2005), 167. The second epigraph is from Alija Izetbegović, acceptance speech for American Center for Democracy Award, New York, March 27, 1997. See Izetbegović, *Sjecanja: Autobiografski zapis* (Sarajevo: TKD Sahinpasic, 2001), 455. This passage was translated by Professor Fikret Karcic, Faculty of Law, Sarajevo University, Bosnia-Herzegovina.

   1. ʿAli B. ʿUthman al-Jullabi al-Hujwiri, *The Kashf al-Mahjub: The Oldest Persian Treatise on Sufiism*, trans. Reynold A. Nicholson (1911; repr., London: Luzac, 1976), 44.

2. Izetbegović, *Sjecanja*, 455.

3. William E. Connolly, *The Terms of Political Discourse* (Princeton, N.J.: Princeton University Press, 1993), quoted in Frank Cunningham, *Theories of Democracy: A Critical Introduction* (London and New York: Routledge, 2002), 3.

4. These systems of government are outlined in book 4 of *The Politics*. See Aristotle, *The Politics*, rev. ed., trans. T. A. Sinclair, translation revised by Trevor J. Saunders (London: Penguin, 1992), 235–94.

5. Aristotle said of the middle class: "This is the class of citizens which is most secure in a state, for they do not, like the poor, covet their neighbors' goods; nor do others covet theirs, as the poor covet the goods of the rich; and as they neither plot against others, nor are themselves plotted against, they pass through life safely. Wisely then did Phocylides pray, 'Many things are best in the mean; I desire to be of a middle condition in my city.'" Aristotle, *The Politics*, trans. Benjamin Jowett, introduction, analysis, and index by H. W. C. Davis (Oxford: Clarendon, 1930), bk. 4, pt. 11. This quotation can be found at http://www.constitution.org/ari/polit_01.htm (accessed June 16, 2009). I am grateful to Professor Stephen Sheppard of the University of Arkansas School of Law for this reference.

6. Cunningham, *Theories of Democracy*, 7. It is often overlooked that Aristotle's acknowledgment of the utility of democracy provides a bridge between the political theories of classical antiquity and Enlightenment utilitarianism.

7. Alexis de Tocqueville, *Democracy in America*, ed. J. P. Mayer, trans. George Lawrence (Garden City, N.Y.: Doubleday Anchor, 1969), 60.

8. Cunningham, *Theories of Democracy*, 9–12.

9. Thomas Jefferson, letter to William Charles Jarvis, September 28, 1820, in *Writings of Thomas Jefferson*, vol. 10, ed. P. L. Ford (New York: Putnam, 1899), 161.

10. Amir Taheri, "Al-Qaeda's Agenda for Iraq," *New York Post Online Edition*, September 4, 2003. Ron Suskind's recent book *The One Percent Doctrine: Deep Inside America's Pursuit of Its Enemies since 9/11* (New York: Simon & Schuster, 2006) reveals that Yusuf al-Ayeri was behind a plot, eventually called off by al Qaeda, to attack the New York City subway system with hydrogen cyanide poison gas. Before his death he was identified by the CIA as the most significant al Qaeda operative in Saudi Arabia. See the article "The Untold Story of Al-Qaeda's Plot to Attack the Subways," *Time*, June 26, 2006, 27–35.

11. Jeremy Waldron, *God, Locke, and Equality: Christian Foundations of John Locke's Political Thought* (Cambridge: Cambridge University Press, 2002), 84–85.

12. Bruce B. Lawrence, *Defenders of God: The Fundamentalist Revolt against the Modern Age* (San Francisco: Harper & Row, 1989), 27.

13. Ibid., 15.

14. Mircea Eliade, *The Sacred and the Profane: The Nature of Religion*, trans. Willard R. Trask (New York: Harcourt, Brace, 1959), 11–13.

15. Sayyid Qutb, *Ma'alim fi al-Tariq* (Beirut: Dar al-Sharq, 2000), 108; this and all translations from Arabic in this essay are mine. This discussion can also be found in the English translation, *Milestones* (Damascus: Dar al-Ilm, n.d.), 87–90. In the widely distributed English version of this work, many of Qutb's key concepts are paraphrased rather than translated directly from the Arabic text. For this reason the page references below are only for the Arabic version. *Ma'alim fi al-Tariq* was written in 1964, two years before Qutb's execution by the Nasser regime of Egypt.

16. Qutb, *Ma'alim fi al-Tariq*, 110.

17. Ibid., 111.

18. Ibid., 112.

19. Sayyid Qutb, *Social Justice in Islam*, trans. John B. Hardie, with revised translation by Hamid Algar (Oneonta, N.Y.: Islamic Publications International, 2000), 37. The idea of Islam as a system or order (*nizam*) appears to have come from South Asia around the time of World War II. In 1943 Mawlana Hamid al-Ansari Ghazi used the term *nizam* to refer to Islam as a political system. The year before, in 1942, Abu al-ʿAla al-Mawdudi (d. 1979) used the Urdu term *Islami nizam* (Islamic order) in a speech about Islamic ideology. Qutb appears to have derived both this concept and that of the neo-*Jahiliyya* from Mawdudi. See Wilfred Cantwell Smith, *The Meaning and End of Religion* (1962; repr., Minneapolis: Fortress, 1991), 274n10.

20. Qutb, *Social Justice*, 42–43.

21. Ibid., 114.

22. Ibid., 115.

23. Alasdair MacIntyre, *Whose Justice? Which Rationality?* (Notre Dame, Ind.: University of Notre Dame Press, 1988), 361–62. The term *epistemological crisis* first appeared in MacIntyre's "Epistemological Crises, Dramatic Narrative and the Philosophy of Science," *Monist* 60, no. 4 (1977): 453–72.

24. MacIntyre, *Whose Justice?* 364.

25. "Aufklärung ist der Ausgang des Menschen aus seiner selbst verschuldeten Unmündigkeit." Cited in Ronald A. Kuipers, *Critical Faith: Toward a Renewed Understanding of Religious Life and Its Public Accountability* (Amsterdam: Rodopi / Vrije Universiteit Amsterdam, 2002), 24 and n. 34.

26. MacIntyre, *Whose Justice?* 362.

27. Jaroslav Pelikan, *The Vindication of Tradition* (New Haven, Conn.: Yale University Press, 1984), 81.

28. In Occidentalism, the mind of the West is often portrayed as a kind of higher idiocy. "To be equipped with the mind of the West is like being an idiot savant, mentally defective but with a special gift for making arithmetic calculations. It is a mind without a soul, efficient, like a calculator, but hopeless at doing what is humanly important. The mind of the West is capable of great economic success, to be sure, and of developing and promoting advanced technology, but cannot grasp the higher things in life, for it lacks spirituality and understanding of human suffering." Ian Buruma and Avishai Margalit, *Occidentalism: The West in the Eyes of Its Enemies* (New York: Penguin, 2004), 75.

29. "Occidentalism is partly a defense of national character, national culture and national life-style against alienation and disloyalty; a popular option against Orientalism as a minority option; a mass culture against Orientalism as an elite culture; an ideology for the ruled against Orientalism as an ideology of the ruler; a liberating device like liberation theology against Orientalism as a dominating device, like church dogmatics." Hassan Hanafi, "From Orientalism to Occidentalism," in *Islam in the Modern World*, vol. 2, *Tradition, Revolution, and Culture* (Heliopolis, Egypt: Dar Kebaa Bookshop, 2000), 400. This article first appeared as the paper "The Self and the Other," Department of English Language and Literature, Cairo University, December 1993.

30. Kevin Avruch, *Culture and Conflict Resolution* (Washington, D.C.: United States Institute of Peace Press, 1998), 14–16.

31. Those who conceive of Islam as a *milla* find justification for their view in the following passage of the Qur'an, where the Prophet Joseph says: "I have forsaken the *milla* of a people who do not believe in Allah and reject the Hereafter. Instead, I follow the *milla* of my fathers Abraham, Isaac, and Jacob. Never was it our practice to associate partners with God" (Qur'an, 12:37–38). Here *milla* refers specifically to the Children of Israel (*Banu Isra'il*), to whom the Qur'an consistently refers in tribal and hence in cultural terms. One is therefore entitled to ask whether the strong communitarian emphasis of contemporary Islamism represents a sort of "Judaizing" of Islamic ideology. Islamism may also be seen as an Islamic version of nineteenth-century European Romanticism in which Qur'anic universalism is replaced by Islamic nationalism. The influence of Romantic concepts of the nation can be observed in the terms that are used for nationalism in the contemporary Muslim world. Territorial nationalism is the basis of the term *wataniyya* (literally, "homeland-ism"); racial nationalism is the basis of the term *jinsiyya* (literally, "genus-ism"); cultural nationalism is the basis of the term *qawmiyya* (literally, "folk-ism").

32. Sherman A. Jackson, *Islam and the Blackamerican: Looking toward the Third Resurrection* (New York: Oxford University Press, 2005), 145.

33. Ibid.

34. Ibid., 145–46.

35. Ibid., 146.

36. Ibid., 150.

37. John Kelsay, "Civil Society and Government in Islam," in *Islamic Political Ethics: Civil Society, Pluralism, and Conflict,* ed. Sohail H. Hashmi (Princeton, N.J.: Princeton University Press, 2002), 8.

38. Ibid., 18.

39. Farhad Kazemi, "Perspectives on Islam and Civil Society," in Hashemi, *Islamic Political Ethics,* 40.

40. Kwame Anthony Appiah, *The Ethics of Identity* (Princeton, N.J.: Princeton University Press, 2005), 71–79; Appiah also calls this model "hard pluralism."

41. I am grateful to Professor Stephen Sheppard of the University of Arkansas School of Law for this insight.

42. Thomas Jefferson, "Notes on a Conversation with Dawson" (January 26, 1808), in *Light and Liberty: Reflections on the Pursuit of Happiness,* ed. Eric S. Petersen (New York: Modern Library, 2004), 66.

43. Quoted in Waldron, *God, Locke, and Equality,* 220.

44. Quoted in ibid., 221.

45. Thomas Paine, *Rights of Man,* in *Collected Writings* (New York: Library of America, 1995), 467.

46. Ibid., 468.

47. Ibid.

48. Ibid., 464.

49. Ibid., 465.

50. Thomas Jefferson, letter to Thomas Earl, September 24, 1823, in *Light and Liberty,* 59.

51. Thomas Jefferson, "Opinion on the Question Whether the President Should Veto the Bill, Declaring That the Seat of Government Shall Be Transferred to the Potomac in the Year 1790" (July 15, 1790), in *Light and Liberty*, 68.

52. Ibid., 74–75. (The quotation from this source combines several statements by Jefferson that were made in 1811, 1812, 1824, and 1826.)

53. Imam Feisal Abdul Rauf, *What's Right with Islam: A New Vision for Muslims and the West* (San Francisco: HarperSanFrancisco, 2004), 104.

54. Ibid., 103; see also F. Forrester Church, *The American Creed* (New York: St. Martin's Press, 2002).

55. Abdul Rauf, *What's Right with Islam*, 106.

56. Ibid.; for the source of these quotations, see Antonin Scalia, "God's Justice and Ours," *First Things: Journal of Religion and Public Life* 123 (May 2002): 17–21.

57. Abdul Rauf, *What's Right with Islam*; see, for example, the chapter "Common Roots," 11–40.

58. Ibid., 86.

59. Ibid., 107.

60. Ibid., 16–17.

61. Ibid., 86.

62. Appiah, *Ethics of Identity*, 79.

63. Muhammad Asad, *The Principles of State and Government in Islam* (Gibraltar: Dar al-Andalus, 1980).

64. Abdul Rauf, *What's Right with Islam*, 86.

65. Ibid., 87; Abdul Rauf could have made his argument stronger if he had relied on the works of Paine and the later writings of Jefferson rather than on the Declaration of Independence.

66. Ibid., 105.

67. Tariq Ramadan, *Western Muslims and the Future of Islam* (New York: Oxford University Press, 2004), 27.

68. John Rawls, *Political Liberalism* (New York: Columbia University Press, 1996), 147.

69. Ibid., 133.

70. Jeffrey Stout, *Democracy and Tradition* (Princeton, N.J.: Princeton University Press, 2004), 74.

71. Paine, *Rights of Man*, 482–83.

72. The text of Qur'an 109 reads, "Say: Oh unbelievers! I do not worship what you worship and you do not worship what I worship. I am not a worshipper of what you have worshipped and you do not worship what I worship. To you your religion and to me mine" (my translation). Although "to worship" is the more accurate translation of the verb *'abida*, which appears frequently in this sura, it is most often translated as "to believe." There are numerous hints in Paine's writings that he may have been aware of the text of the Qur'an in translation.

73. Abdul Rauf, *What's Right with Islam*, 104.

74. Rawls, *Political Liberalism*, 134.

75. Appiah, *Ethics of Identity*, 76–79.

76. Rawls, *Political Liberalism*, 137.

77. Ibid., 136. The social contract can, however, be renegotiated according to the principles set forth in the original contract or constitution.

78. Ramadan, *Western Muslims*, 53; see also Yusuf al-Qaradawi, *Fi Fiqh al-aqalliyat al-muslima* (Cairo: Dar al-Shuruq, 2001).

79. Ramadan, *Western Muslims*, 37; Ramadan calls this hermeneutical context in Arabic *al-waqi'*, "reality" or "actuality" (Fr. *l'actualité*).

80. Rawls, *Political Liberalism*, 220.

81. Abdul Rauf, *What's Right with Islam*, 110.

82. Rawls, *Political Liberalism*, 214.

83. Ibid., 217.

84. *Summary of the Thirteenth General Conference on Islamic Government and Democracy: Differences, Similarities, and the Possibility of Coexistence*, ed. Ghazi bin Muhammad (Amman: Aal al-Bayt Institute for Islamic Thought, 2005), 8.

85. Rawls, *Political Liberalism*, 222–23n9.

The Misrecognition of a Modern Islamist Organization

Germany Faces "Fundamentalism"

KATHERINE PRATT EWING

At the beginning of the twenty-first century, Islamists are seen by many as the primary challenge to the West and to modernity. The more extreme groups reject "the West" and its political, economic, and cultural hegemony. Yet, as Bruce Lawrence showed in his examination of fundamentalism in Christianity, Judaism, and Islam, these "defenders of God" have arisen within the matrix of the modern world.[1] Though many of these groups seek to build communities that reject the trappings and dominance of the West, most do not reject the technologies, science, communications, bureaucratization, and rationalism that are the hallmarks of technological modernity. Lawrence distinguished modernity in this sense from "modernism," which he characterized as a contingent ideology, and thus not a necessary and inevitable accompaniment to modernity. He defined modernism as an ideology that centers on a "search for individual autonomy driven by social values that emphasize change over continuity, quantity over quality and efficient production, power and profit over sympathy for traditional values and vocations."[2] He argued that though fundamentalisms oppose modernism, there is a dialectical affinity between them: fundamentalisms emerge as negative "countertexts" that are shaped by their rejection of and resistance to modernism and that take the form not of nostalgic traditionalism but of a rigorous monotheism that maintains God as an absolute and holistic religious authority.

While I appreciate Lawrence's concern with identifying a configuration of responses to the modern and his attention not only to symbolic/ideological systems but also to social and political practices such as those that marginalize educated young men and make them ripe for political mobilization, I question whether categorizing these groups as resistant to ideological modernism accurately characterizes their position as subjects in the modern world. Positing a divide between modernity as infrastructure and modernism as superstructure obscures the extent to which members of Islamist groups may be modern in ways that go well beyond "modernity" in a technological, utilitarian sense, thereby exaggerating their otherness. I argue that, first, we must take care to distinguish antimodernism from anti-Westernism. Many groups reject various aspects of Western cultures that should be distinguished from ideological modernism as Lawrence has defined it. Furthermore I suggest that under the guise of rejection of certain aspects of Western practice and identification processes there is actually an incitement within many Islamist and other fundamentalist groups to modernize,[3] through an array of practices that constitute a modern subject, which can be characterized by a reflexive, self-conscious interiority, a sense of rupture with a traditional past, and a global, even cosmopolitan, orientation.

Within the past few years, and especially since 9/11, "cosmopolitanism" has emerged as an analytic category that in some respects has supplanted the modern as a way of characterizing a progressive subjectivity. For Kwame Anthony Appiah, in his 2006 "moral manifesto," for example, cosmopolitanism is the foundation of his vision of a harmonious, globalized social order based on pluralism and tolerance.[4] He defines the cosmopolitan in a way that explicitly excludes the "neofundamentalist," thereby marking the fundamentalist as the cosmopolitan's other. I am concerned that such efforts to distinguish "us" and "them" in terms of a fundamentally different kind of subjectivity, like the earlier distinction based on the modern, are in many respects a globalized replication of a discourse about the structure of society that has a very long history. In his lectures titled *Society Must Be Defended*, Michel Foucault argued that since the late Middle Ages, histories have been organized around the idea that society rests on a struggle between opposing forces—understood as races—and is threatened by both internal and external enemies who challenge the very principles of civilization.[5] Could it be that, with the concept of cosmopolitanism, scholars are seeking to find a way to perpetuate this discursive structure, now that neither modernity nor modernism convincingly distinguishes "us" and "them"?

My approach in this paper will focus on the Islamische Gemeinschaft Milli Gorus (IGMG), an Islamic group with roots in Turkey and transnational headquarters in Germany. I argue that groups such as the IGMG not only display the organizational features of modernity, but also participate in the discourse of "modernism" even as they reject some of its most visible features, such as normative German gender relations. Furthermore the misrecognition of them as "not modern" by those who explicitly claim to be a part of the pro-Western modern world comes from demands for conformity to everyday local westernized practices, demands that themselves confuse modernity/modernism with Western cultural hegemony.[6] Many Islamic groups resist subordination to this Western-Christian-secular hegemony, while at the same time inciting their members to constitute and discipline themselves into a reflexive, modern subjectivity that is arguably cosmopolitan.

It is precisely because the Western and the modern are so readily confused that the encompassing of Islamists under the umbrella of the modern has been difficult to imagine for many who identify themselves as Western. As modern subjects we often fail to recognize the extent to which our beliefs and practices are historically and culturally contingent and are not inevitable, rational responses to global capitalism and the hegemony of science.[7] In this paper I first look back to early Turkish Republican efforts to modernize or westernize Islam in ways that confound the two processes in order to foreground such misrecognitions. I then examine some of the recent practices, goals, and interpretive strategies of the diasporic Turkish Islamic IGMG, which is the largest Islamic organization in Germany, in relationship to German and secularist Turkish representations of the group. I demonstrate how the Muslim IGMG subject is misrecognized as nonmodern, and I argue that these misrecognitions are in part a function of the continuing confusion of "Western" and "modern," as well as a function of political maneuvers that draw on this confusion.[8] IGMG projects an alternative vision of the modern, with an organization of space, gender, and time that is different from Western/German arrangements, but it participates fully in the modern as a discursive formation that increasingly appeals to fully modern young people who discipline themselves as Muslim ethical subjects. Having considered the subjectivity of IGMG members in light of Lawrence's 1989 delineation of the modernist, I will in turn consider whether their subjectivity can be subsumed under the umbrella of cosmopolitanism or whether the analytic distinction between self and other represented by this concept has been redrawn in a way that excludes such modern Islamic subjects from the global community of cosmopolitans.

Modernism or Westernism?

Shifts in Euro-American understandings of what is necessary to be "modern" can be seen by looking with an early-twenty-first-century gaze back to the early twentieth century, when the new Republic of Turkey was taking shape. This retrospection can help foreground examples of confusion between what is culturally "Western" and what can be considered a more universally applicable (though also historically contingent and, hence, also cultural) modernism. In the 1920s Turkish intellectuals were struggling with the problem of the place of Islam in a newly formed modern republic modeled on European states such as France (with its secularist ideology) and Switzerland (with its rationalized legal code). Across this temporal gap of more than eighty years from the present, the confounding of cultural practices characteristic of American and Western European societies with features of a global modernity/modernism is transparent, even surprising.

The journal *Moslem World*, published by the Hartford Theological Seminary, which has maintained an Islamic studies program since 1893,[9] published articles on Turkey throughout the period of dramatic religious and social transformation that accompanied the founding of the Turkish Republic in 1923. With its Christian (rather than secularist) orientation, the journal and its authors were particularly concerned with the fate of Islam in the new secularist state, on the one hand fearing that Turkey might go the way of Russia and adopt an atheistic intolerance of all religion and on the other hand asking the question, "Can Islam be reformed?" In an article of that title addressing the "Turkish answer" to this question, written during the height of the legal and social transformation of the place of Islam in Turkey's public sphere, E. Stanley Jones compiled quotations from Turkish sources—mostly local newspapers—that were prescriptions for how Islam could be made compatible with modern civilization.[10] These prescriptions, then, are elements of a discourse that articulate what cultural practices were viewed at that time as essential components of the modern.

Some of these reinterpretations sound absurd to many twenty-first-century ears: "We go less for prayer to the mosque, because our present social habits make it very difficult for us to offer prayer in the customary way. I believe that we ought to be allowed to enter the mosque wearing the shoes we use in walking the streets. We ought to put proper seats in the mosques to sit on. With our present European dress it is impossible to sit on the floor and to take ablutions. One wash early in the morning in our homes ought to be sufficient for the day. O Mohammedans! If we could enter the mosque wearing our shoes, and offer prayers without ablutions, and sit on proper seats, and bow on a desk higher than our seats, and hear educated preachers speaking in beautiful voices in plain Turkish, who would not go to the mosque for worship?"[11]

These are all prescriptions for the reform of everyday practices, for reinscribing the body as a "modern" body that adopts only European postures.[12] These proposals also reject Islamic principles for establishing ritual purity of the body and space as these are laid out in the Qur'an and Sunna, imposing an alien (Christian) cultural logic in which body and spirit are divorced and spirituality is understood as an inner state that does not depend on the condition of the body.[13]

During this period of social transformation in Turkey, even the most basic tenet of Islam was challenged in the name of rationality. Another Istanbul imam published a dialogue in which a "fanatical Moslem" insists to a Swiss Protestant that according to Islam, one must believe in God, Muhammad as a Prophet, the Qur'an, and the next world, and the Swiss replies that he cannot accept things that do not appeal to his reason. The Muslim writer used this dialogue to prove that "no thinking man can believe in Islam as it now is" and advised that "Moslems would insist on the acceptance of one belief only as essential to their faith, namely the creed that 'There is no God but God,'" omitting even the assertion that Muhammad is His Prophet.[14] This proposal for a stripped-down

Islam certainly goes further toward a rationalized monotheism than any Christian faith except perhaps Unitarianism.

Today these suggestions for the reform of Islam are clearly beyond the pale. The first imam suggested that a mosque be transformed into a replica of a Protestant church, and the second suggested a stripped-down "rational" religion more austere than even the Christian Protestant sects, nearly all of which accept Jesus Christ as divinity. For these writers entry into the "modern" world requires the adoption of "civilization," as practiced by the Western nations, in all its detail.

Some of the other recommendations for modernizing Islam in early Republican Turkey, however, are consistent with themes that continue to be important today among Muslim religious leaders: "Islam must be made easier for belief by leaving things out which do not accord with science."[15] The wording of this statement suggests that Islam itself must be changed to fit with science and its rationality, thereby indicating that science is the ultimate arbiter.[16] The relationship between science and Islam continues to be an important theme today, but the rhetoric—and the relationship to the West—has shifted. Far from Islam having to accommodate science, many argue that true Islam is and always has been fully consistent with science. It is emphasized that true Islam encourages humans to know all they can about their world. Some go further and argue that the Qur'an anticipates discoveries made recently by scientists and that Islam is the source of all knowledge and science.[17] To the extent, then, that Islamists see their practices as consistent with science, they can be considered "modern"; from their perspective science is not "Western," but a universal truth. In fact many Islamists, including those who most dramatically excoriate Western society, follow careers in the sciences.

This shift from reforming Islam to fit Western rationality to asserting the primacy and rationality of Islam in opposition to the West is a crucial one, and one that Lawrence foregrounds in his temporal distinction between reformists and fundamentalists. The emergence of Islamic fundamentalisms represents an important shift of power, not away from modernity or even modernism but from a colonizing Western discursive hegemony. There has been a move away from, and definitive rejection of, the presumption that Christianity is superior to Islam and a corresponding embrace of a more universalistic view of science and the modern.

Despite this rhetorical shift, the recommendation to take out of the practice of Islam things that do not accord with science has occurred and persists among Muslims of a wide range of reformist, modernist, and fundamentalist orientations. Elements of Muslim practice such as the use of amulets, the belief in the evil eye, and the spiritual power of dead saints and shrines have been branded as superstition, have been the target of reform, and have achieved the status of being labeled "un-Islamic." What is viewed as proper Islam today is distinguished sharply from what are labeled "ignorant practices" that can still be seen among "the rural and the uneducated." Both the earlier reformist, modernist Islam, as represented by late-nineteenth- and early-twentieth-century thinkers such as Sir Sayyid Ahmad Khan and Muhammad Iqbal in India and Muhammad 'Abduh in Egypt, and what Lawrence and others call Islamic fundamentalism or revivalism, as represented by Sayyid Abu al-'Ala al-Mawdudi of India and Sayyid Qutb of Egypt's Muslim Brotherhood, have led to a more self-conscious practice that incorporates a sense of "pure Islam" as that which has been stripped of local cultural practices. It is precisely these local practices that are most readily dismissed as unscientific.

Like reformists and fundamentalists in other countries with large Muslim populations, Turkish reformists worked to educate the Turkish population to turn away from "ignorant sheikhs who have cheated the people by sorcery and charms,"[18] a project that continues among Islamists today. They also condemned "the Dervish type religion as altogether false," in the context of the Turkish government's shutting down the Sufi brotherhoods in the same year, 1925. This anti-Sufi attitude has moderated today, with some Islamist groups continuing to condemn Sufism and others supporting a reformed Sufism stripped of local "corruptions."[19] In contrast core elements of Islam, such as belief in one God and His Prophet, requirements for prayers and ablutions, *zakat* (charitable giving), fasting during the month of Ramadan, and the pilgrimage to Mecca—in other words, the "Five Pillars"—have crystallized as nonnegotiable requirements of Muslim practice, along with the use of Arabic in prayer, the use of Shari'a as a code for conduct, and, for many, headscarves for women. These elements constitute a rationalized, modern yet timeless, universal Islam based on "fundamentals" that have been purified of local contaminations. Most Islamists apply the same strategy of discursive critique both to local cultures in Muslim lands and to Western cultures. These fundamental requirements, together with the rejection of local "contaminations" from any source, reflect a modernist orientation that is also in some sense cosmopolitan and postnational. The Islamische Gemeinschaft Milli Gorus (an amalgam of German and Turkish words meaning the "Islamic Society of National Vision") is an Islamic organization based in Germany that, like many others, adheres to these fundamentals.

IGMG in German and Turkish Public Discourse

IGMG, like its precursor, Avrupa Milli Gorus Teskilatlari (AGMT, "European National Vision Organization," which was founded in the 1970s), has been under surveillance in Germany as an "extremist" Islamist organization that, according to German Interior Ministry reports, has as its goal the establishing of an Islamic, Shari'a-based government in Turkey. It has ties with the often-banned

and often-renamed Turkish Islamic political party that has been known succes-
sively as the Welfare Party, the Virtue Party, and the Felicity Party, and the
party was headed by Necmettin Erbakan in Turkey until he was banned from
politics (after successfully becoming prime minister for a brief time in the mid-
1990s). *Milli Görüs* (national vision) is the term that Erbakan used to identify
his guiding agenda for bringing an Islamic government to power in Turkey.
Erbakan was accused of advocating Islamic fundamentalism and in the past has
been subject to imprisonment in Turkey for threatening the secularist foundation of the Turkish Republic.[20] The Europe-based IGMG was founded by followers of Erbakan, who were able to operate as an Islamic group more freely in
Germany than in Turkey.

In the early days of the organization in Europe, its primary membership was
the large numbers of Turkish Muslims who had come to Germany, the Nether-
lands, and other countries of Western Europe as guest workers in the 1970s.
Most had the intention of eventually returning to Turkey, and the organization,
in addition to providing makeshift mosques as community spaces for prayer and
socializing in European cities, devoted much of its attention and resources to
the vicissitudes of Islam in Turkish politics. In those early days, there was considerable disagreement over the extent to which members should accommodate
themselves to Western social practices and over the proper tactics for achieving
their central sociopolitical goal of establishing an Islamic government in Turkey.
The more radical element, led by Cemaleddin Kaplan, split off in 1983 and
eventually became Islami Cemaatler Birgili (ICB; Federation of Islamic Associations and Communities). ICB renounced all ties with IGMG and denounced
its members as infidels for their compromises with Western society.[21] ICB was
actually banned in Germany following September 11, 2001, and members were
threatened with deportation, though none had been charged with any specific
crime. It was one of two organizations in Germany that were banned by the
government in the wake of the realization that the extremists who destroyed the
World Trade Center had used Germany as a base of operations.[22] The German
government also put considerable pressure on IGMG, and there were indications for a time that it, too, might be banned in Germany, though there were no
clear indications that either ICB or IGMG had any ties to al Qaeda.

In the 1970s in Germany, AGMT aimed its appeal to workers, who were relatively powerless vis-à-vis the government and the factory, and eventually to
their families newly arrived from rural Turkey. But in recent years IGMG has
been transforming to meet the needs and orientations of the second and third
generations, most of whom are at home in a German world and have no intention of ever returning to Turkey, yet are still struggling with ethnic/racial/reli-
gious discrimination. Members of the second generation generally reject the
"traditional," rural practices of the first generation and embrace either a German

youth culture that has little place for religious concerns or, alternatively, adopt a "conscious" Muslim identity such as that articulated by IGMG.

When I was doing ethnographic research at the organization's headquarters in 2002, Mehmet Sabri Erbakan was its president.[23] He is a member of the "second generation," who grew up in Germany. Though he is a nephew of Necmettin Erbakan, and thus has close ties to the Islamists who sought to create an Islamic government in Turkey, he and his associates devoted much of their energy to establishing a viable community for Muslim minorities in Europe and beyond as the second generation moves into adulthood and into positions of power and influence. The shift created tension between the generations of IGMG leadership but has also led to an array of new strategies for integration into German society, including a citizenship campaign (and consideration of what citizenship means in an increasingly transnational world); a gradual shift away from Turkish to the German language not only in the name of the organization but in publications, activities, and their Web site; and efforts to educate members in "proper" Islam, distinguishing it from what the organization regards as archaic, rural Turkish practices. This often involves young IGMG members and associates educating their parents in what is correct Muslim practice. It is this emphasis on teaching clearly articulated "fundamentals" of Islam and the rejection of "corruptions" that mark them as fundamentalist by Lawrence's, as well as Marty and Appleby's, definitions.[24]

The view of many Germans, including officials such as the interior minister as well as secularists of Turkish background living in Germany, is that IGMG is a fundamentalist group that threatens the German sociopolitical order. What are the features that lead observers to this conclusion about the organization? According to German government *Verfassungsschutz* (protection of the constitution) reports, Islamism, including that espoused by IGMG, has increasingly developed into a threat for Western European countries with large Muslim populations. The annual reports accuse IGMG of trying to establish a society based on the Qur'an and Shari'a for their sympathizers in Germany. The 1999 report, for example, stated that adherents of Islam believe that their religion can only be freely practiced when the governing institutions of the society are themselves dictated by the Qur'an and religious law.[25] The report also argued that the claims by IGMG leaders that their freedom of religion is covered by the Basic Law (the German constitution) are incorrect because the Basic Law only covers the freedom to practice religion within a society organized according to secular democratic principles and not according to Shari'a. Yet the only specific content that this Verfassungsschutz report identified was that IGMG's goal is to change the rules shaping the German public sphere so that Muslims have the freedom to live their own lives in a manner consistent with their interpretations of the Qur'an and Shari'a. The imams of IGMG have issued fatwa-like rulings (that is, interpretations of Islamic law for a specific situation not explicitly covered in the Qur'an or existing law) that clearly accommodate daily practice to the realities of German lifestyle and the German legal system. Despite the continual surveillance of IGMG, recent reports do acknowledge that IGMG does not advocate violence to achieve its political goal of establishing an Islamic political system in Turkey.[26] By the 2005 report, the issue of violence was not mentioned at all, though the report expressed skepticism over IGMG's claims to be focused on integration into German society. Though the Verfassungsschutz report acknowledges that IGMG operates only through legitimate, nonviolent channels, the phantasmic fear is that IGMG will succeed in creating some kind of Islamic state in Germany.[27] The 2005 report expressed concern that their ultimate goal is the establishment of "Islamic civilization" in a "greater Turkey."[28]

For the German public, the most visible threat and point of contention with IGMG is the head scarf that many Muslim groups, including IGMG, maintain is the proper garb for a Muslim woman. The covered Muslim woman has been a key site where the principles of secularism and religious freedom often come into direct conflict, a conflict that has been increasing in intensity in recent years, most visibly in France, where students were banned from wearing the head scarf to school,[29] but also in Germany. Since the establishment of the Republic of Turkey as a laicist state in the 1920s, women have not been permitted to enter state-controlled schools to practice professions such as medicine or law with a head covering in place. Controversy surrounding this prohibition became a visible issue in Turkey in the 1980s and has continued to be so as growing numbers of women explicitly challenge state authority by refusing to remove their head scarves when they attend school. They have done so in the name of democracy and religious freedom, and Necmettin Erbakan's Islamic party was at the forefront of the struggle for the freedom of Muslim women and girls to cover themselves in all circumstances. Thus far in Germany, most specific legal cases addressing this issue have involved situations of Muslim girls being forced to participate in compulsory gym and swimming classes in which wearing a head scarf would be impossible, and these cases have generally been resolved by rulings that exempt covered Muslim girls from such compulsory activities. But in recent years there have been cases of Muslim women who lost their jobs as public school teachers because they insisted on wearing a head scarf in the classroom. IGMG has been involved in training a number of young women to be teachers of Islamic education in the public schools. When I was conducting research between 1999 and 2004, these women were preparing for legal battles as they approached the time to apply for teaching jobs while wearing the head scarf. Controversy surrounded covered teachers because they are seen as a threat to the principle that teachers represent modern secularism in the schools, a key element of the German public sphere. IGMG maintains that the modern principle of religious freedom is being violated by this restriction. A 2003 Federal Constitutional Court ruling, which allowed each state to pass legislation banning the head scarf, was a major setback for teachers who wear them.

IGMG and Modernism

If we consider the debates between the German government and IGMG in terms of what Lawrence has identified as core components of modernism as an ideology that stands in opposition to fundamentalism, does this contrast hold up? Do IGMG's objectives and assumptions demonstrate a rejection of modernism? Following Lawrence's characterization of fundamentalism's antimodernism in terms of a set of dichotomies, does IGMG display modernist values such as: (1) an emphasis on change vs. continuity; (2) the valuing of individual autonomy vs. group conformity; (3) efficient production rather than traditional values; and (4) pluralism vs. a universal revealed truth?

The issue of individual autonomy often comes up in legal discourse as a contrast between a system grounded in the rights of individuals and a system in which rights are granted to groups and in which group members are subject to the rules or laws of the group. Saba Mahmood, drawing on ethnographic research on Egyptian women involved in what she calls a "nonliberal" Islamic movement, disrupts this dichotomy by uncoupling self-realization and agency from autonomy and emancipatory politics.[30] The movement resists the secularization and westernization of Egyptian society, seeking to reorganize public life in terms of Islamic principles. Mahmood effectively uses this case to challenge a universalized notion of agency that is often posited in feminist scholarship, which locates the political and moral autonomy of the subordinate female subject only in resistance to patriarchal authority.[31] Mahmood has demonstrated that agency can more effectively be conceptualized "not as a synonym for resistance to relations of domination, but as a capacity for action that historically specific relations of subordination enable and create."[32] She presents the discursive tradition in which these women participate as one that "holds subordination to a transcendent will (and thus, in many instances, to male authority) as its coveted goal."[33] However, by stressing the discursive distinctiveness of this disciplinary tradition and its roots in centuries of Islamic ethical texts, what she does not emphasize is the extent to which the disciplinary norms and how they are enacted are part of a social movement that is itself shaped by modernism and secularism, not just by being posed in opposition to them, but also by sharing with them specific understandings and practices of subjectivation. Mahmood's conversation is with a certain political feminists who have often used the oppressed Muslim woman, understood as lacking agency and autonomy, as their victimized subject; my conversation in this paper is with a Western public (including many scholars) that sees the Islamic subject as distinctly unmodern, illiberal, and at best parochial.

In Germany considerable public concern has been articulated over the years about the fact that Turkish families, many of whom migrated directly from rural Anatolia to German cities, were reluctant to send their daughters to school and often married them off to relatives when they were still below the legal marriage age in Germany. German fears of IGMG efforts to establish equal rights for Muslims are often conceptualized in terms of these images of the patriarchal rule of the father in the traditional Turkish family. From this perspective the woman's individual rights would be sacrificed to the group's right to maintain its distinctive way of life, including the absolute authority of the father. The IGMG goal of living according to Islamic law is perceived as an effort to subject the young woman to the domination of her family, who will force her to cover, forbid her an education, and force her to marry someone of the family's choosing while she is still a child.

But this perception has little to do with IGMG teachings and goals. In the lengthy conversations I engaged in with young women who were affiliated with IGMG organizations, I heard young women in their early twenties who were working toward college degrees and planned to pursue careers. One young woman whom I met at a meeting of an IGMG women's group told me that she had been through a long fight with her father, who had wanted her to marry a family friend still living in Turkey. It had nearly driven her to a nervous breakdown, until she joined the women's group. There she learned that in the Qur'an, a woman is supposed to choose her own husband. Other women emphasized that it is important for a couple to sign a marriage contract and that IGMG teachers had told them that they should carefully read the contract and be sure that it gives them equal rights in the marriage, including the right to divorce.

IGMG leaders stressed to me that their goal is to help Turkish families integrate successfully into German society by encouraging education and by preaching against traditional Turkish customs that are actually "against Islam." They place stress on the conscience of the individual and on his or her responsibility to choose to live as a proper Muslim. Thus IGMG women are often critical of women who wear "traditional" scarves (which are usually tied under the chin and do not fully cover the hair) out of "habit." But they also emphasized to me (as an uncovered woman) that IGMG does not force a woman to wear a head scarf. When I noted that in photos of various IGMG events and activities, nearly all the women were covered, they replied that there are some who do not cover, but that most women realize within themselves that it is God's will. In one family that I have known for several years, I had the opportunity to observe the youngest daughter make the transition into wearing the head scarf, at age twelve. She had been urged to don it at age eleven, but after a few weeks of trying it out decided that she was not yet ready. Everyone in the family, including the girl herself, talked about the transition in terms of her own decision to cover. Though there was clearly strong family and community pressure for her to cover, the issue was articulated in terms of individual choice, personal autonomy, and inner motivation.

These are just a few of the situations in which Muslims affiliated with IGMG explicitly and comfortably participate in a discourse in which personal autonomy during the socialization process is foregrounded. I never heard the argument of group rights deployed as a way of defending the authority of the organization or of the family to restrict the freedoms of its members. On the contrary the issue of group rights came up in their challenges to what they perceived as discrimination against them as a group, in situations where Christian groups held rights and benefits (such as the right to build churches or the benefit of religious education in the schools) that were denied to Muslims.[34]

As for the modernist value of change over tradition, IGMG explicitly advocates change in many respects. As I have already pointed out, one of its goals is the rooting out of Turkish traditions that group members see as inappropriate in the communities they now live in and, even further, as against Islam. Their understanding of Shariʿa is also dynamic. For the most part, it is not seen as being incompatible with German law. The following minor incident, almost beneath notice, illustrates the sort of spontaneous musings on the issue of German law and Shariʿa that I heard from IGMG members during everyday interactions: While I was visiting IGMG headquarters near Cologne, one young but fairly high-ranking member of the organization reflected on Islamic law in the context of thinking about German traffic laws. It came up because we were looking for another senior member of IGMG whom I wanted to interview. He commented that the man must be in the building because he could not have gone out, since he had lost his driver's license. He explained, "He was speeding. Many of us drive too fast, and it isn't good—it is dangerous. German traffic laws are like Shariʿa—they tell us what is good for us."

IGMG imams stress accommodation to changing times in their interpretation of Shariʿa. One woman whose father is an imam in the organization and issues rulings on how Islamic law should be applied in Germany told me that her father used to be against music of any kind. But now he realizes that music can have many purposes and effects, so now they all listen to the radio and CDs. She felt that he has been wise to recognize that one shouldn't fight an overwhelming presence such as music but rather should adapt to current circumstances.

Another change in practice that has come with the organization's adaptation to Germany and that has clear parallels with the Protestantization of Christianity is the desacralization of ritual objects such as prayer beads. When I was staying near IGMG headquarters with a devout Muslim couple, both of whom had important positions in the organization, I was present one evening when the father and his two teenaged sons set out their prayer rugs and performed *salat*.

After they had finished the formal prayers and were still sitting on their rugs, one of the boys began twirling some prayer beads he had been holding and eventually flung them under a radiator. I was startled at the casual way in which he handled the beads and surprised that his parents did not correct him or comment on it. Later in another context his mother said that part of purifying Islam was to worship nothing but God. She said that beads and other objects may help in worship, but they have no special religious value in themselves.

Similarly IGMG interpreters recognize the need for reinterpretation even of explicit Qur'anic verses. For instance there are key elements of the Qur'an that feminists and Western observers have often used to point out that women are not treated equally in Islam. One of them is Sura 2, verse 282: "And have two of your men act as witnesses, but if two men are not available, then a man and two women you approve, so that in case one of them is confused the other may remind her."[35] When I asked Mehmet Sabri Erbakan how he understood this verse, he provided an interpretation that was consistent with the idea that men and women are equal before the law and thus consistent with German law. Like some translators of the Qur'an, he contextualized the verse, saying that in this particular case two women's testimony had been needed because they were not themselves merchants and thus not expert in the matter being discussed. In the case where a woman's training is equal to a man's, her testimony would carry equal weight.

Clearly in the face of all this change, IGMG nevertheless strives to inculcate basic Islamic principles that anchor the Muslim in his or her relationship to God and in everyday life, from matters of diet to regular prayer, clothing, and participation in the life of their Muslim communities. Muslims associated with this organization and its affiliated mosques adamantly resist German pressures to "assimilate," insisting that their goal is "integration" into German society on their own terms, as is their right according to the principle of religious freedom.

As far as valuing efficient production is concerned, I will touch on this point only briefly. IGMG is fully modern. The organization itself is a remarkably effective machine, sharing many organizational features with the Islamist political parties in Turkey.[36] IGMG is innovative in setting up Web resources, including a multilingual Web site and an Internet radio station, which was just coming online when I visited their headquarters in the summer of 2002. Several of the families I visited were multicomputer households. In Turkey many Islamists are highly successful businessmen, and some of the most successful have ventured into the Islamic market, manufacturing and selling modest clothes for Muslim women as well as Islamic consumer goods.[37] Though groups such as IGMG seek ways to handle their business and personal affairs while avoiding loans that involve interest on the money borrowed or lent, they do not reject capitalist markets.[38] It is true that IGMG seeks to help its members to establish a distinctive way of life that is in some respects quite different from modern German or urban Turkish practices. They reject specific cultural practices such as the consumption of alcohol and the wearing of revealing clothing, and they envision a different arrangement of social space based on gender segregation in many (though not all) settings. They also seek workplace arrangements that enable Muslims to pause for required prayers at intervals during the day. But there is no basis for concluding from these prescriptions that these Muslims do not fully participate in capitalist markets or that their preferred social and spatial arrangements are incompatible with the demands of global capital, any more than are German laws limiting the hours and days that stores can be open. But this insistence on retaining distinctive practices that shape the Muslim mode of being in public, everyday spaces is persistently recognized as evidence of a "nonmodern" orientation by many Germans.

Finally we come to the criterion of pluralism vs. commitment to a universal, revealed truth. One of the attributes of modernism that Lawrence identifies is cultural relativism, which he places in sharp contrast to the universalism espoused by fundamentalist groups.[39] A decade ago this dichotomy played out in public arenas in terms of liberal espousals of multiculturalism as a foundation for policies aimed at accommodating difference in Western nation-states, but multiculturalism as a social policy has itself been increasingly questioned in Western societies in recent years, because of the pitfalls of positing a notion of bounded cultures, which the term "multiculturalism" implies. Today scholars such as Appiah have rejected multiculturalism in favor of cosmopolitanism, a shift that reminds us of the historical contingency of the criteria by which we distinguish self and other. With the concept of cosmopolitanism, Appiah has proposed a model of "conversation between people from different ways of life," where the emphasis is on finding practical points of mutual agreement or accommodation in everyday life rather than on distilling a set of universal, mutually agreeable ethical principles.[40]

IGMG members display a tolerance for other ways of life and are explicit about their project of building Islamic institutions in a plural society, as even the Verfassungsschutz reports acknowledge. The masthead of the *Milli Gazete Europe*, a newspaper with links to the organization, states that the newspaper "is not pursuing the goal of establishing a parallel society, but rather is aiming to build a multicultural, multireligious, multilingual, multiethnic and pluralistic society."[41] The 2005 Verfassungsschutz report is suspicious of these assertions and finds quotations within specific newspaper articles that appear to contradict these principles. However, the enactment of modernism and enlightenment rationalism within Europe is at least as inconsistent. This can be seen in current struggles over the organization of gender. European governments have displayed a marked intolerance for the head scarf, manifest in laws forbidding women to wear them in specific public contexts, even those that fully expose the face, despite Muslim claims that such laws violate Muslim women's religious freedom. Arguments against the head scarf are often made in terms of modernist claims that it violates women's autonomy or principles of secularism. Pressures to assimilate include intense demands for conformity to specific German cultural practices, demands that are particularly evident in the controversial "Muslim Test," a questionnaire introduced in one of the German states that was intended to determine whether Muslim immigrants held attitudes that made them culturally suitable for German citizenship.[42]

Progressive public discourses articulate a tolerance that one might expect to lead to a broader space for Muslim practice. But one may question whether the demands for conformity to a universally applicable code are really lessened in today's pluralistic world. In addition to emerging trends toward a global uniformity of dress and tastes (an important part of the background for an ideological condemnation of the Muslim head scarf as nonmodern), a universalist discourse of human rights enforced by quite specific notions of governmentality, in which the state (along with related institutions) takes on the responsibility of caring for its population,[43] continues to spread across the globe and to penetrate more deeply into the affairs of nations and into formerly private spheres such as the family. These intrusions into the family are justified in the name of goals that are difficult to criticize, such as the protection of the rights and welfare of children and women. But leaders of IGMG also espouse these values, though they differ on some of the details of what these rights should encompass. Positing a dichotomy between (our) cultural relativism and (their) fundamentalist universalism marks the Islamic fundamentalist as other and evades potentially fruitful debate over which universal principles should be espoused in a modern global order. With respect to the core values that characterize modernism, namely, human rights, freedom, and democracy, IGMG has contested governmental practices in both Germany and in Turkey in the name of precisely these values.

IGMG in its ideological stances has specific "flash points" of disagreement with its German interlocutors, most of which are colored by tensions within Turkish politics or by specific conditions in Germany. But key issues in Germany can generally be characterized as points where IGMG and its affiliates have identified inequities within the German political and social order rather than as points where IGMG seeks special accommodation that would violate existing laws based on the requirements of Islam as they interpret it. German responses to points of disagreement often take the form of German espousal of local values in the name of the modern, the progressive, and human rights. When IGMG leaders argue in the name of their own right to equal treatment, the German response is often one of suspicion that these Islamists have a hidden agenda that, if realized, will violate the state's basic constitutional order.

Conclusion

While I have demonstrated that in several key respects an Islamist, fundamentalist group such as IGMG cannot be said to reject "modernism" as an ideology, there is the danger of concluding from this that any differences from the mainstream German or Turkish secularist are only superficial or are merely intended to resist the evermore deeply penetrating sameness of everyday life in the modern world. Though, as I have argued, IGMG maintains discursive practices that shape and discipline a modern Muslim subject, there remain basic differences, such as an alternative vision of how time and space should be organized, raising the question of whether a pluralistic society in which subjects live in differently organized yet overlapping public spaces is possible.

At first glance Islamism's rigorous monotheism might seem utterly incompatible with any kind of cosmopolitanism. Though there is little scholarly consensus on the precise significance of the term, "cosmopolitanism" rests on the notion that the cosmopolitan individual, instead of being bound to a specific cultural tradition and nation, is a citizen of the world. In its most extreme form, it has been taken to mean that the individual adopts a position that is inconsistent with valuing one set of relational ties over another (so that the welfare of individuals on the other side of the world is of equal importance to the welfare of one's own children) or with valuing one way of life over another.[44] Though clearly Islamists cannot be characterized in the latter terms, since they value Islam over other "ways of life," by other definitions of cosmopolitanism, including what Samuel Scheffler has called "moderate cosmopolitanism,"[45] or what Appiah and others have called "liberal cosmopolitanism," there are many members of Islamic movements who can readily be called cosmopolitan in orientation. Appiah's vision of cosmopolitanism, which is based on shared practices and "points of agreement that are much more local and contingent" rather than on robust theoretical agreement at the level of basic principles such as the sources of morality or the universals of human nature, downplays the issue of static, bounded cultures and associated irreconcilable cultural differences (as in multiculturalism), focusing instead on "a form of universalism that is sensitive to the ways in which historical context may shape the significance of a practice."[46] I argue that many Islamists show a cosmopolitan appreciation of the ubiquity of cultural change and a concern not with the purity of a cultural tradition but with its integrity, an attribute of Scheffler's moderate cosmopolitanism and, with Appiah, a perspective that recognizes the contingency of cultural particulars and a pragmatic focus on the points of commonality between the ethical teachings

of Islam and most of the legal and moral demands that a Western state makes
of its citizens and residents on a practical, everyday basis.

It is difficult for the modern subject oriented in terms of rationality, science,
and secularism to avoid the assumption that a theological discourse is necessarily backward looking, a directionality that is implied in the very word "fundamentalism," when it is understood as a turning back to the roots of a religion.
But by arguing that an Islamist discourse such as that espoused by IGMG may
constitute a fully modern subject, I am also suggesting that the concept of God,
as a part of a relationship with a fully modern subject, is something that must be
understood in a fully modern way. People who have been labeled fundamentalist may be a site for new, as yet unimagined visions of a future that transcends
today's dichotomies and even our historically contingent modernism.

NOTES

1. Lawrence defines fundamentalism as "the affirmation of religious authority as
holistic and absolute, admitting of neither criticism nor reduction; it is expressed
through the collective demand that specific creedal and ethical dictates derived from
scripture be publicly recognized and legally enforced." *Defenders of God: The Fundamentalism Revolt against the Modern Age* (San Francisco: Harper and Row, 1989), 27.
Martin E. Marty and R. Scott Appleby, in the first of the multivolume series that
resulted from their "Fundamentalism Project," define fundamentalism in a manner
consistent with Lawrence's, emphasizing active resistance to three dimensions of modern culture: secular rationality, religious tolerance with a tendency toward relativism,
and individualism. "The Fundamentalism Project: A User's Guide," in *Fundamentalisms
Observed*, The Fundamentalism Project, vol. 1, ed. Martin E. Marty and R. Scott
Appleby (Chicago: University of Chicago Press, 1991), vii.

2. Lawrence, *Defenders of God*, 27. Modernism, however, is something of a moving
target in Lawrence's argument, since at other points in the text it comes to include
other attributes such as multiculturalism, a point that will become significant in my
discussion below.

3. This incitement can be understood by means of a rough analogy with Michel
Foucault's analysis of the "repressive hypothesis" in his study of the history of sexual-
ity. *The History of Sexuality*, vol. 1, *An Introduction*, trans. Robert Hurley (New York:
Vintage, 1990), 10.

4. Kwame Anthony Appiah, *Cosmopolitanism: Ethics in a World of Strangers* (New
York: Norton, 2006).

5. Michel Foucault, *"Society Must Be Defended": Lectures at the Collège de France,
1975–76*, ed. Mauro Bertani and Alessandro Fontana, trans. David Macey (New York:
Picador, 2003).

6. One might be led to argue that the specific group I consider in this paper would
not fall within the category of fundamentalism as it is defined by Lawrence, but this
objection raises a difficulty with fundamentalism as an analytic category: it imposes a
scheme of classification that tends to foreground the less-than-productive question of
whether any particular group is or is not fundamentalist by this definition. Lawrence

himself addresses this problem by reference to Wittgenstein's concept of family resemblances (*Defenders of God*, 100). However, I suggest that the concept furthers our apprehension of the world in terms of "us" and "them."

7. Anthropologist Talal Asad has demonstrated the cultural particularity of categories such as religion and secularism in "The Construction of Religion as an Anthropological Category," in *Genealogies of Religion: Discipline and Reasons of Power in Christianity and Islam* (Baltimore: Johns Hopkins University Press, 1993), 27–54; and "Secularism, Nation-State, Religion," in *Formations of the Secular: Christianity, Islam, Modernity* (Stanford, Calif.: Stanford University Press, 2003), 181–201.

8. These disjunctions may also be a product of the fact that IGMG itself is evolving from an organization that fits Lawrence's definition of fundamentalism into something else that transcends existing typologies.

9. Willem Bijlefeld, "A Century of Arabic and Islamic Studies at Hartford Seminary," *Muslim World* 83, no. 2 (1993): 103–17. The journal, which began publication in 1911, was renamed the *Muslim World* in 1948.

10. E. Stanley Jones, "Can Islam Be Reformed? The Turkish Answer," *Moslem World* 16, no. 3 (1926): 238–52.

11. Ibid., 243, quoting from the Turkish newspaper *Millet*, November 17, 1925.

12. Some of the absurdity of these proposals may be particularly clear to us in the twenty-first century because of changes in Western bodily practices. Early-twentieth-century stiffness has been replaced, for example, by a Western tendency to get into all sorts of undignified positions in the name of exercise and a casual lifestyle. The posture for Islamic prayer, which involves prostrating oneself on hands and knees, is surely less subject to being exoticized by today's exercising bodies.

13. Asad, "Religion as an Anthropological Category," 47.

14. Jones, "Can Islam Be Reformed?" 243, quoting in translation from *Millet*, November 27, 1925.

15. Ibid., 241.

16. The effort to accommodate Islam to Western values is characteristic of what Bruce Lawrence calls "Islamic Reformism," one of three periodized stages of Muslim response to the incursions of the European powers into Islamic lands. *Shattering the Myth: Islam beyond Violence* (Princeton, N.J.: Princeton University Press, 1997), 45–50.

17. This reappropriation of science by Islamists can be seen on many Web sites, as in the following quotation from an Islamic Web site: "One of the most remarkable things in the Quran is how it deals with science. The Quran which was revealed in the 7th century to Muhammed (p.b.u.h.) contains unbelievable scientific facts which are being discovered in this century. Scientist are shocked and many times speechless when they are shown how detailed and accurate some verses in the Quran are to modern science." http://www.quran.org/science/ (accessed August 19, 2009). Nevertheless many of those associated with IGMG, like those who established the above Web site, adhere to a "creationist" position with respect to the origins of species and contest the Darwinian theory of evolution, in terms very similar to those of American Christian fundamentalists.

18. Jones, "Can Islam Be Reformed?" 239, quoting from Hikmet Djemal, "The Attitude of the Illuminated," *Djumhuriet*, September 17, 1925.

19. Even Mawdudi, the South Asian founder of the Jamat-i Islami, whose writings continue to serve as a basic source of Islamist thought, did not reject Sufism entirely but rejected its complex institutional structure and redefined it as the inner experience that accompanied outward prayer. Sayyid Abul A'la Mawdudi, *A Short History of the Revivalist Movement in Islam*, trans. Al-Ashari (Lahore: Islamic Publications, 1963).

20. In recent years Turkey's extreme secularism appears to have moderated, allowing Tayyip Erdogan, who had political roots in the Islamic politics of Erbakan's Welfare Party, to come to power as prime minister in 2003. Nevertheless Erdogan has carefully defined his position as conservative and secular rather than Islamist, and though his wife and daughters wear the head scarf, he has not sought to implement Islamic goals such as allowing women to wear head scarves in government buildings.

21. For more detail on this group, see Werner Schiffauer's *Die Gottesmänner: Türkische Islamisten in Deutschland; Eine Studie zur Herstellung religiöser Evidenz* (Frankfurt: Suhrkamp, 2000), and his "Production of Fundamentalism: On the Dynamics of Producing the Radically Different," in *Religion and Media*, ed. Hent de Vries and Samuel Weber (Stanford, Calif.: Stanford University Press, 2001), 453–55.

22. The second organization was the transnational Hizb ut-Tahrir, which was founded in Jerusalem in the 1950s and is particularly popular in central Asia. It seeks to avoid sectarian divisions or entanglement in national politics.

23. He was president from 2001 until 2002, when he was forced to resign for personal reasons.

24. Lawrence, *Defenders of God*, 27, 100; Marty and Appleby, *Fundamentalisms Observed*, ix–x.

25. Bundesministerium des Innen, *Annual Report of the Office for the Protection of the Constitution*, 1999, http://www.en.bmi.bund.de/cln_028/nn_148138/Internet/Content/Common/Anlagen/Broschueren/2000/Annual_Report_of_the_Office_for_id_10268_en,templateid=raw,property=publicationFile.pdf/Anuual_Report_of_the_Office_for_id_10268_en.pdf (accessed August 19, 2009).

26. Federal Office for the Protection of the Constitution, *Federal Ministry of the Interior Annual Report—1998*, 102, http://www.en.bmi.bund.de/cln_028/nn_148138/Internet/Content/Common/Anlagen/Broschueren/1999/Annual_Report_of_the_Office_for_id_10269_en,templateid=raw,property=publicationFile.pdf/Anuual_Report_of_the_Office_for_id_10269_en.pdf (accessed August 19, 2009).

27. See Katherine Pratt Ewing, "Between Turkey and Germany: Living Islam in the Diaspora," *South Atlantic Quarterly*, special issue, ed. Güven Guzeldere and Sibel Irzik, 102 (2003): 405–31.

28. Bundesamt für Verfassungsschutz, *Annual Report for the Office of the Protection of the Constitution 2005*, 214, http://www.verfassungsschutz.de/en/en_publications/annual_reports/vsbericht2005_engl/ (accessed July 8, 2009).

29. See John R. Bowen, *Why the French Don't Like Headscarves: Islam, the State, and Public Space* (Princeton, N.J.: Princeton University Press, 2007); and Joan W. Scott, *The Politics of the Veil* (Princeton, N.J.: Princeton University Press, 2007).

30. Saba Mahmood, "Feminist Theory, Embodiment, and the Docile Agent: Some Reflections on the Egyptian Islamic Revival," *Cultural Anthropology* 16, no. 2 (2001): 202–36.

31. This critique pushes further a rethinking that had begun in the 1970s, when feminist scholars began to broaden notions of freedom in light of the experiences of Native and African American women.

32. Mahmood, "Feminist Theory, Embodiment, and the Docile Agent," 203.

33. Ibid., 204.

34. See Katherine Pratt Ewing, "Legislating Religious Freedom: Muslim Challenges to the Relationship between 'Church' and 'State' in Germany and France," *Daedalus* 129, no. 4 (2000): 31–54.

35. In this translation Ahmed Ali includes a footnote explaining that "the verse deals with a special kind of monetary transaction." It is for this reason that two women are required. Only one serves as the witness, "the other being her helper in case she gets confused. . . . These precautions have not been suggested in the case of a simple transaction face to face about merchandise. . . . The presence of two women does not mean that both are witnesses, or that the evidence of one woman is half that of a man." *Al-Qur'an: A Contemporary Translation*, trans. Ahmed Ali (Princeton, N.J.: Princeton University Press, 1988), 50.

36. See M. Hakan Yavuz, "Political Islam and the Welfare (Refah) Party in Turkey," *Comparative Politics* 30, no. 1 (1997): 77.

37. Yael Navaro-Yashin, *Faces of the State: Secularism and Public Life in Turkey* (Princeton, N.J.: Princeton University Press, 2002), 82–85.

38. See Bill Maurer, *Mutual Life, Limited: Islamic Banking, Alternative Currencies, Lateral Reason* (Princeton, N.J.: Princeton University Press, 2005).

39. Lawrence, *Defenders of God*, 18.

40. Appiah, *Cosmopolitanism*, xxi.

41. Bundesamt für Verfassungsschutz, *Annual Report for the Office of the Protection of the Constitution 2005*, 218, http://www.verfassungsschutz.de/en/en_publications/annual_reports/vsbericht2005_engl/ (accessed July 8, 2009).

42. The following is an example of one of the questions: "In Germany, . . . sport and swim classes are part of the normal school curriculum. Would you allow your daughter to participate?" Charles Hawley, "A German State Quizzes Muslim Immigrants on Jews, Gays and Swim Lessons," *Spiegel Online International*, January 31, 2006, http://www.spiegel.de/international/0,1518,397482,00.html (accessed July 8, 2009). For a discussion of this test, see Katherine Pratt Ewing, *Stolen Honor: Stigmatizing Muslim Men in Berlin* (Stanford, Calif.: Stanford University Press, 2008), 181–84.

43. Michel Foucault, "Governmentality," in *The Essential Works of Foucault, 1954–1984*, vol. 3, *Power*, ed. James D. Faubion (New York: New Press, 1994), 216–17.

44. Appiah has pointed out that even the 9/11 terrorists, like members of some other radical social movements, could be called cosmopolitans—"toxic cosmopolitans"—who were not only widely traveled and well educated but also dedicated to a universalist vision of *ummah* composed of individuals stripped of local, cultural particularities. Appiah, *Ethics of Identity*, 220.

45. Samuel Scheffler, "Conceptions of Cosmopolitanism," *Utilitas* 11, no. 3 (1999): 275.

46. Ibid., 256.

✤

Between *"Ijtihad* of the Presupposition" and Gender Equality

Cross-Pollination between Progressive Islam and Iranian Reform

OMID SAFI

In the political climate of the first decades of the twenty-first century, it is a cliché to begin a discourse on Islam and Muslims with the talk of "crisis."[1] It is not my intention here to add to that unrelenting barrage. Instead I assert that the very matrix that has led to great upheavals among transnational Muslim communities has also created precious opportunity for Muslims who are engaged in processes of reform (*islah*), renewal (*tajdid*), "new religious thought" (*roshanfekri-ye jadid*), critical examination of Islamic thought, and progressive Islam (to offer some of the more prominent labels). As Bruce Lawrence has remarked: "It is the presence of colonialism that linked all Muslim collectivities, throughout the Afro-Eurasian oikoumene, especially in that heavily populated cosmopolitan area south and east of the Mediterranean."[2] The perspective followed in this essay adopts Marshall G. S. Hodgson's global view of Islam as elaborated upon by Lawrence, one of his intellectual heirs. In this essay I wish to explore the opportunity for one fruitful cross-pollination among two prominent contemporary movements among these now linked Muslim collectivities: the North American manifestation of progressive Islam and the Iranian reform movement.

One of the intriguing characteristics of the discourses on Islamic reform is the extent to which the contestations and cross-pollinations are now taking place at a global level, across national and linguistic lines. The cross-pollinations are not without challenge and controversy. Some of the leading scholars of and spokespersons for African American Islam have recently argued that the hegemony of Asian Muslims in America and the resulting "immigrant Islam" has disempowered "Blackamericans" from articulating their own normative view of Islam.[3] Likewise scholars such as Tariq Ramadan have argued that Western Muslims' integration into European societies and the cultivation of a "European Islam" is hindered by attempts to derive identity from Asian and African Islamic models.[4] At the same time, there has been at least a generation of Nile-to-Oxus modern Muslims viewing developments in American Islam with great suspicion, ranging from Ayatollah Khomeini's famous critiques of "Islam-e Amrikai"[5] to the more recent critiques of woman-led prayers by al-Azhar[6] and even Muʿammar Gadhafi's assertion that women leading a mixed congregation of men and women in prayer creates "millions of Bin Ladens."[7]

A further layer of complication is that of the mushrooming discourse of "global jihadist networks." In other words many journalists, scholars, and public policy makers have been interested in mapping out a transnational jihadist or Salafi connection.[8] For the purposes of this essay, I wish to explore a more constructive transnational conversation, namely the possibility that the Iranian reform movement[9] and the movement known as progressive Islam[10] have in fact something to contribute to one another, indeed to learn from one another. By the Iranian reform movement I largely mean the works of figures such as Mohammad Khatami, Abdalkarim Soroush, and the generation of intellectuals who have emerged after Soroush, such as Mohsen Kadivar, Mujtahid Shabestari, Hashem Aghajari, Akbar Ganji, Mehrangiz Kar, and, of course, Shirin Ebadi. In doing so I am not positing either movement as normative or paradigmatic, but rather suggesting that each has investigated some particular areas in greater depth through a sustained engagement, and that both movements can learn a great deal from the strengths of the other. It has certainly been the case that many progressives have been reading the works of Iranian reformers, going back to the groundbreaking work of ʿAli Shariʿati.[11] There is now even more indication that some of the leading Iranian reformers are making themselves familiar with some Western progressives.[12] One of them, Akbar Ganji, has been in the United States since 2007 to undertake interviews with a number of leading progressive Muslims in the West, including Khaled Abou El Fadl and Abdullahi An-Naʿim. Ganji plans to report on these conversations in a multivolume work to be published in Persian. I myself was fortunate enough to receive a grant from the Carnegie Foundation to study the works of the Iranian reformists. This essay aims to advance this conversation.

I propose this cross-pollination not merely as an academic exercise. As someone who considers himself a participant-observer in both movements, it seems to me that both progressive Islam and the Iranian reform movement presently have foundational shortcomings that have to be remedied before each can achieve its potential. I propose to analyze these movements in detail, but in summary it could be stated that the progressive Islam movement has yet to develop a sustained methodological approach to the tradition in the broadest sense. Here I propose that Soroush's explication of the notion of *"ijtihad* of the presupposition" is a potential methodological breakthrough for progressives. As a complement I will use the insights from the progressive Islam movement to argue that the Iranian reform movement has been stalling in the area of gender discourse. I will explore these areas that could benefit from mutual cross-pollination a bit further, but first I will offer a brief overview of each movement.

Who Are the Iranian Reformers?

Iran today is in the midst of a paradox. On one hand the reform movement politically appears to have failed to deliver on its promises, and the new president of Iran, Mahmoud Ahmadinejad, seems to exhibit a strange combination of anti-Semitism, delusion, ignorance, and provincialism.[13] Some have estimated that had things in Iraq not gone so catastrophically bad for the U.S.-led coalition forces, Iran might have already been "target next" in the U.S. agenda of reshaping the Middle East. In spite of the political failure of the reform movement, Iran also is home to one of the most vital and dynamic critical Islamic debates in the world on the nature of religious authority, hermeneutics, the conception of the state, and rights of women. The following is not an exhaustive list of significant Iranian reformers, and one could easily add other figures, but it will suffice to give a sense of the dynamic nature of the reform project there, as well as the extent to which this debate is being discursively pushed on through debate and engagement. While Soroush may be the best known of the "enlightened religious intellectuals" to the Western audience, he is by no means a voice in the wilderness of Iranian reform of Islam.

Mohammad Khatami

Initially the former president of Iran was for most Iranians—particularly the youth—the great symbol of the potential of reform. Eventually he became the manifestation of the inability of the reform movement to deliver on its promises. It is not my purpose to discuss the political troubles of Khatami vis-à-vis hardliners in Iran, but I instead wish to call attention to a few elements of his religious thought. Khatami is a rigorous political philosopher who spent time in Germany, succeeding Ayatollah Beheshti (d. 1981) in the Hamburg Islamic Center. During this time he was well acquainted with philosophy. His *Dialogue among Civilizations: A Paradigm for Peace* contained innovative ideas for inter-civilizational encounters, including those between Iran and the United States.[14] The United Nations developed "Dialogue among Civilizations" as its theme in 2001,[15] only to have it derailed by the horrific tragedy of 9/11 and the subsequent wars in Afghanistan and Iraq.[16]

In seeking a radical departure from Khomeini's characterization of the United States as the Great Satan, Khatami instead argued that "in terms of the dialogue of civilizations, we intend to benefit from the achievements and experiences of all civilizations, Western and non-Western, and to hold dialogue with them. The closer the pillars and essences of these two civilizations are, the easier the dialogue would become. With our revolution, we are experiencing a new phase of reconstruction. . . . This is why we sense an intellectual affinity with the essence of the American civilization."[17]

Abd al-Karim Soroush

If Khatami was the political face of the reform movement, Soroush was surely its intellectual and in many ways public one. Almost every analysis of Soroush in the Western media was obligated to refer to him as the "Muslim Martin Luther," that is, the solitary figure who, single-handedly, was going to rescue and reform Islam.[18] Soroush began his training in pharmacology before taking on the philosophy of science, British rationalism, and then Islamics. He is an indefatigable speaker, and many of his lectures have been transcribed as books, resulting in a truly dazzling range of published works. He gained great prominence through his monumental *Qabz o Bast-e Teorik-e Shariʻat—ya Nazariyeh-ye Takâmol-e Maʻrefat-e Dini* (Theoretical Contraction and Expansion of Shariʻa, or The Theory of Evolution of Religious Knowledge), a tour de force of 681 pages in the original Persian. His main notion in this work was to make a fundamental distinction between religion as such and religious knowledge. Whereas religion was eternal and sacrosanct, all religious knowledge was to be seen as limited, finite expressions of human knowledge.[19] In Soroush's own words:

1. Religion, or revelation, for that matter, is silent.
2. The science of religion is relative—that is, relative to presuppositions.
3. The science of religion is age bound, because presuppositions are.
4. Revealed religion itself may be true and free from contradictions, but the science of religion is not necessarily so.
5. Religion may be perfect or comprehensive, but not so for the science of religion.
6. Religion is divine, but its interpretation is thoroughly human and worldly.[20]

An equally controversial, though lesser-known, interest of Soroush's has been religious pluralism. He began this inquiry with the mischievously titled *Siratha-yi mustaqim* (Straight Paths), the title of which pluralizes the last line of *Sura Fatiha*, the first chapter of the Qurʾan, where humanity pleads with the Divine to guide them to *al-sirat al-mustaqim*, "the straight path." In speaking of *siratha-yi mustaqim*, Soroush acknowledges that there are multiple paths to the Divine.[21] This notion is not new to Islamic thought, having a long and rich history in Sufism in particular. What is relatively new is Soroush's application of this idea to modern debates on Islamic thought.

The idea introduced by Soroush that I will return to as his main contribution to the cross-pollination of progressive Islam is his new conception of *ijtihad* (independent reasoning), which I think pushes the discourse further than it has been so far.

Hashem Aghajari

Hashem Aghajari came to international recognition because of the imprisonment and death sentence that he received in November 2002.[22] While the media coverage has focused on his admonitions that one must not follow clerics "like monkeys" and his background as a war veteran, his writings have received far less attention. In his famous speech given in Hamadan in 2002, he called for the renewal of an "Islamic humanism," which he traces to a conception of a *homo islamicus* independent of color, nationality, race, class, gender, and religion. Aghajari deliberately and explicitly connects himself to the legacy of ʿAli Shariʿati, and his Hamadan speech was given on the occasion of the twenty-fifth anniversary of the passing of Shariʿati. Aghajari's reading of the Qurʾanic verse "indeed we have honored humanity" leads him to conceptualize humanity's worth as being apart from the designation as Muslim, Iranian, Turk, Kurd, male, or female. He emphasizes that his Islam is based on a "divine humanism" (*umanism-e elahi*) and is the legacy of all the *Bani Adam*—"not just Muslims, not just the Shiʿa, not just ayatollahs, and not just jurists." The discussion is far from abstract for him: Aghajari specifically states that it is the height of absurdity to torture a human being in the name of religion where religion should be vouchsafing humanity's dignity.[23]

Aghajari also advocates a notion of *protestantism-e islami*, by which he means the transformation of the relationship of Shiʿa laypersons with the clerics from that of disciples (*murids*) to that of students and seekers of knowledge (*daneshju, moteʿalem*). In his paradigm if/when a student receives knowledge, he is a teacher in his own right and not bound to remain perpetually a disciple. Aghajari is less clear about whether there is a need or space for the Shiʿa clerical institution.[24]

Mohammad Mojtahed Shabestari

Mohammad Mojtahed Shabestari reached the rank of *mujtihad* in the Shiʿa seminary of Qum. Shabestari is a *Hojjat al-islam* (high-ranking Shiʿa cleric) who at an earlier point had been invited by the late Ayatollah Beheshti to take his place at the influential Islamic Center of Hamburg. During his tenure in Hamburg, Shabestari became fully conversant with German philosophy, as well as the works of Paul Tillich and Karl Barth, liberal and neoorthodox Protestant theologians, respectively, in the mid–twentieth century.[25] Among contemporary Iranian Muslim intellectuals, he remains one of the most knowledgeable about

Christian theology. Indeed theology as such looms large in Shabestari's thought, and he articulates one of his goals as arriving at a "new theology" (*'elm-e kalam-e jadid*) that would entail a dynamic and flowing view of religion through human history.[26]

One of Shabestari's main contributions has been the desacralizing of the "tradition" of Islamic interpretation. He specifically argues that *sonnat* (tradition) is not an element of faith or creed (*imani, e'teqadi*) for Muslims and that it can be looked at through an *anthropolojik* lens.[27] Furthermore he argues that in every age Muslims have allowed themselves to understand and comment upon the Qur'an without making the interpretations of the ages before them compulsory upon themselves.[28] He connects this reading to a different notion of time in Islam, since it does not have a "history of salvation" (*tarikh-e nejat*), as in the case of Christianity.[29]

Shabestari is concerned with cultivating a notion of "religious faith" that is fresh and dynamic, developed in the cradle of personal and social freedom. This religious faith, he argues, cannot take root in an oppressive and totalitarian society. Furthermore, for Shabestari true "religious faith" (*iman-e dini*) cannot be developed through blindly imitating (*taqlid-e kur*) "people and traditions." While the notion of "blind imitation" has long been a favorite polemic of many Muslim modernists, it is a radical assertion in the Shi'a intellectual world, which has given primacy to the notion of *marja'-e taqlid*, the necessity of following one supreme *marja'*, or Shi'a scholar, in legal matters.[30]

Lastly he argues that it is imperative for religious faith to be tested and purified in every age. He argues that the "system of beliefs and laws" (*nezam-e e'teqadi va qanuni*) has always to be reconsidered (*tajdid-e nazar*), so that one can strive for purification, perfection, and reform.[31] Shabestari's latest project, *Naqdi bar Qera'at-e Rasmi az Din* (A Critique of Official Reading of Religion), is an equally audacious one, exposing official and canonical readings of religion as hermeneutically simplistic.[32]

Mohsen Kadivar

Like Shabestari, Mohsen Kadivar is another of the Shi'a clerics who has been among the most dynamic voices of reform in Iran. Displaying a deft understanding of modernity through Jürgen Habermas, the influential German philosopher of the Frankfurt school, Kadivar has come to recognize modernity as "an incomplete project," one that every society should be allowed to pursue as its own destination. Rather than attempting to get an idealized version of Islam to live up to a static version of modernity, Kadivar is more invested in whether certain understandings of Islam can be compatible with certain versions of modernity.[33] His ultimate goal is a "critical encounter with modernity—rather than being absorbed in it."[34]

Kadivar's most important contribution so far has been to demonstrate persuasively that the concept of *velayat* (guardianship), essential for any conception of *velayat-e faqih* (Khomeini's theory of "guardianship of the jurist"), has always been a multivalent one in Islamic history. Kadivar meticulously identifies a spectrum of interpretations for the notion of *velayat* in Islamic sources, consisting of linguistic, mystical, theological, juridical, Qur'anic, Sunna-based, *shar'i* conceptions of the *faqih* (the religious jurist), and those derived from the people, before presenting the view of the Islamic republic advocated by Khomeini.[35] In other words he identifies Khomeini's *velayat-e faqih* as but one possible interpretation among many, not necessarily a given and transparent conclusion.

In his subsequent writings, Kadivar has been even more explicit about undermining the religious legitimacy of *velayat-e faqih*:

> The choice between *velayat-e faqih* and democracy, in the event of unresolved incompatibility between the two, is democracy. Through the discourse in answering the first question, we provided that the difference between *velayat-e faqih* and democracy is void of any religious requirement, and a matter of rational evaluation. In which case, the alternative that stands to yield the most benefit is the preferred choice. *Velayat-e faqih* has no credible foundation in Islamic jurisprudence. It is a notion that is formed in the minds of a group of honorable jurists through a specific reading of a handful of Islamic passages. Refuting *velayat-e faqih* does not in any way undermine any of the Islamic teachings, requirements or obligations. I believe democracy is the least erroneous approach to the politics of the world. (Please note that least erroneous does not mean perfect, or even error free.)[36]

Without committing the late-twentieth-century Muslim error of turning democracy into a new idol, Kadivar simply recognizes it as the least imperfect of all the imperfect human political models. As important, *velayat-e faqih* is also exposed as merely the product of human juridical opinion, stripped of all its divine claim to authority—which, just as significantly, also strips its claimants of their authority.

Lastly Kadivar and Soroush have engaged in a vigorous debate about the issue of *pluralism-e dini* (religious pluralism).[37]

Shirin Ebadi

Shirin Ebadi is difficult to classify in many ways, as she is an icon, a social activist, a judge, and an intellectual. Always displaying a concern for the disenfranchised and the marginalized, her advocacy work has moved between standing up for the rights of children, women, non-Muslim minorities, political prisoners, and civilian casualties and other human rights causes.

Ebadi has arguably been the most effective voice in Iran arguing for the compatibility of Islam and international notions of human rights. Her volume *History and Documentation of Human Rights in Iran* provides a detailed juxtaposition of the UN Declaration of Human Rights vis-à-vis the Iranian legal code.[38] She offered a thorough critique of women's rights in the Islamic Republic in her *Hoquq-e zan dar qavanin-e jomhuri-ye Islami-ye Iran.* Furthermore she also showed how she was keenly aware of the multiple processes of marginalization that non-Muslim women in Iran suffer.[39]

One of the intriguing aspects of Ebadi's career is that, while eschewing the language of reform, she argues that her notion of the compatibility of Islam and human rights is nothing other than—indeed, nothing short of—a return to the actual message of Islam. Whereas Soroush, Shabestari, and Kadivar operate in familiar Islamic discourses (philosophy, theology, and law, respectively), Ebadi operates more fluidly outside. It remains to be seen what legacy her work will have for religious reform, as is indeed the case for all the Iranian reformers. One lasting legacy, no doubt, will be as the first Muslim woman to have been awarded the Nobel Peace Prize, in 2003. Her Nobel acceptance speech was a hallmark in speaking truth to power—both the United States and corrupt Muslim regimes.[40] In her speech she talked about the global situation of poverty, prison abuses in Guantánamo Bay, and affirming the rights of people to rise up in situations of oppression. It is perhaps telling that the most explicit Islamic engagement in her text—aside from a reference to the importance of learning in the Qur'an—is to Sa'di's ubiquitous comment on humanity (*Bani Adam*) as being created from one essence. Here we see a reference surely to the Iranian Muslim canon, and yet one decidedly outside the discourses of law and theology that her male counterparts engage.

We turn to a brief overview of progressive Muslims before examining possible mutual reinforcement of goals and methods between the two.

Progressive Muslims

Progressive Islam both continues and radically departs from the 150-year-old tradition of liberal Islam, that of figures such as Muhammad 'Abduh, Jamal al-Din al-Afghani, Rashid Rida, Muhammad Iqbal, and Fazlur Rahman. Unlike some earlier modernists, progressive Muslims are almost uniformly critical of the notion of a teleological modernity that posits the West as the destination of "progress." Progressive Muslims seek to develop a critical and unapologetic "multiple critique" with respect to both Islam and modernity.[41] In distinction to many earlier Muslim modernists, progressives usually display a persistent commitment to oppose colonialism in past and present forms.

Also unlike their liberal Muslim fore*fathers*, progressive Muslims represent a broad coalition of female and male Muslim activists and intellectuals. One of the distinguishing features of the progressive Muslim movement as the vanguard of Islamic (post)modernism has been the high level of female participation and leadership as well as the move to highlight women's rights as part of a broader engagement with human rights.

Progressives measure their success not in developing new and beatific theologies but rather by the amount of change for good on the ground level that they can produce in Muslim and non-Muslim societies. This movement is noted by a number of themes: striving to realize a just and pluralistic society through critically engaging Islam, a relentless pursuit of social justice, an emphasis on gender equality as a foundation of human rights, a vision of religious and ethnic pluralism, and a methodology of nonviolent resistance.[42]

Since many of the progressive Muslim authors, such as Ebrahim Moosa, Kecia Ali, Amina Wadud, Tazim Kassam, Scott Kugle, Saʿdiyya Shaikh, Farid Esack, and Khaled Abou El Fadl, are well known to most readers, I will not go through their contributions in detail here. Instead I will explore some of the particular challenges and dilemmas faced by the progressive movement in North America.

North American or Global?

There is a clear tension in the North American progressive community about whether to conceive of this movement as a fully North American movement or part of a global network of activist/scholars. Some, including myself, have argued that it would be a clear mistake to reduce somehow the emergence of progressive Islam to being a new "American Islam." Naturally it is a dubious exercise to look for Muslims worldwide to identify with a term such as *progressive*, which admittedly does not have ready parallels in a number of important Islamic languages. Yet at the level of commitment to issues of working critically through the tradition, such as social justice and gender equality, progressive Muslims are found in many places in the global Muslim *ummah* (community). When it comes actually to implementing a progressive understanding of Islam in Muslim communities, particular communities in Iran and South Africa are leading, not following, the United States.

My own position in the above debate has not been to deny the importance of one's local context as a layer of a larger, hybrid, or cosmopolitan identity. Indeed one can here fully agree with Bruce Lawrence in stating that the challenge remains for American Muslims to develop a polyvalence that translates mere diversity while coming to terms with the internalized prejudices, including class and racial prejudices, that the immigrant community suffers from.[43] The challenge as I see it is to differentiate between cultivating a meaningful layer of identity that is rooted in and connected to larger American civic traditions (and indeed drawing up on indigenous American justice, aesthetic, spiritual traditions) while resisting the lure of rampant nationalism.[44] I would argue that almost all progressive Muslims are profoundly skeptical of nationalism, whether American, Arab, Iranian, or otherwise. As such they instinctively and deliberately reject the appropriation of this fluid global movement by those who espouse it in order to transform it into an "American Islam" commodity to be exported all over the world. The progressives' firm critique of neocolonialism was also a way to avoid their appropriation by the administration of George W. Bush, which used the language of reforming Islam to justify its invasion of Muslim countries such as Iraq. This appropriation was most explicit in the comments of Paul Wolfowitz's endorsements on *ijtihad*, invoking Michael Wolfe's *Taking Back Islam: American Muslims Reclaim Their Faith* (2002) on the eve of the invasion of Iraq.[45] Wolfowitz also identified the task of the United States with the slogan, "We need an Islamic reformation," thus forming a problematic link between reform movements in Islam and U.S. military hegemony.[46] In other speeches Wolfowitz attempted to co-opt a number of authors, including Khaled Abou El Fadl.[47]

On the other hand, other progressives in North America have been eager to claim and proclaim the movement as an "American Islam" with no precedents, yet another example of a shining *ummah* on a hill to be adored and emulated by the rest of the world. This was exemplified in the ways in which the prayer led by Amina Wadud in New York in March 2005 was advertised by the prayer organizers (not Dr. Wadud herself) as the "first ever" such event of its kind. The controversial Web site MuslimWakeUp.com, the main organizer for the event, went so far as to label it *"the first public Jum'ah prayer of its kind on record* since Prophet Muhammad, upon whom be peace and blessings, reportedly authorized Umm Waraqa to lead her household in prayer" (emphasis theirs).[48] In fact there had been a number of such episodes in South Africa and elsewhere, including in the queer Muslim community al-Fatiha. In an interesting example that confirms Bruce Lawrence's reading of Manuel Castells's argument for the emergence of a "global network society,"[49] an anonymous group of Muslim cybercitizens has taken to providing documentation for examples of women-led prayers prior to the Wadud event.[50]

I would state that it is vital for progressives in North America to realize that the majority of those who have engaged in the most meaningful Muslim struggles on behalf of social justice, liberation, and gender equality have hitherto lived outside of North America, and have in many cases never heard of the terms "progressive Muslim" or "progressive Islam." There are many important movements in places such as South Africa, Iran, Malaysia, Turkey, and Egypt. Connecting with the activists inside these global movements would give us a good chance of correcting our usual North American myopia. Having said that, I continue to believe that the Muslims in North America—African Americans, immigrants, whites, and Latinos—have a unique role to play in the articulation of Islam. The excesses of the American empire, the wide accessibility of Internet technology, and the rise of an educated lay class of Muslim activists, all in the light of the withdrawal of many Salafis from the public domain after September 11, 2001, have created a fruitful space for progressive Muslims from a host of backgrounds to get together and debate new ideas.

There have already been some important victories, and one should not lose sight of them. One of them is in the area of gender justice. Gender justice today is the defining issue, I would argue, for the North American progressive Muslim community. One sign of its success has been in being able to push more conservative communities to make long-overdue corrections. Even in those cases where the mainstream Muslim organizations' response to issues of gender equality has been insufficiently clear (such as the "Women Friendly Mosques" guide[51]), it too is a sign of a move in the right direction. I think it is important to mark these victories, as indeed they benefit all Muslims in our community, regardless of how they self-identify.

Shortcomings and Opportunities for Cross-Pollination

Both the Iranian reform movement and the North American progressive community have serious shortcomings in their present forms, and each can benefit from the strengths of the other.

The Iranian reform movement is suffering from a number of shortcomings internally and externally that may well prove to derail what has been among the most intellectually rigorous and promising Islamic reform movements worldwide. The attention of most Western sources has rightly been on the political tensions that have slowed down and in many cases reversed the accomplishments of the reform movement led by Mohammad Khatami. On the other hand, one can argue that one of the foundational shortcomings of the Iranian reform movement has been its lack of attention to questions of gender equality. It is not the case that the Iran has been lacking in exemplars tackling questions of gender equality. One can begin the conversation with the heroic work of Shirin Ebadi and Mehrangiz Kar, among others. The fundamental problem remains that for many male Iranian reformers, the issue of gender equality has been collapsed into "the woman problem." In the work of most male reformists in Iran, women remain the object of Islamic discourse, not its agents and subjects.

This shortcoming has also been pointed out by Iranian feminists such as Ziba Mir-Hosseini: "Yet among these new religious thinkers, no influential man has yet addressed the issue of gender in Islam."[52] Women's rights activists in Iran have also critiqued this unforgivable silence on gender issues. One of the first to do so was Mehrangiz Kar, in the weekly *Rah-e Now* (The New Way).[53]

One example of the gender shortcomings of male Iranian reformers is seen in Soroush's attempt to engage "the woman problem." He states: "I believe that one of the most important values in the relations between men and women is that a woman should be a woman and a man should be a man."[54] Soroush goes on to state even more explicitly that the nature of manhood and womanhood are fixed and distinct from each other: "The relations between men and women should not impede their attainment of excellence in terms of manhood or womanhood. In other words, these relations must not turn men into women or take women out of the sphere of womanhood." While Soroush is able to answer what he means by "human," he relies on categories on maleness and femaleness without being able to define or quality them. He will go so far as to say that the religious law is like a "temporary husk" protecting the values of religion, and that the religious laws involving women are the "weakest link" of gender relations. Yet for Soroush it remains the case that the only reason to change the laws is that they no longer serve our purpose today. There is nothing inherently unjust or patriarchal about them.[55] Here one has to agree with Ziba Mir-Hosseini that even today "gender equality is a notion to which male intellectuals—whether religious or secular in their perspective—still do not subscribe, so they implicitly agree with the gender model embedded in Shari'a legal rules. For them, gender is not an issue urgent enough to address, but part of a larger problem, and they hope it will go away when their political vision is realized."[56] Kadivar, it should be noted, has recently made some moves in the direction of addressing these shortcomings, but the move as a whole is more a listing of areas of possible inquiry and not a constructive offering of solutions.[57]

As was the case with the Iranian reform movement, the North American Progressive movement presently suffers from some fundamental shortcomings, which I believe can be constructively addressed by seriously engaging the Iranian discourse on reform. Many of the proponents of progressive Islam, including myself, have identified engagement with the tradition (not just with the Qur'an and Sunna but with the full manifestation of Islamic intellectual and poetic praxis) as a sine qua non of the movement. In *Progressive Muslims* I had stated:

> Progressive Muslims insist on a serious engagement with the full spectrum of Islamic thought and practices. There can be no progressive Muslim movement that does not engage the very "stuff" (textual and material sources) of the Islamic tradition, even if some of us would wish to debate what "stuff" that should be and how it ought to be interpreted. . . .
>
> To state the obvious, a progressive Muslim agenda has to be both progressive and Islamic, in the sense of deriving its inspiration from the heart of the Islamic tradition. It cannot survive as a graft of Secular Humanism

onto the tree of Islam, but must emerge from within that very entity. It can receive and surely has received inspiration from other spiritual and political movements, but it must ultimately grow in the soil of Islam.[58]

In spite of the above insistence, there is still a great deal left to be accomplished. Even many of the supporters of progressive Islamic movements in America, including myself, have remarked that the first attempts at translating progressive Islam from an ideal to a communal identity have suffered from insufficient engagement with the tradition, and indeed a methodological vagueness about how to go about engaging the tradition. In fact in a self-critique written on the progressive movement in North America, I identified the five themes as challenges that confront the present movement.

1. Transcending antagonistic attitudes toward mainstream Muslim communities
2. Struggling against secular tendencies in the progressive movement
3. Engagement with the multiple intellectual and spiritual traditions of Islam
4. Reviving the spiritual core of a reform movement
5. Recovering courtesy and spiritual manners[59]

It is not the case that progressives in North America have avoided the question of methodology or engagement with the tradition. Among the most rigorous approaches is that of Kecia Ali, who determines that many Maliki jurists conceived of marriage as an analogy to possession, positing an exchange of right of access to female sexual organs for the promise of male financial protection. Ali does state that future attempts at Islamic law will have to take the question of presuppositions in family law seriously, but she has not yet (and I emphasize *yet*, since I do hope that this is a project she will move to) offered a sense of what that legal tradition would look like if it were to be built on an egalitarian basis.[60] Likewise Scott Kugle has taken on the question of presupposition about sexual diversity more specifically.[61] As is the case in other dimensions of American public life, homosexuality is one of the fault lines of the culture wars, and this call has by and large been met with great hostility among many Muslims, even those who are otherwise sympathetic to the progressive project.

Ijtihad *and Methodology: Reflections of a Cyber-Muslim Citizen*

Many of the mainstream Muslim organizations in the United States have deliberately avoided fruitful *public* conversations with progressives, particularly progressive females. Stripped of a public platform, many progressives have turned to virtual communities, and indeed here is the most intriguing and sustained site of exchange and debate. One particularly noteworthy example is MEISGS, Middle East and Islamic Studies Graduate Students Listserv, a community of 250 young Muslim scholars of Islam (in spite of the name, including both graduate students and younger academics, activists, and lawyers). The debates on the list are unusually cordial for a Muslim Listserv, but also sharp and critical. In addition to a few progressives on the list, there are also a large number of Muslim products of academic programs in Near Eastern languages and civilizations, many of whom have also been brought up in the Hamza Yusuf or Ha Mim Nuh Keller version of Islam with its emphasis on the primacy of the religious schools of thought.

This community has prompted my most sustained engagement over the shortcomings and strengths of the present state of the progressive movement. I describe the audience—acknowledging of course the diversity and plurality of 250 opinionated Muslim academics!—as being sincere in seeking an understanding of Islam that is in some sustainable way authentic and rooted while responsive and dynamic in the world. More than two years of debate and discussion with this virtual community has led me to an important realization: the progressive movement, while very strong in terms of social stances, articulate spokespersons, engagements with Western thought, Sufism, and history, has not yet developed a methodology that is rich enough, sustained enough, and subtle enough to satisfy this demanding and critical audience.

It should not come as a surprise that like many modernists before us, progressives too have turned to the rich reservoir of *ijtihad*, the notion of principled, systematic, and independent reasoning to come up with new answers to new problems. Muslim intellectuals have utilized the conception of *ijtihad* to justify reform for more than a century, as evidenced in the various works of Muhammad Iqbal,[62] Muhammad Sa'id al-'Ashmawi,[63] and others. A great many of these figures have explicitly resorted to the famous report in which the Prophet asked Mu'adh ibn Jabal (d. 627) about how he would settle issues confronting him. Mu'adh—to the delight of modernized Muslims[64]—answered first the Book of God, then the Hadith of the Prophet, and then, if necessary, through his own judgment.

It is not the case that Muslims have not thought through issues of *ijtihad* previously. Muneer Fareed offers a thorough account of the debates on *ijtihad* in legal reform through the nineteenth and early twentieth centuries.[65] Wael Hallaq and others have persuasively argued for a revision of the old myth of the gates of *ijtihad* having been closed, the by now discredited though still pervasive notion that authoritative reinterpretations of Islamic law came to a halt in the medieval times, and that the subsequent centuries are only to refer to the existing set of interpretations rather than coming up with new and fresh answers.[66] Today progressives are more likely to side with S. M. Zafar and against 'Ashmawi that the gates of *ijtihad* are not closed, and indeed many have never been closed.[67] The conversation is less about whether the gates are open or closed, but rather about what can be done with *ijtihad*, who is qualified to undertake this

critical examination, and what aspects and facets of Islam can be subjected to
ijtihad. Many progressives today, including myself, have positioned their endeavor,
indeed their intellectual jihad, as a form of *ijtihad*. However, before we get to
the results of this endeavor, it is important to see first the particular contribution of Soroush, namely the concept of "*ijtihad* of the presuppositions."

Soroush on "Ijtihad *of the Presuppositions*"

A few elements stand out about Soroush's new work on *ijtihad*, which was published in Iran in 1382/2003.[68] For starters this new works takes the form of an
extended conversation, indeed engagement, among various reformist and conservative readings of Islam.[69] Ayatollah H. A. Montazeri had written an article
on facets of Islamic law dealing with jihad, apostasy, the ritual uncleanness of
infidels, and the general ethical formula of commanding good and forbidding
evil (*al-amr bil-maʿruf wal-nahy min al-munkar*). In this essay Montazeri considered the question of whether these interpretations in fact open the door to violent readings of religion, which he answered in the negative.[70] Soroush's essay is
an answer to this essay. In turn his own critique is critiqued by Jaʿfar Subhani.[71]
In addition other scholars, such as Saʿid ʿEdalat-Nezhad, Mohammad Mojtahed
Shabestari, and Ahmad ʿAbedini, also share their thoughts on *ijtihad*.

Soroush's discussion begins by acknowledging that there has been a rupture
in the fabric of time/tradition and that we have left one world and entered a new
one (*ʿalam-e jadid*). Soroush begins by stating that some of the rulings of the
"old world" would have needed no intellectual defense (the example given is the
killing of an apostate), whereas in today's world even those who would want to
argue for upholding such rulings need to articulate a defense and justification
for them. In Montazeri's discourse the defense of the killing of an apostate is
justified by using the analogy of a cancerous tumor: "If a person who has been
raised in Islam becomes openly an apostate, and starts questioning the sanctity
of religious elements, then he is like a cancerous tumor that will gradually spread
to the other healthy parts of the body." Soroush problematizes the cancer analogy as applying to non-Muslims and states that such an analogy is already pre-
figured for a "cure" of removal of the tumor (or to use the other analogy, the
rotting tooth). Soroush creatively suggests that rather utilizing disease/wellness
models, it is more proper to develop a model whereby hybridity is a sign of
strength. In imagining a "society of the religious," Soroush offers the paradigm
of a garden in which there can be many grapevines, with some sour cherries. Or
moving the analogy to a textual level, he suggests thinking of a Persian text with
a few Arabic words.[72]

Soroush then moves from a discussion of apostasy to a slightly broader interrogation of "individual rights" (*haqq-e fard*). He argues that if an individual is to
have the freedom to choose religion, why does one not have the right to be free

of religion? In other words freedom of religion does not end once a person has chosen a religion, and indeed Soroush connects the discussion of apostasy to that of individual rights. He specifically states that the same religious freedoms that apply to a non-Muslim converting to Islam should be applied to a Muslim who converts to another religion.[73]

In expounding upon the notions of freedom of religion, Soroush states that an individual should have the right to hold religious opinions different from others, even the majority. Furthermore an individual should be able to hold different religious opinions than the "lords of power" (*arbab-e qodrat*). Here he is officially taking on the question of who is authorized to offer authoritative opinions on Islam. In doing so he is participating in the same broad tradition of critiquing official readings of religion that Kadivar had begun, although he doesn't go so far as Akbar Ganji in calling these official readings fascist.

Having begun with the issue of religious freedom, Soroush switches to the second of his polemics: the rights, indeed human dignity, of non-Muslims. He begins by critiquing the assertion of certain ayatollahs that the *mukhalif* (here meaning non-Shi'a) deserve no "respect," and it is permissible to engage in talking behind their backs and ridiculing them. In a rare, for Soroush, engagement with gender issues, he critiques ayatollahs who believe that it is permissible to shake hands with non-Muslim women since they don't deserve "human respect" and touching them is akin to touching animals. (However, even here women figure not as agents and subjects but merely objects of Islamic discourse.) At this point Soroush returns to the issue of the innate dignity of human beings, regardless of religious affiliation.

Soroush's questions are direct and explicit: Do human beings leave the circle of humanity because of their beliefs (*'aqidat*)? Do human rights and social advantages change because of a person belonging to this group or that or adhering to one view or another? He cites the ubiquitous verse *La ikraha fi'l-din* ("There is no compulsion in religion," Qur'an 2:256) and dismisses the explanations that would see this verse as being abrogated (*mansukh*). Soroush postulates that so long as the "legal (*fiqhi*) worldview," and in particular its presuppositions (*pish-farzi-haye an*) regarding humanity and rationality (*'aqlaniyyat*), does not undergo a radical rethinking (*tajdid-e nazar-e usuli*), it is inadequate simply to try to deal with contemporary issues in a piecemeal fashion.[74]

Soroush suggests that when we look at the totality of *fiqh* rulings on matters such as the ritual impurity of infidels (*najasat-e kuffar*), the buying and selling of slaves, the killing of apostates, the difference in the rights of slaves and freed people, and the relation between a slave and a master, it becomes clear that "our *fiqh*" is based on a particular view of humanity.[75] He reiterates that unless and until the presuppositions of anthropology (*insan-shenasi*) and epistemology are exposed and laid open to a deep, critical, and explicit critique—something that

Soroush alleges the jurists have yet to do—all of their decrees (*fatwas*) related to life, honor, belief, human freedom, social matters, and the like will always be problematic and should be viewed with suspicion.[76]

Here are Soroush's challenging conclusions to this section: This is the essence of the *ijtihad* that a *faqih* has to undertake, that is to say, *ijtihad* in the *usul* (principles) and not just in the *furu'* ("branches," derived rulings). For Soroush it is insufficient merely to suspend some of the more problematic rulings of Islamic law, since in doing so we have not yet "untangled the knot of *fiqh*, we have not taken any steps forward."[77] Even if the suspension of such a ruling is justified on the basis of *maslaha* ("public good," that darling of modernist Muslims), for Soroush the apostate still remains that human being without the full dignity of being human. He specifically states that the greatest *maslaha* would be the rethinking of our presuppositions and a return to the original sources, the fountainheads *(sar-chashma-ha)*. The metaphor of fountainheads is significant, I believe, because while containing the notion of origin and access to an ever-replenishable source, it also has the sense of producing a dynamic current that flows through time and space.

Comparing Soroush with Tariq Ramadan

The issue of suspension of problematic rulings is one that has been much in the news recently. When Muslim intellectuals have brought the discussion of these topics to the community, they have often been accused of giving in to the forces of "westernization" or even attempting to destroy Islam from within. A particularly noteworthy example has been both the praise and the damnation[78] leveled at Tariq Ramadan when he called for a moratorium on the *hudud*, or religiously mandated punishments. The original call came out in "An International Call for Moratorium on Corporal Punishment, Stoning and the Death Penalty in the Islamic World" on March 30, 2005.[79] The item was quickly picked up by many international news agencies, such as the BBC, which ran a story on it the very same day.[80] In Muslim sources in the West, the reception was far from enthusiastic, even in usually more liberal sources such as the Web site altmuslim.com.[81]

Ramadan's argument is based on working within the parameters of the existing tradition to argue for the nonapplicability of that same system: "The majority of the *'ulamâ'*, historically and today, are of the opinion that these penalties are on the whole Islamic but that the conditions under which they should be implemented are nearly impossible to reestablish. Conditions for the application of these punishments are not met." In other words Ramadan does not deny the ongoing relevance of the *hudud*, nor does he consider the practices inherently problematic. Rather his argument is based on the fact that the conditions that the *hudud* call for are difficult to realize justly in today's society, and as a result the enforcement of the *hudud* must be suspended. It is worth noting that

Ramadan particularly highlights the injustice of the disproportionate application of the *hudud* to the marginalized of society, including women, the poor, and prison inmates: "A still more grave injustice is that these penalties are applied almost exclusively to women and the poor, the doubly victimized, never to the wealthy, the powerful, or the oppressors. Furthermore, hundreds of prisoners have no access to anything that could even remotely be called defense counsel."[82]

The Al-Azhar Legal Research Commission (*lajnat al-buhûth al-fiqhiyya*) issued a statement critiquing Ramadan's statement on April 28, 2005, as follows:

The Commission primarily advances three arguments in its official statement:

1. The statement raises the initial point: "Whoever denies the *hudûd* (Islamic penal code) recognized as revealed and confirmed or who demands that they be cancelled or suspended, despite final and indisputable evidence, is to be regarded as somebody who has forsaken a recognized element which forms the basis of the religion." One of the Members of the Commission, Dr. Mustapha ash-Shuk'a, affirms that "the *hudûd* are a part of the religion, they are Qur'anic and they can be neither subject to debate nor discussion."
2. The point is then raised: "The *hudûd* are known and Tariq Ramadan is demanding that they be stopped because it is hurting the message of Islam: this is a refuted matter."
3. Finally, on the example of Umar Al-Khattab (may peace be upon him), Dr. ash-Shuk'a affirms that "during given periods of time, the Caliph suspended the punishment in instances of war, and then it was re-applied. We are not today in a situation of war which would enable us to suspend these applications. One could suspend the application of *hudûd* in Iraq, because it is a country at war, but this punishment cannot be suspended in Egypt or in other Islamic countries."[83]

In turn Ramadan offered his own countercritique of the al-Azhar critique.[84]

What stands out from Ramadan's view on the *hudud*? He is quite careful to affirm that the *hudud* have been and continue to be a part of the Shari'a corpus. There is nothing fundamentally unjust about the idea of the *hudud*. The only problem for Ramadan, at least in terms of how he articulates the vision, is that the conditions mandated by the *hudud* can no longer be justly realized, thus the practice must be suspended in the interest of *maslaha*. Soroush, on the other hand, living under a regime that is actually likely to apply and enforce corporal punishment and torture against dissidents, wants to use such legal precepts to expose and problematize the presuppositions of such rulings. He then argues for the construction of a new Islamic paradigm that is built upon a humanistic foundation. I would argue that, in the long run, this perspective is likely to have a much more meaningful constructive contribution to the project of *ijtihad*, both in Iran and in the global audience.

Conclusion

Perhaps the most exciting part of the new emerging global Muslim progressive identity is that progressives everywhere are seeking one another out, reading one another's work, collaborating with one another's organizations. This is a fruitful process of cross-pollination. One can point to the influence that 'Ali Shari'ati has had on South African Muslims or the impact the Palestinian struggle has had on South East Asian progressives. Today we are witnessing the emergence of Iranian intellectuals who are fluent in English, German, and French in addition to the expected Arabic. One can only hope that at least some portion of the global Muslim reform audience will learn Persian to engage their imaginative and daring project.[85] Much of this contact is taking place through the Web and e-mail correspondences.

Clearly we are living through a historic phase in the unfolding of Islamic thought and practice. While a great deal of attention has been paid to the instability and even chaos of Muslim societies, this is also an epoch in which incredibly creative movements are responding to the challenging times in which Muslims find themselves. As Bruce Lawrence had accurately predicted, we are witnessing the emergence of multiple Muslim networks, and it is entirely possible that the connection among Iranian reformists and progressive Muslims might be one of these. If this network succeeds in producing the type of fruitful cross-pollination that we have documented here, it might be a crucial step in ushering in a real paradigm shift in the relationship of Muslims to both Islam and modernity.

NOTES

1. Among others, one could mention Bernard Lewis, *The Crisis of Islam: Holy War and Unholy Terror* (London: Weidenfeld & Nicolson, 2003); Bassam Tibi, *The Crisis of Modern Islam: A Preindustrial Culture in the Scientific-Technological Age*, trans. Judith von Sivers (Salt Lake City: University of Utah Press, 1988); and Mahmoud Ayoub, *The Crisis in Muslim History* (Oxford: Oneworld, 2003). Other titles include Ravi Batra, *Muslim Civilization and the Crisis in Iran* (Dallas, Tex.: Venus Books, 1980); 'Abdullah Ashan, *Ummah or Nation? Identity Crisis in Contemporary Muslim Society* (Leicester, U.K.: Islamic Foundation, 1992); Syed Sajjad Husain and Syed Ali Ashraf, *Crisis in Muslim Education* (Sevenoaks, U.K.: Hodder & Stoughton, 1979); Faysal S. Burhan, *The Solution to the Muslim Crisis*, 2nd ed. (Acton, Calif.: Institute of Arabic and Islamic Studies, 1996); 'Abdulhamid Abu-Sulayman, *Crisis in the Muslim Mind* (Herndon, Va.: International Institute of Islamic Thought, 1993); Kamal Hassan, *Islamic Identity Crisis in the Muslim Community in Contemporary Malaysia* (Kuala Lumpur: Pustaka Ilmu Raya, 1981); R. Vasundhara Mohan, *Identity Crisis of Sri Lankan Muslims* (Delhi: Mittal, 1987); Cesar Adib Majul, "The Historical Background of the Muslims in the Philippines and

the Present Mindanao Crisis," paper presented at the second national conference of the Philippine Muslim Lawyers League, December 15–18, 1971.

2. Bruce B. Lawrence, *Shattering the Myth: Islam beyond Violence* (Princeton, N.J.: Princeton University Press, 1997), 25.

3. Sherman A. Jackson, *Islam and the Blackamerican: Looking toward the Third Resurrection* (New York: Oxford University Press, 2005), 131–71.

4. Tariq Ramadan, *To Be a European Muslim: A Study of Islamic Sources in the European Context* (Leicester, U.K.: Islamic Foundation, 1999), 196–98. Ramadan elaborated on this theme in *Western Muslims and the Future of Islam* (New York: Oxford University Press, 2004), which is in many ways more apropos for Europe than it is for North America. For example virtually the totality of African American Islam (and the tensions among immigrant and African American Muslims) is missing from Ramadan. On these tensions, see Bruce B. Lawrence, *New Faiths, Old Fears: Muslims and Other Asian Immigrants in American Religious Life* (New York: Columbia University Press, 2002), 80–86. Lawrence correctly points out this diagnosis from Ali Mazrui, "An Interview on Muslims in America," *Middle Eastern Affairs Journal* 3, no. 1–2 (1997): 177, and Aminah B. McCloud, *African American Islam* (New York: Routledge, 1995). More recently Jackson, in *Islam and the Blackamerican*, has made this same point in more detail.

5. Cited in John Esposito, "Contemporary Islam: Reformation or Revolution?" http://east-westdialogue.blogspot.com/2007/03/contemporary-islam-reformation-or .html (accessed July 19, 2009). Khomeini's denunciation of American Islam extended beyond Islam in the United States and included Gulf regions whose Islam was tainted—in Khomeini's view—with an uncritical infatuation with the West.

6. Shaykh 'Ali Jum'a issued on the Dar al-ifta' Web site a fatwa, Fatwa 4278, dated March 20, 2005. After the issuing of the fatwa, the following clarification was listed under the *fiqh* section of the site:

> F12.27 It is not permissible (O: or valid) to follow an imam who is non-Muslim, insane, in a state of ritual impurity (def: e7,e10), or who has filth *(najasa)* on his clothing or person, *or is a woman leading men,* or someone who omits or mispronounces (def: f8.18) a letter of the Fatiha leading someone who knows it, or a mute, or someone who slurs the words so the letters are indistinct from one another, or someone with a lisp. If after the prayer one finds out that the imam was one of the above, then one must make up the prayer, unless the imam had filth upon him that was concealed, or he was in a state of ritual impurity (N: in which cases one need not make it up).

7. Asra Q. Nomani, "A Gender Jihad for Islam's Future," *Washington Post*, November 6, 2005, http://www.washingtonpost.com/wp-dyn/content/article/2005/11/04/AR2005110402306_pf.html (accessed July 8, 2009).

8. For one example, see Marcia Hermansen's essay "How to Put the Genie Back in the Bottle: 'Identity' Islam and Muslim Youth Cultures in America," in *Progressive Muslims: On Justice, Gender, and Pluralism*, ed. Omid Safi (Oxford: Oneworld, 2003), 303–19, in which she examines the impact of Wahhabi organizations on the American Muslim Student Association organizations that started in the 1960s. The term *Salafi* is a complicated and contested one, but generally it is taken to refer to revivalist movements that posit a "return" to a putative "pure" Islam defined textually through the

Qur'an and the Hadith, often in contradistinction to the existing legal, philosophical, mystical, and theological schools.

9. For a broad overview of the reform movement in Iran, see Said Amir Arjomand, "The Reform Movement and the Debate on Modernity and Tradition in Contemporary Iran," *International Journal of Middle East Studies* 34, no. 4 (2002): 719–31.

10. See Omid Safi, "What Is Progressive Islam?" *ISIM Newsletter* 13 (December 2003): 48–49.

11. In a lecture at Colgate University delivered in March 2003, Farid Esack related the impact that reading Shariʿatiʾs writings had on him and a number of South African progressives. Using a provocative metaphor, he described himself as having drunk milk from Shariʿatiʾs breast.

12. For example in teaching his course on Islamic political philosophy at Princeton during the spring of 2004, Soroush made extensive usage of Charles Kurzman's *Liberal Islam: A Sourcebook* (New York: Oxford University Press, 1998) and *Modernist Islam, 1840–1940: A Sourcebook* (New York: Oxford University Press, 2002). In addition he asked me for essays from the *Progressive Muslims* volume in that same course. Mohsen Kadivar's latest writings on gender seem to be building on Mahmoud Taha and Abdullahi An-Naʿimʾs discussions of Makki/Madani verses of the Qur'an and their relevance today.

13. See Ahmadinejad's speech on the Holocaust as a myth: http://news.bbc.co.uk/2/hi/middle_east/4527142.stm (accessed July 19, 2009).

14. Mohammad Khatami, *Dialogue among Civilizations: A Paradigm for Peace*, ed. Theo Bekker and Joelien Pretorius (Pretoria: Unit for Policy Studies, Centre for International Political Studies, University of Pretoria, 2001).

15. Http://www.unesco.org/dialogue/en/khatami.htm: "The General Assembly of the United Nations has only recently endorsed the proposal of the Islamic Republic of Iran for dialogue among civilizations and cultures" (accessed March 30, 2008).

16. Http://www.un.org/Dialogue/ (accessed March 30, 2008).

17. Christiane Amanpour, "Transcript of Interview with Iranian President Mohammad Khatani," CNN.com, January 7, 1998, http://www.cnn.com/WORLD/9801/07/iran/interview.html (accessed July 8, 2009).

18. Robin Wright, "An Iranian Luther Shakes the Foundations of Islam," *Guardian*, February 1, 1995, 10.

19. For a good English translation of this essay in a mercifully abbreviated format, see Abd al-Karim Soroush, "The Evolution and Devolution of Religious Knowledge," in Charles Kurzman, *Liberal Islam*, 244–54.

20. Soroush, "Evolution and Devolution of Religious Knowledge," 245–46.

21. Soroush, *Sirat-ha-ye mustaqim* (Tehran: Sirat, 1998). This book explicitly lays out the concepts of religious pluralism elaborated by theologians John Hick and Alvin Plantinga.

22. "Profile: Hashem Aghajari," BBC News, July 9, 2003, http://news.bbc.co.uk/2/hi/middle_east/3053075.stm (accessed July 8, 2009).

23. Hashem Aghajari, "Hamadan speech," in Hajizadeh and Hajizadeh, *Aqajari*, 38–39.

24. Ibid., 36.

25. Sadri, "Sacral Defense of Secularism: The Political Theologies of Soroush, Shabestari, and Kadivar," *International Journal of Politics, Culture, and Society* 15, no. 2 (2001): 260.

26. Shabestari, *Iman va Azadi* (Tehran: Tarh-e Nau, 1379/2000), 95.

27. Ibid., 100.

28. Ibid., 104–5.

29. Although Shabestari does not specify this, he seems to have *Heilsgeschichte* in mind.

30. For an earlier attempt to draw this distinction, see Mehdi Bazargan, "Religion and Liberty," in Kurzman, *Liberal Islam,* 79.

31 Shabestari, *Iman va Azadi,* 7–8.

32. Shabestari, *Naqdi bar Qera'at-e Rasmi az Din*—A Critique of Official Reading of Religion (Tehran: Tarh-e No, 2000).

33. Kadivar, "The Principles of Compatibility of Islam and Modernity," http://kadivar .com/Index.asp?Docid=831&AC=1&AF=1&ASB=1&AGM=1&AL=dtv (accessed July 20, 2009).

34. Ibid., 9.

35. Kadivar, *Hokumat-e Velayi* (Tehran: Nashr-e Ney, 1377/1998).

36. Kadivar, "Velayat-e Faqih and Democracy," http://iran-opp.blogspot.com/2005/ 01/mohsen-kadivar-velayat-e-faqih-and.html (accessed July 20, 2009).

37. *Monazara-ye Dr. 'Abdalkarim Soroush va Hojjat al-Islam Mohsen Kadivar dar bara- ye Pluralism-e Dini* [Debate between Dr. Abdalkarim Soroush and Hojjat al-Islam Mohsen Kadivar regarding Religious Pluralism] (Tehran: Salam, 1378/1999).

38. Shirin Ebadi, *Tarikh-che va asnad-e hoquq-e bashar dar Iran* (Tehran: Intisharat-e Rawshangaran, 1373/1994). The English translation that appeared as *History and Documentation of Human Rights in Iran,* trans. Nazila Fathi (New York: Bibliotheca Persica, 1999), is an abbreviation of the massive, 350-page Persian original.

39. Shrin Ebadi, *Hoquq-e zan dar qavanin-e jomhuri-ye Islami-ye Iran* (Tehran: Kitab-khanah-i Gang-i Danish, 2002), 160–63.

40. For the Persian original, see: http://nobelprize.org/peace/laureates/2003/ebadi -lecture-fa.pdf. For an English translation, see: http://nobelprize.org/peace/laureates/ 2003/ebadi-lecture-e.html (accessed June 25, 2009).

41. We have seen a parallel to and an echo of this same notion in Kadivar's writings.

42. Some of the prominent English-speaking progressives were featured in the volume *Progressive Muslims: On Justice, Gender, and Pluralism,* which I edited. I am profoundly grateful to Bruce Lawrence for having introduced me to two of the eventual authors, Farish A. Noor and Ahmad Moussali. Professor Lawrence had also suggested Chandra Muzaffer, who due to his schedule was unable to contribute an essay.

43. Lawrence, *New Faiths, Old Fears,* 137 (also 80–86).

44. For me the paramount American example of drawing on a rich spiritual tradition to combat the triple giant evil of racism, materialism, and militarism remains that of Martin Luther King Jr.—not just the "I have a dream" King but also the 1967 Riverside Church King:

And we must rejoice as well, for surely this is the first time in our nation's history that a significant number of its religious leaders have chosen to *move beyond the prophesying of smooth patriotism to the high grounds of a firm dissent* based upon the mandates of conscience and the reading of history. . . .

Beyond the calling of race or nation or creed is this vocation of sonship and brotherhood. Because I believe that the Father is deeply concerned, especially for His suffering and helpless and outcast children, I come tonight to speak for them. This I believe to be the privilege and the burden of all of us who deem ourselves bound by *allegiances and loyalties which are broader and deeper than nationalism and which go beyond our nation's self-defined goals and positions. We are called to speak for the weak, for the voiceless, for the victims of our nation,* for those it calls "enemy," for no document from human hands can make these humans any less our brothers. (emphasis added; King's speech *Beyond Vietnam* is available online at http://mlk-kpp01.stanford.edu/kingweb/publications/speeches/Beyond_Vietnam.pdf [accessed July 20, 2009]).

45. David Ignatius, "The Read on Wolfowitz," *Washington Post*, January 17, 2003. For a critical review of this concept, see Michaelle Browers and Charles Kurzman, ed., *An Islamic Reformation?* (Lanham, Md.: Lexington Books, 2004).

46. Ibid.

47. Paul Wolfowitz, "Bridging the Dangerous Gap between the West and the Muslim World," speech delivered in Monterey, Calif., May 3, 2002, http://www.defenselink.mil/speeches/speech.aspx?speechid=210 (accessed July8, 2009).

48. MuslimWakeUp.com, http://www.muslimwakeup.com/main/archives/2005/03/make_history_re.php (accessed December 30, 2005).

49. Lawrence, *New Faiths, Old Fears*, 62.

50. See the Wikipedia entry "Women as imams": http://en.wikipedia.org/wiki/Women_as_imams (accessed July 20, 2009).

51. "Resources and References," Council on American-Islamic Relations Pennsylvania, http://pa.cair.com/files/women_friendly_mosques.pdf (accessed July 8, 2009).

52. Ziba Mir-Hosseini, "Religious Modernists and the 'Woman Question': Challenges and Complicities," in *Twenty Years of Islamic Revolution: Political and Social Transition in Iran since 1979*, ed. Eric Hooglund (Syracuse, N.Y.: Syracuse University Press, 2002), 74–95.

53. Mehrangiz Kar, "Roshanfekri-ye dini va Mas'ala-ye 'Zanan'" (Religious Intellectuals and the "Woman Problem"), *Rah-e Now*, 17 Mordad 1377 (August 1998), 32–33, cited in Mir-Hosseini, "Religious Modernists." In the spirit of progressive self-critique, one might note the naive way in which Kar has become affiliated with Benador Associates, a public relations think tank for some of the leading neoconservatives and Islamophobes of the day, including Charles Krauthammer, Michael A. Ledeen, Richard Perle, Walid Phares, Richard Pipes, David Pryce-Jones, and James Woolsey. While there is no questioning Kar's own commitment to women's rights in Iran, when women's rights advocates align themselves with such ideologically triumphalist advocates, it exposes many in the gender equality movement to the charge of being pawns of empire. Benador has quite wisely surrounded its neoconservative members with liberal Muslims who critique the patriarchy and corruption of Muslim regimes—but never that of the American regime or, of course, Israel. For another example, see their inclusion of Saad Ed Din Ebrahim.

54. Abdalkarim Soroush, "Contraction and Expansion of Women's Rights," *Zanan*, 1378/2000, available online through http://www.drsoroush.com/English/Interviews/ E-INT-20000200-Contraction_and_Expansion_of_Womens_Rights.html (accessed July 8, 2009).

55. "It may be the case that our laws are imposing severe social constraints on women, but I believe that they are the weakest links in the chains restraining women. I think that the main issue we need to concern ourselves with is the basic principle of womanhood and manhood. The social contradictions are staring us in the face now and they make it clear that these regulations and commands do not correspond to our social needs and the roles that men and women have taken on in society; in other words, these laws do not meet the needs of the current relations between men and woman." Soroush, "Contraction and Expansion of Women's Rights."

56. Mir-Hosseini, "Religious Modernists and the 'Woman Question,'" 95.

57. Kadivar, "Hoquq-e zanan dar islam-e mo'aser az zaviye-ye digar," http://kadivar .com/Index.Asp?CGID=4&StartDate=3/21/2007&EndDate=3/20/2008&AC=1&AF =1&ASB=1&AGM=1&AL=1&DT=DLY (accessed July 20, 2009).

58. Omid Safi, introduction to *Progressive Muslims*, 7–8.

59. Omid Safi, "Challenges and Opportunities for the Progressive Muslim in North America," *Muslim Public Affairs Journal* 1, no. 1 (2006): 77–83.

60. Kecia Ali, "Progressive Muslims and Islamic Jurisprudence," in Safi, *Progressive Muslims*, 163–89.

61. Scott Kugle, "Sexuality, Diversity, and Ethics in the Agenda of Progressive Muslims," in Safi, *Progressive Muslims*, 190–234.

62. Muhammad Iqbal, "The Principle of Movement in the Structure of Islam," in Kurzman, *Liberal Islam*, 256–57.

63. Muhammad Sa'id al-'Ashmawi, "Shari'ah: The Codification of Islamic Law," in Kurzman, *Liberal Islam*, 55.

64. To recall Sherman Jackson's new term.

65. Muneer Goolam Fareed, *Legal Reform in the Muslim World: The Anatomy of a Scholarly Dispute in the Nineteenth and the Early Twentieth Centuries on the Usage of Ijtihâd as a Legal Tool* (San Francisco: Austin & Winfield, 1996).

66. Wael Hallaq, "Was the Gate of Ijtihad Closed?" *International Journal of Middle East Studies* 16, no. 1 (1984): 3–41; Wael Hallaq, "On the Origins of the Controversy about the Existence of Mujtahids and the Gate of Ijtihad," *Studia Islamica* 63 (1986): 129–41.

67. Charles Kurzman, *Liberal Islam*, 55 and 67–72.

68. The date here refers to the Iranian Shamsi Hijri calendar, not the more conventional Islamic lunar calendar, followed by the Gregorian calendar.

69. For an American observer such as myself, the level of the discourse, critiques, and countercritiques is simply dazzling, and a painful reminder that in the North American there are no comparable sustained engagements across ideological lines.

70. Hussein-'Ali Montazeri, "Dar bab-e Tazahum," *Majalla-yi Kiyan* 45 (1377/1998): 150–51. Quoted in Sa'id 'Idalat-nezhad, *Andar Bab-e Ijtihad* (Tehran: Tarh-e Tau, 1382/2003), 14.

71. Ja'far Subhani, "Falsafa-ye Fiqh," in 'Idalat-nezhad, *Ijtihad*, 65–78.

72. The analogy here of course is an ironic reminder of the attempts under Reza Shah to purge Persian of all the Arabic vocabulary, a failed endeavor. In a way Soroush

is comparing Reza Shah's nationalist linguistic *'asabiyya* to the Ayatollah's religious intolerance.

73. Soroush, *Ijtihad*, 17.

74. Ibid., 21–22.

75. Ibid., 22.

76. Ibid.

77. Ibid., 23.

78. Tariq Ramadan, "An International Call for Moratorium on Corporal Punishment, Stoning and the Death Penalty in the Islamic World," http://www.tariqramadan.com/sphp.php?article264 (accessed July 20, 2009).

79. Ibid.

80. Roger Hardy, "Muslim Thinker Fights Death Penalty," BBC News, March 30, 2005, http://news.bbc.co.uk/1/hi/world/middle_east/4394863.stm (accessed July 8, 2009).

81. Shahed Amanullah, "Shining a Light on the 'White Elephant' of Hudud Punishments," altmuslim.com, April 1, 2005, http://www.altmuslim.com/perm.php?id=1424_0_24_0_M (accessed July 8, 2009).

82. Ramadan, "An International Call for Moratorium."

83. Ibid.

84. Ibid.

85. That rejoinder is also apropos for scholars of Islamic studies. Since the 1979 Iranian revolution, Persian as a language has been severely marginalized in the Western academic study of Islam. I would argue that had Soroush and company been writing in Arabic—or German (!)—there would already be dozens of dissertations on their project.

⚜

Fundamentalism and the Transparency of the Arabic Qur'an

A. KEVIN REINHART

Introduction

This paper arises from two observations, and one—happily ongoing—argument. The two observations are these: (1) Everywhere in Islamdom Arabic books are for sale, and these books are overwhelmingly medieval works. (2) More subjectively, it seems to me that in the Arab world in general the level of conversation about the Qur'an but also about Shariʿa is much less interesting than the discussion I encounter in Turkey and from Pakistanis, Indonesians, Persians, and others. As for the argument: this paper is a salvo fired at my good friend Bruce Lawrence—to which he will no doubt respond—about how to see the connection between the undoubtedly modern phenomenon we call fundamentalism—and particularly the Muslim version of fundamentalism—on the one hand and the premodern textual and intellectual-structural legacy of Muslims on the other. Bruce was among the first, perhaps the first to emphasize the fact of Islamism's modernity.[1] Though I completely agree with his assertion that these various Islamic fundamentalisms are modern (and hope to demonstrate a particular aspect of that modernity below), I want to argue that in at least one respect this modernity is grounded in a medieval anxiety about linguistic and cultural pluralism. This medieval anxiety was no doubt strange to most medieval Muslims, but to Hanbalis, with their self-appointed task of patrolling the borders of Islamic thought, an anxiety about pluralism was an anxiety about authentic Islam. Some Muslim moderns, already susceptible to worry about the nature of authentic Islam are, in a distinctively premodern way, driven to assert the primacy of Arabic and Arabs among the plethora of modern Muslim cultural identities. This, I suggest, leads Arabs in particular to a particular lack of sophistication as they approach the Qur'anic text. Arab fundamentalists are committed to the doctrine of the transparent Qur'anic text, and the illusory experience of this transparency leads them to read it in a distinctively modern way—not in the sophisticated polyvalent way that characterized premodern approaches to the Qur'an and that might characterize a postmodern Qur'anic understanding.

Let me begin with two stipulations:

(1) Fundamentalism, as a comparative term, refers to movements constituted by a set of practices putatively grounded in a distinctive form of hermeneutic. (On this see below.)

The term for the Islamic version of this fundamentalism will be *Islamism*, and in my usage I want to distinguish between Islamic activism of the fundamentalist sort, parallel to, say the Moral Majority in the United States, and jihadists, who are the equivalent of the Michigan Militia, the Aryan Nation, or on the Left, perhaps, the SDS in its later phase. I will be focusing on Islamists, not jihadists.

(2) Fundamentalist Islam, Islamism, has been shaped particularly by historical Salafism—a movement very much at odds with the constellation of movements that today call themselves "Salafī."[2] Yet both forms of Salafism, in the name of an authentic Islam, prune the Islamic intellectual tradition of much of the subtlety, and of course the scholasticism, of premodern Islam. Salafism had one feature that has been decisive and that scholars have not sufficiently attended to. Salafism arose together with Arab nationalism, and it recenters Islamic self-understanding on the Arabs in a way that had not been the case since—perhaps—the tenth century c.e. I will argue that combining the simplification of Islamic scholarship with the (re-)Arabization of Islam has left Arabs particularly prone to fundamentalist readings. In the end, as Chesterton said of another Protestant denomination, this approach to faith leaves not pure religion but a fossil of the full richness of religious life and thought.[3] Further, I will argue, both tendencies—to an emphasized Arabness and to an impoverished hermeneutic—are anticipated by Ibn Taymiyyah (d. 1328), which may tell us something about structural features of Islamist Muslim thought.

This paper is best described as something between a rumination and an essay. It rehearses, if only for my own use, phenomena I have found and wondered about over the last thirty-five years in various places in Islamdom. It is an informal attempt to offer something like an explanation for the phenomena I describe.

Locating Arabic Books

When I visit an Islamic bookstore or book market, what strikes my eye is the enormous number of books by premoderns. This is true throughout the Arab world, and it is true also—though to a lesser extent—in Philadelphia, Istanbul, Lahore, and Paris. The *tafsir* of Ibn Kathir, the massive law work of Ibn Qudamah, the eschatology of Abu Layth al-Samarqandi, and many more such works are given pride of place in the displays, and from the bindings, the quality of the paper, and the number of editions, it is clear these are the prestige items in such stores. Even on corner newsstands, pamphlets and chapbooks are as likely to be produced by someone writing before the Christian eighteenth century as by someone from the twentieth or twenty-first. This strikes me as noteworthy.

It is certainly not the case in Catholic or Protestant Christian bookstores. Anecdotally it is not the case in Jewish bookstores, except among the specialized bookstores of the very frumm. Why the attention to the premodern, especially the Arabic language premodern, among Muslim readers, whether in the Arab world, Iran, or Turkey? (And indeed I'm not even sure I mean readers, since I see such books owned by people who are far from mastering the arcane of medieval scholastic scholarship, and in a few cases, these are owned by people who are not "Arabically" literate.) It is clear that these books are not doing in the consumer's living room what they are doing in the office of scholars such as Wilferd Madelung or Tariq Ramadan. Whatever work they are doing in the house of Ahmad al-Misri or Mehmet Turk, we can say that their presence reflects a prestige that belongs to discourse in Arabic shared even by those whose understanding of it is limited.

Let us begin with what this phenomenon does not signify. It does not mean that Muslims or even Islamists are backward medievals who want to take everyone back to the Middle Ages. There are such people, Romantics of a sort, such as the Aczmendis in Turkey or Corbin's "Templars."[4] They live in a sort of fantasy world, and the dressing up in archaic clothing, proclaiming the faultless glories of *illud tempus*, and a sharing of historically inflected hugger-mugger have a certain aesthetic charm. Of course such groups can also be unpalatable politically, as were similar groups in France in the 1920s and 1930s.[5] But these are insignificant politically and culturally. They certainly are too small to constitute the market for the prolific production of classical texts we see for sale.

The first, but not completely satisfying, explanation for the explosion of premodern religious texts that comes to mind is a sheer consumerist one.[6] These are prestigious books with fancy bindings that look impressive on a bookshelf. "Books do furnish a room," as one of Anthony Powell's characters famously said. Certainly I have visited the homes of people who are far from skilled in Islamic studies, in one case not even literate in Arabic, and found multivolume editions of Tabari's commentary and al-Sarakhsi's great law work, the Mabsut, for instance. Yet this explanation in turn fails to answer the question, Why are these works prestigious while, for example, Jurji Zaydan's multivolume history of Islam or Ahmad Amin's, which one used to see in the homes of people educated in the 1930s and 1940s, have disappeared from the market? And certainly there are first-rate works of Islamic and Islamicate scholarship being produced in Arabic and Turkish, as well as works of popular history. These latter are found in the homes of *intels* in Turkey, for instance, but not in the homes of the identifying religious. When we try to understand this commercial oddity, several explanations suggest themselves.

I have found in conversation with Muslims that there is very often a distrust of the professionally religious. Contrary to recent assertions,[7] it is my impression that the *ulama* are mostly perceived (outside of the Shi'a realm) as remote and bureaucratized figures. Some appear on television or other media and are made thereby present in some sense, but most Sunni Muslims have little if any recourse to the professionally religious. The *ulama* are, in any case, believed to be implicated in the contemporary world, and the more sophisticated one is, it seems, the more one mistrusts the *ulama* as partisan, servile, and unaware of contemporary science, culture, or management techniques. They are seen as foreign, irrelevant, or just ignorant.

Yet Islamic learning per se remains prestigious. Hence for the piously inclined, these works may be talismans of a time when the greats walked the earth, when *'ilm* was *'ilm*, and the formative figures were active and reliable voices. One can turn to these texts for guidance, but also for refreshment from a world that predates the quotidian, with all the banality and corruption that is associated with these times. In this way I am reminded of Soviet Orientalists in Petersburg who boasted of how untheoretical their works were: the less theoretical, the more philological a work was, the more it escaped the banality of Soviet culture—the risks to scholarly integrity on the one hand or to employment and even security on the other. In short the more opaque and technical a work was, the more it insulated scholars from what he or she despised about their contemporary scholarly culture. I think there is something in the Islamic bourgeois attachment to products of medieval scholarship that shares with the Soviets an admiration for the free-floating, the mythic, the uncontaminated work of the premoderns— as they are perceived to be, in any case. One feature of the books of the greats is precisely that they are the "greats." They exist in an alternative time, an undoubtedly Islamic time, which is filtered through a haze of nostalgia that is so different from the fog of battle. Along these lines we might also cynically note that if you want to publish a book on Islam, or buy one, you'll have far less difficulty with state censorship or partisan harassment if the author is safely dead and medieval.

The effect of this bibliographic nostalgia on intra-Muslim conversations we can leave for the moment. It is fair to say, however, that just as American Christian fundamentalism makes it difficult to be a competent biologist, the sanctification of the premodern makes it hard for contemporary Muslims to join in the world conversations about ethics, politics, history, and religion. At the same time, however, this fetishizing of the classic works of medieval Arabic religious scholarship has the effect, in the present climate, of giving to the native Arabic speaker a kind of prestige once reserved only for the learned. A fortiori, the Arabic learned would seem to have some cachet over the non-Arab scholar— however learned he or she might be.

This is an essential methodological point for the study of Muslim fundamentalism at this time: the interest in medieval Islamic scholarship is a creative response to life in the early twenty-first (Christian) century. It is not an attempt by backward people to move society back to medieval times.[8] Yet once that point has been made and absorbed, it is worth reflecting on it again. I want to argue that the heightened status of Arabic scholarship may have a premodern precedent and may suggest something structural, as well as something that is modern. As it turns out, the Islamic utopia of Islamic scholarship, the *illud tempus* to which Islamic utopians seek return or progress toward, involves a special place for Arabic.

Ibn Taymiyyah's Anticipation of Religious Arab Chauvinism

The fourteenth-century Hanbali polymath and polemicist Ibn Taymiyyah in his *Iqtiḍi'* sees non-Arabs as a threat to authentic Islam and as constitutionally inferior to Arab Muslims: "That upon which the people of Prophetic-norms and solidarity [agree] is the belief that the genus of the Arabs is superior (*afḍal*) to the genus of non-Arabs (*al-ʿajam*), whether Hebrew, Syrianic Greek, Persian or any other. . . . The superiority of Arabs . . . is not due merely to the fact of the Prophet's being of them. . . . rather, they are in themselves superior. . . . [Ibn Taymiyyah cites the] *hadith* 'Love of Arabs is faith, and despising them is hypocrisy.'"[9]

In Ibn Taymiyyah's view it would follow as a matter of faith that a Muslim must declare that Arabs surpass non-Arabs, and that this has always been the case.

> When God sent down His book in the Arabic language, and made His Messenger convey from Him the Book and the Wisdom in his Arabic language, and made the early followers of this religion speakers of it, there is no way forward to be correct in religion and in its knowledge except by being precise in this language. And knowledge of it was made a part of religion and use of it for speaking made it easier on people of religion to know the religion of God and closer to undertaking the outward practices (*shaʿaʾir*) of religion.[10]

Consequently even in daily life, normative Arabic ought to be the language of Muslims. Turkish, vernacular Arabic, Syriac, Coptic, Aramaic, or other languages are marks of religious inferiority and even treachery, since non-Islamic practices enter into Islam through contact with foreign Muslims. "It is detestable that a man should become habituated to speaking other than Arabic, because the Arabic language is one of the symbols of Islam and Muslims. . . . To an extent that this other language becomes a habit of a whole city with its dwellers, of an entire household, of a man and his associates, this is undoubtedly detestable."[11]

As I have argued elsewhere, Ibn Taymiyyah's religious ideal is to inhabit, religiously, the mythic era of the companions. Speaking Arabic is one important method for recovering that primordial time.[12] Arabic for him is a precondition for authentic Muslim scholarship and for an authentic Muslim life. To the extent that Islamic emphasis is placed on scriptural texts and their derivatives, Arabic is placed in the center of the ideal Muslim existence. Ibn Taymiyyah's insistence on the primacy of Arabic reflects a medieval decline in its importance, of course. Though Arabic was always to some extent a treasured skill of the Islamically literate, it is well known—if not yet fully accepted in Islamic studies circles—that a plentiful vernacular language tradition, written and oral, supplemented and supplanted the Arabic one, and for "the folk" constituted the whole of the Islamic heritage.[13]

Our task, here, however, is to think about contemporary Islamic intellectual life, and a second starting point might be the category of fundamentalism. To grasp the place of Arabic and its vehicle, the Qur'an, in contemporary Islamic and Islamist movements, it is helpful to think for a moment about such movements comparatively.

Thinking about Fundamentalism in General

Fundamentalism is an unhelpful word in so many ways, and we spend so much time pointing out its shortcomings that perhaps we should consider how the word is helpful as a rubric, one that describes something quite real in various diverse movements. Drawing on Protestant Christian fundamentalism, James Barr, in his foundational work, made an observation that is crucially true for Islamic, as well as Christian fundamentalist movements: Fundamentalists' eimic self-definition is etically false.

> Fundamentalists indeed suppose that this kind of religion is theirs because it follows as a necessary consequence from their acceptance of Biblical authority. But here we have to disagree and say that the reverse is true: a particular type of religious experience, which indeed in the past was believed to arise from the Bible, has come to be itself dominant. This religious tradition on the one hand controls the interpretation of the Bible within fundamentalist circles; on the other hand it entails, not as its source but as its symbol and as an apparently necessary condition of its own self-preservation, the fundamentalist doctrine of the Bible.[14]

For "Bible" we may substitute Qur'an and the statement remains true. It is an article of faith that "the Qur'an is the solution" or "the Qur'an is our constitution," but when one reads fundamentalist works, the attempt at specifying the Qur'anic basis is rather thin. It may be cultural appropriation that leads fundamentalists to assert that the word *shura* in the Qur'an refers to parliaments. It may be an expansive extension of the Qur'anic meaning when banning *riba* is understood to mean banning automobile insurance. It is precisely because the Qur'an does not say anything about automobile insurance or parliaments that it must be insisted so firmly that it does. And since the text is so noncommittal, it requires an authoritarian commitment to affirm emphatically that these notions are present—obviously—when they are in fact not obviously present.[15] None of this is illegitimate, of course. Religious change is often accomplished by just such procedures. Yet in the case of fundamentalist hermeneutics, it seems to me, there is a naiveté coupled with an authoritarian stance that is illiberal, and it is the naiveté that empowers the authoritarian.

The sustaining myth of the fundamentalist hermeneutic is that the text of scripture is transparent. It is accessible, and it is possible to read it without pre-conceptions to apprehend both its intention and its meaning. One does not have to be a postmodernist to know that the full implication of a written text is not accessible simply from the written (or recited) words. Indeed this is a position held by the great eighth-century Islamic jurist al-Shafi'i.[16] Yet the importance of cultural context, a fundamental insight of Islamic jurisprudence, has been chucked over the side by the fundamentalist ideologues.

In the premodern period it was understood that no text was by itself suffi-cient, and indeed no single genre of texts was sufficient for genuine understand-ing of a text. To understand a part of the Qur'an one had to measure it against its potentially relevant parts, against all possibly relevant Sunna texts, against the "circumstances of revelation" texts, and so on. Far from a transparent process, reading the Qur'an was imagined to be an arduous and necessarily imperfect enterprise, at any rate for Muslims after the first three generations.[17]

Indeed the entire edifice of medieval jurisprudential scholarship that evokes such admiration from moderns is built precisely on the idea of reading the Qur'an against its revelational and historical context—as medievals understood it. This was not, of course, a task for the laity. The ever-growing requirements for schol-arly attainment that were preconditions for approaching the text and discerning its applicability produced a more and more self-destructive hermeneutic. By the twelfth century c.e., it was believed that no one was sufficiently equipped to understand scripture and to apply it as the foundational imams (or for the Imami Shi'a, the *imam ma'sum*) had. Everyone was obligated to defer epistemologically to the masters of the past—this is the meaning of *taqlid*.[18] This interpretative process grew hieratic as well, a process reinforced by developing bureaucratized states throughout Islamdom. In the Ottoman world, the *ulama* were completely integrated into the state bureaucracy. In the Safavid realm, the *ulama* were more or less a creation of the state, which selected and imported *imami* jurists from various parts of Islamdom to serve the state. In India the state produced a defini-tive Hanafi law book to serve as the basis for all subsequent jurisprudential prac-tice in the Mughul realm. The sheer volume of legal understanding amassed by scholars from Islam's beginning until the fifteenth century produced an anxiety that led to a number of efforts to synthesize the tradition in order to control it.[19]

Yet while there were demonstrably changes over time in epistemology and practice, nearly all of premodern discourse on scripture and its application assumed the complexity of hermeneutic practice. The revelation was not identical with the Qur'an "between the two covers."[20] One had to know a whole series of enlarging sources, but also disciplining techniques that prevented capricious understanding (*wahm* or *ahwa'*). In addition—and utterly in keeping with the nature of the Qur'an—the model of reading was actually one of auditing a spoken text. Knowingly and unknowingly the interpreters of religious texts made them their own and read them against what they already knew from their practice of Islamic norms. This method of reading is, as we shall see, a distinctively "un-modern" approach to the religious text.

Soloveitchik on Modern Religious Hermeneutics

The "fundamental" change that makes fundamentalism possible is a change in the way reading is done and in the expectations engendered by the act of reading. Modern reading is not premodern reading, and the two should not be confused. The best exposition of this change of reading and appropriating I've read is in two articles by Haym Soloveitchik.[21]

In these articles he points out that in the premodern world, religious texts were not read by themselves, but they were merely a component disciplined by larger life patterns. "And a way of life is not learned but rather absorbed. Its transmission is mimetic . . . and patterned."[22] But in the modern world the living models become only one of a set of choices, and the process of choosing disrupts the mimetic transmission. What were once practices observed as a matter of course become practices chosen because of the commitments of belief. The practice then becomes a ritual, and "a ritual can no more be approximated than an incantation can be summarized."[23] Its essence lies in its accuracy. We forget that what we scholars view in the premodern world as observance of Shari'a was actually, for most, simply the routine of life. Now, because of choice, we see "the ritualization of what had previously been routine acts and everyday objects. . . . A way of life has become a regula, and behavior, once governed by habit, is now governed by rule."[24]

Similarly while the technique of reading remained superficially the same, in the modern world the understanding of a text became radically different. In the premodern world,

> self-contained presentations of a topic, . . . introducing the reader to a
> subject and explaining it in lay language did not exist. There were few, if
> any, serious works [including Scripture] that could be read independently,
> that is, without reference to another text which is glossed. Indeed the use
> of such a work would have been deeply suspect, for its reader would be

making a claim to knowledge that he had not elicited from the primary texts. Knowledge was seen as an attainment, something that had been wrested personally from the sources. Information, on the other hand, was something merely obtained, passed like a commodity, from hand to hand, usually in response to a question.[25]

In the modern world, the domain in which God's intervention can be expected shrinks, and the "value-driven cosmos is replaced by a mechanistic and indifferent one."[26] The experience of God as a constant presence is diminished, and so zealots "seek to ground their new emerging spirituality less in a now unattainable intimacy with Him than in an intimacy with His will."[27]

Consequently it is texts, more than teachers, that bear the burden of imprinting identity on a person. And so these texts are experienced in a new way—as infallible information, not as sacramental revelation—and one turns to them for knowledge as one turns to a science textbook or a political science primer. The Qur'an remains more authoritative than Huntington or Samuelson, but it is no longer different in kind. If the Qur'an is a constitution, it is being defended or praised or had recourse to in the way one might justify or seek guidance from the Constitution of the Fourth Republic. This fits the claim that the Qur'an can be read without all the apparatus of scholasticism, but it significantly alters the kind of authority attributed to the Qur'anic text. The leading advocates of this putatively naive reading of the Qur'an have been the adherents of the movement called Salafiyyah—in both its early quasi-modernist stage and now in its neotraditionist and, in some cases, jihadist phase.

The Protestantism of Islamic Fundamentalism

Islamic fundamentalism resembles Protestantism (which indeed, I would argue, shaped its nineteenth-century origins) in several respects.[28] It defines practices that are explicitly not scripturally sanctioned as part of a false or impure religion. It sees other Muslims as merely nominal or mistaken Muslims. But at a more interesting level, it reorients Islam in a way that is parallel to the reorientation of fundamentalist Protestantism. Protestant fundamentalism, Barr says, puts the Bible at the center of regard, but not in the way that the fundamentalists purport to do. Barr's description is so acute it deserves to be quoted in (nearly) full.

[For the fundamentalist,] the Bible is thus the supreme tangible sacred reality. . . . The Bible in fundamentalism is comparable to the virgin Mary in Roman Catholicism: it is the human visible symbol involved in salvation: as she through the immaculate conception is free from the contagion of human imperfection, so [the Bible] has a kind of perfection and sublimity that makes it sacrilegious for us to analyze and criticize its seamless fabric. . . . Certain kinds of biblical criticism and theology are felt to threaten the status of the Bible as absolute and perfect symbol of the religion; and in order to protect that symbolic status of the Bible the religion itself has to be adjusted or distorted. . . . On the one hand the religious tradition is the ultimate value for fundamentalists. They do not use the Bible to question and re-check this tradition, they just accept that this tradition is the true interpretation of the Bible. The fundamentalist position about the infallibility and inerrancy of the Bible is an attempt to prevent this tradition from being damaged through modes of interpretation that might make the Bible mean something else. . . . To protect the Bible against other modes of interpretation, [fundamentalism] finds that it gradually has to alter and even abandon essential elements of the very religious tradition from which it started out.[29]

This description works equally well for Islamic fundamentalism. The Qur'an is less problematic as a text than the Bible: there are no Gospels to harmonize, no conflicting epistles to reconcile, and no refocusing of the Hebrew Bible so that it becomes the Old Testament. It is the Shari'a (actually *fiqh*) that has to be justified and protected against inappropriate modes of interpretation (historical, contextual, cultural).

For fundamentalists, then, Shari'a is the secondary religious object that acts as a gravitational attractor pulling Islam and the Qur'an after it, as the Bible does for fundamentalist Protestants. This is not the view of medieval legists, however. That Shari'a was, at least in theory, subject to examination and interrogation. Assertions about it required proof. Demonstrably as it becomes more an object than an inquiry through the course of Islamic history, it becomes more central in Islamic symbolic discourse. But even so the early-twentieth-century jurist still had a monopoly over the sources required to examine and, if necessary, to overturn any particular rule associated with Shari'a.

Yet now, it would seem, the Shari'a is a freestanding body imagined to be immutable, and the whole edifice of scholarship that once undergirded it has become irrelevant, as medical doctors and civil engineers publish fatwas stripped of the structures of justification that once were the essence—often unspoken but no less essential for it—of the fatwa itself. Their enterprise is now grounded not in observance, discovering, and transmitting but in what Mohammad Benkheira calls "l'amour de la loi." It is ritualism, he says, that defines the fundamentalist, not, for example, violence.[30] The Shari'a and *fiqh* have been collapsed into each other, and what were once understood as the efforts of human beings are reified and recognized not as human attempts to act in accordance with God's rule but as rulings ontologically identical with God's rule.

Sadiq al-ʿAzm has pinpointed this detachment by fundamentalists from the teaching of the Qur'an and their retreat into Shariʿa this way: "I noticed also a certain minority of students were seeking in an unconscious way a solution to this problem [of the science-religion conflict] by way of taking refuge in a religious position firmly locked up in its zealousness and constructions, by holding fast to the minutia of religious duties. This minority on every occasion expressed their strong enmity to any progressive or scientific idea and derided any position critical of the Muslim heritage and to everything that might affect the traditional way of life."[31]

Yet if this describes a certain kind of Islamic fundamentalism, we are compelled to notice that al-ʿAzm writes about his students, that is, students of his in the Arab world. These students are heirs of the Salafī movement, and it is not surprising that, even in the words of Gamal Abdul Nasser lamenting the disaster of 1969, we find a mild Salafi Islam invoked to bring him comfort.[32] It is to the conceptual origins of Salafism that we must now turn.

Salafism

If the origins of fundamentalism are indeed located in nineteenth- and early-twentieth-century reform movements that called themselves Salafi, then it is worth noting that Salafism was, at its origin and throughout its history, identifiably a movement that took place in the Arab world and that it had as one of its goals the recentering of Islam in the land from which it had arisen—now identified not with Arabia but with the Arabic-speaking nation. This is not to say that there were not Salafi movements elsewhere, but it is notable that, in a way that has been much studied, the stimulus to these movements came from the Arab world or from time spent in the Arab world—particularly in the al-Azhar school in Cairo.[33]

As their patron saint, the Salafis had Ibn Taymiyyah.[34] Whether Ibn Taymiyyah and Hanbali thought created Salafism or the Salafis chose the Hanbalis because they were congenial is unanswerable. What is clear is that the Hanbalis had long ago, as we have seen above, rehearsed a doctrine of Arab superiorism that was comfortable in the mixed Arab/Islamic nationalism of late-nineteenth- and early-twentieth-century Syria and Egypt.[35]

It is no surprise, then, that we find everywhere in Salafi literature an exaltation of the Arabs and their place in Islam. Knowing Arabic was of course the key to their other doctrine—that being a Muslim did not require the scholasticism of the medievals, much less the *ilham* (mystical inspiration) of the Sufi. The early Damascene Salafi ʿAbdal Hamīd al-Zahrawi asserted that "anyone who knows Arabic can understand [the Qur'an], for it addresses all believers from the time of its revelation to the present."[36] In the Salafi account of *fasad al-zaman* (the corruption of the times) it was non-Arabs, especially Turks and Persians, who had corrupted the pure, that is, Arab, form of Islam.[37]

For Salafīs the only prerequisite to reading the Qurʾan and understanding it was a knowledge of Arabic—grammar, lexicon, and style. Yet because of the emphasis on the Qurʾan as an Arabic document, and because Arabic language mastery is the only prerequisite to understanding and then implementing the Qurʾan, Arabic itself becomes disproportionately privileged in the creation of a pure Islam.[38] Moreover scholarship not produced in Arabic, whether Islamic or non-Islamic, cannot be authentic, cannot be significant, because it lacks the single qualifying characteristic of important religious scholarship. The place of Arabic in contemporary Islam may have parallels to the place of sacred language in other contemporary traditions—perhaps Hebrew for Judaism, or Sanskrit for Hinduism—but it has consequences quite particular to Islam, especially Middle Eastern Islam, that have no parallel, I think, in other traditions. I think that its entanglement with Arab nationalism is a decisive feature in its construction—from the beginning through the present.

At present the modernizing liberalism of the Salafis has been replaced by the fundamentalist Islam of the neo-Salafis, such as the Muslim Brethren.[39] Though many features of proto-Salafism remain—the assertion of *ijtihad*'s primacy over *taqlid*, for instance, or the condemnation of Sufism—arguably the one utterly consistent feature of neo-Salafism that links it to prototypical Salafism is its unreconstructed Arabism. Salafism, at present, is a self-designation for a form of Islam that is functionally identical with Wahhabi perspectives. It is scripturalist and purist; it understands itself to be literalist in its hermeneutic, but it is also relentlessly anti-imperialist, chauvinistic, and constantly on the alert for "insults" to Islam's honor. Though this is quite different from the Salafism of the movement's founders, who were progressive, antitraditionalist, and in many ways modernist, they too were anti-imperialist (or anticolonialist) and concerned with policing the boundaries of Islam.

This anti-imperialism and defensive chauvinism confirms the shared roots of Salafism with Arab nationalism—itself a movement of resistance to the colonial presence. Arab nationalism was a nationalist chauvinist movement that, even for Christian Arab nationalists, harked back to the Qurʾanic Arabic as culture marker. All Arab nationalists honored Islam's first several centuries as the nation's most glorious era; all shared a decline paradigm that asserted that Islam's decline (and therefore the Arabs') was due to the corruption of pure Arabism by foreign elements. It needs to be remembered also that Salafism arose in a context in which issues of preferment and professional advantage were at stake. In general the anti-Salafists were supporters of the Ottoman caliphate, the Salafists were critics of it and often were separatists.[40] It is not surprising that Salafis often found common cause with Arab nationalists and that the form of Islam most comfortable to nationalists was a Salafi one, one uncontaminated by foreign influences such as Sufism and authoritarian interpretation. The Arab nationalists (like the Salafis) sought to reinsert Arabs into a central position in history's grand narrative. Though by the First World War Arab nationalism and Salafism had moved in quite different directions, it seems to me that they continued to reinforce each other. And as Salafism evolved into the radical movement it has become, even as it has internationalized, it has retained this Arabo-centrism in its DNA.

Arab Muslims and the Myth of Qurʾanic Transparency

The potency of Salafism, like that of other "recuperative movements," arises from the way it is perceived to transcend the mundane temporalism of modernity. It is at the core of modern self-understanding to see any historical era as distinct from another and particularly to distinguish ourselves from the historic Other. For the premodern (or the member of the philosophy department) Aristotle is not a fourth-century B.C.E. Greek but is a colleague in, as it were, another room; he is a colleague who has ideas to appropriate, to clarify, and to refute but whose works stands outside of the constraints of culture and time. But if the historical facticity of Aristotle was unproblematic for the medieval scholar, the text became quite problematic and could not be understood apart from a tradition, a magisterium of interpretation. What the Roman Church did with the Bible and what the scholastic tradition did with the Qurʾan was effectively to locate it in a past (a hermeneutical, not historical past) that stipulated and required that certain disciplinary tools and auxiliary sources of knowledge be used to understand the texts.

What the Protestant Reformation contributed, both through its approach to the Bible and through its authorized translations into the vernacular, was to produce a return to a mythic hermeneutic. Christians were again in the room, as it were, with the apostles. And for the Salafis, particularly the Arab Salafīs, the disciplining hedge around the Qurʾan was pruned almost to the ground and Muslims were once more in Medina, hearing the Qurʾan and its summons, as they supposed it had been delivered to their co-nationalists, the Salaf, in Arabia 1,200 years before. Consequently—especially in the generation after the Damascene religious reformer Jamaladdin al-Qasimi (1866–1914), when Salafism become a more popular, journalistic endeavor rather than a scholarly critique of the scholastic approach—the Qurʾan and also the enormous corpus of the Sunna (the Hadith) were read by Salafīs without attention to their complexities of transmission, of contradictions, of idiom. As a result, for example, a small subset of popular *hadiths* became canonized and were read as simple, journalistic accounts of the Prophet's speech.

There were, of course, two problems with traveling this path. The first was historical—the text of the Qurʾan is a seventh-century product of a certain kind, not a cookbook or a science textbook or a constitutional primer of the nine-teenth- and twentieth-century sort. Secondly the scholastic literature of *fiqh* has arisen because of a set of genuine problems with the texts—adequacy problems, scope problems, problems of interpretation—that Muslims who were committed to a nonarbitrary application of scripture to Muslim life had attempted to solve by developing the very methods that the nineteenth- and twentieth-century Salafis tossed out. What remained was the powerful sentiment of Qurʾanic devotion—a scripturalist devotion that, as Geertz said, tested not what you believe but how firmly you believed it—set against modern problems with no sophisticated way to go from text to problem.

This is the point of the observations I have made of the link between Arab nationalism and Salafism. Salafism is not merely an attempt to move Arabs and other Muslims from "the margins of history" and to "reclaim [the Arab] right to make history and to lead the world."[41] This is the purport of nationalisms every-where. For the historian of religion, the most interesting point is that Arabism convinces Arabs above all other Muslims to imagine that the Qurʾan as a text to be read effortlessly, transparently, in the modern fashion Soloveitchik describes.

Here we come to the most speculative part of this paper, a part that is the ori-gin of my concern. When I read the *dīn* section of Arab newspapers, when I read the reports of Arab congresses on one or another feature of Islam, I am struck by the embarrassing thinness of the conversation. It is hard to see these pallid articles and arguments as anything more than thin broth made from the bones of great Muslim scholarship of the past. Arabic Islamic scholarship can be very good in its self-contained world, but when engaging the larger world as a whole, it is, as al-ʿAzm points out, characterized by great rhetorical firmness grounded in little more than wordplay and assertion.[42] By contrast some of the religious journalism one reads on the Web from Pakistani journals or Indonesian sources, and certainly a good deal of (often critical) religious thought from Iran as well as from Turkey,[43] has a degree of subtlety and engagement. This simply seems not to be found in the Arab Islamic-world discussions of Islam in the world.

I'd like to suggest that what non-Arab Muslims have that Arabs do not is the ability to see the Qurʾan and its exegetical penumbra as text—to get a certain distance from it (a distance that is largely imposed by language) that liberates them from the *amour de la loi.* The Qurʾan for Turks, Persians, Indonesians, and Indians seems to be on the one hand sacrament—the recited text is as revered outside the Arab world as within it. But on the other hand, for them it is ideas, orientations, trajectories. It is less likely to be mistaken for a science textbook, civics guide, or social recipe. It is no surprise that while Salafism arises from a slightly dodgy Persian ("Al-Afghani"), neo-Salafism arises from the Egyptians Rashid al-Ridaʾ and Hasan al-Banna. Modernism arises in India; jihadism in Egypt, Lebanon, or Arabia. Compare the pronounced obliqueness of ʿAli Shariʿati toward the tradition and his willingness to reinvent it to the recuperative attitude of Hasan al-Banna.[47] And note the realism and agility of Islamically oriented parties in Turkey, in contrast to the stodginess of the Jordanian, Egyptian, or Palestinian Ikhwan (Muslim Brotherhood).

It is of course absurd to offer monocausal explanations of anything, and Bernard Lewis and Samuel Huntington have done much by their own examples to make clear the lameness of crude cultural determinism. Yet I hope that the next generation of scholars will, in the spirit of Bruce Lawrence's willingness to ask big questions, help reflect in a disciplined way on the consequences of what seems to me a categorically different relation to the text between Arabophone Muslims and those who make up Islam's majority.

NOTES

1. Bruce B. Lawrence, *Defenders of God: The Fundamentalist Revolt against the Modern Age* (San Francisco: Harper & Row, 1989), chap. 1; see also Bruce B. Lawrence, *Shattering the Myth: Islam beyond Violence* (Princeton: Princeton University Press, 1998), 23–26.

2. Which Schulze and I, following him, call "neo-Salafi." See Reinhard Schulze, *A Modern History of the Islamic World* (New York: Tauris, 2000), 95.

3. G. K. Chesterton, *As I Was Saying: A Chesterton Reader* (New York: Dodd, Mead, 1936), 52–54.

4. See S. M. Wasserstrom, *Religion after Religion: Gershom Scholem, Mircea Eliade, and Henry Corbin at Eranos* (Princeton: Princeton University Press, 1999), 8, 48.

5. See Wasserstrom, *Religion after Religion,* for the political-religious milieu of Henri Corbin and Mircea Eliade.

6. Gregory Starrett, *Putting Islam to Work: Education, Politics, and Religious Transformation in Egypt* (Berkeley: University of California Press, 1998); Gregory Starrett, "The Political Economy of Religious Commodities in Cairo," *American Anthropologist* 97, no. 1 (1995): 51–56. David McMurray first called my attention to this paper, which led me to Starrett's other excellent and illuminating work.

7. See, for example, Richard T. Antoun, *Muslim Preacher in the Modern World: A Jordanian Case Study in Comparative Perspective* (Princeton: Princeton University Press, 1989); Muhammad Qasim Zaman, *The Ulama in Contemporary Islam: Custodians of Change* (Princeton: Princeton University Press, 2002).

8. A point Bruce Lawrence has made numerous times.

9. T. A. Ibn Taymiyyah, *Kitāb iqtidā' as-sirāt al-mustaqīm mukhālafat ashāb al-jahīm.* Edited by Muhammad Hāmid al-Fiqī (Cairo: Maktabat al-sunnah al-muhammadiyyah, 1369/1950), 148. I have used, and in some cases considerably modified, the translations in T. A. Ibn Taymiyya, *Ibn Taimīya's Struggle against Popular Religion,* trans. Muhammad Umar Memon (The Hague: Mouton, 1976).

10. Ibn Taymiyyah, *Kitāb iqtidā',* 162–63.

11. Ibid., 205 (Arabic text) /203 (English text).

12. A. Kevin Reinhart, "Cosmopolitan Islam: The Standard Islam of the Scholars," in *Lived Islam: Colloquial Religion in a Cosmopolitan Tradition* (forthcoming).

13. There is a good case to be made that in fact Persian was another "canonical" Islamic language, as well as being a supremely important Islamicate one.

14. James Barr, *Fundamentalism* (Philadelphia: Westminster, 1978), 11.

15. K. Abou El Fadl, *And God Knows the Soldiers: The Authoritative and Authoritarian in Islamic Discourses* (Lanham, Md.: University Press of America, 2001).

16. Joseph E. Lowry, *Early Islamic Legal Theory: The Risala of Muhammad ibn Idris al-Shafiʿi* (Leiden & Boston: Brill, 2007), 104.

17. A. Kevin Reinhart, "The Qurʾan in Islamic Jurisprudence," in *The Blackwell Companion to the Qurʾan*, ed. Andrew Rippin (Oxford: Blackwell, 2006).

18. *Islamic Law and Society*, special issue on *ijtihad* and *taqlid*; A. Kevin Reinhart, "Transcendence and Social Practice: Muftīs and Qāḍīs as Religious Interpreters," *Annales Islamologiques* 27 (1994): 5–28.

19. This is surely the impulse behind Fatāwa ʿĀlimgīrī, Waranshirīsī, other Mālikī works of Nawāzil, the state specification of the madrassa curriculum in the Ottoman world, and other attempts at synthesis that took place at about the same time.

20. Reinhart, "The Qurʾan in Islamic Jurisprudence," 434–38.

21. Haym Soloveitchik, "Migration, Acculturation, and the New Role of Texts in the Haredi World," in *Accounting for Fundamentalisms: The Dynamic Character of Movements*, ed. Martin E. Marty and R. Scott Appleby (Chicago: University of Chicago Press, 1994), 197–235; Haym Soloveitchik, "Rupture and Reconstruction: The Transformation of Contemporary Orthodoxy," *Tradition* 28, no. 4 (1994): 64–130. I am grateful to my colleague Susannah Heschel, who called my attention to "Rupture and Reconstruction."

22. Soloveitchik, "New Role of Texts," 197.

23. Ibid., 201.

24. Ibid.

25. Ibid., 210.

26. Ibid., 205.

27. Ibid., 215.

28. Commins also uses the term *protestant*. See D. D. Commins, *Islamic Reform: Politics and Social Change in Late Ottoman Syria* (New York: Oxford University Press, 1990), 58. The study of missionary influence particularly on protomodernist apologetics—and then on the Salafis—is a potentially disturbing but essential study in the history of modern Islam. India, the Levant, and Anatolia all seem to be venues where critiques of Islam were heard, and it was there and in the metropolitan centers that protestant Islam was formulated in response. One can infer this process, which is otherwise unstudied, from Selim Deringil, *The Well-Protected Domains: Ideology and the Legitimation of Power in the Ottoman Empire, 1876–1909* (London: Tauris, 1998), and also from Troll's account of Ahmad Khan's ongoing dialogue with the missionary William Muir. C. W. Troll, *Sayyid Ahmad Khan: A Reinterpretation of Muslim Theology* (New Delhi: Vikas, 1978), 112–27. On the shift in authority entailed by this Islamic protestantism see A. Kevin Reinhart, "Legitimacy and Authority," in *Enemy Combatants, Terrorism, and Armed Conflict Law: A Guide to the Issues*, ed. David K. Linnan (Westport, Conn.: Praeger Security International, 2008), 172–78. See also the essay by Omid Safi in this volume.

29. Barr, *Fundamentalism*, 36–37.

30. M. H. Benkheira, *L'amour de la loi: Essai sur la normativité en Islam* (Paris: Presses universitaires de France, 1997), 5–8, 12. This is a very important book, of which I have

found not a single mention in English-language scholarly literature. It deserves our attention.

31. Sādiq Jalāl al-ʿAzm, *Naqd al-fikr al-dini*, 5th ed. (Beirut: Dar al-Talīʾah, 1982), 160.

32. Ibid., 7.

33. Indeed it has seemed normal to both Arabs and Orientalists, such as those who edited the *Encyclopedia of Islam*, to cover Salafism only in the Arab world and to attribute its rise in Syria, Tunisia, and Algeria to visits of the Egyptian Muhammad ʿAbduh (*Encyclopedia of Islam*, 2nd ed., s.v. "Salafiyya"). Similarly the second edition gives twenty-three pages on "islāh" to the Arab world but fewer than four pages to Iran, two pages to Turkey, and an astonishing one-and-one-eighth pages to India!

34. Weismann sees the turn to Ibn Taymiyyah from al-Jazaʾiri's attachment to Ibn ʿArabi as the moment when we can speak of Salafiyyah rather than mere *islāh* (reform). See Itzchak Weismann, "Between Sūfī Reformism and Modernist Rationalism—a Reappraisal of the Origins of the Salafiyya from the Damascene Angle." *Die Welt des Islams* 41, no. 2 (2001): 206–37, esp. 229.

35. Commins, *Islamic Reform*, 124–40. It is only Commins, to my knowledge, who gives this intermingling its due. He shows that Syrian religious reforms shared a conceptual world with Arab nationalists. Like the Arab nationalists, the Salafīs at first welcomed the reforms of the Ottoman Committee on Union and Progress following the 1908 revolution. They then turned against the committee when the cultural chauvinism of the CUP became clear. In describing events from 1910 onward, Commins uses the term *Salafī-Arabist* (meaning Arab nationalist) as referring to a single entity.

36. Commins, *Islamic Reform*, 57; Malcolm H. Kerr, *Islamic Reform: The Political and Legal Theories of ʿAbduh and Rashid Rida* (Berkeley: University of California Press, 1966), 173.

37. Kerr, *Islamic Reform*. 173.

38. The early Salafi al-Qasimi thought that Arabic was the most important tool for *ijtihad* but also believed that one should know "the principles of legal theory." Commins, *Islamic Reform*, 73.

39. The coinage is Reinhard Schulze's in Schulze, *Modern History of the Islamic World*, 95.

40. Amal Ghazal, "Sufism, Ijtihad and Modernity, Yūsuf al-Nabhānī in the Age of ʿAbd al-Hamīd II," *Archivum Ottomanicum* 19 (2001): 239–72; Commins, *Islamic Reform*.

41. Ghada Talhami, "An Interview with Sadik al-Azm," *Arab Studies Quarterly* 19, no. 3 (1997): 113–27.

42. al-ʿAzm, *Naqd al-fikr al-dini*, 24.

43. Demokratik hukuk devleti: Abant Platformu, Din-devlet ve toplum: Abant platformu 2; Abd al-Karim Soroush, *Reason, Freedom, and Democracy in Islam: Essential Writings of ʿAbdolkarim Soroush*, ed. and trans. Mahmoud Sadri and Ahmad Sadri (New York: Oxford University Press, 2000). I am grateful to Jenny White, who first drew my attention to the Abant conference proceedings.

44. We have to note, though, the brilliance of his social welfare provision and the effectiveness of the institutions that support it.

Can We Define
"True" Islam?

African American Muslim Women Respond to Transnational Muslim Identities

JAMILLAH KARIM

The mistake that a lot of African Americans make when they see foreigners [is that] they are feeling that these people know Islam. They don't. They have to study just like we do. They may be fluent in Arabic, but they are not knowledgeable about the *din* [religion]. Because if you go to some Muslim countries, they are being taught cultural Islam or hearsay Islam. They are not being taught the actual Sunnah [Prophetic example].

> Noni, an African American
> Muslim woman

I learned more Islam in this country than in India. I mean true Islam.

> Nasreen, a South Asian
> immigrant Muslim woman

"Islam is many things," writes Bruce Lawrence. "Just as there is no single America or Europe or the West . . . , so there is no single place or uniform culture called Islam."[1] Why, then, does Nasreen refer to a "true" Islam discovered in America? Noni also alludes to this "true" Islam found in America, contrasting it to a "hearsay" Islam brought to the United States via "foreigners" from Muslim countries. Their comments raise the question, How is the notion of a "true" Islam framed by a specifically American context? First, the idea of a "true" Islam would naturally develop as a prominent part of American Muslim discourses given that the fabric of American Muslim life took substantial form in the twentieth century, at the same time as the global rise and influence of Salafi Islam, marked by its focus on a return to the "pure" practice of the religion among the early Muslims. But also the newness of Islam in America led Muslims to imagine it as a space where Islam could emerge free of any cultural baggage. Salafi Islam shaped this notion, of course, as it renounced the cultural expressions of Islam that had formed in long-standing Muslim societies.

Immigrant Muslims, like Nasreen, who experience a religious reawakening assert that living Islam in America has moved them beyond cultural Islam, that is, Indian or Egyptian Islam, and brought them to "true" Islam. African American Muslims, on the other hand, tout that their roots in a society with no historical ties to Islam make their practice of Islam free of 1,400 years of cultural corruptions and closer to the precedent of the Prophet Muhammad. While these assertions are made, they do not represent the complexity of Muslim identity formations in the United States.

In *Islam and the Blackamerican*, for example, American Muslim scholar Sherman Jackson describes how the African American Muslim experience has been shaped by two major cultural traditions: "Black Religion" and "Immigrant Islam." By the 1960s Islam had attracted thousands of African Americans by claiming the legacy of Black Religion, a legacy of "protest, resistance, and liberation."[2] Through the Nation of Islam especially, Islam protested racism, addressed the suffering of African American people, and offered them an alternative experience and identity.[3] After the change in the Nation's leadership in 1975, however, the majority of African American Muslims identified not with the Nation of Islam but with Sunni Islam.[4] African American Sunni Muslims could no longer base their authority and legitimacy as Muslims on Black Religion exclusively. Now legitimacy had to be claimed on the basis of Sunni tradition. Given the multigeneration Muslim status of immigrants, in contrast to the convert status of African Americans, immigrants were "assumed to have superior knowledge" of the Sunni tradition. "The introduction of Immigrant Islam into the collective space of Blackamerican Muslims," Jackson argues, "resulted in the latter's loss of their interpretive voice."[5] In this narrative of African American Muslim identity, Jackson dispels any myths of "true" Islam as he shows African American Muslim practice shaped by both the religious expressions emanating from black American experience and the cultural Islam of immigrants.

Immigrant Islam, what Noni refers to as "hearsay" Islam, has certainly affected the ways in which African American Muslims define their religious perspective and practice.[6] However, instead of pointing to a loss of interpretive voice, my research demonstrates how African American Muslims have also fashioned identities and discourses that resist Immigrant Islam, and that do so by regularly speaking to an understanding and practice of "true" Islam as opposed to cultural Islam.

African American Muslim responses to Immigrant Islam vary, but also do the immigrant Muslim identities to which African Americans are responding. For this reason the concept "transnational Muslim identities" might be more helpful than "Immigrant Islam." While the latter term is useful when speaking broadly of the trend in which immigrants have transferred their cultural versions of Islam to the American context, it does not account for the nuance and complexity of immigrant Muslim identities, particularly how they constantly shift in the American context.

Immigrant Islam, Jackson argues, "merely *transfers* 'true' Islam from one location to the next."[7] But what is transferred is also *transformed* in the process of movement. As African, Asian, and Arab Muslims immigrate to the United States, they transport cultural practices and religious ideologies to their new American context. However, these cultural Muslim practices do not always remain the same during their transport. "Cultural forms change through the act of moving from one social context to another," writes Peter Mandaville. Transnational anthropology theorizes and traces this change.[8] Anthropologist Aihwa Ong states that the *trans* in *transnationalism* "denotes both moving through space or across lines, as well as changing the nature of something."[9] Transnational identity indicates not only the transport of Muslim cultural forms from one context to another, from Lahore, Pakistan, to Atlanta, Georgia, for example, but it also indicates response to new structures of social interaction, structures of power, and structures of economy within the new context.

South Asian and Arab immigrants to the United States reproduce Muslim culture, they modify cultural symbols, they invent meaning and value, and they imagine new possibilities. These new possibilities represent Islam "when it travels." When Islam travels, new questions are asked and new forms of knowledge and practice are produced.[10] For many immigrant Muslims, this travel of Muslim identity brings about the discovery of "true" Islam. In reality, however, this new knowledge is culturally circumscribed and "produced within particular structures of meaning about family, gender, nationality, class mobility, and social power."[11] This paper analyzes transnational Muslim identities produced "within structures of meaning" about gender especially. In other words I use gender as a category of analysis for mapping out transnational Muslim identities and contestations of "true" Islam. First I show how immigrant Muslim women, particularly South Asians, transport Muslim gender notions to the American context at the same time that they create new meaning into gender structures. They imagine new possibilities for themselves as Muslim women related to mosque attendance, dress, and work.

Second I show how African American Muslim women respond to this repositioning. They often respond with alternative interpretations and practices of Islam that reflect and accommodate their own cultural and historical experiences. "Within any set of ideas, then, there will be multiple and often competing discourses on the nature of the 'true' (or originary) idea. Part of traveling theory's task is to capture this sense of fragmentation. Muslims in translocal spaces often come into contact with other Muslims who interpret and practice Islam in disparate fashions. There often ensue debates about the nature of 'real' Islam."[12] African American women's responses to immigrant identities illustrate this fragmentation and debate. But also do South Asian immigrant women's responses to traditional South Asian gender norms. As immigrant Muslim women reassess and modify gender norms related to mosque attendance, dress, and work, and as African American Muslim women respond to this repositioning, both groups of women create important Islamic feminist discourses seeking gender justice and women's agency based on the Islamic sources of the Qur'an, the Hadith, and *fiqh* (Islamic jurisprudence). These feminist discourses also contest "the nature of 'real' Islam" as they project the interpretive voices of Muslim women, both immigrant and African American.[13] For both groups "real" Islam is understood as one that advances women's rights, whereas cultural Islam is widely accepted as one that harms women. In reality, however, we will see how cultural experiences in the United States frame women's interpretations of "true" Islamic gender justice. I based my analysis primarily on ethnographic research conducted on Muslim women in several U.S. cities, including Atlanta, Chicago, and Durham, North Carolina. I also collected data from online sources such as Sawnet (South Asian Women's NETwork), a restricted e-mail list for women interested in issues pertinent to South Asian women.[14]

Women's Mosque Attendance

"Women in Pakistan are not in the public sphere the way they are in North America," comments Seema, a Pakistani immigrant woman. "Coming to North America includes or even is a step into the public sphere for such women, I think. Going to *masjid* might be part of that step."[15] In South Asia most women pray in the privacy of their homes. Most had never attended the mosque until coming to the United States. "I love it [the *masjid*]," said Amira, a recent Bangladeshi immigrant. "It is my dream because I came from country where women can't go to mosque. Mosque is only for man. I'm so happy. Allah, thank you. I am so happy I go to mosque. Every *jum'ah*, I am here."[16] South Asian women's increased mosque attendance in the American context can be attributed to several factors, including their desire to create social networks with other South Asians and to instill Islamic values within their children. As one Indian American woman notes, "The social element of attending mosque becomes more important when you are living in the West. . . . It may be one of the few spheres where you mix with others from your own religion/ethnic community. So the network of those attending mosque helps replace the extended family or neighborhood network that was lost with the move."[17]

As immigrant Muslim women migrate to another social context, "religious symbols and languages may become invested with new meanings, but they still function to provide a framework of familiarity and a sense of identity."[18] South Asian women's mosque attendance reflects innovation and cultural repositioning in the American context. Yet how these women accommodate gender divides in American mosques indicates the transport of familiar South Asian gender norms, that is, gender segregation, into the new context. While classical Islamic jurisprudence requires that men and women pray in separate sections, the method of gender segregation varies by mosque. The Prophetic precedent is for women to pray in a section behind men but in a shared, partition-free prayer area. In most majority–South Asian mosques in the United States, however, men and women are separated by a curtain, wall, or partition. Sometimes men and women are located on different levels of the mosque. This means that even as the mosque takes on new meaning for women in America, the gender curtain retains for South Asian women the privacy of all-female prayer space.

But even with the gender curtain, women's mosque attendance often represents Islamic feminist resistance. Their attendance challenges the practice of prohibiting women from attending the mosque.[19] While this practice occurs more in South Asia than in the United States, we still see remnants of it in the U.S.: "There is a large Mosque in Sacramento, which permits worship by women, but since the Lodi Mosque is not large enough to have separate facilities for them, women are not permitted there."[20] While cases of absolute prohibition are rare in the United States, inadequate accommodations for women are not uncommon. More often than not, women have smaller, less desirable worship spaces in American mosques. This can be attributed partly to the fact that many immigrant communities are not accustomed to women's presence in public worship space.

South Asian Muslim women increasingly challenge this custom and draw from Islamic sources to claim their right to mosque space. In particular women refer to the Prophet's command, "Do not prevent the female servants of Allah from Allah's mosques."[21] Many women interpret this Hadith as granting women the right not only to attend the mosque but also to have good accommodations. In a growing number of cases, as in the famous mosque movement of Asra Nomani, South Asian women are insisting that mosque officials end "the segregation of women into separate and unequal quarters."[22] A few South Asian women even question the way in which women sit behind men in the mosque. While this Prophetic practice tends to be the most pragmatic arrangement, even in mosques with favorable accommodations for women, it can appear misogynistic to women attending the mosque for the first time. Atteqa, for example, wrote, "The first time I prayed communally in a mixed gathering was at an Iftar gathering in Oxford where I was not happy with the realization that women had to stand behind the men in a group and pray. I am quite sure this practice has no Qur'anic sanction."[23]

Atteqa's comment highlights another way in which women's mosque attendance can function as an Islamic feminist practice. By attending the mosque, women begin to access and study Islamic sources in a way that enables them to question, challenge, and perhaps accept Muslim gender norms with greater confidence and authority. Growing up in majority-Muslim contexts in which women treated Islam as a cultural norm rather than a self-determined religious choice, many South Asian Muslim women did not feel as compelled to study their religion actively as they now do in a non-Muslim-majority context. "I have enjoyed my religion. I have learned much more since I left my country because I understand real Islam," stated Tayyiba, a Muslim woman from India. "In my country, it was mostly what I was taught by other people, and there were so many misunderstandings about Islam. Things became so much clearer when I started attending the Islamic sessions here in America."[24]

Several immigrant women indicated a new practice of reading Qur'an to understand what they imagine as the "real" Islam. "[Before] I didn't listen to the Qur'an's meaning. I just listened to [the] Arabic [recitation]. . . . Now if a question comes, I dig in Qur'an. Before, in India, I pray five times, and that's enough," commented Nasreen.[25] When I asked Nasreen how living in America makes her "dig" in the Qur'an, she instantly responded, "Here I go to mosque. Over there I did not." As South Asian women begin to learn Islam in the formal setting of the mosque, they witness imams and scholars drawing from the Qur'an, Hadith, and *fiqh* manuals. This new access to the epistemological methods of Islamic practice enables women to engage gender norms and introduce new practices.

Women's Dress

Donning the *hijab* (head covering) is one new practice inspired by knowledge gained in the mosque. Women are usually expected to don the *hijab* when they enter a mosque, and once in the mosque, women are often taught to wear the *hijab* in all public spaces. The words of an imam (prayer leader) during a Friday sermon gives an example of this instruction: "Islam sets limits, and those limits remain no matter where we are. If you say that we live in America and women are wearing bikini, then we can wear bikini. No! Women are supposed to cover everything except face and hands."[26] Ironically many South Asian Muslims never knew these "limits" until they came to America. Women who had never covered their hair in India, Bangladesh, and Pakistan are now covering for the first time in the United States. As more South Asian women attend American mosques, they adopt the view that the *hijab* is required. The comments of Fareeha, a Pakistani woman, illustrate this modified position: "Even now, it is hard for me to do *hijab*," she said, "because [back home] I was raised with the importance of covering my body but not my head, and now I realize that is the best part—to do *hijab* for a woman."[27] Nasreen made a similar comment: "I learned more Islam in this country than in India. I mean true Islam. There I didn't know that women should cover hair and why they should cover hair." Her comments underscore how women often express their discovery of "true" Islam in gender terms, and in terms of women's dress codes in particular.[28]

In her research of mosque communities in Houston, Denise Al-Johar also observes that "as women attend prayers and Quranic studies at mosques, they learn of and identify with tenets of Islam that may have been overlooked, de-emphasized, or unknown to them 'back home.' They incorporate this knowledge into their identities."[29] Immigrant women incorporate new knowledge about the *hijab* into their South Asian identities. For example many wear what I refer to as the *dopatta hijab*, a distinctly South Asian *hijab* style. The *dopatta* is a long, rectangular, almost sheer scarf that South Asian women often wear across the shoulders or neck. When worn as a head covering, women loosely drape it around the hair and neck, but with a small amount of hair and ear occasionally exposed. Other South Asian immigrant women who adopt the *hijab* wear a more conservative style, what is referred to as the triangle *hijab*. In this style square fabric is folded into a triangle, draped, and pinned to cover hair, ears, and neck.[30] South Asian immigrant women who incorporate non–South Asian styles of *hijab* such as the triangle still tend to maintain South Asian culture in their dress by wearing the *shalwar kamiz*, the South Asian pants and tunic suit, usually vibrant in color.

Women's Work

South Asian Muslim women in America redefine cultural expectations about women and public space not only by attending the mosque but also by working on a scale that they were unaccustomed to in South Asia. Although women do work in South Asia, the layers of opportunity and the extent of compensation expand in the American context. South Asian Muslim women often draw on their notions of "real" Islam to support their choice to work outside the home. Fareeha, for example, stated that there was "nothing wrong with women working outside," though she qualified: "as long as she wears proper dress."[31] Amira, who works in the computer field, justified women's work by drawing on female models in the life of the Prophet Muhammad. "When Prophet Muhammad lived, women worked the fields and women went to work with men. Fatima even worked," she said, referring to the daughter of the Prophet Muhammad. Like Fareeha, Amira also adds a stipulation for women's work. She stressed the importance of proper interaction with men: "Working women should not mix freely with men."[32]

Fareeha's and Amira's stipulations indicate a consciousness about proper male-female interaction in public space, a consciousness that can be interpreted as Islamic feminist in that it justifies rather than limits their public work. This consciousness does, however, cause ambivalence for some South Asian women as they negotiate an American cultural context in which men and women interact freely. Fauzia, for example, does active community work in a Muslim outreach organization in Chicago. She takes issue, however, with the way in which men and women sit on the same programming committees, what Fauzia called "part of this whole American thing."[33] Fauzia prefers separate-gender committees, but the American-born converts have insisted on mixed-gender committees to ensure that women participate fully in the decision-making processes of the organization. But, Fauzia protests, "in Islam, the mixing of two genders is not so recommended. It's hard to have them together in a proper way that won't create *fitnah* [temptation]. That's my only concern. The Qur'an says to lower the gaze. When you are talking at a table face to face, how do you do that?" At the same time, she agrees that women who want to serve on the same committees as men should be accommodated, though she remains uncertain about how it can be done "within Islamic guidelines."

Through increased work opportunities, South Asian women redefine expectations of women not only in public space but also in domestic space. More presence outside the home translates as less time to do work inside the home. South Asian Muslim women not only reassess their commitment to domestic space but also challenge their men to modify their expectations of women. Tayyiba stated, "We have migrated to this country, and the men want to live in America like the Americans, but they want to treat their wives how women were treated over there, [where] the woman is expected to come home and do everything. [There, the women] had servants, or they had help to do things for them. Men have moved to this country thinking they are going to have maids and servants, but now they expect their wives to do everything, though she might be working, she might be having a full time job, and that is causing a lot of stress on the family. . . . I think these are ignorant men. . . . This is the basic problem because they don't know much about Islam, and if we were aware of the real Islam, then we wouldn't have this problem."[34] Here Tayyiba articulates a clear Islamic feminist position as she contests notions of Islam held by some South Asian immigrant men and states that "real" Islam requires that men take into account the needs and challenges that women face as they work.

African American Women's Resistance

The ways in which South Asian immigrant women transport but also reimagine their gender roles and behavior indicate the range of South Asian Muslim women's identities. As African American Muslim woman encounter their immigrant female counterparts at mosques, during *'Eid* (holiday) prayers, at grocery stores, or at work, they come into contact with various forms of South Asian American female Muslim identity. However given the limits of interethnic

encounters due to the ethnic separation in American Muslim communities and
also the boundaries between blacks and immigrants in the larger society, African
American Muslim women tend to see and emphasize cultural differences over
cultural similarities.[35] Many African American women often see South Asian
women as monolithic, going as far as to group them with Arab women. Referring to South Asian women as the foreigners, the immigrants, or the Pakistinis,
some African American Muslim women view South Asian Muslim women as
passive and submissive. Several social facts reinforce such attitudes, including
the fact that African American Muslim women work outside the home more than
do South Asian Muslim women, pursue divorce more, worship at the mosque
more, and are more likely to attend a mosque without a wall or curtain between
men and women.

Gender disparities in immigrant mosques especially inform how African
American Muslim women perceive South Asian and Arab women. "In 81 percent of immigrant mosques, women pray behind a curtain or in another room,
but in only 30 percent of African American mosques do women do this."[36]
Therefore African American women tend to perceive the gender curtain as an
immigrant influence. Some actively resist the gender curtain and critique other
African Americans who adopt immigrant gender norms. We see this type of
resistance through the narrative of Zakiyyah, an African American woman who
attends a majority–African American mosque, Masjid Bilal in Atlanta.[37] At Masjid
Bilal women share the prayer hall with the men. They do sit behind the men,
but no curtain separates them. On occasion Zakiyyah visits a majority–South
Asian mosque in Atlanta, Masjid Uthman, where the women pray separately on
the lower level. Due to this gender setup, Zakiyyah does not like to attend
Masjid Uthman. "It's not Islam," Zakiyyah said, "to put the sisters in the base-
ment. That's not Islam. When I first moved here in '94, I was too scared to go
on the other side where they are serving food where the brothers were. But now
after *jum'ah*, I walk right over there."[38] By crossing gender boundaries in immigrant mosques, African American Muslim women claim their Islamic right to
shared prayer space. As South Asian immigrant women contest South Asian cultural Muslim norms and redefine Islam, African American Muslim women contest transnational Muslim practices and also define what is and what is not Islam.

Zakiyyah not only contests gender lines at Masjid Uthman, but also she questions the way in which African American women who regularly attend Majsid
Uthman assimilate immigrant culture. "If their orientation is with Arab Muslims," she said, "they [meaning African American women] dress like Arabs. If
they come through the Pakistanis, they learn the Arabic with the Urdu accent,
and they dress Pakistani style." Zakiyyah described the demeanor of one African
American woman at Masjid Uthman. "She carries herself more as a Saudi in her
mannerisms: in the way she speaks, the way she lowers her voice and the way

her eyes are held down." Zakiyyah criticizes the way in which African American Muslim women who attend Masjid Uthman learn and adopt immigrant cultural norms, including passive traits from some of their female immigrant counterparts. Zakiyyah stated that such African American women "want to be like the Arab women. . . . It is sort of like the little black girl saying I'm not black, I'm really white, and I have a white doll because this is what I want to be."[39]

According to Zakiyyah, these women are "losing" their black identity because they think that in order to be Muslim they must look and act Arab or South Asian. Zakiyyah, however, believes that African American Muslim women can and should embrace Islam without compromising black culture and consciousness. She stated, "We are African American women who have made the conscious choice to become servants of Allah. We answer to Allah. However I think we also need to understand that we do have a history. We have a history of racism in this country—what it has done to us and our people as African American women and what it is still doing to us. What it is still doing to us all over the world. It is exploiting not only our people but other peoples as well." By speaking these powerful words, Zakiyyah, along with other African American convert women, claims Islam. Doing so, these women define Islam as another space in which to mobilize women to resist race and class injustices, and particularly to resist the ways in which these injustices affect them. Therefore, in the eyes of some African American Muslims, assimilation into immigrant Muslim communities translates as a means to silence their resistance to race, class, and gender injustices.

Noni, an African American Muslim woman in Chicago, similarly comments on the way in which African American Muslim women internalize and perpetuate race and gender discrimination when she sees women "running to Pakistanis and Arabs."[40] Noni remarked, "I have actually heard sisters tell me things like they would never marry an African American man. It's self-hatred. By you saying, 'I don't want to be around this or I don't like black men,' you are saying that you don't like yourself, or you are saying that Allah made a mistake. Well, Allah doesn't make mistakes. You have to love yourself. I'm not saying be arrogant. I mean accepting who you are: your hair, your color, your legs, whatever you are. You are a black woman. There is something beautiful in that, just like an Arab woman is beautiful in her right, a Pakistani woman in her right. And then you are Muslim. *Alhamdulillah* [praise God], that is something more beautiful. You cannot let other people tell you what you are and what you are not, or what you can be and what you cannot."

Noni's description of African American Muslim women who internalize racism echoes Barbara Smith's black feminist analysis of African American women's self-hatred. "How was I to know that racism and sexism had formed a blueprint for my mistreatment long before I had ever arrived here? As with most black women, other's hatred of me became self-hatred, which has diminished over the years, but has by no means disappeared." Black feminist analysis, however, has "given us the tools to finally comprehend that it is not something that we have done that has heaped this psychic violence and material abuse upon us, but the very fact that, because of who we are, we are multiply oppressed." This multiple oppression emerges at the intersection of race, gender, class, and other forms of discrimination. "We are not hated and abused because there is something wrong with us, but because our status and treatment is absolutely prescribed by the racist, misogynist system under which we live."[41]

Noni's resistance represents the way in which African American Muslim women modify and expand black feminist consciousness to create black *Muslim* feminist consciousness. Black, female, *and Muslim*, African American Muslim women resist racism not only in mainstream America but also in the American *ummah* (Muslim community). "It's like this," Noni explains. "You're already being beaten down, torn down, discriminated by the white majority. Now here comes this beautiful way of life. This beautiful thing that Allah, *subhanahu wa taʿala* [glorified and exalted], gave you: Islam. You see this as being the only solution to your problems. Yet you have a group of people that follow the same belief system, or they profess that they follow the same system, and yet they are discriminating against you. You already have a problem with trying to belong, and now they are telling you, 'We don't like you either.'"[42] As a result African American women's conversion to Islam often translates as movement from one form of discrimination to another. Surrendering to immigrant authority in a shared American *ummah*, some African American women internalize South Asian and Arab supremacy in the way that they formerly internalized white supremacy. It used to be "the white person," Noni explained, but "now you put the Arab over you. You put the Pakistani over you. But they are not over you. They are equal to you in Islam."

Noni's resistance represents black *Muslim* feminist consciousness also in how she uses her understanding of Islam to construct a positive image of African American women. Especially she draws from her belief in Allah as the perfect God who created all human forms beautiful, including African American women. She draws from her vision of Islam as a gift from God that enhances women's beauty. And she draws from her understanding that God will help African American Muslim women as they resist self-hatred. "Allah says that He will change the condition of a people when they change it within themselves. You have to look inside yourself. Some people don't have this problem, but if you don't like being who you are, then you have to cry. You have to ask Allah, *subhanahu wa taʿala*, to help me, and through the Sunnah of the Prophet Muhammad, *sallallahu ʿalayhi wa sallam* [may God bless him and grant him peace], deal with this. I mean, Allah created you in the way that He created you for a purpose."

Noni's words represent the emergence of black Muslim feminism, a form of Islamic feminism in which African American Muslim women define and appropriate Islam to address black women's specific experiences of race and gender discrimination.

Contesting Dress

Given her resistance to African American women who assimilate into majority-immigrant mosques, Zakiyyah respects African American women who attend majority–African American mosques. She especially admires how they define African American Muslim identity through their dress. "They have such creative and diverse ways of covering. You know as long as you are covered, you can create your own style or manner of covering." Zakiyyah's comments present another important way in which African American women define Islam counter to transnational Muslim identities. She and many other African American women believe that Islam allows for different cultural expressions of *hijab* and that the Qur'an, while commanding general modesty, does not specify style of dress. African American Muslim women cover their hair in various styles. These styles reflect African, Arab, South Asian, and American cultural influences, sometimes a combination of them all. The head wrap style, which tops the head and leaves a woman's ears and upper neck exposed, reflects African American Muslim women's African heritage. Another popular style among African American women is a head covering that falls down over the back and shoulders, also leaving ears and neck revealed. This style resembles the wimples of Catholic nuns and therefore reflects women's American cultural context.

Many African American women who wear distinctly African American *hijab* styles, especially the head wrap, feel that immigrants look down upon their dress. Take Maryam, a woman in her midthirties, as an example. "Our dress is not Islamic enough for them," she stated, referring to Arab and South Asian women. It upsets her that Arab and South Asian dress is considered more authentic Islamic dress. But the issue of authentic Islamic dress is not simply an issue of culture. It is also an issue of modesty. Arab and South Asian women who cover tend to wear a *hijab* that drapes down and covers the ears and upper neck. Many immigrants believe that Islamic law requires that they cover the ears and neck. When African American women wear a wrap, they do not meet these criteria. Maryam knows that the question of acceptable dress has to do with not only cultural style but also criteria of modesty. But to her even standards of modesty must develop from within her African American community. "We must define" modesty "within our own selves" based on "what is appropriate and what's inappropriate according to what Allah tells us," rather than "someone forcing us," she said.[43] In this way Maryam not only challenges the way in which men might force women to cover, but also the way in which one ethnic

Muslim group imposes dress standards on another. In this way she sets an Islamic feminist agenda that advocates not only for women's choice to cover but also for women's autonomy to cover in a way that represents their ethnic expression and their personal and spiritual comfort.

Young college-aged African American Muslim women also challenge the ways in which immigrant dress standards are imposed on them. Many of these women feel that their second-generation South Asian and Arab American peers question African American Muslim dress because it does not conform to their cultural ideas of Islam. Even though they grow up in the United States and wear American dress such as jeans and T-shirts, some second-generation Muslim women judge African American Muslim women based on *hijab* norms set within Arab and South Asian American Muslim culture. Tiyya, an African American Muslim college student who wears the head wrap, stated, "Dress is a huge issue that African Americans are dealing with in the Arab and Asian communities. We feel like they judge us on how we appear. They tell us, 'This is not the proper way. You should wear the traditional *hijab*.' But their dress is not the standard. There is no dress code per se in Islam."[44] In other cases second-generation Arab and Asian American women who wear strictly Arab or Asian dress challenge African American women who dress American, even if they are modest. Naimah described how an Arab American Muslim peer who wears the *jilbab* (traditional Arab overgarment) once told her that "it doesn't matter if you wear *hijab* because you don't wear a *jilbab*." Naimah protested that there are other ways outside the *jilbab* to cover modestly. "I don't wear tight jeans. I wear long shirts. What are you saying? That's not going to count with God?"[45]

However, a few second-generation American women have adopted African American Muslim dress practices, especially post-9/11. After 9/11 the *hijab* made Muslim women easy targets of anti-Muslim as well as anti–South Asian and anti-Arab backlash. Fearing harassment or assaults, some women modified their hair covering in ways that made it harder to identify them as Muslim, South Asian, or Arab. Sadiyah, a young African American Muslim woman, witnessed this practice among some of her South Asian and Arab American peers. "After September 11, some of the girls started wearing theirs tied behind, the African American way."[46] Previously they had been wearing their *hijab* down over the ears and neck, but they "switched because a lot of women were getting attacked, and so they started wearing it up. Now some of them feel comfortable with it that way. It's their style." Unlike the triangle and *dopatta hijab* styles that the women had worn previously, the head-wrap *hijab* does not necessarily indicate Muslim identity. Rather it is a popular fashion among both non-Muslim and Muslim African American women. The multiple meanings behind the head-wrap *hijab* made it an obvious choice for women who wanted to maintain the *hijab* without looking like a Muslim immigrant. The way in which 9/11 pressures eventually led some second-generation American women to adopt the head-wrap *hijab* indefinitely demonstrates transnational Muslim identities in the second generation as women negotiate two cultures, the culture of their parents and the culture of birth.

Women's Work: A Shared Dilemma

Above I have focused on the ways in which African American Muslim women resist pressures to conform to immigrant expressions of Islam. However, there are many examples in which African American Muslim women respond favorably to transnational Muslim identities. For example they share similar experiences with South Asian women as they constantly reposition themselves between domestic work and public work. I conclude with an example of how Zakiyyah responded to transnational female Muslim identity in a way that affirms her philosophy that Islam elevates and ennobles women.

During one of her visits to Masjid Uthman, Zakiyyah started a conversation with a Bangladeshi woman, Samiya. "I love that outfit," Zakiyyah said to Samiya, referring to her *shalwar kamiz*. As the two women of different ethnic backgrounds continued to talk, Samiya emphasized the importance of staying at home to raise her daughters. Samiya said, "I used to work, but I want to be with my daughters more. I feel like it's a full-time job." Zakiyyah replied, "You're blessed, though, because so many women have to work." "I know, I know," Samiya responded. "And still it is hard because I know it will be better for my family if I worked, but my husband says Allah will provide."[47]

After their conversation Zakiyyah later expressed to me the emotions she felt when talking to Samiya. "I was happy for Samiya," she said, "but at the same time the other side of me reflected back on when I was going through a painful process of not having that when my husband left and I had to do it all alone." Zakiyyah wished that she could have had the choice to do what Samiya is doing: in Zakiyyah's terms, "making the choice of not doing anything else but being a good mother." Zakiyyah believes that ideally women have the right to stay at home rather than work. She believes that Islam gives women this right; however, she blames men for not taking care of the responsibilities that make it possible for women to exercise it. "If a male is not fearing Allah," she said, "and doing his part to stick with that family and nurture that family and help that family, then he puts the woman in a situation where she has to be the role *man* model, where she has to be assertive and aggressive to survive, and take care of the children. And it's hard. It's very difficult."[48]

Zakiyyah's desire to restore traditional gender roles that present men as providers and women as mothers and caretakers of the home resonates with aspects of black feminist thought. Many African American women blame slavery and racism for undermining functional gender roles in African American families and communities. As Zakiyyah indicated African American women have carried the double burden of fulfilling both male and female roles, and therefore they want "freedom from having to 'do it all.'"[49] As a result many African American women reclaim traditional gender roles as a way to restore their communities. Rather than always stepping out into the public sphere to work, some women imagine greater rights for women when they can choose to stay home with their children. Zakiyyah and other African American women value this choice based on their distinct struggles as African American women. When they see immigrant Muslim women such as Samiya also making this choice, it affirms their philosophy that Islam restores rights to women.

Conclusion

Neither immigrant nor African American Muslim identities are static or monolithic. Transnational in nature, immigrant Muslim identities take on multiple, evolving forms. African American Muslims respond to these forms in different ways, sometimes conforming to transnational Muslim practices but at other times resisting them. Muslim women's perspectives on Muslim gender norms provide a window into transnational Muslim formations and African American Muslim responses. As both immigrant and African American Muslim women redefine Islam and Muslim gender norms based on their new religious knowledge and ethnic American experiences, they often generate Islamic feminist consciousness and practice. While this paper focuses primarily on African American women's responses to immigrant women, both Muslim female experiences increasingly interact and impact each other.

NOTES

1. Bruce B. Lawrence, *Shattering the Myth: Islam beyond Violence* (Princeton, N.J.: Princeton University Press, 1998), 4.

2. Sherman A. Jackson, *Islam and the Blackamerican: Looking toward the Third Resurrection* (New York: Oxford University Press, 2005), 32.

3. For information on early Sunni African American groups that existed alongside the Nation of Islam, see Robert Dannin, *Black Pilgrimage to Islam* (Oxford and New York: Oxford University Press, 2002).

4. On the Nation of Islam's change to global Sunni Islam, see Zafar Ishaq Ansari, "W. D. Muhammad: The Making of a 'Black Muslim' Leader (1933–1961)," *American Journal of Islamic Social Sciences* 2, no. 2 (1985): 245–62; Mattias Gardell, *In the Name of Elijah Muhammad: Louis Farrakhan and the Nation of Islam* (Durham, N.C.: Duke University Press, 1996), 99–118; Lawrence H. Mamiya, "From Black Muslim to Bilalian: The Evolution of a Movement," *Journal for the Scientific Study of Religion* 21 (June 1982): 138–52; Clifton E. Marsh, *From Black Muslims to Muslims: The Transition from Separatism to Islam, 1930–1980* (Metuchen, N.J.: Scarecrow, 1984), 89–124; and Jane I. Smith, *Islam in America* (New York: Columbia University Press, 1999), 89–93.

5. Jackson, *Islam and the Blackamerican*, 69, 70.

6. I come to similar conclusions in the article "Between Immigrant Islam and Black Liberation: Young Muslims Inherit Global Muslim and African American Legacies," *Muslim World* 95 (October 2005): 497–513.

7. Jackson, *Islam and the Blackamerican*, 12.

8. Peter Mandaville, *Transnational Muslim Politics: Reimagining the Umma* (London and New York: Routledge, 2001), 39, 30.

9. Aihwa Ong, *Flexible Citizenship: The Cultural Logics of Transnationality* (Durham, N.C.: Duke University Press, 1999), 4.

10. Mandaville, *Transnational Muslim Politics*, 109.

11. Ong, *Flexible Citizenship*, 6.

12. Mandaville, *Transnational Muslim Politics*, 87.

13. Ibid.

14. I use pseudonyms for all of the women mentioned.

15. Sawnet, April 18, 2000.

16. Interview with author, April 10, 2000, Durham, N.C.

17. Sawnet, April 18, 2000.

18. Mandaville, *Transnational Muslim Politics*, 112.

19. South Asian women on Sawnet and other online forums described how women are prohibited from attending the mosque: "Southasian women in southasia don't attend mosques because, for the most part they are not allowed to. In the past some years there have been groups of intrepid women in Lucknow and Kerala who have tried to enter mosques and to ask for arrangements to be made to allow for a praying space for women in the mosques. They have had mixed success and progress is slow and patchy," Sana, Sawnet, April 18, 2000. Zeenat Shaukat Ali, a professor of Islamic studies, also writes about this prohibition and indicates some exceptions: "Bohra women in India have been offering prayers at mosques for several years." Zeenat Shaukat Ali, "God Knows No Gender," *Indian Express*, February 10, 2005, http://www.indianexpress.com/full_story.php?content_id=64370 (accessed July 8, 2009).

20. Julia Priest, "Lodi's Pakistani Women Struggle with Clash of Cultures," *Lodi (Calif.) News-Sentinel*, http://www.lodinews.com/pakistan/html/women.shtml (accessed March 3, 2008). Also see Umm Zaid Saraji, "Why Every Mosque Should Be Woman-Friendly," in *Taking Back Islam: American Muslims Reclaim Their Faith*, ed. Michael Wolfe (Emmaus, Penn.: Rodale, 2002), 108–10.

21. *Characteristics of Prayer* (*Sahih Bukhari*), no. 832, Center for Muslim-Jewish Engagement, University of Southern California, http://www.usc.edu/dept/MSA/fundamentals/hadithsunnah/bukhari/012.sbt.html (accessed March 3, 2008).

22. Asra Q. Nomani, "Being the Leader I Want to See in the World," in *Living Islam Out Loud: American Muslim Women Speak*, ed. Saleemah Abdul-Ghafur (Boston: Beacon, 2005), 142.

23. Sawnet, April 18, 2000.

24. Interview with author, April 26, 2000, Raleigh, N.C.

25. Interview with author, April 8, 2000, Raleigh, N.C.

26. Author's notes, March 31, 2000, Durham, N.C.

27. Interview with author, March 28, 2000, Durham, NC.

28. Jasmin Zine critiques the way that Islamic spirituality is reduced to the issue of the *hijab*. Jasmin Zine, "Unveiled Sentiments: Gendered Islamophobia and Experiences of

Veiling among Muslim Girls in a Canadian Islamic School," *Equity and Excellence in Education* 39, no. 3 (2006): 249.

29. Denise Al-Johar, "Muslim Marriages in America: Reflecting New Identities," *Muslim World* 95 (October 2005): 567.

30. This popular U.S. style is most likely a transport from Muslim cultures abroad. The triangle *hijab* is popular in many places, including North Africa, Greater Syria, and Malaysia.

31. Interview with author, March 28, 2000, Durham, N.C.

32. Interview with author, April 10, 2000, Chicago.

33. Interview with author, June 20, 2002, Chicago.

34. Interview with author, April 26, 2000, Chicago.

35. A 2000 American mosque study indicates this ethnic separation. The study found that "sixty-four percent of mosques have one dominant ethnic group. In most cases, this one group is either African American or South Asian." As for the remaining 36 percent of mosques, most have a combination of two ethnic groups, most often South Asian and Arab. See Ihsan Bagby, Paul M. Perl, and Bryan T. Froehle, *The Mosque in America: A National Portrait, a Report from the Mosque Study Project* (Washington, D.C.: Council on American-Islamic Relations, 2001), 19.

36. Karen Isaksen Leonard, *Muslims in the United States: The State of Research* (New York: Russell Sage Foundation, 2003), 78. See Ihsan Bagby, "A Profile of African-American Masjids: A Report from the National Masjid Study 2000," *Journal of the Interdenominational Theological Center* 29, nos. 1–2 (2001–2): 205–41.

37. Mosque names are pseudonyms.

38. Interview with author, December 8, 2001, Atlanta.

39. Remarks by this research participant have been used in a previous publication by the author. Jamillah Karim, *American Muslim Women: Negotiating Race, Class, and Gender within the Ummah* (New York: New York University Press, 2008), 196–98.

40. Interview with author, July 9, 2002, Chicago.

41. Barbara Smith, "Some Home Truths on the Contemporary Black Feminist Movement," in *Words of Fire: An Anthology of African-American Feminist Thought*, ed. Beverly Guy-Sheftall (New York: New Press, 1995), 262.

42. This remark by a research participant has been used in a previous publication by the author. Karim, *American Muslim Women*, 36.

43. Parts of this passage have been used in a previous publication by the author. Karim, *American Muslim Women*, 192.

44. Interview with author, August 22, 2002, Chicago.

45. Interview with author, August 22, 2002, Chicago.

46. Interview with author, June 4, 2002, Chicago.

47. Author's notes, November 3, 2001.

48. Parts of this passage have been used in a previous publication by the author. Karim, *American Muslim Women*, 197.

49. Carolyn Moxley Rouse, *Engaged Surrender: African American Women and Islam* (Berkeley: University of California Press, 2004), 51.

Rethinking Religion

Social Scientific and Humanistic Perspectives

Who Are the Islamists?

CHARLES KURZMAN
AND IJLAL NAQVI

Bruce Lawrence famously noted that fundamentalism grows out of the encounter with modernity. It is not the atavistic movement that unsympathetic observers often take it to be, but rather a product of modern processes such as colonialism and postcolonial state formation, industrialization and economic inequality, and contemporary shifts in popular identity. The social bases of fundamentalist movements in Muslim societies, he argues, are consistent with this modern context: "The groups that have mobilized as fundamentalists are not the most wretched but those who have had some contact with the West, who understand the horizons of possibility denied them by the inequities of the world system."[1]

Lawrence bases this observation in part on sociologist Saad Eddin Ibrahim's widely cited 1980 article in the *International Journal of Middle East Studies*, which examined the social background of several dozen imprisoned Egyptian Islamists.[2] Ibrahim's study has served as a sort of license for endless generalizations about the social bases of Islamist activism worldwide, many of them far less well-informed than Lawrence's observations, which grow out of his long and far-flung experiences with Muslim communities around the planet. But for all the interest that scholars have shown in Islamist movements, there is relatively little empirical analysis of its social origins. Several important ethnographic field studies have noted that Salafi leaders in Jordan are from poorer neighborhoods,[3] and that Egyptian Islamists are primarily from lower-middle-class communities.[4] Systematic data on this subject is less well known and has never been subjected to a meta-analysis of the sort that we present in this paper, which reviews biographical encyclopedia entries, quantitative case studies, and survey data to review the state of our knowledge about the social bases of Islamist leaders, activists, and supporters.

For present purposes we use a simple definition of *Islamist* that is parallel to Lawrence's more general approach to the concept of *fundamentalist:* a person or movement expressing "the collective demand that specific creedal and ethical dictates derived from scripture be publicly recognized and legally enforced."[5] In the case of Muslims, these demands seek to implement particular provisions of the Shariʿa as the basis for the nation-state. Notice that this definition makes no distinction between those who seek to do so through violent means and those who repudiate violence, despite the competition and hostility between Islamist movements with varying strategies. It makes no distinction between different sects and schools within Islam. However, this definition of Islamist does distinguish between those who seek to establish the Shariʿa through the state and those who seek to establish it outside of the state—through a renovation of personal piety, for example. It distinguishes between those who favor a scripturalist interpretation of Shariʿa and those who defend the incorporation of local customs into Islamic practice. It distinguishes between those who believe that the Shariʿa contains within it all the basic principles needed for governance and those who believe that the Shariʿa is silent on important topics of governance and leaves these to human ingenuity.[6]

With this definition in mind, let us turn to three categories of Islamists: leaders, activists, and supporters. We find that Islamist leaders are split into two categories, one group trained in secular schools and one in religious seminaries, many of them from provincial backgrounds. Activists, on the other hand, largely received secular schooling, with increasingly diverse levels of education and varied social backgrounds. Supporters, in elections and surveys, tend to be less educated, poorer, and more rural in some—but not all—countries. The best correlate for Islamist attitudes is country of residence rather than socioeconomic characteristics within any given country.

Islamist Leaders

There appear to be two typical careers of Islamist leaders. One is epitomized by Hasan al-Banna (1906–1949), founder of the Muslim Brotherhood in Egypt. Banna came from a clerical family—his father taught at the local mosque—but received his advanced education at a secular school, the Teacher's College in Cairo. In college he was exposed to Western scientific training and also to European accounts of the rise and fall of Western civilization. As a result of this contact with Western education, he become more overtly activist, helping to found a Young Men's Muslim Association in 1927 and the following year, after his graduation, creating the organization that would become the Muslim Brotherhood. After several years of cultural activism in defense of Islam, he turned in the early 1930s to political activism, seeking to implement the Shariʿa through state intervention in addition to changes in personal mores.

The second career is epitomized by Imam Ruhollah Khomeini (1902–1989) of Iran. He was born into a devout family in a provincial town, where social practices were regulated in large part by religious principles. He was trained first in traditional religious schools, not in state-run elementary schools, and then in a recently rejuvenated institution of advanced religious training, the seminaries of Qom. Khomeini turned to antimonarchic activism at Qom against the wishes of the leaders of the institution, who placed him under virtual house arrest for several years in the late 1950s. Even during the Iranian Revolution of 1979, in which Khomeini was the undisputed leader, many of his fellow Shi'a Muslim theologians were less than eager to participate in antimonarchic activism, a position for which Khomeini frequently chided them.

These two career paths overlap in the provincial roots of the Islamist leaders, their advanced educations, and their defense of Islam against encroachments by Western culture. However, Banna, following the first career path, turned to Islamism as a response to contact with Western culture, primarily through secular higher education. Khomeini, on the second career path, turned to Islamism as a response to traditional Islamic scholarship, which he saw as ill suited to modern challenges.

Of the forty-two contemporary Islamist leaders profiled in the *Encyclopedia of Islam and the Muslim World* and the *Oxford Encyclopedia of the Islamic World*—we define contemporary as 1970 and later—about half conform to each type (see table 1).[7] It is striking that almost all of these leaders have advanced educations, a relatively rare accomplishment in Muslim-majority societies, as everywhere. Only two have little or no advanced education: Zaynab al-Ghazali of Egypt and Juma Namangani of Uzbekistan. Al-Ghazali attended public high school and received certificates in several Islamic subjects, while Namangani appears to have moved quickly from Soviet military service to Islamist revolutionary movements in Tajikistan and Afghanistan. As opposed to the internationally renowned figures in our sample, however, Islamist leaders at the local level may be more likely to lack advanced educations.[8] Approximately twenty-one of forty-two Islamist leaders in our sample attended secular universities with degrees in engineering, management, law, philosophy, and other fields. For these scholars, as for Banna, Islamist activism represents a response to the westernized approach to knowledge that is dominant at secular universities. 'Abbasi Madani of Algeria, for example, who earned a doctorate in England, wrote a book titled *The Crisis of Modern Thought and the Justifications of the Islamic Solution* (1987), in which he identified Islamist activism explicitly as a response to Western ideologies: "By their action, they have put us in a situation of reaction."[9] Similarly Abdessalam Yassine, who was trained in French colonial schools in Morocco (as well as having an Islamic education), began his book *Islamicizing Modernity* (1998) with a discussion of the work of French sociologist Alain Touraine, in which he attempts to sift through the positive and negative aspects of Western notions of modernity.[10]

This finding corresponds closely with case studies of Islamist leaders in several settings. Secularly educated professionals constituted two-thirds of leaders

TABLE 1. Advanced Education of Selected Islamist Leaders

Secular Education	Seminary Education	Both/Neither
Ahmadinejad, Mahmoud, Iran, 1956, engineering	ʿAbdel Rahman, Omar, Egypt, 1938	ʿAzzam, ʿAbdullah, Palestine, 1941
Bin Laden, Osama, Saudi Arabia, 1957, management	Belhadj, ʿAli, Algeria, 1957	Erdoğan, Recep, Turkey, 1954
Erbakan, Necmettin, Turkey, 1926, engineering	Bin Baz, ʿAbd al-ʿAziz, Saudi Arabia, 1909	Ghazali, Zaynab al-, Egypt, 1917
Faraj, ʿAbd al-Salam, Egypt, 1954, engineering	Buti, Saʿid Ramadan al-, Syria, 1929	Gumi, Abu Bakr, Nigeria, 1922
Ghannushi, Rashid al-, Tunisia, 1941, philosophy	Fadlallah, Muhammad, Iraq & Lebanon, 1935	Kadivar, Muhsin, Iran, 1959
Gül, Abdullah, Turkey, 1950, economics	Hakim, Muhammad Baqir al-, Iraq, 1939	Namangani, Juma, Uzbekistan, 1969
Hekmatyar, Gulbuddin, Afghanistan, 1947, engineering	Hashemi-Rafsanjani, ʿAli-Akbar, Iran, 1934	Yasin, Abdessalam, Morocco, 1928
Izetbegović, Alija, Yugoslavia-Bosnia, 1925, law	Khamenei, ʿAli, Iran, 1939	
Kısakürek, Necip Fazıl, Turkey, 1904, philosophy	Khomeini, Ruhollah, Iran, 1902	
Madani, ʿAbbasi, Algeria, 1931, philosophy/psychology	Kishk, ʿAbd al-Hamid, Egypt, 1933	
Maryam Jameelah, U.S. & Pakistan, 1934, religious studies	Marwa, Muhammad, Cameroon & Nigeria, 1920s	
Masri, Abu Hamza al-, Egypt & U.K., 1958, engineering	Mawdudi, Abu al-Aʿla, India & Pakistan, 1903	
Mustafa, Shukri, Egypt, 1942, agronomy	Mutahhari, Murtaza, Iran, 1920	
Turabi, Hasan al-, Sudan, 1932, law	Nasrallah, Hasan, Lebanon, 1960	
Zarqawi, Abu Musʿab al-, Jordan, 1966, biotechnology	Omar, Muhammad, Afghanistan, 1959	

TABLE 1. (*continued*)

Secular Education	Seminary Education	Both/Neither
Zawahiri, Ayman al-, Egypt, 1951, medicine	Qaradawi, Yusuf al-, Egypt & Qatar, 1926	
	Sadr, Muhammad Baqir al-, Iraq, 1935	
	Sadr, Muqtada al-, Iraq, 1970s	
	Yasin, Ahmad, Palestine, 1937	

of the Jamaat-i Islami of Bangladesh in the early 1980s and half of the founders of the Islamic Action Front in Jordan in the 1990s.[11] Over the decades the leaders of the Jamaat-i Islami of India and later Pakistan increasingly were professionals,[12] as was the membership of the Guidance Council of the Muslim Brotherhood in Egypt in the 1950s.[13]

About twenty-four of the forty-two Islamist leaders in our sample attended religious universities such as al-Azhar in Cairo and the more informally structured seminaries of Najaf, Iraq; Qom, Iran; and Delhi, India. For these scholars Islamist activism frequently represents a response to the scholasticism of traditional religious learning. Abu al-Aʿla Mawdudi, for example, never publicized his religious education and "criticized the institution of the ulama openly and at times sharply," since "he did not believe in the effectiveness of traditional Islam . . . in addressing the predicaments that had brought him to the study of religion in the first place"—the challenges facing Muslims in the modern world.[14] Shaykh ʿAbd al-Hamid Kishk was blunt about his alma mater, al-Azhar, the ancient Islamic university in Cairo, which he felt was too passive in confronting the problems of the day: "al-Azhar slumbers the deepest sleep, in unparalleled dishonour!"[15]

Several Islamist leaders combined both secular and religious training, such as ʿAbdullah ʿAzzam (who studied agronomy before attending the University of Damascus's seminary college), Recep Erdoğan (Imam Hatip religious high school and Marmara University's Department of Economics and Management), Abu Bakr Gumi (British colonial schools and Islamic seminaries), Muhsin Kadivar (one year at the University of Shiraz's Department of Electronic Engineering, then the seminaries of Shiraz and Qom), and Abdessalam Yassine (French colonial schools and Islamic seminaries).

Like Banna and Khomeini (who is included on this list because his activities continued past 1970), these figures are largely provincials who migrated to the capital—of the thirty-nine leaders for whom place of birth can be identified, only eight were born in the capital of their home country, evenly split between the secularly and religiously educated; all but six of the forty-two later came to the capital at some point in their career. Of the twenty-eight figures whose family background is available, twelve are the children of religious scholars (eight of these following in the same profession themselves). Seven come from middle-class backgrounds with secular educations (six of them pursuing secular educations themselves), five from poor rural families (evenly split between secular and religious educational tracks), and three from poor urban families (two of them seminary trained). Only one was born rich: Osama bin Laden, whose father was a major industrialist.[16] In sum this sampling of Islamist leaders shows a relatively even split between two career paths, seminary scholars and secular college graduates, both of them originating primarily in well-educated families in the provinces.

Islamist Activists

Turning from leaders to activists more generally, we find relatively little systematic evidence available. Indeed the classic work in this tradition, Saad Eddin Ibrahim's "Anatomy of Egypt's Militant Islamic Groups," was intended only as a preliminary study. Its sample size is only thirty-four, and its method of sampling—interviewing suspected militants under arrest—allows the government to select respondents and biases the sample in the direction of whatever political concerns the government may be suffering. For example the high proportion of university students and graduates in this sample (85 percent) may be exaggerated by governments' heightened sensitivity to university-based unrest. It may also reflect government agents' ability to infiltrate university settings more easily than other settings. In any case the study offers a striking image of Islamist activists: among the students a majority have earned spots in elite majors, and almost all are in scientific and technical fields. All of the activists lived in large cities, but 62 percent had migrated from smaller cities or rural areas. However, this does not mean that the activists come from uneducated or peasant backgrounds; a majority of the activists' fathers had a secondary or higher education, and most worked in civil service or professional occupations. Upward mobility is evident among the activists, if not dramatic peasant-to-university mobility.[17]

A second study by Ibrahim, published fifteen years later, suggests that the social basis for Islamist activism in Egypt had shifted from universities to shanty-towns. He mentions a group of thirty Islamists "arrested, tried, and convicted for attacks on tourists," seven of whom received death sentences in December 1993, but the reported statistics appear to come from a larger sample of arrestees whose size is not reported. The usual caveats regarding arrest sampling apply. Ibrahim argues that the composition of Islamist activism has changed considerably, with arrestees now younger and less educated (only 20 percent were college students or graduates). He notes that 54 percent of militants arrested and charged for acts of violence in the 1990s reside in shantytowns and rural areas as compared to 8 percent in the 1970s, and speculates that the alienation and discontent that fueled university Islamists in the 1970s has spread throughout Egyptian society. He does not state whether educated Egyptians are now less likely to be Islamist activists or whether they are participating at the same rate as before but are now outnumbered by less-educated Islamists.[18]

To what extent are Ibrahim's foundational studies confirmed by other research on the social bases of Islamist activism? We have located twenty-five studies that offer quantitative data on the social background of Islamist activists (see table 2 and figure 1). These studies do not use the same definition of *Islamist* that we propose in this paper, namely, state implementation of Shariʿa. Some focus on "terrorists"—several on suicide terrorists specifically—one on guerrilla fighters, and three on more peaceful forms of activism: Hermassi on the Islamic Tendency Movement in Tunisia, Dekmejian on open-letter signatories in Saudi Arabia, and Schbley on marchers in a Hizbullah demonstration (whom Schbley calls "terrorists"). The Amraʾi study, which examines fatalities in Tehran during the Iranian Revolution, included activists whose goals were more liberal or leftist than Islamist, as well as bystanders who were not activists at all.[19] In general it appears that the social bases of nonmilitant forms of Islamist activism, such as providing social welfare, are studied more rarely than overtly confrontational activists, but we believe that these definitions overlap enough with our definition of Islamists to make useful comparisons. In addition the sampling methods differ in these works: nine studies derive their samples from government arrestees, ten from militants who died during movement activities, one from signatories of open letters (Dekmejian), one from a survey of members of an Islamist organization (Hermassi), and one from a survey at a refreshment stand at a Hizbullah demonstration (Schbley). We do not have enough studies to tell whether particular methods bias the findings in the direction of one social basis or another.

These studies confirm Ibrahim's initial analysis that Islamist activists are more likely to have some higher education than the population of Muslims at large. In only three of the twenty-two studies was the percentage of highly educated Islamists lower than the percentage of highly educated adults in the population at large: the small sample of Islamist revolutionaries arrested in Singapore, only one of thirty-one of whom had some higher education, as compared with 7 percent of all Singaporeans (the percentage for Muslim Singaporeans is not available); and two studies of Hizbullah in Lebanon, which estimated the percentage of highly educated activists as lower than 20 percent, as compared with 21 percent of all Lebanese (not broken down by confessional group).[20] Even if we compare Islamist activists specifically with young adult Muslims—since most activists tend to be young adults—only the Singapore and Lebanese samples

TABLE 2. Quantitative Studies of the Social Background of Islamist Activists

Year(s) Covered	Source	Sampling Method	Sample Size	% with University Education	Social Background
AL QAEDA CENTRAL STAFF					
1990s–2000s	Sageman (2004)	Public reports about terrorists	32	92	86% upper and middle class
EGYPT					
1970s–90s	Fandy (1994)	Members of the Islamic Group in southern Egypt	N.R.	Most	Largely peasant
1977–79	Ibrahim (1980)	Arrested Islamist militants	34	85	62% sons of government employees; 61% provincial
1981	Ansari (1984)	Arrested Islamist militants	280	56	74% provincial
1986	Ismail (2000)	Arrested members of Islamist groups	101	35	Poor neighborhoods of Cairo
1990s	Ibrahim (2002)	Arrested, wounded, killed Islamists	N.R.	?	Largely provincial
1991–93	Ismail (2000)[1]	Arrested Islamist militants	N.R.	51	Poor neighborhoods of Cairo
IRAN					
1971–77	Abrahamian (1982)	Dead members of Islamic Mojahedin and other Islamic guerrillas	91	69[2]	Provincial middle-class families
1978–79	Amra'i (1982)	"Martyrs" of the Iranian Revolution in Tehran whose families later registered with the Martyr Foundation	742	7	19% high school students; 41% working class; 48% born outside Tehran
IRAQ					
1979–80	Wiley (1992)	Executed Islamists	29	51	N.R.
LEBANON					
1982–94	Krueger/ Maleckova (2003)[3]	Articles on deceased Hizbullah fighters	129	14	28% poverty rate; 42% from Beirut
2001	Schbley (2003)	Questionnaire at Hizbullah parade	341	~15	Family income < $20,000; provincial
LEBANON AND PALESTINE					
1980–2003	Pape (2005)	Public reports about suicide bombers	38	62	N.R.

TABLE 2. (*continued*)

Year(s) Covered	Source	Sampling Method	Sample Size	% with University Education	Social Background
MAGHRIB NETWORK					
1990s–2000s	Sageman (2004)	Public reports about terrorists	53	43	52% upper and middle class
MASHRIQ NETWORK					
1990s–2000s	Sageman (2004)	Public reports about terrorists	66	57	80% upper and middle class
MOROCCO					
1984	Munson (1986)	Arrested members of Association of Islamic Youth	71	Most	Not poor
1984	Munson (1986)	Arrested associates of ʿAbd al-Salam Yasin	5	80	Not poor
PAKISTAN					
1990–2004	Fair (2008)	Interviews with family of deceased militants	141	19	26% unemployed
PALESTINE					
1993–2005	Kimhi/Even (2006)	Interviews with surviving suicide bombers, families, friends	60	N.R.	N.R.
1993–2004	Merari (2005)	Interviews with family of suicide bombers, surviving attackers, and captured recruiters	N.R.	N.R.	Economic status similar to society as a whole.
1993–2000	Pedahzur (2005)	Reports about suicide bombers	33	50	30% unemployed
2000–2004	Pedahzur (2005)	Reports about suicide bombers	150	32	42% unemployed
Late 1980s–2003	Berrebi (2007)	Biographies of martyrs and leaders from Hamas and Palestinian Islamic Jihad Web sites	335	57	84% not poor; 90% employed full-time
1996–1999	Hassan (2001)	Interviews with failed suicide bombers and families/trainers of successful suicide bombers	~250	N.R.	Not poor or uneducated
SAUDI ARABIA					
1991	Dekmejian (1995)	Signatories of open letter	52	40	64% from Najd region
1992	Dekmejian (1995)	Signatories of open letter	107	60	72% from Najd region
1990–2004	Lacroix/ Hegghammer (2004)	Militants mentioned in Saudi police statements or jihadist publications	50	Minority	N.R.

TABLE 2. (*continued*)

Year(s) Covered	Source	Sampling Method	Sample Size	% with University Education	Social Background
SINGAPORE					
2001–2	Singapore government (2003)	Arrested members of Jemaah Islamiyah and the Moro Islamic Liberation Front	31	3	N.R.
SOUTHEAST ASIAN NETWORK					
N.R.	Sageman (2004)	Public reports about terrorists	21	88	83% upper and middle class
SYRIA					
1976–81	Batatu (1982)	Arrested Islamists	1,384	49	N.R.
TUNISIA					
1987	Burgat/Dowell (1993)	Convicted Islamists	78	48	N.R.
1970s–80s	Hermassi (1984)	Survey of Islamic Tendency Movement members	~50	80	69% from Tunis region; 75% of fathers primary educated or less; 46% of fathers working class

N.R. = Not reported.

1. Reporting findings from Hisham Mubarak, *Al-Irhabiyun Qadimun! Dirasah Muqaranah bayna Mawqif al-Ikhwan al-Muslimin wa-Jamaʿat al-Jihad min Qadiyat al-ʿUnf, 1928–1994* (Cairo: Markaz al-Mahrusah li'l-Nashr wa al-Khidmat al-Suhufiya, 1995).

2. The percentage rises to 82 percent if office workers are included.

3. Analyzing data from Eli Hurvits, *Ha-Dereg ha-Tsevai shel Hizballah* (Tel Aviv: Merkaz Mosheh Dayan le-Limude ha-Mizrah ha-Tikhon ve-Afrikah, Universitat Tel-Aviv, 1999).

Sources: Ervand Abrahamian, *Iran between Two Revolutions* (Princeton, N.J.: Princeton University Press, 1982); Sohbatollah Amraʾi, "Barresi-ye Moqeʿiyat-e Ejtemaʿi-ye Shohada-ye Enqelab-e Eslami az Shahrivar 1357 ta Akharin-e Bahman 1357" (master's thesis, University of Tehran, 1982); Hamied Ansari, "The Islamic Militants in Egyptian Politics," *International Journal of Middle East Studies* 16, no. 1 (1984): 123–44; Hanna Batatu, "Syria's Muslim Brethren," *MERIP Reports* 12, no. 9 (1982): 12–20, 34, 36; Claude Berrebi, "Evidence about the Link between Education, Poverty and Terrorism among Palestinians," *Peace Economics, Peace Science and Public Policy* 13, no. 1 (2007): art. 2; François Burgat and William Dowell, *The Islamic Movement in North Africa* (Austin: Center for Middle Eastern Studies, University of Texas at Austin, 1993); R. Hrair Dekmejian, *Islam in Revolution: Fundamentalism in the Arab World*, 2nd ed. (Syracuse, N.Y.: Syracuse University Press, 1995); C. Christine Fair, "Who Are Pakistan's Militants and Their Families?" *Terrorism and Political Violence* 20, no. 1 (2008): 49–65; Mamoun Fandy, "Egypt's Islamic Group: Regional Revenge?" *Middle East Journal* 48, no. 4 (1994): 607–25; Nasra Hassan, "An Arsenal of Believers," *New Yorker*, November 19, 2001, 36–41; Mohammed Elbaki Hermassi, "La société tunisienne au miroir islamiste," *Maghreb-Machrek*, no. 108 (January–March 1984): 1–54; Saad Eddin Ibrahim,

"Anatomy of Egypt's Militant Islamic Groups: Methodological Note and Preliminary Findings," *International Journal of Middle East Studies* 12, no. 4 (1980): 423–53; Saad Eddin Ibrahim, "The Changing Face of Islamic Activism" [1995], in *Egypt, Islam and Democracy: Twelve Critical Essays* (Cairo: American University in Cairo Press, 2002), 69–79; Salwa Ismail, "The Popular Movement Dimensions of Contemporary Militant Islamism: Socio-Spatial Determinants in the Cairo Urban Setting," *Comparative Studies in Society and History* 42, no. 2 (2000): 363–93; Shaul Kimhi and Shemuel Even, "The Palestinian Human Bombers," in *Tangled Roots: Social and Psychological Factors in the Genesis of Terrorism*, ed. Jeff Victoroff (Amsterdam: IOS, 2006), 308–23; Alan B. Krueger and Jitka Maleckova, "Education, Poverty and Terrorism: Is There a Causal Connection?" *Journal of Economic Perspectives* 17, no. 4 (2003): 119–44; Stéphane Lacroix and Thomas Hegghammer, *Saudi Arabia Backgrounder: Who Are the Islamists?* Middle East Report no. 31 (Riyadh & Brussels: International Crisis Group, 2004); Ariel Merari, "Social, Organizational and Psychological Factors in Suicide Terrorism," in *Root Causes of Terrorism: Myths, Reality, and Ways Forward*, ed. Tore Bjørgo (London: Routledge, 2005), 70–86; Henry Munson Jr., "Social Base of Islamic Militancy in Morocco," *Middle East Journal* 40, no. 2 (1986): 267–84; Robert Pape, *Dying to Win* (New York: Random House, 2005); Ami Pedahzur, *Suicide Terrorism* (Cambridge: Polity, 2005); Marc Sageman, *Understanding Terror Networks* (Philadelphia: University of Pennsylvania Press, 2004); Ayla Schbley, "Defining Religious Terrorism," *Studies in Conflict and Terrorism* 26, no. 2 (2003): 105–34; Government of Singapore, *The Jemaah Islamiyah Arrests and the Threat of Terrorism* (Singapore: Ministry of Home Affairs, 2003); Joyce N. Wiley, *The Islamic Movement of Iraqi Shi'as* (Boulder, Colo.: Rienner, 1992).

FIGURE 1.

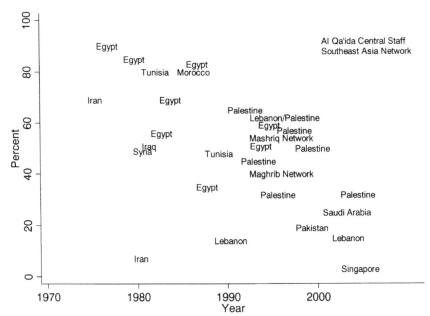

have rates of higher education lower than the tertiary school enrollment ratios reported in the World Bank's World Development Indicators database. All of the other studies show considerably higher rates of tertiary education among Islamist activists than among young adults in the populations from which they are drawn.

At the same time, it is worth noting the inconsistencies in these studies' estimates of educational attainment among Islamist activists. For example there is a large discrepancy between educational levels of the Jemaah Islamiyah samples in Singapore and in Sageman's Southeast Asia network (only two of whose members were Singaporean), and between the various samples of Palestinian attackers. Similarly three studies of Egyptian Islamists report levels of higher education at 85 percent in the late 1970s (Ibrahim), 66 percent in the early 1980s (Ansari and several other studies using the same published list of government detainees),[21] and 80 percent in the mid-1980s (Fandy), using different samples. All are far higher than the percentage of Egyptian adults with higher education (around 5 percent in the 1980s) and the percentage of young adults enrolled in higher education (under 16 percent in the 1980s)[22]—but the Ansari study complicates Ibrahim's conclusions about the downward trend in higher education among Islamists over time. Notwithstanding the uncertainty in these samples, however, it appears that this trend is generally confirmed. Four of the six least-educated samples are from the past decade, while five of the eight highest-educated samples are from earlier periods. Of course we cannot rule out the possibility that this trend is an artifact of the locations that happened to be selected for study at different periods. Another observation that emerges from figure 1 is the increasing variation in levels of higher education over time. Samples from the past decade now range from under 10 percent to over 90 percent with higher education, as compared with somewhat smaller ranges in earlier periods. Again this trend may be due to the selection of sites for study, but it may suggest that Islamist movements are now much more diverse in terms of social bases than they were in the 1970s and 1980s.

One of Ibrahim's main points is that Egyptian Islamist activists came increasingly to be drawn from far poorer social circles than they were in the 1970s. Few of the studies that we have located give systematic data that would confirm or disconfirm this hypothesis, so we cannot produce a chart analogous to figure 1 for the social background of Islamist activists. However, several studies give hints that there has always been substantial variation in this background. Abrahamian's study of Islamic guerrillas in 1970s Iran notes that activists came predominantly from middle-class households, as does Munson's study of 1980s Morocco.[23] More recently data collected by Eli Hurvits on Lebanon and Claude Berrebi on Palestine found that Islamist activists are not drawn from the poorest communities—they tend to have incomes above the poverty line, according to Hurvits, and hold steady jobs, according to Berrebi.[24] A widely cited paper by Krueger and Maleckova, which uses data from both of these studies, offers the more general conclusion that poverty does not breed Islamist terrorism.[25] At the same time, other samples find poorer backgrounds for Islamist activists. Hermassi's study of Tunisia reports that 46 percent of Islamist movement members in the 1970s and early 1980s came from families of urban or agricultural workers. A series of studies of university students has found that supporters of Islamist ideals and movements tend to be from poorer backgrounds than other students.[26] Sageman finds that the Maghrib Islamist terrorist network is evenly divided between middle-class and lower-class family backgrounds, as distinct from the predominantly middle-class backgrounds of the networks that lie farther east.

Another aspect of social context is the location of recruitment into Islamist organizations. Sageman reports that 70 percent of the members of what he calls the global Salafi jihad were recruited outside of their country of origin: al Qaeda central staff bonded through common experiences during the Afghan war against the Soviets,[27] while the Maghrib and Mashriq networks (Sageman calls the latter the "Core Arab Network") are dominated by Arabs who were either first- or second-generation immigrants in Western Europe and felt excluded from full participation in European society. (This process is identified also in Wiktorowicz's study of second-generation Muslim immigrants who were recruited into Al Mohajiroun in the United Kingdom, where the experience of racism formed a cognitive opening for later membership.)[28] By contrast Sageman writes that the Southeast Asian network was recruited largely domestically, especially through two Islamist boarding schools in Indonesia and Malaysia.[29] Similar boarding schools are associated with the Taliban, particularly the Dar-ul-Ulum Haqqania, near the Afghan border, where activists were recruited and trained from among the Afghan refugee population.[30] There is no evidence on what proportion of madrassas contribute to the recruitment of Islamist militants, but enrollment numbers for Pakistani madrassas in general are limited to 0.02–1 percent of enrolled children in most of the country and slightly over 4 percent in a belt bordering Afghanistan.[31] While Pakistani madrassa enrollment is marginally related to household income and the education level of the head of household, the biggest impact on school choice is access to private and public schools. Only in settlements with no public or private schools are the poor substantially more likely (4 percent versus 2.5 percent of enrolled children) to enroll their children in madrassas—though total enrollment plummets under such conditions. While few studies have found systematic evidence about the social bases of either madrassa students or Taliban activists,[32] this pathway to activism seems to differ considerably from the European-based experience of certain other Islamist movements.

These differing social bases of Islamist mobilization are symbolized by the contrast between al Qaeda and the Taliban. Western news reports frequently confuse the two, on the basis of the alliance that they forged during the 1990s, but the two draw on quite distinct pools of recruits. Would-be militants who showed up in Afghanistan to join the jihad "had to take a complex entrance exam," a former member of al Qaeda told U.S. officials. "It involved what sounded like an IQ test. Those who scored high, like Max [the code name for the informant], were sent to bin Laden's intelligence training program. Those who scored lowest were sent to fight against the Northern Alliance on the front lines."[33] Al Qaeda leaders denigrated the Afghans as "a simple people with a simple culture," according to an Egyptian Islamist. "They didn't believe the Taliban had an ability to grasp contemporary reality, politics and management."[34] Taliban leaders, for their part, were irate at al Qaeda for its global campaign of violent attacks and media publicity, according to a Pakistani journalist who interviewed them regularly. The Taliban worried—correctly, as it turned out—that al Qaeda's activities would provoke the United States and threaten Taliban rule in Afghanistan.[35] The sociopolitical distinctions between the two groups extended also to religious matters, notwithstanding their overlapping interest in establishing an Islamic state. Mullah Muhammad ʿUmar, leader of the Taliban, literally wrapped himself in the cloak of the Prophet one day in 1996— the cloak is a cherished relic in Qandahar—and consistently refuses to be photographed. Bin Laden and other globalists, by contrast, denounce the worship of relics and are comfortable in front of a camera, even distributing videotapes of themselves to the media.[36] Of course the two movements were able to cooperate. Similarly globalists and localists conspired together to kidnap and murder American reporter Daniel Pearl in Pakistan, including "members of at least three different Pakistani groups, none of which had ever shown much previous interest in international jihad."[37]

Certain other nationality- and communal-based Islamist movements, however, do not fall so clearly into this dichotomy. Palestinian Islamists, for example, are territorially limited in their activities, like the Taliban, but mobilize broader segments of the local population than the Taliban appeared to do. Studies of Palestinian militants, listed in table 2, show that they are fairly representative of the education levels of Palestinians at large. Similarly a 1998 survey of educated young adults in Gaza found that economic well-being—self-reports of a five-point scale ranging from "We are a lot poorer than most" to "We are a lot richer than most"—was not significantly correlated with willingness to engage in future protest.[38] One possible explanation for this representativeness could be the role of retribution for the loss of family members as a motivation for Palestinian militancy, since several studies have identified revenge as an element in the motivations of some Palestinian suicide attackers.[39] Revenge-based activism resulting from experiences of sustained violence may be more randomly and broadly distributed in the population than more ideological forms of motivation for activism.

Supporters

Finally let us turn from activists to more passive supporters of Islamist movements. One indicator of support is voting for candidates whose platform includes state implementation of Shariʿa. In more than sixty national parliamentary elections since 1970 in which such candidates have participated, they have never received a majority of votes.[40] However, Islamist candidates have been well represented in parliament on several occasions, including Algeria in 1991 (47 percent of votes and 81 percent of seats in the first round, which was soon canceled by the military), Bahrain in 2002 (48 percent of seats), Jordan in 1989 (41 percent of seats), Kuwait in 1999 and 2003 (40 and 42 percent of seats), Palestine in 2006 (44 percent of votes, 58 percent of seats), and Turkey in 1995, 2002, and 2007 (21, 34, and 47 percent of votes; 29, 66, and 62 percent of seats). More commonly Islamists receive 10 percent or less of the vote, though they might have received more if the state had not handicapped them in various ways. These vote levels do not appear to be correlated significantly with any social characteristics at the national level—both high and low vote levels appear in both more industrialized and less industrialized countries, more educated and less educated, and so on. Within countries there is fragmentary evidence that poorer districts vote slightly more frequently for Islamist candidates. In Turkey, for example, the Islamist party has done best since the 1970s in areas with lower socioeconomic development,[41] and recent ethnographic studies from Istanbul suggest that Islamist parties have targeted their mobilizing efforts at poor neighborhoods with large numbers of migrants from the provinces.[42] In Jordan, too, Islamists appear to have received more votes in poorer districts, where they focused their campaigning, though factors such as tribal or local identity may have been more important than wealth in accounting for the Islamists' performance.[43] In Pakistan and Malaysia, the provinces where Islamists have been most successful and actually formed provincial governments are among the most peripheral regions of these countries: Baluchistan and Northwest Frontier Province in Pakistan and Kelantan and Terengganu in Malaysia.

Cross-national survey findings partly confirm the electoral results. In 2000–2002 the World Values Survey asked Muslims in seven countries with significant Muslim populations and active Islamist movements (as well as sixty-eight other countries)—Algeria, Bangladesh, Egypt, Indonesia, Jordan, Nigeria, and Pakistan—whether they thought that "good government . . . should implement only the laws of the *shariʿa*."[44] The percentage agreeing or strongly agreeing ranged from 44 percent in Bangladesh and 50 percent in Indonesia to 62 percent in Pakistan, 72 percent in Algeria, 79 percent in Jordan, and 80 percent in Egypt.[45] Within each country the least educated were the most likely to support state implementation of Shariʿa, and this relationship held up in almost every

country even when controlling for other socioeconomic variables. The poorest
third of respondents were most likely to agree in three countries (Bangladesh,
Nigeria, and Pakistan), but in the countries with the highest rates of support
(Algeria, Egypt, and Jordan) the middle third was most likely to agree. Only in
Indonesia was the wealthiest third the most likely to agree. In every country in
the sample, residents of towns and small cities were more likely than residents
of big cities (over half a million in population) to agree. The oldest respondents
were among the most pro-Shariʿa, though the youngest generation (ages fifteen
to thirty-four) were slightly more pro-Shariʿa than middle-aged respondents in
five of the seven countries. In sum the image of Shariʿa supporters that this survey presents is that they are less educated and somewhat poorer, less metropolitan, and older. However, the variation within countries is less prominent than
the variation across countries: the nations with lower levels of overall support
for Shariʿa tend to have lower levels of support across all categories of education, income, city size, and age, and the range of national averages is considerably more dispersed than the range across subnational categories within any
given country.[46]

But what does it mean to say that one favors Shariʿa? The question may
mean different things to different people. For example, 71 percent of Indonesians agreed that "the government must make obligatory the implementation of
shariʿa," according to a survey in 2002. Sixty-seven percent agreed that "government based on the Qurʾan and Sunnah under the leadership of Islamic authorities such as *kiai* or *ulama*, is best for a country like ours." But only 46 percent
agreed that "in elections we must choose the candidate who fights for the implementation of *shariʿa*." Only 21 percent agreed that "in elections there should
only be Islamic parties."[47] In parliamentary elections in 2004, only 18 percent
actually voted for Islamist parties (PPP, PKS, PBB). In Turkey, by contrast, survey questions about Shariʿa have predicted electoral results more closely: in the
1990s a series of surveys found support for a Shariʿa-based state at 20 to 27 percent, matching the 21 percent of votes received by the Islamist party (Fazilet
Partisi) in national elections in late 1995.[48] However, fewer than one third of the
supporters of the party agreed that Turkish civil law on divorce or inheritance
should be changed in accordance with "Islamic law."[49] In Palestine 60 percent
of a 1999 survey said they found no incompatibility between democracy and a
political system based on Shariʿa.[50]

Similarly in the World Values Survey, most people who supported Shariʿa also
agreed or strongly agreed with the statement that "democracy may have problems but it's better than any other form of government."[51] Interestingly the percentage is lowest in Indonesia and Nigeria (69 percent), which are among the
countries with the lowest levels of support for Shariʿa, and highest in Egypt (98
percent), Bangladesh (97 percent), and Jordan (91 percent), two of which (Egypt

and Jordan) are among the countries with the highest level of support for Shari'a. If we examine respondents who are both pro-Shari'a and antidemocracy, there are no consistent findings with regard to socioeconomic characteristics. Higher income is negatively related with these attitudes in Pakistan, as is metropolitan residence in Algeria—but most countries display no significant pattern. Again the bigger difference is between countries, not within countries, ranging from 1–2 percent of respondents in Bangladesh and Egypt to 15 percent of respondents in Indonesia and 17 percent in Nigeria. Support for democracy is so widespread— 79 percent of all Muslims in the World Values Survey[52]—that it outweighs the correlations between particular social categories and support for Shari'a.

These findings are visible also in a second cross-national survey, conducted by the Pew Global Attitudes Project in 2002, which asked respondents in ten countries with significant Muslim populations (along with thirty-four other countries)—Bangladesh, Indonesia, Jordan, Lebanon, Mali, Nigeria, Pakistan, Senegal, Turkey, and Uzbekistan—"How much of a role do you think Islam *should* play in the political life of our country—a very large role, a fairly large role, a fairly small role, or a very small role?"[53] If we take the response "a very large role" as most closely approximating our definition of Islamists, we once again find tremendous cross-national variation, from 18 percent of Muslim re-spondents in Uzbekistan and 24 percent in Turkey to 59 percent in Mali and 82 percent in Pakistan. Within-country variation was fairly consistent but less dra-matic: the poorest segment of most countries' samples was more likely than others to select this response, and in only one case (Indonesia) marginally less likely; college-educated respondents were less likely than others in half the sam-ples (only in Indonesia were the college-educated marginally more likely); and metropolitan respondents were less likely in a few countries.[54] Parallel to the overlap between support for Shari'a and democracy in the World Values Sur-vey, the Pew survey found that most people who said that they wanted Islam to play "a very large role" in political life also said that "democracy is not just for the West and can work well here" (only in Turkey was this portion just below 50 percent).

Similar variation emerges from single-country surveys (see table 3). The rates of support for Islamism are relatively consistent within each country, despite the use of different indicators, but vary greatly between countries. The demo-graphic characteristics of these supporters also differ by country: they are less urban than other survey respondents in Bangladesh, more urban in Turkey, and less or equally urban in Indonesia, according to different studies. Islamist sup-porters are inconsistently differentiated by age, education, and wealth as well, not just between countries but also within each country. Different surveys of Palestinians, for example, found Islamist supporters to be older, similar in age, or younger than other respondents. Different surveys of Indonesia found Islamist

TABLE 3. Social Background of Islamist Supporters, as Compared with Other Survey Respondents

Year	Source	Type of support	Percent Islamist	Compared with Other Survey Respondents			
				Urban	*Age*	*Education*	*Wealth*
BANGLADESH							
1983	Banu (1992)	Select religious figures as political representatives	27	less	N.R.	less	N.R.
EGYPT							
1988	Tessler (1997)	Four questions about the role of religion in politics	20	N.R.	younger	more	N.R.
1988	Tessler/Jesse (1996)	Support current organized Islamic movements	40	N.R.	similar/ younger	similar	N.R.
2005	Moaddel/ Karabenick (2008)	Twelve questions about Islamicattitudes	N.R.	N.R.	N.R.	similar	less
INDONESIA							
1999	Liddle/Mujani (2007)	Support United Development Party (PPP)	11	similar	N.R.	similar	N.R.
2002	Mujani/Liddle (2004)	Fourteen questions about Islamic attitudes	14	less	N.R.	less	less
2004	Liddle/Mujani (2007)	Support United Development Party (PPP)	8	similar	N.R.	similar	N.R.
2004	Webber (2006)	Support United Development Party (PPP)	N.R.	less	N.R.	less	less
KUWAIT							
1988	Tessler (1997)	Four questions about the role of religion in politics	47	N.R.	similar	more	N.R.
1988	Tessler/Jesse (1996)	Support current organized Islamic movements	49	N.R.	similar	similar/ more	N.R.
PALESTINE							
1986	Shadid/Seltzer (1988)	Favor state based on Shariʿa	26	N.R.	older	less	N.R.
1994	Tessler/Jesse (1996)	Support Hamas or Islamic Jihad	16	N.R.	similar	similar	N.R.
1994– 1998	Tessler/ Nachtwey (1999)	Support Hamas or Islamic Jihad	13–20	N.R.	similar/ younger	similar	N.R.
SAUDI ARABIA							
2005	Moaddel/ Karabenick (2008)	Twelve questions about Islamic attitudes	N.R.	N.R.	N.R.	similar	more
TURKEY							
1998	Akgün (2002)	Support Virtue Party	14	more	younger	less	less
2002	Başlevent et al.(2005)	Support Justice and Development Party	19	more	younger	similar	N.R.

TABLE 3. (*continued*)

Sources: Birol Akgün, "Twins or Enemies: Comparing Nationalist and Islamist Traditions in Turkish Politics," *MERIA Journal* 6, no. 1 (2002): 17–35; U. A. B. Razia Akter Banu, *Islam in Bangladesh* (Leiden: Brill, 1992); Cem Başlevent, Hasan Kirmanoğlu, and Burhan Şenatalar, "Empirical Investigation of Party Preferences and Economic Voting in Turkey," *European Journal of Political Research* 44, no 4 (2005): 547–62; R. William Liddle and Saiful Mujani, "Leadership, Party, and Religion: Explaining Voting Behavior in Indonesia," *Comparative Political Studies* 40, no. 7 (2007): 832–57; Mansoor Moaddel and Stuart A. Karabenick, "Religious Fundamentalism among Young Muslims in Egypt and Saudi Arabia," *Social Forces* 86, no. 4 (2008): 1675–710; Saiful Mujani and R. William Liddle, "Politics, Islam, and Public Opinion," *Journal of Democracy* 15, no. 1 (2004): 109–23; Mohammed Shadid and Rick Seltzer, "Political Attitudes of Palestinians in the West Bank and Gaza Strip," *Middle East Journal* 42, no. 1 (1988): 16–32; Mark Tessler, "The Origins of Popular Support for Islamist Movements: A Political Economy Analysis," in *Islam, Democracy, and the State in North Africa*, ed. John Entelis (Bloomington: Indiana University Press, 1997), 93–126; Mark Tessler and Jolene Jesse, "Gender and Support for Islamist Movements: Evidence from Egypt, Kuwait and Palestine," *Muslim World* 86, no. 2 (1996): 200–228; Mark Tessler and Jodi Nachtwey, "Palestinian Political Attitudes: An Analysis of Survey Data from the West Bank and Gaza," *Israel Studies* 4, no. 1 (1999): 22–43; Douglas Webber, "A Consolidated Patrimonial Democracy? Democratization in Post-Suharto Indonesia," *Democratization* 13, no. 3 (2006): 396–420.

supporters to have less education or similar levels of education, as compared with other respondents. No universal profile of Islamist supporters emerges from these studies.

Conclusion

The primary finding from this review of the social bases of Islamism is variation. Some Islamist leaders are trained in seminaries, while others are products of secular state school systems (and a few have both or neither background). Most migrated from the provinces to the capital of their home countries, but not all. Islamist movements of the 1970s drew largely on middle-class university students and graduates, with the exception of the Iranian Revolution, but in more recent years the educational and social background of activists is increasingly mixed. Surveys from the past decade suggest that Islamist attitudes are most widespread among the least educated and poorest residents of rural areas, but these are only marginal distinctions—plenty of well-educated, wealthy metropolitans voiced the same opinions as well. The short answer to the question in our paper's title, "Who are the Islamists?," is anybody. We find no strong demographic predictors of Islamist leadership, activism, or sympathy.

The bigger explanatory feature is country of residence. Some countries— Egypt, for example—generate considerably higher rates of Islamist activism and support than other countries.[55] Regardless of social background, education, or urban/rural distinctions, Egyptian Muslims seem to be more supportive of

Islamist attitudes than their neighbors, and this difference appears to be related to religiosity in general. According to recent surveys, 99 percent of Egyptians consider themselves "a religious person," compared with 85 percent in Jordan and 62 percent in Saudi Arabia.[56] Cross-national differences extend from the rate of support for Islamism to the social bases of support. In Egypt the middle third of the income distribution was most likely to tell survey researchers that they support state implementation of Shari'a, while in Pakistan it was the lowest third and in Indonesia the highest third. Islamist movements seem to differ by country. The most consistent feature of support for Islamism across countries is the view that democracy and a state based on the Shari'a are compatible, and this view is also broadly held across all segments of the national populations. The social bases of Islamism seem to be less important than the national bases.

This nonfinding is important as a counterweight to grand theories about the social bases of Islamism. The evidence reviewed in this paper suggests that we should be careful about generalizing from the study of any one movement, even Saad Eddin Ibrahim's studies of militant Islamism in Egypt. Ibrahim's research—confirmed by several other studies on Egypt—concludes that Islamist activists of the 1970s came from well-educated, middle-class provincial families, and that this profile changed in subsequent decades to include less-educated, poorer shanty dwellers. This trajectory is not easily corroborated in other countries, because there are few similar studies. But the evidence we do have suggests that Islamist militants in other countries are more varied than Ibrahim's classic 1980 paper would imply. International jihadi groups, for example, continue to draw disproportionately from well-educated middle classes, while other movements appeal to less-educated and poorer populations as well as the educated middle class.

This is not to say that Islamist movements have ceased to be "modern" in the sense that Bruce Lawrence and others have used the term. Even as Islamist activism and opinion has spread beyond the educated middle class, so too has the "contact with the West" and understanding of "the horizons of possibility denied them by the inequities of the world system," to return to Lawrence's phrases. Yet there is little evidence that the spread of Islamism matches the spread of globalization and relative deprivation: we would need far more detailed evidence than this paper has located to understand, for example, why rural folk in some Muslim societies are so much more likely than rural folk in certain other Muslim societies to express support for Islamist attitudes. The cross-national variation in the scale and social bases of Islamism suggests that global factors are not so important as local ones.

Perhaps another argument of Lawrence's is more appropriate here. Lawrence begins his comparative study of fundamentalism, *Defenders of God*, with a sharp attack on social-scientific approaches that fetishize "hard data, evidence capable of observation and measurement in models or graphs." This "need for hard data, that is, recurrent behavioral evidence in the public sphere, . . . minimizes the significance of soft data, such as scriptural references, creedal assertions, and biographical analyses, all of which are messy, admit of a thousand exceptions, and, of course, preponderate in the private sphere." Hard data, in Lawrence's argument, is part of the modernist effort at "domesticating" fundamentalism by objectifying it and reducing it to social—nonreligious—causes. "Most social scientists, especially sociologists, mirror the Enlightenment categories [of religion and academic scholarship] in a manner that precludes, even while seeming to permit, self-criticism."[57]

Yet social scientific methods are self-critical in at least one way that humanist analyses are usually not: for more than half a century, social scientists have struggled to come to terms with the fallibility of their own observations of the world around them, and they have institutionalized this struggle through constant concern for representativeness. Humanists who mock the pretenses and limitations of "nationally representative samples" may be missing the underlying anxiety that these samples are intended to address: the concern that human observations may be biased and self-serving. The search for random and representative samples is an admission of this personal failing, and an attempt to transcend it. Perhaps transcendence is folly, but so is the humanists' lack of reflexivity—or lack of published accounts of reflexivity—about how they discovered and selected the evidence that they present.

In addition a number of social scientists have in recent years attempted to challenge the objectivist approach to the study of Islam—and other themes—arguing that understanding the worldviews of one's subjects may trump the attempt to explain their attitudes or actions.[58] In this view the empiricist collection of "hard" data may be harnessed for the same analytical purposes that Lawrence's humanistic approach intends. The evidence reviewed in this paper, for example, does not point to a single set of socioeconomic determinants of Islamism but rather to a varied set of social conditions that have been activated in a variety of contexts. The result is a social-scientific call for further humanistic research into the self-understandings of Islamists—so long as the findings of this research are subjected to the checks and balances of all available evidence, including "hard" data.

NOTES

1. Bruce B. Lawrence, *Defenders of God: The Fundamentalist Revolt against the Modern Age*, with a new preface by the author (Columbia: University of South Carolina Press, 1995), 237.

2. Saad Eddin Ibrahim, "Anatomy of Egypt's Militant Islamic Groups: Methodological Note and Preliminary Findings," *International Journal of Middle East Studies* 12 (December 1980): 423–53.

3. Quintan Wiktorowicz, *The Management of Islamic Activism: Salafis, the Muslim Brotherhood, and State Power in Jordan* (Albany: State University of New York Press, 2001), 127.

4. Carrie Rosefsky Wickham, *Mobilizing Islam: Religion, Activism, and Political Change in Egypt* (New York: Columbia University Press, 2002), 158; Salwa Ismail, "The Popular Movement Dimensions of Contemporary Militant Islamism: Socio-Spatial Determinants in the Cairo Urban Setting," *Comparative Studies in Society and History* 42 (April 2000): 372–73, 379–93.

5. Lawrence, *Defenders of God*, 27.

6. On these distinctions, see Charles Kurzman, *Liberal Islam: A Sourcebook* (New York: Oxford University Press, 1998).

7. Richard C. Martin, ed., *Encyclopedia of Islam and the Muslim World* (New York: Macmillan Reference USA, Thomson/Gale, 2004); John L. Esposito, ed., *Oxford Encyclopedia of the Islamic World* (New York: Oxford University Press, 2009).

8. Ismail, "Popular Movement Dimensions of Contemporary Militant Islamism," 384.

9. Mustafa Al-Ahnaf, Bernard Botiveau, and Franck Frégosi, *L'Algérie par ses islamistes* (Paris: Karthala, 1991), 79. The original publication was 'Abbasi Madani, *'Azmat al-fikr al-hadith wa mubarrirat al-hall al-islami* (Mecca: Maktabat al-Manara, 1987).

10. Abdessalam Yassine, *Islamiser la modernité* (Rabat, Morocco: al-Ofok Impressions, 1998); translated by Martin Jenni as *Winning the Modern World for Islam* (Iowa City: Justice and Spirituality, 2000).

11. U. A. B. Razia Akter Banu, "Jamaat-i-Islami in Bangladesh: Challenges and Prospects," in *Islam, Muslims, and the Modern State*, ed. Hussin Mutalib and Taj ul-Islam Hashmi (New York: St. Martin's Press, 1994), 86–87; Hani Hourani et al., *Islamic Movements in Jordan* (Amman: Al-Urdun Al-Jadid Research Center, 1997), 103.

12. Seyyed Vali Reza Nasr, *The Vanguard of the Islamic Revolution: The Jama'at-i Islami of Pakistan* (Berkeley: University of California Press, 1994), 83–84. A list of the founding members and their educational background is available online at Jamat-i Islami, "The Profile of the Founding 75 Members," http://jamaat.org/overview/profile.html (accessed July 10, 2007).

13. Eric Davis, "Ideology, Social Class, and Islamic Radicalism in Modern Egypt," in *From Nationalism to Revolutionary Islam*, ed. Said Amir Arjomand (Albany: State University of New York Press, 1984), 142.

14. Seyyed Vali Reza Nasr, *Mawdudi and the Making of Islamic Revivalism* (New York: Oxford University Press, 1996), 12–19, 29.

15. Gilles Kepel, *Muslim Extremism in Egypt: The Prophet and Pharaoh*, trans. Jon Rothschild (Berkeley: University of California Press, 2003), 183.

16. A similar pattern emerges in a study of Syrian Islamist leaders: seven professionals, most from middle-class backgrounds, and five religious scholars, three from clerical families. See R. Hrair Dekmejian, *Islam in Revolution: Fundamentalism in the Arab World*, 2nd ed. (Syracuse, N.Y.: Syracuse University Press, 1995), 114–15.

17. Ibrahim, "Anatomy of Egypt's Militant Islamic Groups."

18. Saad Eddin Ibrahim, "The Changing Face of Islamic Activism" (1995), in *Egypt, Islam and Democracy: Twelve Critical Essays* (Cairo: American University in Cairo Press, 2002), 69–79.

19. Of the seventy "martyrs" whose families offered an assessment of their political ideology, twenty were not focused on establishing an Islamic state. Sohbatollah Amra'i, "Barresi-ye Moqe'iyat-e Ejtema'i-ye Shohada-ye Enqelab-e Eslami az Shahrivar 1357 ta Akharin-e Bahman 1357" (master's thesis, University of Tehran, 1982), 218. For a discussion of the Amra'i study, which has been banned in Iran, see Charles Kurzman, *The Unthinkable Revolution in Iran* (Cambridge, Mass.: Harvard University Press, 2004), 176–77.

20. National comparison data are drawn from the Task Force on Higher Education in Society, *Higher Education in Developing Countries* (Washington, D.C.: World Bank and UNESCO, 2002).

21. Nazih Ayubi, *Political Islam: Religion and Politics in the Arab World* (London: Routledge, 1991), 164; Dekmejian, *Islam in Revolution*, 101; Nemat Guenena, "The 'JIHAD': An 'Islamic Alternative' in Egypt," *Cairo Papers in Social Science* 9 (Summer 1986): 100.

22. Robert J. Barro and Jong-Wha Lee, *International Data on Educational Attainment: Updates and Implications*, Harvard Center for International Development, Working Paper no. 42 (Cambridge, Mass.: National Bureau of Economic Research, 2000).

23. Ervand Abrahamian, *Iran between Two Revolutions* (Princeton, N.J.: Princeton University Press, 1982), 481; Henry Munson Jr. "Social Base of Islamic Militancy in Morocco," *Middle East Journal* 40 (Spring 1986): 267–84.

24. Eli Hurvits, *Ha-Dereg ha-Tsevai shel Hizballah: Deyokan Hevrati* (Tel Aviv: Merkaz Mosheh Dayan le-Limude ha-Mizrah ha-Tikhon ve-Afrikah, Universitat Tel-Aviv, 1999); Claude Berrebi, "Evidence about the Link between Education, Poverty and Terrorism among Palestinians," *Peace Economics, Peace Science and Public Policy* 13, no. 1 (2007): art. 2; available online at http://www.bepress.com/peps/vol13/iss1/2 (accessed July 8, 2009).

25. Alan B. Krueger and Jitka Maleckova, "Education, Poverty and Terrorism: Is There a Causal Connection?" *Journal of Economic Perspectives* 17 (Fall 2003): 119–44.

26. Kiren Aziz Chaudhry and Peter McDonough, "State, Society, and Sin: The Political Beliefs of University Students in Pakistan," *Economic Development and Cultural Change* 32 (October 1983): 29; Nilüfer Narli, *Unveiling the Fundamentalist Women: A Case Study of University Students in Malaysia* (Istanbul: Isis, 1991), 117–27; Nilüfer Narli, "The Rise of the Islamist Movement in Turkey," *MERIA Journal* 3, no. 3 (1999): 42; Nasr, *Vanguard of the Islamic Revolution*, 74; Carrie Rosefsky Wickham, "Political Mobilization under Authoritarian Rule: Explaining Islamic Activism in Mubarak's Egypt" (Ph.D. diss., Princeton University, 1996), 380–83.

27. For an overview of Afghan "alumni," see Yoram Schwaitzer and Shaul Shay, *The Globalization of Terror* (Herzliya, Israel: Interdisciplinary Center; New Brunswick, N.J.: Transaction, 2003).

28. Quintan Wiktorowicz, *Radical Islam Rising: Muslim Extremism in the West* (Lanham, Md.: Rowman & Littlefield, 2005).

29. See also Sidney Jones, *Al-Qaeda in Southeast Asia: The Case of the "Ngruki Network" in Indonesia*, Asia Briefing no. 20, rev. ed. (Jakarta & Brussels: International Crisis Group, 2003).

30. Muhammad Amir Rana, *A to Z of Jehadi Organizations in Pakistan* (Lahore: Mashal, 2004), 528; Ahmed Rashid, *Taliban: Militant Islam, Oil, and Fundamentalism in Central Asia* (New Haven, Conn.: Yale University Press, 2000), 90–92; Jessica Stern, "Pakistan's Jihad Culture," *Foreign Affairs* 79, no. 6 (2000): 123.

31. Tahir Andrabi, Jishnu Das, Asim Ijaz Khwaja, and Tristan Zajonc, "Religious School Enrollment in Pakistan: A Look at the Data," *Comparative Education Review* 50, no. 3 (2006): 446–77.

32. Estimates of madrassa support for Pakistani Islamist movements appear in Rana, *A to Z*, 511–33; and estimates of the family background of Pakistani madrassa graduates—based on the honorific titles of their fathers—appear in Jamal Malik, *Colonialization of Islam: Dissolution of Traditional Institutions in Pakistan* (New Delhi: Manohar, 1996), 241–44, 322–23.

33. John Miller and Michael Stone, with Chris Mitchell, *The Cell: Inside the 9/11 Plot, and Why the FBI and CIA Failed to Stop It* (New York: Hyperion, 2002), 282.

34. Abdel-Fattah Fahmy Ahmed, quoted in Alan Cullison and Andrew Higgins, "Strained Alliance: Al Qaeda's Sour Days in Afghanistan," *Wall Street Journal*, August 2, 2002.

35. Rahimullah Yusufzai, "Osama bin Laden: The Man and His Cause," *Gulf News*, September 24, 2001.

36. Charles Kurzman, "Bin Laden and Other Thoroughly Modern Muslims," *Contexts* (American Sociological Association) 1, no. 4 (2002): 13–20.

37. Jason Burke, *Al-Qaeda: Casting a Shadow of Terror* (London: Tauris, 2003), 240.

38. Brian K. Barber and Joseph A. Olsen, "Adolescents' Willingness to Engage in Political Conflict: Lessons from the Gaza Strip," in *Tangled Roots: Social and Psychological Factors in the Genesis of Terrorism*, ed. Jeff Victoroff (Amsterdam: IOS, 2006), 215, 220.

39. Robert J. Brym and Bader Araj, "Suicide Bombing as Strategy and Interaction: The Case of the Second Intifada," *Social Forces* 84 (June 2006): 1979; Shaul Kimhi and Shemuel Even, "The Palestinian Human Bombers," in *Tangled Roots: Social and Psychological Factors in the Genesis of Terrorism*, ed. Jeff Victoroff (Amsterdam: IOS, 2006), 313.

40. This subject is covered in more detail in Charles Kurzman and Ijlal Naqvi, "Islamic Party Participation in Parliamentary Elections," unpublished paper.

41. Ergun Özbüdün, "Voting Behavior: Turkey," in *Electoral Politics in the Middle East*, ed. Jacob M. Landau, Ergun Özbüdün, and Doğu Ergil (London: Croom Helm; Stanford, Calif.: Hoover Institution Press, 1980), 125–28; Sencer Ayata, "Patronage, Party and State: The Politicisation of Islam in Turkey," *Middle East Journal* 50 (Winter 1996): 53; Ali Çarkoğlu, "The Geography of the April 1999 Turkish Elections," *Turkish Studies* 1 (Spring 2000): 149–71; Haldun Gülalp, "Social Bases of Turkey's Welfare Party," *International Journal of Middle East Studies* 33 (August 2001): 433–48; M. Hakan Yavuz, *Islamic Political Identity in Turkey* (New York: Oxford University Press, 2003), 219.

42. Jenny B. White, *Islamist Mobilization in Turkey: A Study in Vernacular Politics* (Seattle: University of Washington Press, 2002); Cihan Tuğal, *Passive Revolution: Absorbing the Islamic Challenge to Capitalism* (Stanford, Calif.: Stanford University Press, 2009).

43. Abla M. Amawi, "The 1993 Elections in Jordan," *Arab Studies Quarterly* 16, no. 3 (1994): 15–27; Hanna Y. Freij and Leonard C. Robinson, "Liberalization, the Islamists, and the Stability of the Arab State: Jordan as a Case Study," *Muslim World* 86 (January 1996): 1–32; Glenn E. Robinson, "Can Islamists Be Democrats? The Case of Jordan," *Middle East Journal* 51 (Summer 1997): 373–87; Curtis Ryan, "Elections

and Parliamentary Democratization in Jordan," *Democratization* 5 (Winter 1998): 194–214.

44. The question is worded as follows in different languages: "Al-hukuma al-jayyida yajibu an tatbaqa qawanin al-shariʻa al-islamiyya faqat" (Arabic); "Nimne bornito duto'r moddhe konta bhalo sorkar bole apnar mone hoe? . . . Shudhumatro desh porichalito hobe shoriayat ayin onuari" (Bengali); "Un bon gouvernement . . . ne devrait mettre à effet que les lois de shariʻa" (French in Algeria); "Pemerintahan yang baik . . . seharusnya hanya menjalankan hukum agama Islam (syariah)" (Indonesian). Only the English-language questionnaires are available for Nigeria and Pakistan in the survey documentation. European Values Study Group and World Values Survey Association, *European and World Values Surveys Integrated Data File, 1999–2002, Release I: Data Collection Instruments*, Second ICPSR Version (Ann Arbor, Mich.: Inter-university Consortium for Political and Social Research, 2005), 61 (Algerian/English), 89 (Algerian/French), 283 (Bengali), 867 (Egypt/English), 1530 (Jordan/Arabic), 1926 (Indonesian), 2052 (Pakistan/English), 2102 (Nigeria/English).

45. Nancy J. Davis and Robert V. Robinson, "The Egalitarian Face of Islamic Orthodoxy: Support for Islamic Law and Economic Justice in Seven Muslim-Majority Nations," *American Sociological Review* 71 (April 2006): 178.

46. Weak findings for demographic variables appear also in a 2003 survey of 256 Shiʻa Muslim Lebanese's attitudes toward Hizbullah. See Simon Haddad, "The Origins of Popular Support for Lebanon's Hezbollah," *Studies in Conflict and Terrorism* 29 (January/February 2006): 30–31.

47. Saiful Mujani and R. William Liddle, "Politics, Islam, and Public Opinion," *Journal of Democracy* 15 (January 2004): 114. According to another survey in Indonesia, with a nonrandom sample, 63 percent agreed that "the spirit of fundamentalism is constructive rather than destructive." See Riaz Hassan, *Faithlines: Muslim Conceptions of Islam and Society* (Oxford: Oxford University Press, 2002), 135.

48. Ali Çarkoğlu and Binnaz Toprak, *Türkiye'de Din, Toplum ve Siyaset* (Istanbul: Türkiye Ekonomik ve Sosyal Etüdler Vakfı, 2000), 16–17.

49. Ibid., 72–75.

50. Audra K. Grant and Mark A. Tessler, "Palestinian Attitudes toward Democracy and Its Compatibility with Islam: Evidence from Public Opinion Research in the West Bank and Gaza," *Arab Studies Quarterly* 24, no. 4 (2002): 9.

51. European Values Study Group and World Values Survey Association, *European and World Values Surveys Integrated Data File*, 59 (Algerian/English), 86 (Algerian/French), 279 (Bengali), 863 (Egypt/English), 1528 (Jordan/Arabic), 1923 (Indonesian), 2048 (Pakistan/English), 2098 (Nigeria/English).

52. Pippa Norris and Ronald Inglehart. "Islamic Culture and Democracy: Testing the 'Clash of Civilizations' Thesis," *Comparative Sociology* 1, nos. 3–4 (2003): 235–63.

53. Andrew Kohut et al., *Questionnaire: Pew Global Attitudes Survey, 2002* (Washington, D.C.: Pew Research Center for the People and the Press, 2003), 25. Only the English-language questionnaire is available in the survey documentation.

54. Similar findings emerge from another Pew question about whether "suicide bombings and other forms of violence against civilian targets are justified in order to defend Islam from its enemies." Variation among countries was large, while the effects of poverty and education were small and mixed. See C. Christine Fair and

Bryan Shepherd, "Who Supports Terrorism? Evidence from Fourteen Muslim Countries," *Studies in Conflict and Terrorism* 29 (January/February 2006): 62, 65–68, 70–71; Ethan Bueno de Mesquita, *Correlates of Public Support for Terrorism in the Muslim World*, Working Paper (Washington, D.C.: U.S. Institute of Peace, 2007), 36–37, 44.

55. Asef Bayat, "Revolution without Movement, Movement without Revolution: Comparing Islamic Activism in Iran and Egypt," *Comparative Studies in Society and History* 40 (January 1998): 136–69.

56. Mansoor Moaddel, "The Saudi Public Speaks: Religion, Gender, and Politics," *International Journal of Middle East Studies* 38 (February 2006): 84.

57. Lawrence, *Defenders of God*, 7, 13–14.

58. Kurzman, *Unthinkable Revolution in Iran*; Charles Kurzman, "Can Understanding Undermine Explanation?" *Philosophy of the Social Sciences* 34 (September 2004): 328–51; Ali Hassan Zaidi, "A Critical Misunderstanding: Islam and Dialogue in the Human Sciences," *International Sociology* 22 (July 2007): 411–34.

Sufism, Exemplary Lives, and Social Science in Pakistan

DAVID GILMARTIN

They are and they aren't; they do and they don't.

Clifford Geertz, *Islam Observed*

As Marcia Hermansen and Bruce Lawrence have noted, *tazkira*s of Sufi saints trace "memory through the lives of heroes."[1] They are heroes because their lives embody many of the most basic ideals of Islamic civilization. Both through the tracing of exemplary genealogy and through stories of exemplary behavior and exemplary power, the lives of Sufi saints embody, in the eyes of many, how God's purposes for mankind have been brought to earth. And yet, for this very reason, critical also to the stories of Sufi saints is their particularity. The stories of Sufis have power precisely because they have dramatized how civilizational ideals—imagined as being shared by vast portions of humanity—have been brought to bear in the most particularistic places and amid the most mundane of experiences. That is why these stories can be used to trace simultaneously the operation of civilizational identities and of the most local—and sometimes competitive—particularistic identities. The historical association of Sufis with particular cities, places, or communities (or even dynasties) provides ample evidence of this.

A consequence is that stories of Sufis also embody, as dramatically as any sources we have, the tensions between civilizational ideals and the operation of local power structures—whether those of states, tribes, kinship networks, or urban patronage—in shaping Muslim lives. Peter Brown noticed long ago these tensions in the lives of saints more generally in commenting on the holy men of early Christianity. Saints were often portrayed as the ideal embodiments of the structures of leadership and authority around which everyday life was structured. They were, as Brown wrote, frequently portrayed in hagiographical writing as patrons par excellence—in a society in which patronage was central to social order.[2] Yet, at the same time, they embodied (or at least allowed their followers to catch a glimpse of) those transcendent ideals that linked everyday life, however tenuously, to the ideal models at the core of civilization. Life in the late Roman Empire, as Brown argued, was marked by a "permanent ache" of "center" and "periphery," between the core values of civilization and of Christianity and the local realities of everyday life. It was in this context that the holy man, whatever his frequent place as a patron in local society, was also a "'Christ-carrying' exemplar," a reminder of those larger divine principles that gave meaning to lives that were defined by pressures and powers of far more mundane sorts.[3]

This duality marked saints in South Asia as well. Life in South Asia was defined by the tension between center and periphery in a variety of senses. In both the Delhi Sultanate and the Mughal Empire, centralized authority was legitimized by appeals to transcendent principles, and yet practical power was built around local negotiation, patronage, tribal power, and mundane networks of influence (and armed strength). For most, central power was distant, and yet its presence was dramatized through a variety of connecting links, sacred genealogies, rituals, and architectural sites that suggested the power and pull of the "center," even on local life. In this context Sufis (and their shrines), like Christian holy men, made locally manifest the principles of central Islamic power on which transcendent power was based—and in the process helped to legitimize the Islamicate state. Yet at the very same time, the particularity of Sufi power (with its powerful local associations) dramatized the periphery's inescapable particularity and intractability. For rulers Sufis were thus, as the writings of many historians have made clear, simultaneously instruments of legitimation and figures of potential political subversion.[4]

The focus of this essay will be on the ways that the stories of Sufi saints can be read as diagnostic of the tensions marking the principles of state authority in South Asia as they have changed over time. The close connections between Sufis and structures of political influence have been remarked by many. Deriving from Persianate rule, the very language of South Asian Sufi power, as Richard M. Eaton has argued, tended both to mirror and to mimic the language of central authority.[5] But by bringing the language of divine power to earth—in relation to particular localities, particular claims to spiritual precedence (hinging on *silsilah* and genealogy), and particular networks of political connection and patronage—Sufi stories also suggested how the inherent tensions between transcendent principle and local power have been negotiated. It is the argument of this paper that in the colonial period and beyond, lives of Sufi saints have continued to provide lenses through which we can examine the tensions inherent in the constitution of political authority within the Islamic tradition as it has changed over time. In particular the changing lives of Sufi saints provide us a window on how the structural changes in politics associated with the emergence of the nation-state in South Asia have been negotiated in their relationship to Islam.

Sufis, Colonialism, and Pakistan

This essay focuses on retellings of the lives of Sufi saints in Pakistan after 1947, and on their relationship to new conceptualizations of Pakistan as a nation. A critical backdrop for this is the structural transformations that marked the British colonial period in South Asia. There is little doubt that colonial rule defined a set of attitudes toward Sufis that were related to changing assumptions about the legitimizing principles of colonial political power. British rule was in some ways, like earlier empires, built on the tensions between center and periphery. The central authority of the British, like that of earlier empires, was linked to a vision of the state as a focal point for civilization in South Asia—the node from which civilization, linked to British visions of science and "modernity," radiated to the intractable "peripheries" of a "traditional" world. Yet in relation to Sufis and Sufism, this new imperial structure was marked by significant contradictions.

At the heart of these contradictions was the fact that the imperial center in this case was not Muslim. This did not mean, of course, that Sufis and Sufi shrines did not continue under the British to be hinges between the central principles of Islamic civilization and India's myriad particularisms. But Sufis and Sufi practices now held a far different relationship to the imperial state. To the extent that Sufi shrines continued to embody the magnetic echoes of a universalizing Islamic civilizational center, this represented a potential threat to the civilizational foundations of British colonial authority.[6] Yet as centers of local cultural influence, Sufi shrines represented important local nodes to which the British sought to link imperial power. As Katherine Pratt Ewing has argued, the British developed strategies of interpretation relating to Sufism that sought to negotiate the tensions inherent in the position of Sufi shrines within the new imperial order. The image of the idealized Sufi as an exemplar of civilizational values was in fact not generally denied by the British (thus legitimizing Sufi shrines as sites of local authority), but the contemporary position of Sufis was inescapably particularized. British writing linked dead Sufis with the image of an Islamic civilization that was now irretrievably *lost*. Sufis (including shrine custodians, *sajjada nishins*), as they actually existed in contemporary India, were portrayed as immersed in local superstition, a manifestation of the "traditionalism" of a local culture that was now echoing not the universal values of Islamic civilization but a particularized Islamic culture that could be readily juxtaposed against the universal values of science and modernity embodied by the British. "This split," as Ewing writes, "was part of a rhetorical strategy, grounded in a modernist ideology. . . . The object of yearning—the Oriental sage—was safely unreachable, while the other who was immediately present was denigrated, abjected."[7] The image of the Sufi as civilizational exemplar was thus split from the Sufi who was firmly embedded in local life.

This split also shaped a growing critique of Sufis among reform-minded Muslims—particularly among the *ulama.* Influenced perhaps in part by Orientalist writings, reformist attacks on Sufis and Sufism reflected the structural transformations between center and periphery that marked British rule. With the political center no longer linked to Islamic values, reformers drew on long traditions of Islamic reform (and fear of worldly corruption) to stress the importance of the internalization of the core values of the Islamic tradition within individual Muslims. In such a view, the center was, in a sense, internalized. Sufi practices thus became emblematic in these circumstances of the new dangers posed by local and internal peripheries to the core of the Muslim self.[8] With Sufism increasingly identified with South Asian particularism—and increasingly divorced from an image of an Islamic civilizational center—it is no surprise that Islamic reform often focused its harshest attacks on what were increasingly viewed as the degraded forms of a particularized South Asian Sufi Islam.[9]

Yet the contradictory position of Sufis within the new colonial framework was shaped not just by the emergence of a non-Muslim imperial center, but also by fundamental structural changes in British rule that challenged the ordering vision of center and periphery as a frame for imperial authority. Fueled, particularly in the late nineteenth and early twentieth centuries, by new state technologies of knowledge and social scientific quantification—and later by new structures of popular representation defined by elected legislatures—center and periphery were increasingly transformed in British India into "state" and "society." Indian (and Muslim) society was increasingly conceptualized—by the British and many Indians alike—as an autonomous and reified entity (shaped by maps, ethnographies, censuses, and social scientific data), not simply as the periphery surrounding a magnetic center. And within this framework, Sufism took on new cultural meanings. It emerged not just as a frame for the embodiment of civilizational ideals within exemplary individuals, but also as a form of Islam that was, far more than the reformist Islam of the *ulama,* embedded in the autonomous (if often hierarchical) society of the "people" themselves. For some Sufism increasingly became a marker of Muslim "popular culture" in India, a sign of the people's cultural autonomy as an imagined entity and thus potentially a key element in imagining a "nation."

This is in no way to suggest that negative valuations of Sufism—either from the British or reformists—disappeared within this context; quite to the contrary. Indeed the ambiguities implicit in the position of Sufis became all the more marked with the movement for creation of a separate Muslim state in British India in the mid–twentieth century. The call for Pakistan was, of course, explicitly justified by Muhammad Ali Jinnah with an appeal to the idea of a distinct Muslim nation in British India. And yet the movement for Pakistan, with its initially highly symbolic (and territorially vague) definition, testified in many respects to the continuing salience in Muslim India of a vision of the state constructed around core and periphery. Indeed it could be argued that the Pakistan movement was an attempt to reinvest the state with Islamic principles, to establish the state, in other words, as a new, political, Islamic center or core, around which the diverse periphery of Muslims in India would be organized and symbolically pulled together. This was, ironically, in some ways implicit in Jinnah's largely deterritorialized "two-nation theory" itself. Nevertheless the structure of politics in late imperial India guaranteed that the vision of Pakistan could only be realized within the framework of a political order, long in formation in British India, organized around territorialized state and society. The importance of provincial elections in the legitimation of the Pakistan demand provides only one example of this.

It is little surprise that the position of Sufis in these circumstances was fraught with ambiguity. In mobilizing the people in support of Pakistan, Jinnah and the Muslim League sought the support of Sufis on a broad scale in the elections of 1946. Whatever the symbolic meanings attached to Pakistan, it was in fact not the *ulama*, with their focus on the internalization of a core of Muslim identity, but Sufis, with their connections to local society and local structures of power, who played the decisive role in mobilizing the support necessary in the elections of 1946 to give victory to the Muslim League and make the creation of Pakistan a reality. But Sufis also embodied the multiple meanings and ambiguities attached to Muslim identity in the transition from empire to independent national state.[10] It is little wonder, in these circumstances, that Sufism subsequently played a critical—if highly contested—role in Pakistan's search for a distinctive "national culture" as colonial rule came to an end.

The State, Sufi Lives, and National Culture

The twists and turns of the story of Pakistan's governmental and nongovernmental efforts to define a national culture are complex and well beyond the scope of this paper. But at the risk of some oversimplification, I would like to compare two distinct approaches to the biographies of Sufi saints—and their relationship to national identity—that were developed by government institutions in the early decades of Pakistan's existence. The first of these institutions, the Department of Auqaf, was established during the rule of Field Marshal Ayub Khan in order to take control of West Pakistan's shrine and mosque endowments. The second, the National Institute of Folk Heritage (IFH, or Lok Virsa), was founded under the government of Zulfiqar Ali Bhutto in the 1970s to study and promote Pakistan's popular culture.

The West Pakistan Waqf Properties Ordinances (1959 and 1961) established the Department of Auqaf with the aim of giving Ayub's government enhanced control over Pakistan's religious institutions.[11] "The auqaf acts were intended," Ewing writes, "to undercut the political power of both the hereditary pir families (the *sajjada nishin*s) and the ulama (scholars of Islamic law)."[12] This was not the first time that the government had attempted to take control of the *auqaf* supporting Sufi shrines; in the 1930s the Punjab Unionist Party, with British support, had unsuccessfully attempted much the same thing. But the aim of these efforts was not simply to give the government greater leverage over religious institutions, but also to use such control to redefine the relationship of Sufism to Pakistani culture. It was thus an answer both to those *ulama* and Islamists who attacked Sufism altogether as a particularistic corruption of pure Islamic principle and to those (including many on the Left) interested in developing in Pakistan a secular national culture. At the heart of the effort was an attempt to manipulate both Sufism and Sufi shrines in Pakistan to help establish a "national" culture linked to Islam and to the people.

As Ewing persuasively argues, the ideology behind the government's *auqaf* policy owed much to the thinking of Muhammad Iqbal.[13] Iqbal, who died in 1938, had in fact been strongly influenced by European writings that had drawn sharp distinctions between the great Sufi masters of the past who embodied Islam's civilizational aspirations and contemporary Sufis, who had become either too otherworldly or too corrupt.[14] But if the British had emphasized this temporally split image of Sufis and Sufism for their own legitimating purposes, Ayub's government now sought to turn it in a somewhat different direction. Though the Sufi masters of the past may perhaps have been separated in time from contemporary Pakistani society, their images could nevertheless be mobilized at Sufi shrines as models for the ideal of Pakistani citizenship. It was not contemporary Sufis but long-dead ones, whose exemplary lives had once brought the magnetic echoes of an Islamic civilizational center to South Asia, who were now to serve as models, through their specifically Pakistani shrines, for the internalized values of a specifically Pakistani nation.

Much of this hinged on the ways that the Auqaf Department managed the shrines it took over. Ewing notes that the Auqaf Department attempted to shift attention away from the authority of the local *sajjada nishin*, usually a lineal descendant of the original saint, and toward the role of the shrine itself as a social welfare institution and center of learning, with research centers and libraries associated with the patronage of the government.[15] Such shifts were also at the heart of the Auqaf Department's management of shrine rituals, such as the yearly *'urs* (or saint's death anniversary), in which government officials now assumed precedence over living shrine custodians. But perhaps most important, these shifts were evident in the department's patronizing the publication of new Sufi lives, or *tazkiras*, that embodied its concern to develop a new Pakistani national identity at the intersection of an imagined Islamic past and modernity. As the director of the Auqaf Department's Ulama Academy at Lahore explained in the foreword to one of the department's publications, "Along with the responsibilities of looking after the important shrines of religious men, the Punjab Auqaf Department feels strongly the need to protect and to spread the religious (*dini*) and learned (*ilmi*) legacy left by these religious men."[16] And as an Auqaf Department pamphlet on the life of Baba Farid explained in the late 1970s, it was a central part of the responsibility of the department to use the "circumstances of the lives and teachings" of the great Sufis of Pakistan to make the people aware of the role these great men played in bringing Islam to the people of the South Asian subcontinent. It was only the efforts of these Sufis centuries ago that had made possible in the mid–twentieth century the emergence of "a great Islamic country" as "Pakistan appeared on the map of the world."[17] The lives of great Sufis were thus linked directly to the emergence of Pakistan as a territorial nation.

To protect themselves from the attacks of scripturalizing reformers, the Auqaf Department tended in analyzing the lives of the saints to use a language strongly shaped by rationalism, with internalized Islamic values emphasized and miracles downplayed. Many (though hardly all) *tazkiras* used the apparatus of modern historical science, including footnoting and references to a wide range of sources. The Islamic learning of saints and their work in *tabligh* (or the popular spread of Islam) tended to be strongly emphasized. This is not to say, of course, that the Auqaf Department ignored entirely the popular stories or local beliefs about well-known Sufis, but these were marginalized. The author of an Auqaf Department publication on the life of Sakhi Sarwar, for example, was well aware of the existence of large numbers of folk stories about this famous saint (many of them collected by the British). But his concern in the *tazkira* was to transcend these folktales to use the story of the saint's life to tell a greater truth about Islam and humanity itself. "There is no shortage of traditional stories about [Sakhi Sarwar]," he says, "but the mention of truth [in these stories] is equal to the amount of salt found in flour."[18] As to particular customs associated with shrines, such as the passage through the *bihishti darwaza* (or gateway to heaven) at the *'urs* of Baba Farid, these were made note of without reference to any of their popular associations.[19]

But at the same time the Auqaf Department understood well the importance of the shrines' local groundedness in shaping their meanings for Pakistanis and Pakistani national identity. Recognition of the specific association of shrines with the territory of Pakistan was in fact central to the department's agenda. Yet this defined as well the difficult contradictions the department had to traverse. In many cases the department found it hard to escape the local political pressures that defined the popularity and influence of many shrines and Sufis in their local political settings. This was evident in the ongoing conflicts between the department and many local *sajjada nishin*s, conflicts embodied in the numerous challenges that the policies of the Auqaf Department faced in Pakistan's courts, where appeals to local customs and traditions sometimes provided powerful grounds for local custodians to resist Auqaf Department takeovers.[20] The tensions between the shrines (and Sufism) as emblematic of locally embedded power and identity on the one hand and as the target of a strongly statist national project on the other in fact lurk beneath the surface in the Auqaf Department's publications. At stake was the very definition of a distinctive Pakistani society that subsumed Sufi shrines in a distinctly Pakistani culture.

But the tensions evident in the Auqaf Department's publication of Sufi lives come into even clearer focus if they are contrasted with the tensions marking the approach toward Sufis of the Institute of Folk Heritage (Lok Virsa). The IFH was established in 1974 under Prime Minister Bhutto as an autonomous government institute whose mission was to preserve and perpetuate "the folk and traditional heritage of Pakistan."[21] On the surface its purpose was thus quite different from that of the Auqaf Department. But the underlying foundation and mission of the IFH disclosed the same concern to define a national culture that underlay many Auqaf Department publications. This was put quite clearly by Uxi Mufti, the institute's director: it is "Pakistan's folklore, popular beliefs, popular religion, attitudes, common values and ideals," he wrote, "which make Pakistan one nation." Like the Department of Auqaf, Lok Virsa from the beginning saw Sufism as central to the meaning of their project. Sufism, as Mufti wrote, was the foundation for "the bulk of Pakistan's folklore," as it was the form of Islam closest to the lives of the people. It had in fact shaped the historical dynamism of Pakistan's folk culture. Though it varied "from region to region," popular Sufism was marked by common messages and desires, embodying the basic values of the people.[22] By grounding Islam in everyday lives, Sufism was thus central, in the eyes of many IFH researchers, to the popular culture defining the Pakistani people.

Yet the approach of the IFH to the study of Sufis and Sufism—and to the relationship between the universal and the particular—differed sharply from that of the Auqaf Department. Though they did not (as far as I have discovered) comment directly—or critically—on the publication program of the Auqaf Department or on their management of shrines, IFH researchers were quick to dismiss the assumptions that led writers of Sufi *tazkira*s, including those of the

Auqaf Department, to devalue oral tradition in favor of a strong emphasis on Sufism's literate heritage and to elide Sufism's local particulars in the name of an ideal model of Sufi piety that could serve as a model for the national citizen. The notion that what is unwritten is less worthy than written traditions, Mufti declared, is "nothing but urban snobbery." Indeed it was the unwritten character of Pakistan's folk heritage that had allowed it to survive as a distinct, vital, and dynamic culture in the face of the ongoing efforts by states over the centuries to control and discipline it. "The fact that Pakistan's folk culture is not written," Mufti declared in 1977, "something inscribed in a book and preserved in cold print, but is actually lived, talked of, believed in, felt and transmitted, ensures its continuity as well as longevity over written cultures."[23] This was, by implication at least, all the more important in the face of state efforts in Pakistan to impose textual visions of normative Islam (and of exemplary Sufis saints) on the Pakistani people. As one Lok Virsa publication noted in 1990 in the wake of the authoritarian and Islamicizing policies of Gen. Zia al-Haq, "The suffering of a people[,] and their contempt for oppression, is expressed powerfully in oral traditions which cannot be banned as easily as written material." Oral popular tradition, here associated with freedom, thus reflected the "unwritten voice of the people."[24]

But the key to turning this vision of a diverse, autonomous, and popular oral culture into a unity—a basis for a national Pakistani identity—was the heavy reliance of the IFH in their research methodology on the universalizing language of social science. Here the contrast with the Auqaf Department was most marked. The search for cultural unity, in the eyes of the IFH, lay not in turning shrines into centers for dissemination of Islamic ideals or in turning the lives of Sufi saints into exemplars of core civilizational values, but rather in using social science to record, study, and give value to the culture and beliefs that defined the modern cultural fabric of the Pakistani people themselves. IFH researchers thus toured Pakistan extensively, interviewing peasants and tribesmen, recording and videotaping their practices and customs. As the institute's director said in describing the institute's mission: "The task is an all-important one of National Reconstruction and National projection through culture. It implies systematic research, re-discovery and re-evaluation of our historic tradition and its re-organization and integration with new elements created by modern conditions."[25] Drawing on international social scientific standards, the deputy director of the institute in 1977 published an Urdu pamphlet detailing the proper methodology for the Pakistani folklorist: "Our effort," he declared, "is that folklore in Pakistan might be given a . . . scientific status. It should be incorporated in school, college and university curricula in the same way as other social sciences."[26] Rather than commission the writings of new Sufi *tazkira*s, as did the

Auqaf Department, the IFH thus published accounts of regional cultures containing a wealth of popular stories about Sufis and other forms of popular culture. They also published the poetry of many of Pakistani's great Sufis, particularly, though hardly exclusively, those based in Pakistan's regional languages (thus bridging to some extent the line between oral and written traditions).[27] By the 1980s and 1990s, the institute had established procedures for cataloging, studying, and archiving masses of "folk" production—artifacts, transcriptions of stories, recordings of songs, videotapes of festivals, and so forth—many of which related to Sufis, festivals, and the lives of Sufi saints. These were preserved in a computerized documentation center and media library, displayed at a museum in Islamabad, and disseminated through a publishing program.[28]

In contrast to the Auqaf Department, Lok Virsa thus traversed the tensions between the universal and the particular in the stories of Sufi saints in a very different way. Rather than trying to adapt creatively an old tradition of *tazkira* writing to modern purposes, the IFH turned to scientific traditions of folk studies, thus adapting a genre of folklore study with deep roots in the development of European nationalism to the study of Islamic popular culture. In some ways these traditions harked back to the British, who had tried to identify the state with an Indian society quintessentially defined by its localisms, even as it had sought to transcend the parochial character of local identities by "explaining" them in terms of generalized scientific theories of social evolution and social organization. But in an independent Pakistan, the political and cultural purposes of the IFH became quite different. Unlike the colonial British, the institute did not disparage popular Sufism but instead sought to use it as a foundation for a popular Pakistani culture simultaneously indigenous and Islamic. Indeed the director of the institute underscored the critical importance of the indigenous study of Pakistani folklore in freeing Pakistan from the "cultural domination" of the industrialized West.[29] It was in fact no accident that the IFH first came into existence in the early 1970s under the Bhutto regime, which had restored democracy to Pakistan and was itself groping for a popular national culture to support its sometimes anti-Western "Islamic socialist" program.

At the same time, the effort of the IFH to define a national culture through folk studies, encompassing both Sufism and Sufi lives, embodied its own contradictions. Whether in attempts to separate a distinctively (oral and autonomous) Pakistani Sufi tradition from the larger Sufi textual tradition (an often problematic undertaking) or in efforts to mobilize international social science in the name of an autonomous popular Pakistani identity, the IFH has, like the Department of Auqaf, sought, not always successfully, to traverse the tensions between the universal and the particular in the attempt to link Pakistan's Islamic past to the definition of a new nation.

The Case of the Shrine of Shah Daulah

The contrast between these approaches to Sufism and Sufi lives can be traced in the life story of one saint, the famous seventeenth-century Sufi Shah Daulah, whose shrine is in the northern Punjab town of Gujrat. As in the modern study of much in Pakistani culture, post-1947 appreciations of this shrine—and of Shah Daulah—have been much influenced by the contradictory attitudes of the British during the colonial period. In fact British interest in the shrine clearly disclosed the same contradictory political and cultural concerns that in the nineteenth and early twentieth centuries motivated colonial attitudes toward Sufism generally. Some British observers saw the shrine as emblematic of the powerful local associations that defined the essence of the traditional in India. In his *Chronicles of Gujrat*, written in 1902, the British deputy commissioner, Capt. A. C. Elliott, devoted two chapters to Shah Daulah and his shrine, noting the saint's local importance as the "guardian of Gujrat." For Elliott the local folk stories about the life of the saint provided a wealth of local history, and he devoted one chapter to retelling the life of the saint and his miracles, including his move from Sialkot to Gujrat on "heavenly instructions"; his construction, with divine help, of numerous bridges, tanks, and mosques in the city; and his miraculous encounter with Jahangir, during which he defied the Mughal emperor's attempts to poison him. All of these helped to define the saint's significance as Gujrat's special protector and patron—and a man worthy of a special place in Elliott's depiction of local Punjabi culture.[30]

Yet at the same time, Elliott's analysis of the saint was deeply affected by his moral view of the seemingly degraded popular practices associated with the shrine. Elliott's views on the shrine, like those of other British administrators, were strongly influenced by its popularity in the nineteenth century as the center of a fertility cult, which was closely associated with the birth of microcephalic, mentally retarded children known as *chuha*s or "rat children," who were kept at the shrine as beggars. People believed, Elliott wrote, that "Shah Daulah as a saint could bring about the birth of a child for any parents," but the price was that "the first child was always a *chuha* and had to be presented to Shah Daulah's shrine as an offering." Though sometimes people vowed to pay money to the shrine instead, if that vow were also forgotten, then "the next child born was, by the influence of the outraged saint, born a *chuha*, as well as all subsequent children, till the vow was performed."

Such customs deeply influenced Elliott's interpretation of the shrine's history and fed into the wider tendency among the British to denigrate contemporary Sufi practices as morally degraded and built on superstition. In fact the association of microcephalic children with the shrine became the subject of a large and continuing British commentary, as M. Miles documented in 1996.[31] Both ethnographers and doctors were fascinated with the shrine, and many speculated on the question as to whether the children were "artificially deformed." Some, such as Captain Ewens, superintendent of the Lunatic Asylum at Lahore, approached the shrine with careful local observation. Ewens visited the shrine at the beginning of the twentieth century and recorded observations on the microcephalic children, assessing the degree of care (and exploitation) that they actually received. But most observers were far more interested in dwelling on the monetary exploitation and possible deformation of the children as illustrative of the debased state of Sufi practices and credulous state of the people.[32] Captain Elliott's conclusions about Shah Daulah himself, whose supposed powers were central to popular beliefs about the saint, were perhaps typical. In spite of his miraculous powers in the aid of Gujrat and his undoubted importance in local culture, Elliott's ultimate appreciation of the saint shaped his own Victorian evaluation of the purposes to which the Shah Daulah's powers had been put. "Many of his acts, which are imputed to him for righteousness," Elliott wrote, could only appear "to western minds" in a far different light. The story of the saint's power and "the popular theory as to the production of chuhas" combined "to give Shah Daulah a character which in these days would render him notorious rather than respected."[33]

Such ambivalence on the part of Elliott with regard to the shrine and the saint reflected British attitudes toward Sufism generally. Such shrines were important to an emerging British vision of society defined by the ethnographic study of local practices. Whether in administrative settlement literature or in local chronicles such as Elliott's, the British in the late nineteenth century increasingly used ethnographic study to give form and meaning to local culture as a critical element in the structure of Indian society under colonial rule. Sufism in a sense embodied these local cultures, and no example illustrated this more clearly than the case of Shah Daulah and Gujrat. At the same time, it was in large part through the denigration of popular Sufi customs such as those associated with Shah Daulah (and their complete detachment from any connection to Islamic universalism) that the British asserted their own identification with a universalist modernity that transcended such localism and defined their control over it.

These attitudes provided the backdrop after Pakistan's creation for the contrasting treatments of the shrine and its *chuha*s by the Auqaf Department and the Institute of Folk Heritage. The shrine of Shah Daulah was in 1960 one of the first to be taken over by the Auqaf Department after the passage of the first West Pakistan Auqaf Ordinance. So well known was the shrine for its particular association with Shah Daulah's "rat children" that the Pakistan Supreme Court, which decided in favor of the Auqaf Department in an appeal lodged by the custodians against the shrine's takeover, made reference to these *chuha*s as the most distinctive mark of the shrine's identity, even though their existence had not been raised in the plaintiff's petition.[34] It is little surprise, in these circumstances, that once the shrine was safely under Auqaf Department control, the department sought quickly to distance itself from these popular practices and published a pamphlet retelling the life of the original saint in a way that was clearly intended to reorient the popular meanings attached to the shrine by redirecting attention back to Shah Daulah himself.[35]

The approach of the department in recounting the life of Shah Daulah in fact reflected the strategies commonly deployed in Auqaf Department *tazkira*s. The foundations of a modern Pakistani culture were now linked to the exemplary behavioral models embodied in the lives of the original saints. Shah Daulah's miracles, which provided the foundation for Elliott's account, were virtually ignored in the Auqaf Department's pamphlet on him, as they were impossible to confirm—and were in any case problematic within the context of rational Islamic principles. Instead the department stressed Shah Daulah's life as a learned Sufi, who in twelve years of study in a Sufi *khanaqah* became well versed in *tasawwuf* (Sufism) and *ma'rifat* (mystical knowledge) and sought "to merge his own ego (*khudi*) in the personality of the *mahbub-i haqiqi* (God)." The popular superstitions at the shrine associated with deformed children were explained not as a product of the concerns of the saint, who himself had cared for the disabled, but as an outgrowth of the propaganda employed by Shah Daulah's successors, who encouraged the popular fertility beliefs associated with the shrine and employed microcephalic children in begging for their own financial gain. This the Auqaf Department strongly condemned, but tellingly it did so in a language of analysis seemingly derived not from the British but from the example provided by the life of Shah Daulah himself. It is "after all enough for us to know," the pamphlet thus declared, that Shah Daulah was a Sufi who spent his life seeking to spread Islam and help the common man, a model any Muslim (and any good Pakistani) might seek to follow. Retelling the story of Shah Daulah's life thus served what the department declared in the pamphlet to be among the central "purposes of *auqaf*": "to raise the standards of religious customs" and "to make holy places [such as these shrines] centers of social, cultural, and spiritual restoration according to the principles of Islam." In political terms, though the department's reinterpretation of the life of the saint fully recognized the saint's local associations, the shrine itself now became a vehicle through which the folk culture of Gujrat could be transformed as its local saint was made to conform to the standards of all the great saints of Pakistan.[36]

Yet the tensions in such a view, which discounted local culture on its own terms, can be seen in comparing the Auqaf Department's approach with one coming from the IFH. In contrast to the Auqaf Department, it was the study of local culture that was at the very heart of Lok Virsa's mission. In fact the very format in which a brief account of Shah Daulah was presented by the IFH—in a compendium of stories and vignettes of Punjabi folk culture—indicated its view of the shrine not as a symbol of a Sufi ideal but as a part of Punjab's general fabric of folk culture. The story of Shah Daulah and his shrine was only one of many contained in an IFH book called *Lok Panjab* ("The Ways of the People of Panjab," as the back cover subtitles it), which, as it described itself, was a reconstruction of the cultural and social milieu of the Punjab, encompassing its "habits, folk tales, proverbs, figures of speech, romance and stories of miracles performed by Sufis and Saints."[37] Indeed in this, the approach of the IFH suggested the importance for Pakistani identity (which grew organically from Pakistan's regional identities) of a popular culture defined fundamentally from below (though necessarily systematized from above by experts and the state). The stories of the miracles of Shah Daulah were related by the IFH (at least in aspiration) as the people of Gujrat themselves had told them, for in the eyes of the IFH, the stories of the people must speak for themselves.

Still in confronting the fertility customs associated with the shrine, the institute ran into its own problems, particularly in defining the relationship between local culture and the universal principles of social science. It was social science, after all, that provided the wherewithal for the IFH to call into existence the image of a unified Pakistani "society" and "nation," whatever the realities of Pakistan's varied local cultures. Social scientific explanations for folk practices and beliefs were thus critical to the IFH's approach. Rejecting a moral explanation for (or condemnation of) the popular customs associated with *chuha*s at the shrine, the author of the IFH account of Shah Daulah thus tried to explain them instead in terms of the universal human impulses that have been identified by modern social and psychological science. Rather than condemn the presence of *chuha*s at the shrine from the perspective either of Victorian morality or from that of an exemplary Sufi idealism embodied by a long-dead saint, the IFH account sought rather to "explain" the shrine's practices by resorting to the "scientific" truths of folk psychology. "It is said that the first child of those women who make vows at Shah Daulah's shrine is a *chuha*. In addition to spiritual agency, there is a scientific (*aqli*, rational) argument in this matter. When you put a picture of a beautiful baby or of an African (*habshi*) in the room of a pregnant woman, then [because it is imprinted on the woman's mind] it is bound to affect the baby about to be born."[38] Here, in building an argument about the births of *chuha*s, the author drew on the common belief in Pakistani society—to which the numerous pictures of babies for sale in the bazaars of Pakistan attest—that pictures of healthy babies in the homes of pregnant women tend to promote healthy births.[39] He continued: "In the same way, when women make vows at Shah Daulah's tomb, they accept in their minds that their first child will be a *chuha.* Consequently, under this psychological (*nafsiyati*) agency, the first child in these women's homes takes on the *chuha* form."

The scientific form of this explanation (whatever the blurring of a line between folk belief and science) points toward its significance for the IFH. Given this explanation, any reform of practices at the shrine must take on a very different significance from that given to it by the Auqaf Department. If the presence of *chuha*s represents a moral problem, it is not to be solved by challenging the validity of popular culture or by assimilating it into a reformed Sufi worldview exemplified by model saints. Rather folk culture evolves according to its own internal dynamics. The most significant modern reform at the shrine is thus one that, as the author of the account tells it, was already well under way at the time he wrote. The gifts of microcephalic children to the shrine were in fact increasingly being replaced by the donations of small, silver replicas of children, which were sold in the lane leading to the shrine's entrance and hung on the shrine by its devotees. In light of the analysis of the shrine put forward by the IFH, this reform had a double significance. On the one hand, it undermined the so-called psychological foundation for the birth of *chuha*s. But perhaps equally important, it did so without challenging the validity of the people's vows and their basic assumptions about the power of the saint.[40]

Such an explanation of ongoing practices at the Shah Daulah shrine suggests the importance to the IFH of having its own methodology for the study and validation of local culture. As social science tells us, popular culture has its own rationality, just as society has its own autonomous dynamics. This is essential for the cultural grounding of the nation, which is Islamic because popular culture (in its *particular* Pakistani form) is Islamic. And yet the tensions between the IFH's explanation and the realities behind the practices of the shrine remained in some ways just as marked in this IFH account as the tension between the Auqaf Department's idealized reformulation of Shah Daulah's life and the realities of local power structures in which the shrine was embedded. Perhaps most important, we can see in both accounts the ways that the definition of the nation and its relationship to Islam has been fought out over the most local and mundane of popular Sufi practices.

Conclusion

The stories of Sufi lives and Sufi shrines have proved critical in a variety of ways to attempts to negotiate the existence of a national culture in Pakistan, rooted in appeals both to universal values and to the particularities of Pakistan. Sufism as a historical phenomenon has long defined itself at the critical—and problematic—intersection of the universal and the particular. Sufi lives in earlier eras exemplified the "permanent ache" between center and periphery that defined the great empires of Islamic civilization in India. But Sufi stories have proved no less important in modern times in negotiating the tensions between the particular and the universal that are central in the definition of state and society in Pakistan— and in the definition of the nation. Contrasting the approaches to Sufi lives of the Department of Auqaf and of the Institute of Folk Heritage, both of which rely on state patronage, has given us a glimpse of this. But this only scratches the surface of this story. As Jamal Malik has argued in analyzing a recent Urdu short story about the shrine of Shah Daulah, modern Pakistani literature as well has struggled with the tensions between the particularities of power and the universal promise of freedom rooted in the structure of Pakistani Sufism.[41] The lives of Sufi saints will undoubtedly continue to provide an important perspective on the tensions between civilizational ideals and the operation of local power structures, both in the construction of state and society and in modern individual lives. Located precisely at the intersection of the universal and the particular, the changing history of Sufi lives, far more than abstract arguments about the relationship of the "nation" and "Islam," provides us a critical window on the often charged relationship between Islam and the national community.

NOTES

1. Bruce B. Lawrence and Marcia Hermansen, "Indo-Persian Tazkiras as Memorative Communications," in *Beyond Turk and Hindu: Rethinking Religious Identities in Islamicate South Asia*, ed. David Gilmartin and Bruce B. Lawrence (Gainesville: University Press of Florida, 2000), 149–75.

2. Peter Brown, "The Rise and Function of the Holy Man in Late Antiquity," *Journal of Roman Studies* 61 (1971): 80–101.

3. Peter Brown, "The Saint as Exemplar in Late Antiquity," *Representations* 1 (1983): 9.

4. See, for example, K. A. Nizami, *Some Aspects of Religion and Politics in the Thirteenth Century* (Delhi: Idarah-i Adabiyat-i Delli, 1978). Some aspects of the tension inherent in "sacred peripherality" are discussed in Pnina Werbner and Helene Basu, "The Embodiment of Charisma," in *Embodying Charisma: Modernity, Locality and the Performance of Emotion in Sufi Cults*, ed. Pnina Werbner and Helene Basu (London: Routledge, 1998), 11–14.

5. Richard M. Eaton, "Court of Man, Court of God: Local Perceptions of the Shrine of Bâbâ Farîd, Pakpattan, Punjab," *Contributions to Asian Studies* 17 (1982): 44–61.

6. Such a view was, of course, not unreasonable, as Sufis were quite prominent in many parts of the world in resistance to the establishment of colonial domination.

7. Katherine Pratt Ewing, *Arguing Sainthood: Modernity, Psychoanalysis, and Islam* (Durham, N.C.: Duke University Press, 1997), 47.

8. This can be seen, for example, in the parallel dangers to Islamic reform posed by the influence of personal passion, local custom, and the pressures of everyday life. See, for example, Barbara Metcalf, "Islam and Custom in Nineteenth-Century India," *Contributions to Asian Studies* 17 (1982): 62–78, and also her translation of Maulana Ashraf Ali Thanwi's *Bihishti Zewar*, titled *Perfecting Women* (Berkeley: University of California Press, 1990).

9. This is, in effect, the argument made so persuasively by Clifford Geertz with respect to Indonesia and Morocco in *Islam Observed* (Chicago: University of Chicago Press, 1971).

10. Some of the contradictions in the Pakistan rhetoric of the 1946 election campaign are discussed in David Gilmartin, "A Magnificent Gift: Muslim Nationalism and the Election Process in Colonial Punjab," *Comparative Studies in Society and History* 40 (July 1998): 415–36.

11. It was later federalized under the terms of the Auqaf (Federal Control) Act of 1976, passed during the administration of Zulfiqar Ali Bhutto.

12. Ewing, *Arguing Sainthood*, 70.

13. Ibid., 68–71. Ewing suggests that Ayub's *auqaf* policy may have been influenced by the publication of *The Ideology of Pakistan and Its Implementation* (Lahore: Ghulam Ali, 1959) by Javid Iqbal, Iqbal's son. The book had a foreword by Ayub Khan.

14. Iqbal's contrast of early and later Sufis took basically two (slightly contradictory) forms. On the one hand, he saw the dynamism of the early Arabs as having been lost in Persian mysticism: "The sufi, who was a hero unrivalled in the service of the Lord; unrivalled in love; peerless in his sense of honour—He has lost himself in the thoughts of Persia; that traveler has lost himself in stages (*maqamat*)," wrote Iqbal in the *Saqi-nama*. On the other hand, he saw the contemporary *sajjada nishin*s of the Punjab as irretrievably corrupt compared with earlier Sufis (including those in the Persianate tradition). In his poem "To the Punjab Pirzadas," he compared Shaykh Ahmad Sirhindi, "whose neck did not bow in front of Jahangir," with Punjab's contemporary *pir*s, who had replaced the "cap of poverty" with the "crested turban" of worldly influence. Whatever the contradictions, the notion of decline and of a lost dynamism was at the heart of Iqbal's vision of Sufism. D. J. Matthews, trans., *Iqbal: A Selection of the Urdu Verse: Text and Translation* (London: School of Oriental and African Studies, University of London, 1993), 113–21, 125.

15. Ewing, *Arguing Sainthood*, 73.

16. Muhammad Yusuf Goraya, foreword to Hamid Khan Hamid, *Tazkirah-yi Hazrat Sakhi Sarwar* (Lahore: Ulama Akedami, Mahkama-yi Auqaf, 1975), 3.

17. Department of Auqaf, Ministry of Religious Affairs, *Baba Farid al-Din Ganj-i Shakar* (Islamabad: Administrator General of Auqaf, Ministry of Religious Affairs, Government of Pakistan, 1977), 1.

18. Hamid, *Tazkirah-yi Hazrat Sakhi Sarwar*, 6.

19. Department of Auqaf, *Baba Farid al-Din Ganj-i Shakar*, 15. For a discussion of passage through the *bihishti darwaza* (a small door into the tomb) during Baba Farid's *'urs*, and an analysis of its meanings through the lens of the tragedy that occurred in 2001 during a stampede at the shrine, see Robert Rozehnal, "*Faqir* or Faker? The Pakpattan Tragedy and the Politics of Sufism in Pakistan," *Religion* 36 (March 2006): 29–47.

20. For an example that shows the ongoing tension between the "public" claims on *auqaf* as defined under the West Pakistan Waqf Properties Ordinances and the claims of long-standing local custom in the operation of shrines, see the important legal battle over control of the shrine of Data Ganj Bakhsh in Lahore, *Haji Ghulam Rasool and Others vs. The Chief Administrator of Auqaf, West Pakistan*. Supreme Court Appeals nos. 127–67 of 1969, *All Pakistan Legal Decisions*, vol. 23 (1971), 376–93.

21. Institute of Folk Heritage, *Directory of Cultural Institutions in Pakistan* (Islamabad: Institute of Folk Heritage, 1980), 9–15.

22. Uxi Mufti, "The Folk Heritage of Pakistan," in National Institute of Folk and Traditional Heritage, *Folk Heritage of Pakistan, 1977* (Islamabad: Institute of Folk Heritage, 1977), 30.

23. Uxi Mufti, "The Crises in Folklore," in National Institute of Folk and Traditional Heritage, *Folk Heritage of Pakistan, 1977* (Islamabad: Institute of Folk Heritage, 1977), 25

24. "Lok Virsa—the National Institute of Folk and Traditional Heritage," in Institute of Folk Heritage, *Heritage 90* (Islamabad: Institute of Folk Heritage, 1990), 9.

25. Mufti, "Crises in Folklore," 25

26. Mazhar ul-Islam, *Foklor ki Pahli Kitab* (Islamabad: Institute of Folk Heritage, 1977), iii. The international connections of the IFH have subsequently been strengthened through collaborations with UNESCO.

27. By publishing some of the mystical poetry of the Indus region's great Sufis, Lok Virsa has, in effect, tried to claim them for Pakistan's "folk" tradition. See, for example, Karam Haidari, trans., *Pir Mahr Ali Shah: Panjabi aur Farsi Kalam, Urdu tarjama* (Islamabad: Lok Virse ka Qaumi Idarah, 1980); Sharif Kunjahi, trans., *Kahe Farid* (Islamabad: Lok Virse ka Qaumi Idarah, 1978); Lok Virsa, *Sachal Sarmast: Sindhi, Panjabi, Farsi aur Urdu Kalam, Urdu tarjama* (Islamabad: Lok Virse ka Qaumi Idarah, 1981). To support this appropriation, the claim was sometimes (though not always) made that the poetry was originally oral and written down only by followers.

28. As the director wrote in the 1980s, "Within a decade, Lok Virsa has grown from a fledgling endeavor to create a science of folklore." It had become "a complex whose projects and activities span over the roots of the entire nation." Uxi Mufti, *Documentation of Performing Arts and Crafts in Asia and Computer Retrieval Systems* (Islamabad: Lok Virsa, [1988?]), 5.

29. Mufti, "Crises in Folklore," 24. Though closely modeled on international principles, the effort to "indigenize" social science has thus remained an important Lok Virsa concern. See, for example, Salahuddin A. Khan, *Anthropology as Science: The Problem of Indigenization in Pakistan* (Islamabad: Lok Virsa / Lahore: Sang-e-Meel, 1996).

30. A. C. Elliott, *The Chronicles of Gujrat* (Lahore: Civil and Military Gazette Press, 1902), 53–65. All the quotes from Elliott in the paragraphs that follow are from this source. Similar attitudes among British officials appear in earlier administrative documents as well. In his 1861 land settlement report, Capt. Hector Mackenzie linked the settlement of Shah Daulah at Gujrat with the town's emergence as an important center in Mughal times. "The place grew in importance as time went on," he notes, "but chiefly during the reign of the Emperor Shah Jehan. It then happened that a Peer of great virtue and sanctity named Shah Dowla, took up his residence here. As the offerings made to him were large, so was his expenditure lavish, and a good deal was laid out on the improvement of the Town and suburbs." Hector Mackenzie, *Report of the Revised Settlement of the Goojerat District in the Rawulpindee Division* (Lahore: Hope, 1861), 11. The significance of Shah Daulah as a local patron has more recently been noted. As Abdul Rehman and James Wescoat write, "Although not unique, Shah Daulah represents one of the very rare cases where Sufi mysticism was combined with public works, for he was a famous builder of bridges and public works." Abdul Rehman and James L.

Wescoat Jr., *Pivot of the Punjab: The Historical Geography of Medieval Gujrat* (Lahore: Dost, 1993), 12.

31. M. Miles, "Pakistan's Microcephalic *Chuas* of Shah Daulah: Cursed, Clamped or Cherished?" *History of Psychiatry* 7 (1996): 571–89. Whether kept at the shrine or not, microcephalic children (and adults) in Punjab were generally associated with Shah Daulah and called *chuhe* or *Shah Daulah ke bachhe*.

32. "Unfortunately," Miles writes, "Ewens's positive, detailed and expert observations were missed or ignored by almost all later reporters, possibly because they were confined to a medical journal." Miles, "Pakistan's Microcephalic *Chuas* of Shah Daulah," 579. The common British attitude toward these children is evident in the words of an earlier settlement officer, who referred to "those loathsome idiots called 'Chuhas.'" Leslie S. Saunders, *Report of the Revised Land Revenue Settlement of the Lahore District* (Lahore: Central Jail Press, 1873), 49. When the continuance of the shrine's endowments came up for government discussion in the early twentieth century, some noted the shrine's microcephalic children with deep concern, suggesting that the custodians might have encouraged the children's "artificial deformation." The Gujrat settlement officer himself dismissed this as "doubtful" but allowed "that deformed children who are congenital idiots are kept at the shrine, and profit is made by sending men in charge of the children to tour the country [in order to beg]. It is suspected," he said, "that the children are not well-treated." H. S. Williamson (Settlement Officer, Gujrat) to Commissioner, Rawalpindi, April 19, 1915, Punjab Board of Revenue, file 131/1616.

33. In fact Elliott harbored far deeper suspicions about the shrine. Alluding to the speculation that the children were artificially deformed so that they could be used for begging and to provide income to the shrine, he noted darkly that there was a large file in the district office on the subject of the shrine's children. But "the matter has been treated always 'confidentially,'" he said, "and had better remain so." Miles dismisses Elliott's implication, since, as he argues, later officials who must have had access to the district files came to discount the artificial deformation theory. Miles, "Pakistan's Microcephalic *Chuas* of Shah Daulah," 588.

34. *Pir Rashid-ud-Daula and Three Others vs. The Chief Administrator of Auqaf, West Pakistan.* Supreme Court Appeal no. 13 of 1965, *All Pakistan Legal Decisions*, vol. 23 (1971): 401–30.

35. Mahkama-yi Auqaf, *Hazrat Sayyid Kabir ud-din Shah Daulah Darya-yi Ganj Bakhsh* (Lahore: Mahkama-yi Auqaf, 1965?). All quotations in the following paragraph are from this pamphlet.

36. The degree to which Auqaf Department control has in fact served to change popular attitudes or practices at the shrine is another matter. As Ewing notes, begging by fakirs using "Shah Daulah's chuhas" continued even after the Auqaf Department's takeover, and their strong association with the shrine remains. Ewing, *Arguing Sainthood*, 79.

37. Mazhar ul-Islam, *Lok Panjab* (Islamabad: Institute of Folk Heritage, 1978), back cover.

38. Ibid., 25–30. All quotations in this paragraph are from this book.

39. Miles provides evidence that the popular belief in such "visual influence" on pregnancy had been noted by British observers at the shrine as early as the mid–nineteenth century. The general belief that visual images could influence the children

of pregnant women was noted by a number of amateur ethnographers in the Punjab, such as H. A. Rose, comp., *A Glossary of the Tribes and Castes of Punjab and North-West Frontier Province*, 3 vols. (Patiala: Languages Department, Punjab, 1970), 1:738. Miles, "Pakistan's Microcephalic *Chuas* of Shah Daulah," 573.

40. Compare this with Miles's efforts to interpret the role of the shrine as a premodern welfare institution.

41. Jamal Malik, "The Literary Critique of Islamic Popular Religion in the Guise of Traditional Mysticism, or the Abused Woman," in *Embodying Charisma: Modernity, Locality and the Performance of Emotion in Sufi Cults*, ed. Pnina Werbner and Helene Basu (London: Routledge, 1998), 187–208. Malik's article focuses specifically on a story by Ahmad Nadim Qasimi.

☽

Formations of Orthodoxy

Authority, Power, and Networks in Muslim Societies

RICHARD C. MARTIN AND
ABBAS BARZEGAR

In light of shifting political and economic realities at both global and local levels, contemporary Islam appears to be facing unprecedented challenges to its orthodox institutions of authority. These include (a) the dissolution of "place" and traditional boundaries as globalization increasingly affects Muslim communities and networking abilities around the globe; (b) the challenges to traditional modes of authority by nontraditional voices using media such as the Internet and satellite television; and (c) the fallout from the self-fulfilling prophecies of a "clash of civilizations" between Islam and its historic "other" (Christendom/the West). Given such contexts of dislocation, this paper examines these conditions to understand some of the processes of formation and authentication of the "orthodox" or "normative" in contemporary Islam in light of some historical parallels in premodern Islamicate history.[1]

While the sociology of knowledge shaped by the Internet and globalization is unique and unprecedented in premodern history in many respects, the challenge of social and political change to orthodox institutions and ways of being religious is not, which raises these questions: What do we mean by *orthodox* or normative religious institutions and practices in the first instance? By what process does orthodoxy—as recognized and affirmed by Sunni, Shi'a, and indeed Sufi communities—form? What are its sources? Does orthodoxy, by definition, constitute a more or less stable set of norms throughout history by which variations are judged and brought into line? What relationships do rising popular religious ideas and movements, such as discourses and disputes now aired on the Internet, have to traditional, orthodox institutions and religious authority?

As historians of religion, we are also interested in the comparative question of whether a general theory of orthodox formations applies to other traditions as well. The central task of this investigation, however, will be to interrogate

concepts of orthodoxy in religious studies with respect to the dynamic of continuity and change, with the main focus on formations of orthodoxy in Islam.
This approach challenges the commonsense view that popular, that is, nontraditional or informal, religious movements are simply a degradation or corruption of high religion—the Great Tradition—or orthodoxy. The argument here
is that, to the contrary, popular religious ideas and movements are often vital
sources of evolving new orthodox discourses. We concur with our Emory University colleague Abdullahi An-Naʿim when he says: "Every orthodox perception that believers take for granted today began as a heresy from the perspective
of some other doctrine and may well continue to be considered heretical by
some believers."[2] In fact An-Naʿim's claim echoes that of early church historian
Walter Bauer's that "heresy precedes orthodoxy."[3] By and large scholars today
have abandoned conceptions of an essential "orthodoxy" or "heresy," opting
instead for an appreciation of the two as forever mutually embedded, dialectical
discourses subject to social and political change.[4] A corollary of this argument
is that orthodoxy historically is actually about power; therefore analyses of new
formations of orthodoxy in the age of globalized Islam should focus particularly
on shifts in power and authority. Recalling Peter Brown's thesis in *The Cult of
the Saints*, that popular religious movements can be the source of orthodoxy in
religion and are not necessarily the result of corruption of and straying from
orthodoxy, we propose in the pages that follow to apply that thesis to a recon-
sideration of orthodoxy in Islam.[5]

Many of the ideas discussed here have grown out of two and a half decades of
conversations with Bruce Lawrence about the academic understanding of religion, and especially Islam, in the present contentious global climate. It is an ongoing conversation, of which this essay and volume are part. We continue to
resist his thesis that modernity is primarily if not solely responsible for the shape
Islam, especially fundamentalist Islam, has taken in recent decades, for such
insightful but narrow focus leads him to leave largely unexamined the heritage
of indigenous Islamic conflicts, debates, and discourses in the premodern era.
On the other side, his vigorous investigations into the sources and consequences
of violence and conflict confronting Islam since the Iranian Revolution, in works
such as *Shattering the Myth* and, most recently, *The Qur'an: A Biography*, have
opened up conversations that historians of religion needed to have.[6] Much of
what we have to say about Muslim networks below has been inspired by his volume with that title, coedited with miriam cooke.[7]

The case we shall make in this paper has an ethical dimension that needs to be
stated here briefly, for it arises in any attempt to explain and interpret violence
associated with religion. The dilemma of outsiders intervening in the theological and political discourses of Islam has become more apparent to this generation than in the past. Historian Bernard Lewis has famously written that Islam,

when compared to modern, secular democracies in the West, has taken a different, more troubled, violent, and anti-Western path into the modern age.[8] Lewis became the dean of neoconservative policy makers in the presidential administration of George W. Bush and the think tanks in Washington, D.C., that support the administration, and he has influenced the rhetoric of Islamophobic ideologues and religious leaders such as David Horowitz, Norman Podhoretz, the Reverend Pat Robertson, and the Reverend Franklin Graham. The majority of scholars trained in Islamic studies have reacted to this general assault on Islam and sought ways to come to the defense of Islamic civilization, its historical past, and its precarious present. This defense has spilled out of the classroom and moved beyond scholarly monographs and refereed journal articles—the normal venues of scholarly discourse—to appear on the Internet and, even more significantly, in the popular media. Increasingly since the Iranian Revolution in 1979, colleagues have raised their voices also in the public sphere, where scholars empathetic to Islam are free to speak but have no special authority or guarantee of influence. One move made by some scholars has been to make the good Muslim / bad Muslim distinction, popularized by President Bush in the immediate wake of the attacks on the World Trade Center and the Pentagon on September 11, 2001.[9]

Another move by empathetic scholars is to downplay extreme public focus on Muslim acts of violence as a way of understanding Islam by seeking alternatively to explain their social causes in the Muslim experience of colonialism and post-colonial corrupt governments. Critics complain that such moves tend to side-step rather than deal directly with the moral status of unethical acts, such as the killing of noncombatants and innocents. At a conference on Muslim heretics convened by modernist and progressive Muslims in Atlanta in March 2008, one Muslim speaker observed that many empathetic scholarly defenders of contemporary Islam bend so far over backward to understand the causes of religiously inspired violence among some jihadists that they bang the backs of their heads on the floor.[10] On the other side, A. Kevin Reinhart has cautioned non-Muslim scholars of religion to be careful not to seem to be silent, in their statements about religion, regarding unethical acts that they would not condone if *they* were adherents of that religion.[11]

This cautionary note is expressed in statements by Lawrence and others who offer sympathetic interpretations of strident Islamic movements but who have nonetheless (uncharacteristically in scholarly discourse) rebuked Osama bin Laden for the consequences of his interpretation of Islam. The dilemma this poses for the scholar of Islam and Muslim societies is that it advances a position, not only on what is or is not humane and ethical, which is surely justified, but also on what is or is not authentically Islamic, which is more complicated. Muslim jurists and intellectuals such as Khaled Abou El Fadl remind us that many of the issues raised by jihadist Salafi Muslims who may be sympathetic to bin Laden and al Qaeda have deeper roots in Muslim legal and theological debates.[12] Taking Lawrence's condemnation of bin Laden as fundamentally justified on ethical grounds, we nonetheless caution reticence when speaking and writing as scholars; our main task when we wear our scholarly hats is not to enter intra-Islamic debates and participate in making theological judgments about bin Laden and those Muslims who support him to some degree, however remotely. Rather our first task is to try to account for and understand intra-Islamic disputes, in order to be able to explain, for example, why social movements such as al Qaeda have become successful transnational influences, especially among younger Muslims turning to religion. In other words we have to account for the fact that even the most ardent jihadist Muslims, no matter how alienated some may seem from mainstream Islam as we know it, are still Muslims nonetheless, at least by their own lights.

It is important to stress that such a methodological posture is not advocated solely for the sake of academic objectivity. Rather attempting to understand Muslim displays of power in terms of Islamic discourses enables an analysis of violence that can better inform contemporary fluctuations in Muslim regimes of authenticity and authority. In the contemporary moment, it seems befitting that scholars of Islamic civilization might best serve their colleagues and audiences with insights about how current events relate to historical precedents and discourses within the Islamic tradition itself. Such an analytic orientation, delinked from an immediate ethical-political project, may in fact be indispensable in understanding the tremendous forces shaping the Muslim world today and in discerning the scholar's location in relation to them.

In the remainder of this essay, we will argue that orthodox religion—as defined and understood, for example, at al-Azhar University in Egypt (Sunni) or Qom in Iran (Twelver Shi'a)—is not static or timeless but evolving: it has a social and political history, and it has its sources in what we might broadly call popular religion, that is, religion that devolves not from existing orthodox institutions but rather evolves from gradual changes going on in society at large. This claim runs against the grain of post-Enlightenment *Religionswissenschaft*, on which historians of religion usually base theories and methods in religious studies. We argue instead that popular and nonestablishment religions are not necessarily the result of a deterioration of orthodoxy but rather are often the source of it.

An interesting Islamic case can be seen in the ninth-century standoff between the 'Abbasid caliph al-Ma'mun (r. 813–833) and the scholar-hero Ahmad ibn Hanbal (d. 855), wherein the role of popular piety in the resistance to the ruler's enforced attempt to standardize orthodox belief about the Qur'an proved to lay the groundwork for a newer, more populist form of Sunni orthodoxy by the second half of the century. We will also deal briefly with why we think orthodox or

established Islam is being made, in the present moment, in the discourses aris-
ing on the Internet and other media linked to globalization. Finally we will
argue that the seminal work by Lawrence and his colleagues in the Muslim networks project referenced above provides a framework for analyzing the formation of orthodox institutions and movements.

Defining Orthodoxy

How is the term and concept of *orthodoxy* to be understood for the purposes of
this essay? As we understand that term applied to Islam in the modern period,
it does not mean a static, reified, universal Sunni definition of Islam (the traditional *ahl al-sunna wal-jama'a*) as distinct from a dynamic, contentious modern
Islam. Rather in more general terms it often refers to the idea of local authority of established Sunni and Shi'a communities and their institutions, including
those communities in which Sufi ideas and *tariqa*s may predominate, as found
in Egypt, Iran, Indonesia, and other Muslim states.[13] In other words normative
Islam is seen very differently by the *ulama* in Tehran, Cairo, and Riyadh, with
normally only limited charges of heresy, or even error, between them. This suggests adopting the more accurate, if inelegant, plural reference to "Islams" while
continuing to stress that within Hanbali Sunni, Shafi'i Sunni, Ithna-'Ashari
Shi'a, Isma'ili Shi'a, and *tariqa* Sufi movements are normative institutions of
authority as well variations and contestations of belief and practice among con-
stituents. In other words the schools of legal reasoning (*madhdhahib*) and Sufi
brotherhoods (*turuq*) had been sources of identity for Muslims in premodern
Islam and largely remain so today. Nonetheless Lawrence and others have
shown that traditional institutions are being challenged by global and Internet
Islam, as well as the newer classes of Muslim intellectuals from the professions
previously unrelated to religious authority, such as medicine, technology, and
engineering.[14] At the same time, however, traditional Muslim institutions adapt
and appropriate these changes in an effort to secure and expand their conventional spheres of influence. Another challenge to the analysis of modern orthodoxy is the sizable and growing Muslim diasporas in Europe, North America,
and other lands where Muslims have become a significant minority.[15] These
diasporas have given rise to independent intellectuals who do not shy from challenging Islam's historical centers of hegemony.

The inclusive dimensions of this descriptive definition of orthodoxy will not
be acceptable to most Muslims, who understandably regard themselves as right-
believing, committed adherents of a particularly correct interpretation of Islam.
It may also seem too fluid to those at home with more essentialist understandings of the nature of religious traditions. The reply must be that the historian
of religion takes his or her critical stance outside the tradition, whence he or she
cannot fail to notice many forms of Islam claiming normative authority; thus

anything the scholar says about normative authority (orthodoxy) must come to terms with that plurality and those variants. Many Muslim scholars, including those contributing to this volume, along with their obvious personal insights as insiders and/or as entrenched participant-observers, nonetheless practice the kind of critical scholarship we are alluding to.

The application of the term *orthodox* to Islam in the early and medieval periods was judged not to apply as well to Islam as it did to Christianity by Western scholars. Writing in the 1920s, Ignaz Goldziher was one of the first to make this observation:

> There is no parallel between dogma in Islam and dogma in the religious system of any Christian church. In Islam there are no councils and synods that, after vigorous debate, fix the formulas that henceforth must be regarded as sound belief. There is no ecclesiastic office that provides a standard of orthodoxy. There is no exclusively authorized exegesis of the sacred texts, upon which the doctrines of a church, and the manner of their inculcation, might be based. The consensus is the highest authority in all questions of religious theory and practice, but it is a vague authority, and its judgment can scarcely be precisely determined.[16]

Montgomery Watt later reaffirmed what had by then become a commonplace in Western scholarship, that the term *orthoprax*—pointing as it does to predominance of practice and performance over adherence to creed in Muslim life—is more accurately applied to normative Islam than is *orthodoxy*.[17]

Nonetheless creedal statements did evolve and contend with each other in the early centuries of Islam, as they did in early Christianity. When the history of the formation of a Muslim creed is compared to the first five centuries of the Common Era and the contentious work of the Christian ecumenical councils at Nicea (325 C.E.), Constantinople I (381 C.E.), Ephesus (431 C.E.), and Chalcedon (451 C.E.), we see interesting differences.[18] Indeed orthodoxy, both in the general sense of a theologically normative and politically authoritative tradition as well as the specific sense of the Eastern Orthodox churches, was the work of the ecumenical councils, collectively fixed in space and time by the state. In Islam authority in judicial and theological matters was determined by consensus among scholars who were partisans of those schools that eventually prevailed over a plurality of others and agreed to disagree in matters of legal interpretation. There was no central authority invested in a single religious leader or authorized council. This proved to be a system that had its advantages for a nascent religion that spread widely and quickly beyond the effective control of the caliphate, which by the tenth century failed politically to establish universal theological authority across the larger Muslim body, or *ummah*.[19] Nor was there much tolerance in Islam, as we shall see below, for rulers, such as Constantine at Nicea, presiding over or even convening councils of clergy at which doctrine was hammered out.[20]

Finally the sense of Islamic orthodoxy or "orthodoxies" suggested above is supported by reading the narratives of orthodoxy through the lenses of critical theory. Talal Asad observed in 1986 that the claim of orthodoxy is a reflex of power and performance. More recently cooke and Lawrence have argued that this means that "moments of exchange and conflict complicate a monolithic narrative of Islamic orthodoxy precisely to the extent that they specify and localize knowledge production."[21] In other words orthodoxy is the exercise of power through the production of knowledge in interpretive institutions, in book publishing, and in local communities that remain connected to the larger Muslim world through specific means of communications, such as the annual pilgrimage or hajj to Mecca and, more recently, electronic media, including the Internet.

Asad's focus on *power* and *performance* as the central features of religious orthodoxy provides a useful way to address the problem of discerning the formations of orthodoxy in contemporary Islamic societies. For Asad power is not something that an individual, group, or institution owns or *has* in its possession. Rather social, political, and discursive power flows between individuals and groups. It is dynamic. It flows between *ulama*, the sultan, and minority groups as they contest with one another for control. Like Michel Foucault and Alasdair MacIntyre, Asad thinks of orthodox power as nexuses within *discursive traditions*. In one insightful passage, he explains: "Clearly not everything Muslims say and do belongs to an Islamic discursive tradition. Nor is an Islamic tradition in this sense necessarily imitative of what was done in the past. For even where traditional practices appear to the anthropologist to be imitative of what has gone on before, it will be the practitioners' conceptions of what is *apt performance*, and how the past is related to present practices, that will be crucial for the tradition, not the apparent repetition of an old form."[22] Asad adds: "Wherever Muslims have the power to regulate, uphold, require, or adjust *correct* practices, and to condemn, exclude, undermine, or replace *incorrect* ones, there is the domain of orthodoxy.[23] Steven C. Caton suggests that "Asad's definition of discursive tradition allows for what might be called a 'gap' between the instructional texts as given in the Qur'an, the hadith and concrete Islamic practices."[24] This echoes Jonathan Z. Smith's definition of ritual as "a means of performing the way things ought to be in conscious tension with the way things are."[25] Like ritual, orthodoxy as performed religion draws followers toward the norm, while at the same time the realities of life hold the ideal at bay.

We turn now from this brief description and comparison of the Islamic phenomena of orthodoxy to the equally important problem of theorizing orthodoxy. How are we to account for religious communities and whole traditions such as Islam achieving an orthodox consensus and identity? How did Muslim

intellectuals construct normative understandings of the "other," the heresy movements, and what used to be called the low, vulgar traditions, that are seen not to
rise to the level of orthodoxy and may be seen by those who claim authority over
orthodox beliefs and practices as dangerous and even in need of correction?

Toward a Theory of the Formation of Orthodoxy

In *The Cult of the Saints: Its Rise and Function in Latin Christianity*, Peter Brown
argued against the standard view of popular religion as a corruption and degeneration of the orthodox high tradition. Brown made the case that in fact the normative traditions of medieval Christendom had evolved out of popular religious
practices and ideas; popular movements such as saint worship, which was not
authoritative in the patristic period, proved to be generative factors in the formation of late medieval orthodox religion. In the case of Islam, the formation
of normative ideas and practices out of popular movements can be seen, for
example, in the rise of Ash'arism and Islamic traditionalism, which began as
populist reactions under the charismatic leadership of men such as Ibn Hanbal,
to the rising court influence that Mu'tazili rationalism had attained by the middle of the ninth century.[26]

History of religions and its many Western disciplinary sisters inherited from
the Enlightenment a theory of high religion constantly struggling to rise and
remain above popular, low, or vulgar religion. In *The Cult of the Saints*, Brown
traces the prevailing tendency to construe religion in terms of orthodoxy and
popular religion to thinkers of the Enlightenment such as the philosopher
David Hume (1711–1776) and the historian Edward Gibbon (1737–1794). In
Brown's words, "The religious history of late antiquity and the early middle ages
owes more than we realize to attitudes summed up so persuasively, in the 1750s,
by David Hume, in his essay, *The Natural History of Religion*."[27] Hume can now
be criticized for having very little on-the-ground knowledge of the actual social
history of religions. Brown observes that the influence of Hume's writing about
religion "drew on evidence that lay to hand in classical authors, which all men
of culture read and would read up to our own times. . . . He placed this evidence
together with such deftness and good sense that the *Natural History of Religion*
seems to carry the irresistible weight of a clear and judicious statement of the
obvious."[28] Thus Hume's model of popular religion as the devolution of orthodox high religion was to become commonplace among scholars of religion by
the nineteenth century. Henry Hart Milman, writing at the turn of the twentieth century about the spread of Christianity throughout early medieval Europe
along with the spread of barbarian tribes, concluded, "Now had commenced
what may be called, neither unreasonably nor unwarrantedly, the mythic age of
Christianity. As Christianity worked downward into the lower classes of society,
as it received the crude and ignorant barbarians within its pale, the general effect

could not but be that the age would drag down the religion to its level, rather than the religion elevate the age to its own lofty standards."[29]

The larger issue for Enlightenment philosophes was to account for the origins and variety of religious thought. Until the eighteenth century, Christian philosophical theology commonly held that humans were natural monotheists who had "lost, through sin, the original simplicity of faith in the Supreme Being that had been granted to Adam and the Patriarchs."[30]

Hume critiqued that view of orthodox Christianity as the high tradition against which all else was to be measured with an argument remarkably similar to that of the Basra school of the Mu'tazila in tenth- and eleventh-century Islamic Iraq and Iran, about which we will have more to say below. He held that "theism . . . depended on attaining a coherent—and so, rational—view of the universe, such as might, in turn, enable the enlightened mind to deduce from the order of the visible world the existence of, and the forms of worship due to, a Supreme Being." Hume reasoned that the vulgar masses were incapable of attaining the conditions of rational theism, not simply because they lacked the intellect, but because they lived in social and cultural environments that were hostile toward rationality. The historical patterns of relations between rational and vulgar, or monotheistic and popular, religion that Hume saw were ones not simply of decline and lapsing from high to low religions, but rather were a history of constant tensions between "theistic and polytheistic ways of thinking." As he put it, "It is remarkable that the principles of Religion have had a flux and reflux in the human mind, and that men have a natural tendency to rise from idolatry to theism, and to sink again from theism to idolatry."[31]

Brown referred to this standard form of conceptual analysis of high and low religion as the "two-tiered" model.[32] It is a model that was conceived and applied beyond European post-Enlightenment historiography and religious studies. In medieval Islamic historical and theological writing, it was common to distinguish between the *'awamm* and the *khawass*, the common people and the upper-class elites—a categorical social and class distinction that the *mutakallimun*, or "theologians," frequently used to explain the differences between orthodox beliefs and misguided popular diatribes about beliefs. Philosophers (*falasifa*) and theologians debated whether the common people were capable of understanding the doctrines and arguments for the teachings of their religion; some thought it quite dangerous to allow untutored commoners, the *'awamm*, to address such matters in public. The ninth-century litterateur and theologian Abu 'Uthman 'Amr b. Bahr, known as al-Jahiz ("the google-eyed"), satirized the dangers of theology in the hands of common folk:

> There is another field which is unknown to the common people and throws the mob into confusion. . . . If a scholar stands up in the main street or the

marketplace and discusses grammar and prosody, or discourses on the law, astronomy, mathematics, medicine, geometry, or the crafts, only specialists will gather round and dispute with him. But let him say so much as a word about predestination, or mention the Knowledge and Will [of God], or "capacity" and responsibility [of human agency], or consider whether or not God created unbelief, and there will be no fool of a porter, no down-and-out wretch, no tongue-tied idiot or ignorant blockhead who will not stop and argue and contribute his [two cents' worth].

Jahiz went on to comment: "These sorts of people ought not to associate with the aristocracy (*khawass*) [which included most jurists, theologians, and other scholars]; and furthermore, however good their intentions may be, they lack the attainments needed for understanding and discrimination."[33] Philosophers such as al-Farabi (ca. 890–950) and Ibn Sina (Avicenna), worried about this same two-tiered problem of common people and elite intellectuals within the framework of the convergence of Neoplatonism and Aristotelian philosophy that had evolved in the Islamic Middle Ages and Plato's concept of the philosopher-king in *The Republic*. Muslim philosophers and theologians of such a mind argued that the rational understanding of divine laws and truths in the minds of prophets and philosophers was rendered available to common folk in the form of symbolic narratives expressed in divine revelation. Thus was comity between the truths of reason and revelation preserved.

One characteristic that Islamic theological and philosophical analyses of religion among the masses and the elites share with the Western two-tiered model described by Brown is that the vulgar masses of common folk and their religion can only be understood in reference to an orthodox premise of high monotheism.[34] Brown argued it was time to abandon the two-tiered model of Hume, Gibbon, Milman, and the many scholars of religion they were to influence in subsequent generations down to modern times. He proposed standing the traditional Enlightenment model on its head and suggested that what scholars like to refer to as popular religion in fact possesses a dynamic of its own and should be seen as a source of orthodox religion in its own right. That is, contrary to understanding popular religions as lower forms that devolved from high monotheism, Brown found more explanatory power, at least for Latin Christendom in the Middle Ages, in the hypothesis that orthodox religion at any given moment in history is the result of the historical evolution of competing popular religious ideas and practices.[35] It is this hypothesis, applied beyond the Latin Middle Ages, that we propose to try to think with in our attempt to understand the Muslim experiences of globalization and the new forms of religious expression appearing in cyber-Islam and in transnational Islamic social movements. An example from the ninth to eleventh centuries in Islam demonstrates that

Brown's description of Latin Christendom has relevance, and it sets up a different kind of comparison between premodern and modern Islam.

A Premodern Moment in the Historical Production of Orthodox Islam

Orthodox theology (*kalam*) for the majority of traditional Sunni Muslims is grounded in the doctrines of the Ash'arite school, whose chroniclers trace its teachings to the tenth-century dialectic theologian Abu l-Hasan al-Ash'ari (d. 935). In contrast to the Mu'tazili school that had prevailed in the first half of the ninth century, Ash'arism fused the rationalist methods of disputation of the Mu'tazilites with a staunch fidelity to the priority of revelation over reason in the determination of human morality, the nature of God, the boundaries of human free will, and other pertinent theological questions. Al-Ash'ari, however, was not the founder of the way of thinking about *'ilm al-kalam*, "the science of dialectical theology," that gained popular support in early and medieval Islam, but rather, as Wilferd Madelung has shown, he was the theological spokesman for a popular movement that had begun nearly a century earlier in Baghdad with Ibn Hanbal.[36]

That movement, which eventually became synonymous with orthodox Sunni Islam and would claim the affiliation of the likes of al-Ghazali (d. 1111), appeared on the stage of 'Abbasid history as a challenge to earlier forms of religious intellectualism that were in many ways a continuation of older established forms of Near Eastern rationalism.[37] Near Eastern religious intellectualism confronted early Muslims, especially in the work of converts on the eastern frontiers of Islam rule, such as Iran, Samarkand, and Khurasan. On the eastern periphery of Muslim rule, older religious theological and social systems such as Nestorian Christianity, Orthodox and Monophysite Christianity, Manichaeanism, Zoroastrianism, Buddhism, and Hinduism still held sway even as the new religion of Islam was sweeping the countryside. Ash'arism can be understood as a compromise doctrine grown out of the standoff between rationalism, represented by the Mu'tazilite school and the philosophers, on the one hand, and the traditionalists, represented by Ibn Hanbal, on the other.[38]

That Hanbalis and Ash'aris might have a common genetic link is counterintuitive to some Islamic historians, given the tension that continued between the schools in medieval Islam and the low esteem in which Mu'tazili rationalism is held by many Sunni Muslims in the modern period. However, such a relationship is better understood through a paradigm of orthodox formation as outlined above rather than through a positivist history of doctrine, intellectual history, and evolving religious institutions.

The Mu'tazilites, however, were more successful than the Ash'arites in meeting the older cultural and religious systems head on. They succeeded in establishing a place for Islamic teaching among the plural expressions of rationalism

and theological engagement with other traditions that existed in the cosmopolitan atmosphere of ninth-century Islamicate society. By the early ninth century,
Muʿtazili theological rationalism had become well established and influential in
the salons of the men of the ruling and social elite. Yet the first generations of
Muʿtazilite theologians modeled their discourse on the older forms of religious
rationalism that were deeply entrenched in Near Eastern cultures and with
which they frequently disputed and defended Islamic doctrine.

In the first half of the ninth century, Muʿtazili theologians were frequent ad-
visers, lecturers, and disputants in the caliphal court in Baghdad. Thus they had
privileged access to the institution of caliphal authority and the machinery of
punitive power that went with it. This was epitomized by the inquisition of civil
servants who did not support state-sponsored theological doctrine. Known as
the *mihna*, the infamous inquisition established by Caliph al-Maʾmun in 833
required civil servants in Iraq to subscribe to the well-known Muʿtazili doctrine
of the created Qurʾan (*khalq al-qurʾan*), which violated more popular notions of
Qurʾanic piety and framework for understanding that the Qurʾan was the eternal word of God. Ibn Hanbal, the ninth-century icon for populist opposition to
Muʿtazili forms of orthodoxy, is heralded as something of a folk hero for his
resistance to al-Maʾmun's pressures. His arrest in turn triggered widespread resistance to official state doctrine of the created Qurʾan. It is one of the great historical narratives of theological and political contest in early medieval Islam. Ibn
Hanbal was imprisoned for more than two decades for refusing to subscribe to
state-supported theological doctrine. Popular support for Ibn Hanbal in the
streets surrounding the various prisons where he was incarcerated exposed a
much wider expression of popular piety and religious sensibility that eventually
triumphed in the suspension of the *mihna* and ultimate reversal of state doctrine
toward a more traditionalist-oriented posture. This signaled the simultaneous
fall from official state grace of the Muʿtazili school, but not, as often is concluded,
their disappearance from local spheres of influence.

Tilman Nagel has argued that this drama of inquisition was evidence of a
popular movement or movements of traditionalists and Sufi theologians such as
al-Muhasibi (d. 857), and of popular dialectic theologians such as al-Ashʿari and
his followers, who in reaction to the older rationalist schools of thought produced a new, distinctively Islamic form of piety and religious thought.[39] What
began as popular resistance to the doctrines of court theologians and to the
ʿAbbasid court itself within a century developed into what we now recognize as
one of the pillars of Sunni Islam. Whether one pursues a Hegelian dialectic that
sees Ashʿarite Sunnism emerging out of the contest between Muʿtazili rationalism and Hanbali traditionalism or sees traditionalism winning out over, but
not entirely defeating, rationalism, something new evolved out of popular
movements, and that, we would submit, was the formation of the new Sunni

orthodoxy—or perhaps one should say more cautiously, *a* new orthodoxy, for at the same time the Imami (Twelver) Shiʿa and other sects were forming their own authoritative ritual and discourse communities out of popular dissenting religious movements within the ʿAbbasid Empire.

The history of the tenth-century rise of Ashʿarism, Sufism, and Twelver Shiʿism out of popular movements is of course much more complex and nuanced. Nonetheless we contend that the history of early Islamic theological disputes such as the one just narrated offer a good illustration of Brown's revisionist reading of the medieval European cult of the saints: popular religion not as an aberration of orthodox religion grounded in beginnings but as a source of orthodoxies, evolving nuances from popular religious movements that contend with the old guard.

What light can the medieval Christian cult of the saints and the historical evolution of medieval Islamic theology shed on the fate of orthodox Islam in the age of the Internet and globalization?

Is Global Islam a Problem of Culture?

To answer that question, we may turn to contemporary studies of political Islam, where what is happening religiously on the margins of society is seen to have a profound effect on the more orthodox center. In a poststructuralist study of political Islam in the Sudan, Abdou Maliqalim Simone, a social psychologist, argues that "every society is in some way obligated to its margins for its existence." The author goes on to explain, echoing Talal Asad,[40] "The margins exist partially as a space to which [society] can relegate thinking and discourses it considers dangerous and destabilizing."[41] This is how state and orthodox religious authorities, as nexuses of power, keep tabs on ideas and movements they wish to control, and conversely Simone's insight also recognizes the importance and influence of marginal forces on institutional authority.

In *Globalized Islam: The Search for a New Ummah*, Olivier Roy treats the problem of orthodoxy in ways similar to the insights of Brown. He makes a persuasive case for seeing globalized Islam as expanding well beyond traditional political and theological borders and, through revival and re-Islamization movements, enabling Muslims in the West to adopt new identities. At the same time, Roy reminds us, as Bruce Lawrence did earlier, that even in countries of the Middle East and elsewhere that are predominantly Muslim, Islamic movements are rising out professional classes trained in medicine, science, and technology and less so from professionally trained and employed religious scholars. In recent Islamist discourses, often coming from these new professional classes, the restoration of a nonstate, nonterritorial, Muslim *ummah*, led by a caliph, is frequently imagined.[42]

Benedict Anderson's widely influential theory of the nation as an "imagined community" has a counterintuitive twist in contemporary Islam among groups that Roy classifies as neofundamentalist.[43] Roy defines neofundamentalism as "a closed scripturalist and conservative view of Islam that rejects the national and statist dimension in favour of the *ummah*, the universal community of all Muslims, based on the *sharia*."[44] He distinguishes between the more radical and violent Islamist groups such as al Qaeda that pursue a deterritorialized transnational modus operandi, on the one side, and the more established Islamist movements seeking to establish the *ummah* locally, in conflict with postcolonial secular governments, such as those in Egypt and Algeria, on the other. It is the shared vision of re-Islamization of westernized and secular Muslim lands and creating a global Muslim *ummah* that unites these two forms of Islamic neofundamentalism. Thus it is the practice of creating a new imaginary for Muslim identity that sustains the various Islamist political projects, whether they be radical and violent, pragmatic and conservative, or liberal and moderate.

An important aspect of Roy's thesis is his rejection of the notion that modern Islam should be understood as a civilization or culture. It is worth quoting at length a passage in which he lays out his answer to Samuel Huntington's political "clash of civilizations" and Lewis's Orientalist "what went wrong" constructions of modern Islam. Roy shifts the global strife from territorial to mental boundaries, which does not destroy Huntington's concept of a clash between Islam and the West so much as relocates it:

> At a time when the territorial borders between the great civilizations are fading away, mental borders are being reinvented to give a second life to the ghosts of lost civilizations: multiculturalism, minority groups, clash or dialogue of civilizations, *communautarisation* (communitarisation),[45] and so on. Ethnicity and religion are being marshaled to draw new borders between groups whose identity relies on a performative definition. . . . These new ethnic and religious borders do not correspond to any geographical territory or area. They work in minds, attitudes and discourses. They are more vocal than territorial, but all the more eagerly endorsed and defended because they have to be invented, and because they remain fragile and transitory. Deterritorialisation of Islam leads to a quest for definition, because Islam is no longer embedded in territorial cultures.[46]

Elsewhere in the same work, Roy points out that "it makes no sense for a traditional *alim* [religious scholar] to speak about Muslim culture"—a central concept for Huntington[47]— because in the Western academic discourse of multiculturalism and demarcated civilizations, to accept identity as one among many cultures or world civilizations is to buy into secularism and the relativism of cultures and creeds.[48]

For Huntington, Lewis, the early Francis Fukuyama, and other neoconservative intellectuals, the problem since the end of the cold war has been to explain the rise of religious fundamentalism and specifically the perceived emergence of Islam as a threat to Western political and economic dominance.[49] Drawing from an oft-quoted statement by Daniel Moynihan on the relation of culture to politics, Huntington explained that, contrary to other approaches, the cultural approach follows a subjective sense in which culture is seen as an independent variable that helps to explain why some societies are more progressive than others with roughly the same material and economic resources. In his words, "If cultural factors do affect human progress and at times obstruct it, however, we are also interested in culture as a dependent variable, that is, Moynihan's second truth: How can political or other action change or remove cultural obstacles to progress?"[50] In other words how can political science and public policy research serve the interests of the state? Another form of the "cultural" analysis has been to ask, as Lewis has, "what went wrong" with Islam in modern times, and why is *Islam* as such a problem for the modern West?

Contemporary Formations of Islamic Orthodoxy

That new ways of construing authentic Islam are emerging from what Roy terms neofundamentalist forms of popular Islam (and perhaps from modernist and progressive Muslim reactions) is apparent to most historians and social scientists studying Islam. While it is tempting for the historian of religion to turn prophet and venture into predictions about the future of religion in the age of globalization, that is not a legitimate task for scholarly investigations, as we have argued above. Nonetheless in concluding this paper, it may be useful to summarize the forces and conditions influencing the formation of group identities and nexuses of power claiming normative, if not orthodox, status, with an eye toward better insight into the nature of the process. It would be presumptive to conclude, as some scholars have, that the simple use of modern technologies of communication would teleologically lead to more moderate, liberal forms of Islam, for as Lawrence has shown, the use of technology and the Internet is also a modus operandi in modern forms of fundamentalism.

One important result of globalization, as we have seen, is that a growing number of Muslims "no longer have," in Roy's words, "a relationship with a territory or given society." Deteritorrialization, he goes on, "means that religion has to define itself solely in terms of religion: there is no longer any social authority or social pressure to conform. . . . It has to define itself in comparison with all 'others'—other religions, other values, other environments."[51] This is the "world religions" syndrome of modern religious identities, a product of post-Enlightenment secularism and especially nineteenth-century Orientalist scholarship (in the broader sense of *Religionswissenschaft*) that establishes religions on a global scale. One implication is that globalized Islam does not have to be seen by its proponents as a strange new postmodern mutation of premodern Islam. Indeed finding the way back to the precepts and lifeways of what are seen as traditional religious teachings is what most of the major actors in the contemporary Islamic world are calling for. In other words the current conditions of transnational, global Islam can be and are seen by many Muslims as an *opportunity* for renewal within the present framework, not the *loss* of an imagined past. This recalls Asad's statement above, that rituals are not mere repetitions of old forms but productions in new circumstances. Globalization ironically provides Islamists and neofundamentalists in the twenty-first century with a remedy for the years of cultural westernization during the colonial and postcolonial periods of the nineteenth and twentieth centuries. In the new communal and social spaces in traditional Muslim lands, and perhaps even more so in the growing Muslim diasporas of Europe and the Americas, "an opportunity presents itself to reconstruct a Muslim community based solely on Islamic tenets."[52] The project of neofundamentalists is to rebuild the Muslim *ummah* from the ruins of the traditional worlds, East and West, that seem to be disappearing under the impact of globalization.

The strength of the deterritorialization thesis in liberating Muslims to construct authentic Muslim identities and bases of power is also its weakness, for it entails the lack of territorial, cultural, ethnic, or economic bases (ironically, a connotation of the Arabic term al Qaeda [*al-qa'ida*]) on which to scaffold and build a new transnational Islamic *ummah*. The ideological attraction of this condition of prenational Islamic universalism is why the imaginary reconstitution of the caliphate (*khalifa*), the transnational *ummah*, and the connectedness of Muslims in the new globalized Islam without the usual infrastructures, has had the appeal it has had among neofundamentalists. However, as Roy points out, in its most extreme expression, globalized Islam is capable of producing violent nonstate underground spin-off organizations, such as al Qaeda and its sisters. An important corollary is his observation that modernization and westernization do not influence dogma and beliefs as such. "What is changing is not religion but religiosity—that is, the personal relationship between the believer and his faith and creed, the way he formulates and performs it." To which Roy adds perceptively: "The contemporary history of Christianity and Judaism is the best proof that modernization does not automatically entail more liberal views regarding what believers should think and how they should behave."[53]

Muslim Networks as a Framework for Orthodox Formations

A difficulty running throughout this analysis has been that globalization theory has developed within a very strong Western social science discourse, with emphasis on political economy. The response to those interpreters of Islam, such as Huntington and Lewis, who see Islam as a political problem for the West (in terms of violence) and Western ways of life (in terms of the "problem" for many Western observers, including feminists, of Muslim male treatment of Muslim women) easily turns defensive and reactive, a point we have discussed above. One conclusion of this paper is that scholarship on Islam and globalization needs a more constructive framework in which to expose and understand the distinctively Islamic features of globalized Islam. Such a constructive framework is suggested by the concept of Muslim networks. J. R. McNeill and William H. McNeill have theorized a concept of human history as woven together by human social networks.[54] In their one-volume overview of human history as world history, the authors focus on "webs of interaction in human history" as the new wine to be mixed with older ways of narrating and writing world history. They define *web* as "a set of connections that link people to one another."[55] These include a wide range of social interconnections, such as "kinship, friendship, common worship, rivalry, enmity, economic exchange, political cooperation, even military competition." This local and global spread of "information, items, and inconveniences, and human response to them, is what shapes history."[56] Taking world history by historical periods that are subdivided into cultural regions, the McNeills show how in the lands of Christendom and Islam, as well as in China, South Asia, and elsewhere, webs of communication, exchange, and conflict became, over more than two millennia, progressively complex and culturally idiomatic, down to the era of civilizations converging upon each other through the process of globalization during the past century. What contribution does the narration of human history through an analysis of the complex of human relationships and interactions make to our understanding of globalization and the problem of recovering, imagining, and constructing orthodox Islam in the modern era?

Lawrence and his Duke University colleagues miriam cooke and Ebrahim Moosa established the Center for the Study of Muslim Networks (CSMN) in the spring of 2001 to explore just this question.[57] A recent product of the CSMN consortium is a volume edited by cooke and Lawrence titled *Muslim Networks from Hajj to Hip Hop*. If the hajj is seen by the editors and several of the contributors as the root symbol of the ancient ritual connectedness and communicative interaction of Muslims from the far-flung domiciles of Muslims in Asia and Africa, the Internet and modern telecommunications and global art forms such as hip-hop music and poetry epitomize effective modern networks. Cooke and Lawrence nuance the McNeills' characterization of the human web by defining Muslim networks as "phenomena that are similar to institutionalized social relations, such as tribal affiliations and political dynasties, but also distinct from them, because *to be networked entails making a choice across recognized boundaries.*

'Muslim' refers to a faith orientation, but also to a social world in which Muslims are not always dominant. Both the networked nature of Islam and the impact of Muslim networks on world history are pivotal. Yet neither has received its due from scholars."[58]

The central unifying theological concept of the historical Muslim network is the *ummah*. Like the more modern political notions of the state, the *ummah* is also an imagined community.[59] In its ideal form, in the view of some Islamists, a caliph should once again govern the universal *ummah*. Yet this globalized vision of orthodox and orthoprax Islam is contextualized in local or "glocalized" environments—a ritual community of Muslim believers as distinct from immediate and near neighbors who claim other religious identities or none. As cooke and Lawrence have argued, the *ummah* is at once all of Islam at the highest level of religious identity Muslims may experience, and yet the ritual reinforcements of this larger identity—such as the global daily prayer oriented on Mecca, the annual pilgrimage to Mecca, and breaking the fast during Ramadan with family and friends—are moments when normative Islam is *embodied*, that is, experienced by the human body in local environments.[60] The hajj, which epitomizes the character of Muslim networks, is itself a complex of ritual, travel, educational, and commercial networks, which amounts to a vast network of human communication about religious and political identity as well as occasional disputes about differences. In premodern times the *ulama* (the religious notables, men of the pen, or by the Middle Ages, patrician scholars and their families)[61] were the primary exemplars of the shared values of the larger Islamic societies they served, and thus they were often both the creators as well as the custodians of Islamic orthodoxy.

In modern (since the nineteenth century) and contemporary (since the Iranian Revolution in 1979) Islam, both the hajj and the *ulama* remain important networks of communication. Newer networks have emerged, however, as we have shown above, and within the social and intellectual spaces provided by the Internet and the dispensation of religious knowledge and fostering of new social movements by Muslim professionals independent of the *ulama*, nontraditional religious intellectuals are interpreting Islam on their own. Yet careful observers of the discursive practices of contemporary nontraditional social movements and voices on the Internet reveal that they deploy the form and stylistics of the *ulama*, such as *fatwa*s (nonbinding legal opinions) and theological treatises citing the Qur'an, Hadith, and the precedents of early Islamic history, with some adaptation to format required by modern print and electronic publication. We have argued here that it is from this phenomenon of popular or common religious speculation and interpretation that conventions of orthodoxy are likely to emerge in future.

Conclusion

The theoretical claim of this paper, that popular Islam is not a degeneration of orthodox Islam but often a source of it, to be useful must be qualified and partially deconstructed. The main thrust of the argument, inspired by a reading of Brown's *The Cult of the Saints*, is that Enlightenment formulations of religion were mistaken; Hume and Gibbon inaccurately held that orthodox religion (primarily Christianity) was the highest form of religion and that popular or vulgar expressions of religion were to be understood as degenerations of orthodoxy. We used that thesis as a lens through which to view and interpret the rise of Hanbali traditionalism, Ashʿarite theology, and the more orthodox forms of Sufism as popular movements that contributed to the formation of orthodoxy in the tenth and eleventh centuries. We also deliberately left the definition of orthodoxy large enough to encompass normative forms of Shiʿa and Sufi Islam where these have established authoritative discourses within their own communities.

In making this argument, we have tried to shift the analysis away from the "culturalist" claim that Islamic extremism and anti-Westernism are ingrained in Islamic value systems, and as such those who pursue radical Islamist agendas need to be isolated and defeated, either by Western governments using direct force or indirectly by supporting "good" Muslims, who accept the West, democracy, women's rights, and so forth, against "bad" Muslims. This study has sought to extend the more productive analyses of Olivier Roy, who sees the struggles between Islamist, liberal, and progressive Islamic movements in the larger context of Islamic history not only in the colonial and postcolonial periods but in medieval Islam as well. An important dimension of the larger context of Islamic history has been the many educational, social, and economic networks that have made adaptation to the Internet a natural move, even for the most traditional Muslim groups and movements.

The raison d'être of this exercise, thus, has been to explore ways of understanding the profound changes that seem to be taking place among and within Muslim communities in the era of globalization and the Internet. Is it possible to see in Islamic social movements such as Salafism, progressive Islam, and even al Qaeda not the degeneration of orthodox Islam but rather the components in a dialectic that will engender the orthodoxies of the future? In this regard it is important to note the changing responses to political Islam in Western academic and policy circles. It was not long ago that Egypt's Muslim Brotherhood was considered the monolithic bedrock of Sayyid Qutb's jihadist ideology, yet today leading policy experts see in the Brotherhood an opportunity for constructive engagement.[62]

Are strident yet non-jihadist Islamist movements the new norm in emerging expressions of authentic Islam? If so it is important to concentrate on the ways in which these movements, no matter how disparate, have adapted standing discursive traditions to new mediums of communication. This begs the larger question, to what extent are the *media* of the Internet and telecommunications, as Marshall McLuhan might have said, the *message* that is framing not only the content of orthodoxy but also the ways it will be socially transmitted? Who will receive and make use of these forms of electronic madrassa education? How will new formations of orthodoxy establish authentication? In whose hands will power lay in the age of globalized Islam?

This paper brings us to the edge of these problems without attempting to resolve them. That will require more debate and considerable scholarly effort. The main problem here has been in part to establish what the debate is about. Another way to test the claims of this paper is to ask whether or not the points made above help us to identify what we are looking for in the matter of orthodox religious authority in the age of electronic globalized Islam, and how to look for it. That much of what seems like popular, even heterodox, religion in the first decade of the twenty-first century may contain important elements for Islamic orthodoxies in the future seems a sizable enough endeavor to merit further analysis.

NOTES

1. The term *Islamicate* is used here in Marshall Hodgson's sense of reference "not directly to the religion, Islam, itself, but to the social and cultural complex historically associated with Islam and the Muslims, both among Muslims themselves and even when found among non-Muslims." See Marshall G. S. Hodgson, *The Venture of Islam*, 3 vols. (Chicago: University of Chicago Press, 1974), 1:59.

2. Abdullahi Ahmad An-Naʿim, *Islam and the Secular State: Negotiating the Future of Shariʿa* (Cambridge, Mass.: Harvard University Press, 2008), 275.

3. For a review of Bauer's work and theses, see Daniel J. Harrington, "The Reception of Walter Bauer's Orthodoxy and Heresy in Earliest Christianity during the Last Decade," *Harvard Theological Review* 73, no. 1/2 (1980): 289–98; and Thomas A. Robinson, *The Bauer Thesis Examined: The Geography of Heresy in the Early Christian Church* (Lewiston, N.Y.: Mellon, 1988).

4. See, for example, Daniel Boyarin, *Border Lines: The Partition of Judaeo-Christianity* (Philadelphia: University of Pennsylvania Press, 2006); and Marina Rustow, *Heresy and the Politics of Community: The Jews of the Fatimid Caliphate* (Ithaca, N.Y.: Cornell University Press, 2008).

5. Peter Brown, *The Cult of the Saints: Its Rise and Function in Latin Christianity*, Haskell Lectures on History of Religions, n.s., no. 2 (Chicago: University of Chicago Press, 1981).

6. See Bruce B. Lawrence, *Shattering the Myth: Islam beyond Violence* (Princeton, N.J.: Princeton University Press, 1998); and Bruce B. Lawrence, *The Qurʾan: A Biography* (New York: Atlantic Monthly Press, 2006).

7. miriam cooke and Bruce B. Lawrence, eds., *Muslim Networks from Hajj to Hip Hop* (Chapel Hill: University of North Carolina Press, 2005).

8. Bernard Lewis, *What Went Wrong: Western Impact and Middle Eastern Response* (New York: Oxford University Press, 2002). See the review by Juan Cole in *Global Dialogue*, January 27, 2003, available at http://www.juancole.com/essays/revlew .htm (accessed December 13, 2007).

9. See the excellent study of this move, largely by non-Muslims, to judge between good examples of Islam and bad by Mahmoud Mamdani, *Good Muslim, Bad Muslim: America, the Cold War, and the Roots of Terror* (New York: Pantheon, 2004). Richard C. Martin has also addressed the implications of the good Muslim / bad Muslim distinction in his paper "September 11: Clash of Civilizations or Islamic Revolution?" in *Roads to Reconciliation: Approaches to Conflict in the Twenty-first Century*, ed. Amy B. Brown and Karen M. Poremski (Armonk, N.Y.: Sharpe, 2004), 69–86.

10. See the Web site of the Muslim Heretics Conference, http://www.hereticmuslims .com/ (accessed April 6, 2008).

11. From the oral introduction to a paper by Reinhart at the conference "Islam in Theory and Practice," Duke University, January 7, 2006.

12. Khaled Abou El Fadl, *The Place of Tolerance in Islam*, ed. Joshua Cohen and Ian Lague (Boston: Beacon, 2002), 3–23, 93–111.

13. See Talal Asad, "Modern Power and the Reconfiguration of Religious Traditions," interview by Saba Mahmood, *Scandinavian Economic History Review* 5, no. 1 (updated February 27, 1996), http://www.stanford.edu/group/SHR/5-1/text/asad.html (accessed January 25, 2008).

14. Lawrence makes the case in the chapter 1 of his classic *Defenders of God: The Fundamentalist Revolt against the Modern Age* (New York: Harper & Row, 1989), 23–42.

15. On Muslims in Europe, especially France, see Olivier Roy, *Secularism Confronts Islam* (New York: Columbia University Press, 2007). On Muslims in the United States, see Muqtedar Khan, *American Muslims: Bridging Faith and Freedom* (Beltsville, Md.: Amana, 2002).

16. Ignaz Goldziher, *Vorlesungen über den Islam* (1925), translated by Andras and Ruth Hamori as *Introduction to Islamic Theology and Law* (Princeton, N.J.: Princeton University Press, 1981), 162–63.

17. W. Montgomery Watt, *The Formative Period of Islamic Thought* (1973; repr., Oxford: Oneworld, 1998), 5–6, cited in John B. Henderson, *The Construction of Orthodoxy and Heresy: Neo-Confucian, Islamic, Jewish, and Early Christian Patterns* (Albany, N.Y.: State University of New York Press, 1998), 194. See a more recent, similar conclusion by Josef van Ess, *The Flowering of Muslim Theology* (Cambridge, Mass.: Harvard University Press, 2006), 16, 38. For a critique of Watt and the standard Orientalist view, see Sherman Jackson, *On the Boundaries of Theological Tolerance in Islam* (Oxford: Oxford University Press, 2002), 30.

18. Henderson, *Construction of Orthodoxy*, 49.

19. For a highly accessible survey of the many groups and forces involved in the changing theological and political landscapes of early Islam, see Patricia Crone's *God's Rule: Government and Islam; Six Centuries of Medieval Islamic Political Thought* (New York: Columbia University Press, 2004).

20. An important textual record and commentary on the evolution of a Muslim creed, that is, on theological attempts to define the content of doctrine, was summarized and analyzed by A. J. Wensinck in his *The Muslim Creed: Its Genesis and Historical Development* (Cambridge: Cambridge University Press, 1932).

21. Talal Asad, *The Idea of an Anthropology of Islam* (Washington, D.C.: Center for Contemporary Arab Studies, 1986), 15, as cited in cooke and Lawrence, *Muslim Networks*, 9.

22. Cited in cooke and Lawrence, *Muslim Networks*, 9.

23. Cited in cooke and Lawrence, *Muslim Networks*, 15; emphasis in original.

24. Steven C. Caton, "What Is an 'Authorizing Discourse'?" in *Powers of the Secular Modern: Talal Asad and His Interlocutors*, ed. David Scott and Charles Hirschkind (Stanford, Calif.: Stanford University Press, 2006), 43.

25. Jonathan Z. Smith, "The Bare Facts of Ritual," in *Imagining Religion from Babylon to Jonestown* (Chicago: University of Chicago Press, 1982), 63. The cited passage continues: "Ritual relies for its power on the fact that it is concerned with quite ordinary activities. . . . But it relies as well for its power on the perceived fact that, in actuality, such possibilities cannot be realized."

26. This argument is made by Tilman Nagel, *Die Festung des Glaubens: Triumph und Scheitern des islamischen Rationalismus im 11. Jahrhundert* (Munich: Beck, 1988). See note 39 below.

27. Brown, *Cult of the Saints*, 13.

28. Ibid.

29. Henry Hart Milman, *A History of Latin Christianity: From the Birth of Christ to the Abolition of Paganism in the Roman Empire*, 3 vols. (London: Murray, 1903), 3:417; cited in Brown, *Cult of the Saints*, 16.

30. Brown, *Cult of the Saints*, 13.

31. David Hume, "The Natural History of Religion," in *Essays Moral, Political and Literary*, 2 vols., ed. T. H. Green (Cambridge: Longmans, Green, 1875), 2:334; cited in Brown, *Cult of the Saints*, 14.

32. Brown, *Cult of the Saints*, 17.

33. Translated from the Arabic in Charles Pellat, *The Life and Works of Jahiz: Translations of Selected Texts*, trans. D. M. Hawke (London: Routledge & Kegan Paul, 1969), 79. Specifically he meant those trained in *'ilm al-kalam*, the *mutakallimun* or theologians.

34. Brown, *Cult of the Saints*, 19.

35. Ibid., 20–22.

36. See Wilferd Madelung, "The Vigilante Movement of Sahl b. Salama al-Khurasani and the Origins of Hanbalism Reconsidered," *Journal of Turkish Studies* 14 (1990): 331–37.

37. On this point, see H. A. R. Gibb, "An Interpretation of Islamic History," in *Studies in the Civilization of Islam*, ed. Stanford J. Shaw and William R. Polk (Boston: Beacon, 1962), 10–14.

38. For a history of early *kalam* and further references, see Richard C. Martin and Mark R. Woodward, *Defenders of Reason in Islam: Mu'tazilism from Medieval School to Modern Symbol* (Oxford: Oneworld, 1997), esp. chap. 1.

39. See Nagel, *Festung des Glaubens*, 85–119, on the new popular piety.

40. See note 13 above.

41. T. Abdou Maliqalim Simone, *In Whose Image? Political Islam and Urban Practices in Sudan* (Chicago: University of Chicago Press, 1994), 204–5. We are indebted to Abdul Rashied Omar for calling this and other works dealing especially with the conflicted nature of globalization to our attention in his 2005 Cape Town University dissertation, "Religion, Violence and the State: A Dialogical Encounter between Activists and Scholars."

42. Olivier Roy, *Globalized Islam: The Search for a New Ummah* (New York: Columbia University Press, 2004).

43. See Benedict Anderson, *Imagined Communities: Reflections on the Origins and Spread of Nationalism* (London: Verso, 1991).

44. Roy, *Globalized Islam*, 1.

45. Roy defines *communitarisation* in its French context as a term used to "describe the trend in which people want to be recognized first as a group (usually ethnocultural) and only second as individual citizens, which means ethnocultural identity stands between the state and the individual. It is a negative term for multiculturalism." Roy, *Globalized Islam*, 20n16.

46. Roy, *Globalized Islam*, 20.

47. See Huntington's introduction to Lawrence E. Harrison and Samuel P. Huntington, eds., *Culture Matters: How Values Shape Human Progress* (New York: Basic, 2000).

48. Roy, *Globalized Islam*, 33.

49. For a useful history of the neocon anti-Islamist movement, see Gilles Kepel, *The War for Muslim Minds: Islam and the West*, trans. Pascale Ghazaleh (Cambridge, Mass: Belknap, 2004), esp. chap. 3.

50. Huntington, introduction to *Culture Matters*, xv.

51. Roy, *Globalized Islam*, 38.

52. Ibid., 29–30.

53. Ibid., 30.

54. J. R. McNeill and William H. McNeill, *The Human Web: A Bird's Eye View of World History* (New York: Norton, 2003). For a discussion of earlier scholarship in the social sciences on the concept of human networks, see Charles Kurzman, "The Network Metaphor and the Mosque Network in Iran, 1978–1979," in cooke and Lawrence, *Muslim Networks*, 69–83.

55. McNeill and McNeill, *Human Web*, 3.

56. Ibid., 3–4.

57. A Web site was established and for a couple of years maintained to announce the programs sponsored by the CSMN: www.duke.edu/sweb/muslimnets (last accessed December 18, 2001). The CSMN in effect succeeded the Carolina, Duke, Emory Institute for the Study of Islam, established in 1996 at a meeting convened by Lawrence and cooke in their home by scholars from Duke University, Emory University, the University of North Carolina, and North Carolina State University for the purpose of establishing a regional graduate program exchange and cooperative in Islamic religious studies.

58. Cooke and Lawrence, *Muslim Networks*, 1; emphasis added.

59. See Peter G. Mandaville, *Transnational Muslim Politics: Reimagining the Muslim Umma* (London: Routledge, 2001), summarized in cooke and Lawrence, introduction to *Muslim Networks*, 1–28.

60. cooke and Lawrence, *Muslim Networks*, 2.

61. cooke and Lawrence offer "men of the pen" on page 6 of *Muslim Networks*. Richard Bulliet adopts the term *patrician* to describe the social standing of the *ulama* and their families in Nishapur in the ninth to eleventh centuries. Richard Bulliet, *The Patricians of Nishapur: A Study in Medieval Islamic Social History* (Cambridge, Mass.: Harvard University Pres, 1972).

62. See, for example, Robert S. Leiken and Steven Brooke, "The Moderate Muslim Brotherhood," *Foreign Affairs* (March/April 2007): 107–21.

Caught between Enlightenment and Romanticism

On the Complex Relation of Religious, Ethnic, and Civic Identity in a Modern "Museum Culture"

LOUIS A. RUPRECHT JR.

As if in a museum some figure streaked & pocked, a "Roman copy of a lost Greek original," and looked at for decades by none but anatomy students, had suddenly been discovered to *be* the original . . .

James Merrill, *The (Diblos) Notebook*

Preliminaries

Modernity is not constituted by the Enlightenment alone. Rather the modern age is constituted both by the Enlightenment and the specific forms of contention it generated. Modernity, then, may be constituted politically by the ideals of the French Revolution, as well as by the Napoleonic Wars and their aftermath.[1] Philosophically, and presumably religiously as well, our modernity is constituted by Enlightenment science, rights-language, and secularism, on the one hand, as well as by the first roundhouse rejection of those same values. I am thinking primarily of the *Romantic* rejection. The thesis proposed in this essay is that "modernity" is best imagined as "caught between" the discrepant value systems embedded in Enlightenment and Romanticism. And I wish to situate the split between Enlightenment and Romantic values in one preeminently modern institution: the national public art museum. Certain important trajectories follow from that analysis, in conclusion. In the first part of this essay I lay out some of the main intellectual sources for this project—in the work of Marshall Hodgson, David Hollinger, Bruce Lawrence, and Alasdair MacIntyre. I then turn to an analysis of the construction of the modern public museum in relation to the emerging conception of national identity.

Much as was the case with James Merrill's fanciful statue, I am uncertain these days about how to distinguish the copy from the original, the reaction from the revolution, since we live on the far side of these seismic developments. If this view of the modern age is even roughly correct, then Romanticism is not only the first coherent quarrel with Enlightenment values; it is also a telling premonition of later religious movements that understood themselves, as Lawrence has suggested, as "revolt[s] against the modern age."[2] And yet fundamentalists today also have one foot planted squarely in each of two discrepant value systems; they too are "caught in between." That is the sense I have made of Lawrence's challenging and provocative suggestion, one highlighted by most of the contributors to this volume, that contemporary fundamentalists are modern without being modernists.[3] Given spatial and temporal restrictions, my analysis will be somewhat schematic, more suggestive than comprehensive. The fuller argument may be found in two forthcoming books inspired by the initial request for this essay.[4]

From Old World to New

Marshall Hodgson took the project of world history very seriously indeed. He believed that any credible attempt to discuss a world religion such as Islam required some clear conception of the ebb and flow of world history, how one civilization communicates and conflicts with others, and how all of them are changed by such cultural contact. Hodgson insisted—and all the maps and tables in the three impressive volumes of *The Venture of Islam* are sure testimony to this belief—that one needed to keep the entire world consciously in view whenever one endeavors to think or speak responsibly about any part of it. Beyond the display of raw intellect and fierce discipline, it is the moral seriousness and humanistic urgency of the work that grabs me still.

The two most singular innovations in Hodgson's venture may best be understood when viewed through a Romantic periodization: "the ancients and the moderns." Arguably the two greatest novelties of Hodgson's approach to Islamic civilization had to do with his interpretation of the period of Islamic formation ("the ancients") in the first volume and with his analysis of modernity and modernization in the third. One of Hodgson's single-handed contributions to the formation of a field was his emphasis on the centrality of Persian language and Persianate culture to the emergence of what he called Islamicate civilization. Hodgson went so far as to refer to Islamdom as the product of an "Irano-Semitic"[5] complex in literature, politics, and culture. This did much to cut against what he called "the Arabist bias"[6] in previous Islamic scholarship in the Occident, most of which we now deem Orientalist and Orientalizing. What has been less well remarked is the way Hodgson's own commitment to comparative methods resulted in this surprising conclusion. By comparing the period of early Christian formation to the Islamic case, Hodgson noted an Islamicate parallel to the Christian case of cultural formation. If Christendom was the result of an

"Helleno-Semitic" complex (the "Jews and Greeks" of whom Paul and others spoke repeatedly), then Islamdom was similarly "Irano-Semitic" in its inception. That insight has borne rich fruit, precisely to the degree that it was neither Eurocentric nor Christocentric.

But the real conceptual centerpiece of Hodgson's venture was his analysis of what made modern Europeans *Modern* (with a capital *M*), that seismic series of global revolutions he referred to as "the Great Western Transmutation" (GWT).[7] Two things are especially noteworthy about that account; both reveal Hodgson's intellectual debt to G. W. F. Hegel and to Max Weber. First there is the emphatic globalism of his approach. Hodgson makes the remarkable observation that the GWT is so far from proving any inherent superiority of Occidental culture (the Eurocentric "West is best" story) that it actually counts decisively *against* the effort to privilege one oikoumene over the others. The four most significant technological innovations that fueled the GWT, in Hodgson's view, were all invented in China, not in Europe; he is speaking of gunpowder, the compass, the printing press, and the civil service exam.[8] Hodgson plays brilliantly with the Hegelian attempt to sift through the alternatively accidental and necessary developments in world history.[9] "It just so happened" is a repeated refrain in these defining pages of *The Venture of Islam*. China *just so happened* to be separated from the Americas by a sea three times the size of the Atlantic. The Europeans *just so happened* to use their compasses to get there first. The Chinese writing system *just so happened* to lend itself less easily to block printing. So the Europeans *just so happened* to engage in the emblematically modern projects of scriptural dissemination and political pamphleteering first. The case of gunpowder is more interesting, for the simple reason that gunpowder can be put to so many different uses. As Hodgson repeatedly emphasizes, there is far more to the rise of the European gunpowder empires and their global hegemony than gunpowder. Gunpowder may be used for fireworks and pyrotechnic displays. It may be ignited in cannon without projectiles to create deafening and terrifying noises. But the Europeans *just so happened* upon the devastating military innovation embodied in a well-disciplined infantry armed with individual, handheld firearms. That development was destined to change the nature of modern warfare and quite literally altered the global map.

Taken together, the ways in which these Chinese technological developments were put to innovative new uses in Europe paint a surprisingly different picture of the modern. Hodgson believed that we are heir to the emergence of a new social ideal: that of a fully autonomous individual, one at the same time more intimately connected to the collective. Such a symbiotic image of the individual and the community is evidenced in Hegel's mature philosophical system, which is what "just so happens" to make Hegel the first modern philosopher. His was the first systematic attempt to theorize the sociopolitical impact and the ethical implications of the GWT. Hegel, too, was caught importantly "between Enlightenment and Romanticism."[10]

The invocation of Hegel is telling for another reason—namely the confusion over the reception of his views that broke out between Left and Right Hegelians in the mid–nineteenth century. Hodgson, like Hegel, has what seems to me a far subtler and far less polemical theory about what has been happening in the world over the course of the past four hundred years. His conceptualization of the GWT suggests that certain crucial developments in Europe between 1350 and 1550 coalesced in a way that gave the European gunpowder empires rather sudden global preeminence. For the first time in world history, one oikoumene outstripped all the others, and the "rough parity" that had previously existed millennially between different Afro-Eurasian oikumenai broke down once and for all, with, as Hodgson notes, "results that were disastrous almost everywhere."[11] Innovation was institutionalized in ways that increased the rate of scientific, moral, and political change to such a degree that the rest of the world's oikumenai were trapped in a game of catch-up they were doomed eternally to lose. Still Hodgson refuses to reduce modern developments to technological or material concerns, in much the same way that Weber uses Hegel to nuance materialist analyses, Marxist and otherwise. Hodgson notes that the real issue lying at the very heart of the GWT is not technology; it is *technicalism*.[12] This new ideology, Hodgson noted, presented unique new challenges to religious communities and their conception of both authority and tradition. At the heart of the GWT, then, is a "rationalizing calculativeness," that "depended, especially at first, on *an expectation of continuous innovation*: on encouraging an attitude of willingness to experiment, taking as little as possible for granted what had already been thought and done, rejecting established authority of every sort, and running the inherent risks of error that such rejection entails. . . . By the end of the eighteenth century . . . some of the most important institutions in the Occident had come to embody frankly and zealously the very principle of change, of innovation. . . . In the new social organization, innovation was institutionalized."[13] Hegel *just so happened* to begin his philosophical career at precisely the time when these institutional renditions of technicalism were secured and, in Hodgson's view (though this last is debatable), inevitable.

Long a student of South Asia and of Hodgson's ideas, Bruce Lawrence's recent work has focused more explicitly on the postcolonial context[14] and the turmoil created by the increasing politicization of identity categories.[15] He also extends his work in Islamic studies to the Americas, as Hodgson did not live to do. As we turn to the Americas, two perplexing developments come into focus. The first is the language of "identity" itself, and the way in which this paradigmatically Romantic rhetoric aided the Romantics in displacing more traditional religious values. Now link personal identity to ethnic identity, and we discover the intellectual and political fits to which that notion often leads in postcolonial contexts: How many nation-states to create out of the wreckage of a collapsed empire? If there is to be no Yugoslav federation, then should we create five countries, or seven, in its wake? And how many countries should the former Soviet Union contain? These intractable questions are answered differently depending on whom you ask, what their implicit conception of a people or a nation is, and thus they have not come to rest in our own day.

David Hollinger's *Postethnic America* addresses itself to these problems by cutting more emphatically against the intellectual grain.[16] It is a book about the New World—a world not even present on most of Hodgson's maps. And the book invites us to think "*beyond* multiculturalism," at a time when most North Americans think we are not close to achieving our multiculturalism yet. Hollinger suggests that there is no coherent way to achieve it. How to move beyond multiculturalism, then, when we are not yet multicultural? Hollinger's suggestion is intriguing: he notes that the Americas clearly *are* multicultural, if by that we mean that they are constituted by an increasingly diverse civic population. Multiculturalism, on this view, is simply a statement of fact. But multicultural*ism* as a political ideology now regnant in North America is, at best, a fuzzy-headed attempt to make moral sense of the facts of such pluralism. Its record to date has not been a promising one. You will note the echo once again of Lawrence's important distinction between moderns and modernists; here Hollinger is distinguishing between a multicultural political space and a theory of multiculturalism.

The virtue of Hollinger's book lies in the way it articulates several alternative destinations that warrant serious consideration for any thoughtful modern citizen or scholar. It also makes the crucial point that intellectual history matters to these deliberations, and that our failure to attend to such history has been disastrous. Hodgson had argued in much the same way, but it is intriguing to see the same point applied with equal passion to the Americas. "The United States is not a young country," Hollinger opines. "No other major nation in the twenty-first century operates on the basis of a constitution written in the eighteenth."[17] And it just so happens that we are now in a position to see some of the unintended logic of the Founders' political aspirations, and their moral vision:

> The United States now finds itself in a position to develop and act upon a cultural self-image as *a national solidarity committed—but often failing—to incorporate individuals from a great variety of communities of descent, on equal but not homogeneous terms, into a society with democratic aspirations inherited largely from England.* There is much more to the United States than this. But if one were obliged to sum up in one sentence what a history of the United States is a history *of,* this sentence has much to recommend it beyond its simple

truthfulness. It emphasizes the liberal and cosmopolitan elements of the national self-image without denying the parts of American history that are not liberal and are not cosmopolitan.[18]

I want to devote the remainder of this essay to an attempt to grapple with these observations and their historical resonance. The United States is not a young country. It has a history. And its history wants desperately to be the history *of* something, too. As we will see, the fulcrum around which everything turns, in Hollinger's judgment, is an ancient ideal whose pedigree may be traced back to the Hellenistic age: the cosmopolitan ideal most commonly associated with Stoicism. It is arguable that the cosmopolitan ideal, in a form roughly like the one Hollinger articulates, may be the best available option for splitting the difference, as it were, between our twinned political commitments to Enlightenment and Romanticism. Civic cosmopolitanism[19] has been upheld by many recent political theorists as an alternative to other forms of religious or ethnic nationalism, ideas that, at least as much as freedom, seem to be "on the march."

From Enlightenment to Romanticism

On this view the history of the United States since its founding charters has been the history of the movement from Enlightenment to Romanticism, and the conflict that emerges quite naturally from their deliberate juxtaposition. I wish to gesture briefly to two books that help bring this thesis into focus. The first is Bruce Lawrence's *Defenders of God*, which is dedicated to Marshall Hodgson and is true heir to the latter's humanism. Lawrence proposes a bold thesis: namely that "fundamentalism," which seemed for all the world like a local North American creation,[20] is in fact a far-reaching *global* phenomenon. It may have been most dramatic and visible in Iran, but it is truly global in its scope and orientation. Lawrence called it a religious "revolt against the modern age." There would not be Fundamentalism, with a capital *F*, except for the fact of Modernity, with a capital *M*. The first half of Lawrence's book is devoted to painting a picture not only of the modern age, but also the accompanying ideology of modern*ism*. Lawrence's conclusion is very clear: fundamentalism is a symptom of a pervasive crisis *within* the modern.

The second book I wish to mention agrees with that thesis for a very different reason: it is Alasdair MacIntyre's *After Virtue*.[21] MacIntyre proposed an astonishing thesis (he himself called it a "disquieting suggestion," but he means us to feel far more than disquiet). MacIntyre suggests that modern (and "Western," in his view) moral languages are in such disarray that we are no longer capable of seeing how incoherent our moral arguments have become. We have inherited bits and pieces of various moral languages—words such as *virtue* and *duty*, *courage* and *compassion*—but we have lost sight of the context in which those words once made sense. MacIntyre's word for that moral context is *tradition*, and he goes so far as to lay this entire problem at the feet of the Enlightenment. The Enlightenment was a profoundly antitraditional movement, he argues, one that misunderstood itself *as* a tradition.[22] It is not. The Enlightenment took a wrecking ball to traditional social practices, ways of life, and worldviews, MacIntyre argues, and has failed over the course of two hundred years to put anything intelligible in its place. The country that puts this incoherence on display better than any other, he clearly believes, is the United States. It is in this country that we see the inevitable failure of what he calls "the Enlightenment Project"—the attempt to ground morality in universalizable and context-free legal norms—writ large, and writ wrongly.

So these two books work in opposite directions but move toward the common purpose of situating the contemporary culture of contestation in the Americas. Lawrence begins with an American coinage, *fundamentalism*, and ends by making a global point about the modern age and its distress. MacIntyre begins by telling the story of the history of Western moral thought, yet his critique comes to rest (and fruition) in the Enlightenment-run-amok that he sees as the essence of U.S. culture. I want to try to work in both directions in the remainder of this essay, and I wish to emphasize what neither Lawrence nor MacIntyre discusses: Romanticism.

I begin in North America. The Declaration of Independence and the U.S. Constitution are preeminent Enlightenment documents, enshrining time-honored Enlightenment ideals of political equality and citizens' rights against the coercive power of cultural or religious majorities, as well as the governments they serve and sponsor. Romanticism, surely a ragbag category if ever there were one, was critically suspicious of all that. So is MacIntyre, as I have already noted. "The truth is plain," he says, intending to shock us into new awareness: "there are no [natural or human] rights, and belief in them is one with belief in witches and in unicorns."[23] As the title of this essay indicates, I am trying to develop a historical perspective on some of the concepts that inform these political developments and this critique.

In a word I locate modern moral disarray elsewhere than in Enlightenment, suggesting that mainstream culture in the United States today is "caught between" two competing and probably inconsistent sets of political commitments, those of the Enlightenment and those of Romanticism. The United States is uniquely located at that nexus, where these competing sets of political commitments inevitably collided. The country emerged in the years (1776–87) when Enlightenment ideals were nearly secured, and just before their Romantic counterideals came to more prevalent expression (1790–1830). We see this tension embedded in the conflict of metaphors in domestic U.S. politics—the old-style image of the "melting pot" versus the aspiration toward a more Canadian brand of "multiculturalism"[24]—and we see it positively bedevil U.S. foreign policy, where appeals to "human rights," and the international bodies created for their protection, slam up against a peculiarly modern interest in securing borders and national autonomy. We often do not seem to know quite how to conceive of the proper relationship between that eminently Romantic conception—the modern nation-state, as defined by a national identity grounded in an ethnic history—and that preeminently Enlightenment body of internationalism, the United Nations.

If the Enlightenment stood for anything politically, then it stood for a fairly critical stance vis-à-vis traditions, whether they be cultural or historical, political or religious. Here is the spirit of Hodgson's "technicalization," the sheer institutionalization of cultural restlessness, and "the expectation of continuous innovation." The Enlightenment made the status of the human being qua human being a potential political trump card—something that guaranteed and secured certain self-evident rights, something that also entailed certain vague but heartfelt moral obligations. Being human as such came to matter more than being human in this way, in this region, in this tradition, in this religion. Enlightenment ideals, then, embody the very culture and color blindness that most associate with what is most admirable in a more-than-two-hundred-year-old global experiment with pluralistic democracy. This Enlightenment commitment to political autonomy flies in the face of other common notions, however—what we might term a collective "identity," though it seems clear to me that this language was unavailable in the eighteenth century, at least until very near its end.[25] Nor, for that matter, was the language of "race," a concept first given a scientific meaning by these same Enlightenment thinkers in these same decades. Enlightenment universalism embodied a bracing and liberating set of political ideas, fueling the North American revolution well before it did the French (the Greek Revolution of 1821 was another matter, an eminently more Romantic matter, as we shall see). The U.S. Constitution is, as Hollinger notes, arguably the first and most long-lived political expression of these Enlightenment political ideals and constitutional commitments. It articulates a conception of civic nationalism against which later Romantic nationalisms were arrayed—ethnic and religious nationalism especially.

Sir Isaiah Berlin devoted his later years to studying that hodgepodge of literary, philosophical, and religious movements that coalesced in what we call "Romanticism," and while he was never able to complete the book on Romanticism he envisioned, the decision was made shortly after his death in 1997 to publish his Mellon lectures on the topic. *The Roots of Romanticism*[26] is a superb presentation of the central thesis with which I am working here: namely, that Romanticism was clearly the first, the most coherent, and also the longest-lived reaction against Enlightenment in Europe. As Charles Taylor has argued with great subtlety and elegance, Romanticism is still one of the premier "sources" of the modern conception of selfhood and—here is that word again—of the modern "identity."[27]

If the Enlightenment was sometimes characterized by a crude scientism, then this was due to its overly optimistic views on the possibilities and expanding horizons of human knowledge. Enlightenment thinkers were tempted by the claim that all human questions were by definition answerable, Berlin suggests, and that such answers could not come into conflict.[28] Politically speaking, the commitments to liberty, fraternity, and equality cannot work at cross-purposes. And religiously speaking, the commitment to God's revelation in a scriptural canon and God's ongoing presence, as Spirit, in the interpretive life of the community should not, either. These are precisely the points of view that the early Romantics—especially in Germany, and to a lesser degree in England as well—found ludicrous. The world of the Romantics does not cohere. It is fraught with demonic forces and irredeemable conflicts, many of them the creation of Nature's most demonic character of all: "man." The tension between that demonic individual and the collective that sought to restrain him must inevitably erupt into collisions, conflicts, and revolutions. Hegel recognized this; Nietzsche reveled in the fact.

If Enlightenment thinkers wrote encyclopedias, attempting to fit the entire planet into a single scheme and a single story, then the Romantics were more comfortable with local histories and local grammars and contented themselves with more local compendia—of national folklore, national literature, and even national languages. What we are witnessing, I think, is the reassertion of the primacy of local, rather than global, belonging. Berlin clearly enunciates the fundamental dichotomies that were partly the result of this Romantic reaction: human identity versus a national identity; law as color blind versus custom as culturally and ethnically coded; future orientation versus a nostalgic privileging of the past; reason versus irrationalism; secular versus quasi-pagan; optimism versus pessimism; and so on. A new conception of (ethnic) nationalism was born of this selfsame constellation of ideas. The U.S. polity was originally relatively free of this rhetoric, but that situation has changed dramatically of late, under the aegis of a surprising array of forces: fundamentalism, multiculturalism, and the politicizing of identity.

It is important to recognize precisely how the Romantics reconceived the concepts of nationalism and of national identity. Their work of collecting national literatures, folklores, languages, and dialects was part of a larger project, also vaguely Romantic in origin: the articulation of a national character. This presumption still lies at the very heart of most contemporary arguments about nation formation—nowhere more so than in the long-suffering lands formerly under Ottoman control. One vast, tragic political question persists: If a large landmass is not going to be one nation, then the question of how many it ought to be instead is especially charged. The Ottoman collapse and recolonization after the First World War presages many of our contemporary troubles. "National identity"—some conception of a people, defined by its explicit history and inscribed by its implicit borders—has served as the most influential recent answer to questions about the formation of nationhood, peoplehood, and partition. Its Romantic roots have not been sufficiently remarked, however. The Romantics invited the assumption that there was a place on a map—let's call it "Germany"—and that "a people" had lived there for a very long time. These people had a continuous language, a continuous history, and a clearly recognizable set of national characteristics that rendered them recognizable, even at a great distance, in the past. Access to that past was gained through the language and its literature, as well as through archaeology, that eminently Romantic "science" of human and/or cultural origins. If the Enlightenment was forward looking and utopian, then Romanticism returned to history and the authority of a (largely fictive) originary past.

We know one of the roads—and I should emphasize that it was not the only road—that emerged out of that potent constellation of ideas: it was fascism.[29] It led, in its strangest forms (and precisely in those nation-states that were formed latest and whose national "identity" was least secure), to the idea that Germany or Italy was in fact a far larger entity than the current map of Europe indicated, precisely by arguing that there were "Germans" living in other regions. Complex appeals that linked history to national character and race culminated in annexation, ethnic cleansing, invasion, and attempted genocide. It is precisely this "blood and soil" conception of national identity that had such a shattering effect on twentieth-century politics and twenty-first-century attempts to derive lessons therefrom. But the roots of this too may be found in Romanticism.

The Romantic Museum

I am especially intrigued by what might almost be called the "co-birth" of four paradigmatically modern phenomena and by the new institutions that came to be associated with each of them. I want to mark a decisive connection between the birth of modern archaeology, the construction of the modern public museum, an emerging conception of national identity, and the ragbag movement we now call Romanticism—all of which contributed, among other things, to my own profession of comparative religion. No doubt this will seem like an odd list. But I have come to believe that viewing these four phenomena together may assist us in understanding each of them better,[30] as well as assist us in better comprehending the long-standing appeal of another nineteenth-century creation: Greece itself. And I intend that claim quite literally, for Greece was formed as an independent nation-state, replete with a Bavarian king, only after a long war of independence against the Ottoman Empire (1821–30), a war it would not have won so easily (if at all) had the European powers not elected to intervene at several decisive points.[31] Why they chose to intervene, and to do so decisively, is one of those unanswerable questions, reflection upon which helped give birth to this essay. European rivalry with the Ottomans, especially Russian and Austrian rivalry, does not fully explain this, and the alleged antipathy between European Christendom and the world of Islam explains even less.

That religious values and spiritual aspirations played a role in the Greek War is clear. But religion must be reconceived in the very broadest terms—the way the Romantics conceived it—if this claim is to be made meaningful. Four centuries of speculative flirtation with pagan antiquity, coupled with two centuries of figural pilgrimage to Catholic and pagan Italy—and two decades of pilgrimage to Greece—provide a subtler context. As the traveler's reports and guidebooks make abundantly clear, Europeans had always known, in many cases, where Greek antiquities lay. They had been underground for a very long time, and they were often exposed in the ruins of temples still marking the place of certain prominent ancient sites. The question is, Why was there such a sudden explosion of interest in, and the requisite commitment of enormous monetary and human resources to, the recovery of Greek (and other) antiquities in the first three decades of the nineteenth century? Napoleon may have initiated this vast industry during his Egyptian campaigns in 1798 and 1799, but the British and Bavarians perfected the ploy. And Greece, though a later destination to an originally Italian "Grand Tour," eventually became the Europeans' premier cultural laboratory. Archaeology itself, then, was quite literally one of the most influential discoveries of the nineteenth century.

What followed next needs special emphasis: public museums were one logical outgrowth of this vast scientific industry; they too were quite new. There had been collections of antiquities before, private collections, housed especially in the well-appointed villas of countless church cardinals in Rome. A still more immediate precursor for my purposes was the establishment of the Capitoline Museum by the Vatican in 1734, and the "Museo Profano" within the Vatican complex itself by Clement XIII in or around 1761.[32] That the self-professed leader of European Christendom would sponsor a public collection of pagan art indicates that something strange was afoot. It was the commitment of public monies to the purchase of antiquities and their housing in a place designed for free public access that constitutes the real revolution. The debate in the House of Commons regarding the purchase of the Elgin Marbles is illustrative of many of the issues implicit in this innovation.[33] Its outcome, of course, resulted in the creation of one of the first public museums of ancient art in the modern world. I have already tried to tell its story in tandem with the creation of its rival and distant cousin, the Glyptothek Museum in Munich.[34]

The religious valence of such collections had already been remarked by poets, from Keats to Byron, in their dramatically different ways. Both men made "pilgrimages" to see such things, after all. Keats describes his visit to the first of the Elgin pieces in London as a kind of spiritual awakening that takes him very nearly to a place past words.

> Haydon! forgive me that I cannot speak
>   Definitively on these mighty things;
>   Forgive me that I have not Eagle's wings—
> that what I want I know not where to seek . . .

The poet resolves this dilemma with two stunning images: one of worship and the other of time. Pilgrims who come to the Elgin marbles will almost inevitably fall into a state of worshipful, ecstatic inspiration and Romantic epiphany. What such aesthetic pilgrims witnessed most clearly was proof of the vagary and fragility of time:

> So do these wonders a most dizzy pain,
>   That mingles Grecian grandeur with the rude
> Wasting of old Time—with a billowy main—
>   A sun—a shadow of a magnitude.[35]

Similarly Byron framed his two-year trip to Greece (1809–11) as a literal pilgrimage;[36] at times it seems almost as if the entire country were a museum turned inside out. But for those who had neither the means nor the time to manage a trip such as that, the public museum offered an alternative (and infinitely easier) pilgrimage site. Such a museum, it was argued, served a profoundly civic function, by bringing a modern citizenry into closer contact with ancient beauty, an aesthetic value now more closely connected to truth and civic virtue. It was Keats who concluded (while looking at a Grecian urn, no less) that "'Beauty is truth, truth beauty'—that is all / Ye know on earth, and all ye need to know."[37] But is that really enough?

There must be something else at work here. I want to suggest that one of the chief legacies of Romanticism, in addition to its aestheticizing of morality and politics, is a new way of talking about nationalism and national identity—and that this dramatic shift was housed most effectively in modern public art museums. It is still so close to us, still so much a part of the way we talk about politics and identity, that we fail to notice its strangeness. The political reorganization of this planet in the nineteenth and early twentieth centuries tells a story of the collapse of empires and the creation of nation-states out of their former colonial holdings. Greece, like the United States, is a fairly early example of an ongoing "postcolonial" trend. But Greece was a Romantic construction at its inception, as the United States was not.

What is most striking about this general agitation for national independence is just how loose the reigning conceptions of ethnic or national identity actually were. (Greek borders have in fact proven to be as elastic and as fungible as U.S. borders—and for reasons just as suspect.) The elaborate "national" collections of the Romantics were designed to underline the importance of the concept of ancestry in the construction of such a Romantic national identity. The invocation of history, and a privileged past, was the key: the people who had lived in this place *had always been* Greeks, or Germans, or what have you (only indigenous Americans could venture this claim, as we will see). We are witnessing the subtle introduction of ethnic identity, and the almost spiritual power of some prior notion of ancestry, into the construction of modern nationalism. Fascism notwithstanding, these political, religious, and historical trends have not to come to rest in our own time.

What the Greeks had to do with any of this was complicated. For another idea emerged among Romantic historiographers in Europe in the nineteenth century, one seen quite clearly in Hegel's *Lectures on the Philosophy of History*. Here we meet the idea that Greece was the "childhood" of Europe, as Rome was her young adulthood. The matter of Greek and/or Roman ancestry mattered enormously to modern Greek and Italian identity, of course. Yet it seemed to matter every bit as much to the British and French and Germans, and sometimes more. Why? Because the ancient Greeks were now invoked as the "ancestors" of the modern West. Greco-Roman culture embodied a brand of nonsectarian spirituality that attracted many disaffected Romantics. Greek religion—in tandem with its sculptural images—just might be made to belong to everyone. Flirting with the Muses might not be the same thing as flirting with pagan gods, after all. The modern public art museum (deriving from the Greek term *mouseion*) was literally conceived as a "shrine to the Muses."

Such museums traded in one commodity that has rarely if ever been given its due, a commodity that still enjoys overwhelming currency at the dawn of a new millennium: identity itself, whether ethnic or religious or national, and usually all three at once. The birth of the modern public museum had everything to do with the emergence of a new way of talking about identity, one whose roots also lay in Romanticism. And that raises a singular dilemma in the Americas, for their inhabitants were not exclusively European. The current prominence of multiculturalism rather than melting pots in our political discourse, coupled with an increasing awareness of the various cultural influences—indigenous, European, and west African—at home in the New World, make this abundantly clear. But then why invest so heavily in Greek art here, in the Americas? Remarkably the story I have been tracking, a story that began in the early nineteenth century in Rome and then led to London and Munich, culminates in the fairy-tale landscape of Malibu, where we find what is arguably the greatest institutional investment in ancient art the Euro-American world has ever seen: at the Getty Villa.[38] What has not yet been explained, nor thought on sufficiently, is what we are really investing in, and why.[39]

Old World Museums, New World Bones

I want to shift the scene now—closer to the Balkan peninsula, and thus closer to Greece—in order to trace the subsequent development of such museums at twentieth century's end. In September 1995 I found myself in Skopje, the capital city of the Former Yugoslav Republic of Macedonia (FYROM). It was the day tension in that city finally dissipated due to the dramatic signing of a Greco-Skopjan agreement in Manhattan, and I was attending an impromptu press conference hastily organized to announce the formalizing of U.S.-Skopjan relations and the preliminary opening of a U.S. embassy in what had formerly been, of all things, a kindergarten. The fight had been about—what else would it be about?—ancestry and national identity. The flash points were, unsurprisingly, a constellation of images and of names.

The Macedonians had succeeded where every other Yugoslav republic had failed. They had declared their independence from the Milosevic regime without a bloodbath. The country gained its independence peacefully in 1993, but that is where things stalled. The Greek government blocked NATO and UN recognition of the fledgling country in protest over their choice of a national flag and a name. The flag utilized a symbol, the Vergina Star, embossed on a bright, blood-red background. That star had originally been discovered in the early 1980s on a golden ossuary in northern Greece, one that possibly held the remains of Alexander the Great's father, Philip. The two hailed from a region, ancient Macedon, that was claimed by the modern Greeks as "Greek," despite the fact that the father and son swooped down out of the north and conquered a confederation of Greek cities opposed to them. Alexander was thus a foreign conqueror of "Greece" before he became "Great." But histories that are designed to underwrite modern notions of identity deal in amnesia as often as they do in ancestry.[40] The Greeks prevented political recognition and the establishment of diplomatic ties with the fledgling state, pending resolution of the name of the country to be so recognized. In the very next year, the small athletic contingent from Skopje was still forced to march into Atlanta's Olympic Stadium under *F* (FYROM) rather than *M*. "Macedonia," the Greeks insisted, was a Greek name, and the southern Slavs could not have it. The employment of such names in the Balkans, the Greeks argued with far greater justification, had inspired programs of territorial annexation and even invasion repeatedly since 1903, when Macedonia was home to the first modern anticolonial terrorist organization[41]—one aimed precisely at propagandizing for "national" independence.

More intriguing to me than the press conference, which seemed forced and silly, were the three museums I had visited on the previous day. None of them was completed, yet all three were already open to the public. They needed to be, for they were designed to display the very overlap between political propagandizing and the modern museum culture that has been one of my chief preoccupations in this essay. The first museum, the Museum of Skopje, was simply a collection of old photographs, chronicling the history of the automobile industry in this city since 1905. The Archaeological and Ethnographic museums held greater interest, though the building in which these collections were being assembled had not yet been completed. Here one witnessed the enormous political project of manufacturing a coherent identity out of what Balkaners themselves refer to as the multicultural Macedonian "salad." The Ethnographic Museum boasted a collection of some sixty local costumes and musical instruments, many of which were identical to the sorts of things one might find across the modern border, in northern Greece.

Of the three the Archaeological Museum was most fascinating for the archaeological layers it privileged. There was a great deal made of the Neolithic record here, a historical record presumably free of modern identity claims (though, as we shall see shortly, even that is not always so—in the New World). After a gloss of the Bronze Age, Iron Age, Hellenistic, Roman, and Byzantine periods (the term *Greek* was never used), the visitor was shuttled into two full rooms dedicated to the agitation for independence around 1903 and the Balkan Wars of 1912–13.[42] The cumulative effect of all this was plain enough: a very selective modern identity was being manufactured out of bits and pieces of the past. It seemed as bizarre to this U.S. observer as the original Greek protests over the country's name had been just one year earlier.

Lest I be taken to be merely writing off such things as silly and propagandizing, I want to shift venues once again and to move west, from the old Ottoman Empire to the New World. I want to track a surprisingly similar debate about ancestry that emerged at roughly this same time in the state of Washington. This debate over cultural and ethnic identities also wound up in a museum. Historically speaking, as I have said several times already, the United States and its founding documents were pretty clearly innocent of Romantic ideas. They were simply conceived too early. Moreover a self-styled "nation of immigrants" will logically have a very hard time articulating a sense of national identity that asserts the primacy of "blood and soil" to the conception of ancestry. But that older, North American narrative of the melting pot, the conception of the nation as a collection of immigrants, notoriously excluded two major ethnic groups: those west Africans who were not immigrants, precisely because they did not come here by choice, and those indigenous peoples who were gradually rendered invisible through the long, bloody course of the mechanized march across a continent. Of these two groups, the Romantic ideas I am tracking here lend themselves far more powerfully and poignantly to Native American peoples. Indeed one hears with astonishing consistency from such indigenous peoples that their own most "Romantic" ideals—of ancestor worship, reverence for nature, and a sacred tie to the land—simply cannot be harmonized with the regnant Enlightenment ethos enshrined in the U.S. Constitution. The tentative political rapprochement in the United States has essentially granted this point and ceded certain territories to indigenous peoples as a place in which to practice their politics and their religion in their own way. A separate people, a separate place, and a separatist politics.

Yet the notion that cuts to the very heart of ethnic and national identity, so conceived, has received insufficient attention: the concept of ancestry itself. The idea has such an obviousness about it that it seems not to require much in the way of explanation. For that very reason, I suspect that it does—and the twentieth-century experience of fascism demonstrated its potential danger. As Jeffrey Stout puts the point with sharp eloquence, "the solidarity of an aggrieved people can be a dangerous thing."[43]

One year after my return from Skopje, in 1996, a 9,000-year-old skeleton was discovered along the Kennewick riverbank in Washington state. Developments over the next decade bordered on the surreal.[44] After discovery of the skeleton in July, and an initial radiocarbon dating that indicated its age at somewhere in the neighborhood of 9,500 years, the U.S. Army Corps of Engineers intervened, since the city of Kennewick leases the riverbank where the bones were found from the federal government. The corps took possession of the skeleton in September, denied all further scientific requests to study it, and expressed its intention to return the bones to a coalition of five tribes as required by the 1990 Native American Graves Protection and Repatriation Act (NAGPRA).[44] Having cast its lot almost immediately with the tribes, the corps permitted five different religious rituals to be conducted near the remains, in at least two cases permitting the depositing of organic material and more bones with them, thereby rendering subsequent radiocarbon dating impossible. Despite temporary court restraining orders and federal legislation designed specifically to prohibit it, in the spring of 1998 the Army Corps of Engineers then covered the entire Kennewick site under several tons of rubble and 3,700 new Russian olive trees, unusual for their speedy growth and deep roots (all at a cost of $170,000), clearly intending to prevent the possibility of any further discoveries on this site. Finally on August 30, 2002, the U.S. District Court in Portland, Oregon, issued a decision, finding primarily in favor of the eighteen scientists who had brought suit against the Corps of Engineers, the U.S. Department of the Interior, and by implication, against the claims of the tribal federation that they had been assisting.[45]

While the legal issues raised were complex, the moral and political stakes in this debate are clear enough. The case turned decisively on the definition of "Native American" under the NAGPRA, a definition that in turn assumes some conception of "ancestry"—the proposed relationship between a nine-thousand-year-old corpse and a contemporary tribal federation. The Army Corps of Engineers proposes to define any human remains dated prior to confirmed European contact (that is, five hundred years or more ago) as Native American by definition. This definition admittedly has a certain Romantic obviousness about it. But the scientists were calling for a more nuanced conception of ancestry, one grounded in an allegedly more scientific conception of ethnicity—or rather, of race. For the morphology of this skeleton suggested that it was neither European nor Native American. Research paleoanthropologists suggest that this skeleton could contribute to a new thesis about early settlement and migration patterns in the Americas. The idea is that such settlement took place in waves and originated in various foreign locales. If the Kennewick Man "belongs" to anyone as an "ancestor," they suggested, such people likely live either in Polynesia or among the Ainu of Hokkaido Island, Japan. So it is that the Romantic ideas of ancestry and national identity, on the one hand, and the Enlightenment conceptions of race and the scientific study of global migration patterns, on the other, came into inevitable conflict on the battleground of human remains. The trouble is that both sets of ideals have been asked to play an essential role in defining the "identity" of this skeleton as determined in our courts of law.

Religion also played a subtler role, since the confederated tribes of the Umatilla asserted in an amicus brief that modern science simply cannot adjudicate what are essentially premodern religious ideas: "We already know our history. It is passed on to us through our elders and through our religious practices. . . . From our oral histories, we know that our people have been a part of this land since the beginning of time. We do not believe that our people migrated here from another continent, as the scientists do."[46] Now, this claim—with its studied refusal of any distinction between religious "belief" and scientific "argument" (and its strange assertion of autochthony)—sounds remarkably close to Bruce Lawrence's conception of fundamentalism, with its embattled spirit of anti-Enlightenment antimodernism. What I am noting in this essay is how utterly Romantic such claims also are. Debates about the "identity" of the Kennewick Man by 2001 were well on the way to constituting a latter-day Scopes trial,[47] one made more difficult of resolution by the multicultural and anticosmopolitan veneer that has been attached to these remains.[48] The bones languished in—where else?—the Burke Museum at the University of Washington in Seattle, which sponsored a conference dedicated to further study in February 2006 but which served merely as a holding area for remains still "belonging" to the federal government of the United States.

Concluding Trajectories

At this point I simply reiterate, bullet-point-fashion, several of the broader trajectories to which this essay may be pointing. First I have attempted to trace the Romantic lineage of much, if not most, contemporary "identity" talk. And I am especially intrigued by the manner in which modern museums became one of the sites in which such "identities" were and continue to be contested. Second I argue that Romanticism was in fact a premonition for many later forms of antimodernism, "religious fundamentalism" included. Third, given my longstanding interest in the appropriations of "classical" cultures and modern museums as important institutions in the project of identity formation, I have become more concerned about the dominance of aesthetic metaphors in contemporary political and moral theory. I worry about the degree to which the "aestheticizing of morality" is itself part of a larger North American belief that "personal experience" is the ultimate arbiter for moral judgments. This is precisely what Alasdair MacIntyre decries as modern "emotivism." The notion that intense feeling "counts" as moral argument is one of the more pernicious legacies of Romanticism and a continuous challenge in the comparative religions classroom. Fourth, however, this is clearly not a singularly North American issue; it too is global. While most of my work tends to focus on regions that are not as strictly "Western" as we are invited to imagine them (Greece, Italy, the Balkans, and the United States), my work possesses clear implications for the emergence of modern Islamicate nation-states in the postcolonial twentieth and twenty-first centuries. Attending to when and how such nations construct their own public art museums and ministries of culture, and what stories they choose to foreground, may serve as one way to reclaim important but muted Muslim voices now lost in the cacophony of international debates about war and security, detention and terror (Carl Ernst's fascinating analysis of "civilizational Islam" offers a crucial theoretical corrective to such matters). Finally, and in the spirit of cross-cultural inquiry, I have tried to develop the thesis that modern geopolitics and some of our most prominent moral debates are caught between the not-very-compatible commitments of Enlightenment and Romantic values. I have concluded that a certain conception of cosmopolitan world citizenship—the notion of a civic, rather than ethnic or religious, nationalism—does decidedly better in the face of such conflicts than the now-regnant language of multiculturalism and identity, a rhetoric that tends to underwrite the very conflicts (and reify the categories) it was designed to resolve. I have also tried to show how such problems play out with surprising similarity in the Old World and the New, from Kosovo to Kennewick.

NOTES

1. This is one important implication, I take it, in Marshall G. S. Hodgson's decision to refer to the modern age as a creation of "the generation of 1789," rather than simply as a product and epiphenomenon of the French Revolution. See *The Venture of Islam: Conscience and History in a World Civilization*, 3 vols. (Chicago: University of Chicago Press, 1974), 3:205–8.

2. This important phrase derives from Bruce B. Lawrence, *Defenders of God: The Fundamentalist Revolt against the Modern Age* (San Francisco: Harper & Row, 1989), reprinted with a new preface in 1995 by the University of South Carolina Press.

3. Ibid., 17, 23–42.

4. Louis A. Ruprecht Jr., "Winckelmann's Secret History: The Birth of Art History and the Vatican's First Profane Museum," and "Shrines to the Muse: A *Religious* History of the Modern Public Art Museum" (both forthcoming).

5. Hodgson, *Venture of Islam*, 1:60–62, 103–4, 117n9, 233–40.

6. Ibid., 1:39–45, 62–63.

7. Ibid., 3:176–222.

8. Ibid., 3:197.

9. This is developed most clearly in Hegel's introduction to his *Lectures on the Philosophy of History*, trans. J. Sibree (New York: Dover, 1956), 1–79.

10. For a related interpretation of Hegel's contemporary relevance, see Jeffrey Stout, *Democracy and Tradition: Religion, Ethics and Public Philosophy* (Princeton, N.J.: Princeton University Press, 2004), 185.

11. Hodgson, *Venture of Islam*, 3:200.

12. This also seems one of the crucial sources for Lawrence's distinction between moderns and *modernists*; see *Defenders of God*, 1–2, 23–42, 247n1.

13. Hodgson, *Venture of Islam*, 3:193.

14. Bruce B. Lawrence, *Shattering the Myth: Islam beyond Violence* (Princeton, N.J.: Princeton University Press, 1998).

15. Bruce B. Lawrence, *New Faiths, Old Fears: Muslims and Other Asian Immigrants in American Religious Life* (New York: Columbia University Press, 2002).

16. David A. Hollinger, *Postethnic America: Beyond Multiculturalism*, rev. ed (New York: Basic Books, 1996).

17. Ibid., 217.

18. Ibid., 216; emphasis in original.

19. Kwame Anthony Appiah has argued forcefully for what he terms a "rooted cosmopolitanism" in *The Ethics of Identity* (Princeton, N.J.: Princeton University Press, 2005), 213–72, and again in *Cosmopolitanism: Ethics in a World of Strangers* (New York: Norton, 2006).

20. See Nancy T. Ammerman, "North American Protestant Fundamentalism," in *Fundamentalisms Observed*, The Fundamentalism Project, vol. 1, ed. Martin E. Marty and R. Scott Appleby (Chicago: University of Chicago Press, 1991), 1–65.

21. Alasdair MacIntyre, *After Virtue*, 2nd ed. (South Bend, Ind.: University of Notre Dame Press, 1984). No one has worked harder to represent MacIntyre's views fairly,

and to show that modern liberal democracies nonetheless do embody coherent traditions in their own right, than Jeffrey Stout. See his *Democracy and Tradition*, 120–31.

22. See MacIntyre, *After Virtue*, 51–61, as well as *Whose Justice? Which Rationality?* (South Bend, Ind.: University of Notre Dame Press, 1988), 326–69.

23. MacIntyre, *After Virtue*, 69.

24. See Charles Taylor, *Multiculturalism: Examining the Politics of Recognition* (Princeton, N.J.: Princeton University Press, 1994), 52–61.

25. Michel Foucault pointed in this direction in the first two volumes of his *History of Sexuality*, trans. Robert Hurley (New York: Vintage, 1978–1986). For a short summary of this argument, see my essay "Sexual Identities," in *Encyclopedia of Religion and North American Cultures*, ed. Gary Laderman and Luis Lèon (Santa Barbara, Calif.: ABC-CLIO, 2003), 2:667–69. Katherine Ewing's contribution to this volume extends this Foucauldian metaphor in some highly suggestive ways.

26. Sir Isaiah Berlin, *The Roots of Romanticism*, ed. Henry Hardy (Princeton, N.J.: Princeton University Press, 1999).

27. Charles Taylor, *Sources of the Self: The Making of the Modern Identity* (Cambridge, Mass.: Harvard University Press, 1989), 355–90.

28. Berlin, *The Roots of Romanticism*, 57–67, 120–22.

29. A telling case in point may be found in Albert Speer's recollections of prewar Germany, *Inside the Third Reich*, trans. Richard and Clara Winston (New York: Macmillan, 1970), 94–97. For an interesting comparative analysis of such fascist fascination, see Umberto Eco, "Ur-Fascism," in *Five Moral Pieces*, trans. Alastair McEwen (New York: Harcourt, 2001), 65–88.

30. Louis A. Ruprecht Jr., *Was Greek Thought Religious? On the Use and Abuse of Hellenism, from Rome to Romanticism* (New York: Palgrave Macmillan, 2002), began to make the case for this connection.

31. For a highly readable account, see David Brewer, *The Greek War of Independence: The Struggle for Freedom from Ottoman Oppression and the Birth of the Modern Greek Nation* (London: Overlook, 2001), esp. 247–57, 325–36.

32. This is the story I endeavor to tell in my forthcoming book, "Winckelmann's Secret History."

33. See Arthur H. Smith, "Lord Elgin and His Collection," *Journal of Hellenic Studies* 36, no. 2 (1916): 163–372, for a superb summary of the questions this inquiry raised and ultimately answered.

34. Ruprecht, *Was Greek Thought Religious?* 125–39.

35. Both poems, "To Haydon" and "On Seeing the Elgin Marbles," appear in *The Works of John Keats* (Ware, Eng.: Wordsworth Poetry Library, 1994), 293.

36. Lord Byron, "Childe Harold's Pilgrimage" in *The Works of Lord Byron* (Ware, Eng.: Wordsworth Poetry Library, 1994), 174–244.

37. John Keats, "Ode on a Grecian Urn," in *Works of John Keats*, 234.

38. Mike Davis, *City of Quartz: Excavating the Future in Los Angeles* (New York: Vintage, 1990), 22, 78–80.

39. See the timely remarks made by George Steiner, *In Bluebeard's Castle: Some Notes towards the Redefinition of Culture* (New Haven, Conn.: Yale University Press, 1971), 110–11.

40. This is an antinostalgic political argument I first offered in *Afterwords: Hellenism, Modernism and the Myth of Decadence* (Albany: State University of New York Press, 1996). I had already applied the idea to the Macedonian question in "Of Coins and Carnage: Rhetorical Violence and the Macedonian Question," *Soundings* 77, nos. 3–4 (1994): 331–66.

41. Duncan Perry, *The Politics of Terror: The Macedonian Revolutionary Movements, 1893–1903* (Durham, N.C.: Duke University Press, 1988).

42. The newly formed Carnegie Foundation issued a report about human rights abuses in these two wars, one that has now been reprinted. See George F. Kennan, ed., *The Other Balkan Wars* (Washington, D.C.: Carnegie Endowment for International Peace, 1993).

43. Stout, *Democracy and Tradition*, 1.

44. For a superb and comprehensive time line of events, see Heather Burke, Claire Smith, Dorothy Lippert, Joe Watkins, and Larry Zimmerman, eds., *Kennewick Man: Perspectives on the Ancient One* (Walnut Creek, Calif.: Left Coast Press, 2008), 26–37.

44. See Alison Dundes Renteln, "Repatriation," in *Encyclopedia of Religion and North American Cultures*, ed. Gary Laderman and Luis Lèon (Santa Barbara, Calif.: ABC-CLIO, 2003), 1:221–23.

45. Two excellent accounts of the sometimes maddening scientists' views in this case are James C. Chatters, *Ancient Encounters: Kennewick Man and the First Americans* (New York: Simon & Schuster, 2001), and the biography of Doug Owsley in Jeff Benedict's *No Bone Unturned: The Adventures of a Top Smithsonian Forensic Scientist and the Legal Battle for America's Oldest Skeleton* (San Francisco: HarperCollins, 2003).

46. *Bonnichsen v. United States of America*, Civil No. 96-1481-JE, page 5.

47. For the argument that the real issue here is not religion but politics, and the question of who gets control of history and its artifacts, see David Hurst Thomas, *Skull Wars: Kennewick Man, Archaeology, and the Battle for Native American Identity* (New York: Basic Books, 2000).

48. For a more sympathetic account of similar arguments about cultural posterity and religious value made by Hawaiian islanders, see Greg Johnson, "Ancestors before Us: Manifestations of Tradition in a Hawai'ian Dispute," *Journal of the American Academy of Religion* 71, no. 2 (2003): 327–46.

Rethinking the Subject

Asian Perspectives

The Subject and the Ostensible Subject

Mapping the Genre of Hagiography among South Asian Chishtis

TONY K. STEWART

In an essay titled "The Chishtiya of Sultanate India: A Case Study of Biographical Complexities in South Asian Islam," Bruce Lawrence has argued that for South Asian Sufi masters, Clifford Geertz's notion of "enacted biography" must give way to a more complex act of "retrospective biography."[1] Sufi masters—*shaykhs* and *pirs*, that is, "saints"—were understood to inherit in some undefinable way the spiritual charisma (*baraka*) of the Prophet, whose image served them as a model for emulation. While Muhammad's daily actions (*sunnat-i nabi*) constituted the most significant standard of righteous conduct, or *adab*, the self-image of saints was in no way based on a simple replication of his acts. Sufi *shaykhs* have patterned and continue to pattern their behavior on Muhammad, but they also develop their own images to reflect the innovators and exemplars in the *silsila* (lineages) who came before them, which is a decidedly more complex process than simple emulation of the actions of the Prophet.[2] Because the function of the *shaykh* is different from the Prophet, models of emulation are not as sharply defined; each *shaykh* must respond to the successful patterns of action handed down through the *silsila*, while discovering for himself what captures the religiosity that guides his heart. The boundedness of the model provided by Muhammad, with its myriad examples in Hadith, has no precise analog among the *shaykhs*. Each *shaykh* then modifies his action in a dynamic process that constantly looks to the past but at the same moment reshapes the memory of the past. The historically observable confirmation for this dual patterning on the life of Muhammad and the lives of the *shaykhs* in the *silsila* produces a biographical tradition that is retrospective.

Lawrence further observed that at the heart of each saint's image lay a set of complementary, often strangely juxtaposed, characteristics that revolve around the twin poles of genuine humility and extraordinary religious accomplishment. The permutations of these combined characteristics are myriad, accounting for differences among the *shaykhs*, but in every case each characteristic is understood to multiply the profundity of the others. For example demonstrations of religious accomplishment were often translated through the disciplined display of power (*karamat*), the practice of exceptional scholarship, the observance of strict orthodoxy, or the occasional manifestation of ecstasy. Humility was frequently seen to manifest itself in actions of self-abnegation or chastity or in the performance of menial tasks, especially those charitably, but selflessly, done for others. All of this in turn serves to counter the public elevation of the *shaykh*, a good antidote to the hubris that might ensue from wielding *karamat*.[3] These seemingly countervailing characteristics provide a model of piety for everyone, from layman to *murid* to later *pirs*. Unfortunately, most hagiographical models stop with the simple cataloging of these characteristics, but Lawrence was led in this essay to ask why some saints emerge from the *silsila* to dominate the popular imagination while others seem to be little more than caretakers. I will suggest that it may not be the individual as much as the model of piety itself that takes hold. The mechanism that accounts for this shift lies in the structure of hagiography itself and its dynamic perpetuation by the community.

The naive form of retrospective biography would argue that a simple cumulative model of emulation (with each *shaykh* following all the actions of his predecessors) must be rejected, because choices made by these *shaykhs* lead to different models of piety. Retrospective biography can never simply look to the past for inspiration and guidance; it must interact with the past, requiring judgments of value. As a result of these choices, a greater prominence is afforded to certain *shaykhs*, a greater recognition in the community as well as among later *shaykhs*; others of great accomplishment often languish in relative obscurity. Lawrence does not immediately accept the obvious alternative to the naive accumulation model when he refuses to attribute the popularity of the saint to a direct measure of the *shaykh*'s demonstrations of *karamat* or corresponding (proportional) humility, which rest on reputation as much as anything. The answer, he suggests, is the way the memory of the *shaykh* is circulated within the community that tends his shrine, his tomb, and, with the tomb, his biographical legacy. It is this particular observation I would like to extend in an effort to isolate some of the mechanisms within the hagiographical corpus by which the community promotes the saint's memory. To see what happens to that memory will allow us to isolate some of the ways that followers synthesize the competing images of religiosity.

The Biographical Process and the Issues of Memory and Relevance

In order to get at Lawrence's questions, we might be led to ask not only what is significant about the complex image of the saint that gives rise to a following, but we may also ask a concomitant question about how that memory is perpetuated.

By what mechanism or mechanisms does it take shape and persevere? When a *shaykh* emerges to dominate, the easy assumption is that the individual was extraordinary, that his personal actions and teachings were superlative, that his personal religious accomplishments were self-evident and therefore widely acclaimed (the catalog of set characteristics is often invoked at this juncture). Most approaches conclude that the *shaykh* possesses that mysterious attraction indicated by the shorthand expression "charisma," an indefinably vague term indicating an articulable allure or appeal.[4] Once established, or more accurately, asserted, the biography and collected teachings are marshaled for historical reconstruction, and the life history becomes indexical to the tradition's history. But the seemingly simple assumption that the record somehow matched the lived reality masks the complex process by which biographical images are constructed, and likewise, it obscures the role of religious biography in shaping the religious community itself, that is, in instantiating the ideal among the faithful. For this reason Lawrence's insistence on the role of the community invites us to see what drives the biographical process.

There is no reason to doubt that when a *shaykh* developed a following, he somehow conducted himself in a way that was religiously laudable, for such a figure would build his reputation over a lifetime of service. Too many would have witnessed his accomplishments to propose that the accounts were baseless. But what captures the imagination of followers is the *way* the individual is portrayed as much as the *quality* of the accomplishments themselves. It has to be the "biographical image," the perpetrated image and memory of the person, to which people respond. Following Reynolds and Capps, the biographical image is constituted by a blending of the features of the individual life with the articulation of a religious ideal supported by those actions.[5] The subject of a hagiography can never be portrayed without that connection, so the historical *shaykh* as glorified object is seen to embody some timeless religious truth in his action, in speech, in thought—and this is ultimately a reflection of the author's perspective. It is generally the work of religious biography to produce this image, and it is the image that inspires his following. The memory of the *shaykh* can never be the memory of him as an individual alone, rather it is of the *shaykh* as he embodied ideals of his tradition. The memory itself, however, will of necessity reflect, or perhaps more accurately "highlight," selected virtues and actions, those that reflect something deemed of value to the individual or community, which is another way of saying the memory will cling to and be shaped by what is deemed relevant by the author. It was perhaps Dilthey who was the first to argue this point systematically with respect to biography, for relevance is by his definition a concern of the moment, of the biographer's here and now. Dilthey proposed that biography reconstructed the past according to issues that are immediately relevant to the author at the time of writing, a position now widely accepted; as the issues changed, the later written history that inevitably changed to reflect new concerns. As Talal Asad has more recently argued, this discursive tradition does not simply conduct a monologue with the past but reconstitutes itself, repeatedly and continuously, in negotiation with an ever-changing present, with its new forms of authority, power, and knowledge.[6] It is this dynamic process in which the hagiographer engages. And again following Dilthey: while engaging the past, the author seeks to shape the future; his discovery of patterns in (or imposition of them on) the actions of the biographical subject provides a template for future action.[7] In the case of the Sufi hagiography, this template of action, captured in the biographical image, becomes typological and thus predictive. *Typological* here does not mean the static taxonomy of virtues or characteristics suggested by Digby and Schimmel. It indicates a more dynamic structure that suggests possible future trajectories of the tradition, laying down parameters of the discursive arena in which subsequent *shaykhs* can fashion their own religiosity.[8] The hagiographer sets the limits of possibility and in some cases suggests a preferred direction; others later will take that suggestion and bend it to their own needs as the relevant issues change. In the history of Islam, one can observe this tendency from the historical record's inception to the point where we can argue it exists as a generalizable feature of all Islamic religious hagiography.

Ibn Ishaq's Sira *and the Changing Fortunes of the Early Community*

To illustrate the issue of relevance in the writing of Islamic biography, let us turn to the earliest sustained biographical treatment of Muhammad, the *Sira* of ibn Ishaq (A.H. 85–151 [= 707–773 C.E.]).[9] There are fragments of earlier texts that have survived, especially among the *maghazi* war narratives, but ibn Ishaq's is the earliest extant connected chronological treatment of Muhammad's life. The text is divided into three distinct books: *Mubtada'*, *Mab'ath*, and *Maghazi*. The *Mubtada'* is the book of the beginning, the genealogy of Muhammad starting with Adam and stretching until, but not including, his advent. The second book, *Mab'ath*, begins with Muhammad's birth and ends with the start of fighting in Medina. The third book of war stories, *Maghazi*, appears to have been compiled from numerous eyewitness accounts and follows the military campaigns through to the burial of Muhammad. In its early formation, the *Sira* was probably not dissimilar to the Hadith, vignettes of proper action, which in their atomistic and anecdotal form provided the foundations for Sunna. Yet the *Sira* eventually concatenated those discrete elements into a narrative, which contextualized the actions of Muhammad and provided a model for subsequent religious biography or hagiography in the tradition. The distinction is important.

The Hadith carry a legal force, which ultimately grounds the tradition in law; they constitute a freestanding, encyclopedic compilation of proper practice and,

therefore, a model for imitation. The assumption that makes these compila-
tions possible is that Muhammad's character was fully formed and unchanging
throughout his life, thereby creating an essentialized, seamless model of perfection (although the tradition could not admit perfection on his behalf, but the
closest thing to it): Muhammad is *insan al-Kamil*, the "complete man." The *Sira*,
on the other hand, portrays the life of Muhammad in a chronotopic narrative,
attempting not only to portray what he did (as a basis for later practice), but the
meaning of his presence as prophet (*nabi*) and apostle (*rasul*). In Bakhtin's terms
we can see a contrast between the epical figure of Muhammad, a timeless figure
whose essential character is revealed through each and every act, as opposed to
a more chronotopic narrative that situates Muhammad in a specific historical
time and place. Though I am not willing to push this except to develop the contrast, it demonstrates a kind of discovery, if not maturation or development, of
his character.[10] The life narrative provides the framework for the first extended
history of the early tradition. In its depiction of right action in context, it provides the basis for subsequent biographical treatments (an issue immediately
germane to the *malfuzat* and *tazkirah* of the Sufi saints) and for establishing patterns of right action, rather than atomistic, autonomous, or discrete action. Each
Sufi master will have to demonstrate the character traits similar to those that
can be divined from Muhammad's actions as cataloged in the Hadith (leading to
the lists such as those compiled by Digby and Schimmel). But it is the *Sira* that
would seem to serve as the dominant precursor for Sufi hagiography, because it
pays close attention to the historical placement of actions and the characteristics they reveal, context resolving the apparently competing images of saintliness
demonstrated by each *shaykh*. That the *Sira* serves as the historical precursor,
however, is not the issue; for the prominence of the text allows us to assume this
easily enough (whether in a general or more specific way is immaterial, for the
biographical treatment of Muhammad will by definition affect later depictions).
What is significant for our current argument is the way in which the text was
composed and subsequently redacted by ibn Ishaq's editor, 'Abdu'l-Malik b.
Hisham (d. A.H. 213 or 218).

Guillaume's interpretive introduction reveals an urge to read the text as history, a kind of historicism that, it should be noted, occasionally loses sight of
the nature of the text as a hagiographical document. He also moved to establish
a sound intertextuality in a heroic effort to trace precursor texts and their contribution to the *Sira*. Based on these reconstructions, he argued that the text
was profoundly shaped by contemporary political events that cannot be overtly
acknowledged. The text as we have it today must be read in the light of the
tragedies of Karbala' (A.H. 61) and the sack of Medina (A.H. 63), both of which
occurred after the *Sira*'s original composition. Guillaume observed that by the
time ibn Hisham edited the text, there was a palpable shift in tone, the editor

asserting Ansar claims to priority in the life of Muhammad.[11] Religious biographies, as a rule, are decidedly not about recording a history that can be reconstructed in positivist terms, although they are forced into that role willy-nilly and may contain verifiable historical data. Nor are religious biographies literary masterpieces exploring the construction of imagined religious worlds, although one can clearly profit from the attempt to apply literary critical techniques to the narratives.[12] Both of these approaches inevitably become reductionist in ways that blunt our understanding of the power of these documents—if not simply miss their point altogether—unless they recognize that the genre is inherently political and that the chronotopic narrative is itself subject to manipulation.[13] And even though Guillaume does not set out to establish the political dimension, its inescapable presence is what he discovered, uncovering in the process one of the most fundamental features of religious biography.

Intentionally or not, religious biographies are political. They are political because the genre itself is not designed to reflect the ruminations of the author for his private consumption, but for community. The texts in this genre are automatically rhetorical, seeking to persuade others of the truth and validity of the embodied religious ideal. These texts articulate theological and practical ideals not in a vacuum but for a specific community for which they often, if not inevitably, become charter documents for theology and praxis. As charter documents these hagiographies function as an integral part of the group's canon, officially sanctioned or otherwise, as will be obvious in the Sufi *khanqah.* As canonical documents they articulate the values of the followers—or serve coercively to enforce those values.[14] As articulators of value, their political power serves to organize the tradition, often implying or even spelling out an explicit internal organization of the community, according to its hierarchy of ideals. While arguably the result of extraordinary piety, the commissioning, writing, and circulation of these religious biographies nearly always serves to define what it means to be properly religious according to the tradition, providing a blueprint for instantiating the religious ideal. When viewed this way, we see exposed in the writing of the text of the *Sira* a fundamental tension in the nature of the genre of hagiography itself, and this manifests to a greater or lesser extent specifically in subsequent Sufi hagiographies.

In ibn Ishaq's original *Sira*—and here I am relying on Gordon Newby's reconstruction of the first book[15]—the orientation is clearly retrospective. The initial third of the biography moves to justify Muhammad's position as *rasul* and *nabi* and focuses on his connection to the line of prophets that stretched from the beginning of humanity, ultimately culminating in his person. That justification inevitably conditions the reading of the last two books of the *Sira.* The tone is one of justification, and the context is a fledgling monotheism seeking to establish itself among the other monotheistic traditions to which it is related. Ibn

Ishaq sought to adapt Muhammad's monotheism to the preexisting traditions, demonstrating how Muhammad extended them in the process of finalizing monotheism once and for all: Muhammad becoming then the *khatam an-nabiyin*, or Seal of the Prophets. While the document seems to be confident, it still expends much energy to make the case for legitimacy, which is carried out with a rather heavy hand in the genealogical sections of the opening book and in the portrayals of the lives of other prophets, whose actions Muhammad somehow mirrored but superceded or at least brought to fruition. When ibn Hisham edited the text decades later, the religion and polity promoted by Muhammad have been firmly established and, in that dominance, no longer need to be justified, merely noted. So ibn Hisham's version of the text excised a huge portion of the first book, the *Mubtada'*, and focused on the religion of the Prophet as new pattern for action; Muhammad was *insan al-Kamil* and the model of the ideal Muslim. Justification of the monotheistic modality of Islam as a tradition—separate from the other monotheistic traditions—was no longer necessary. The text was now prospective in its orientation, and its tone clearly anticipated the future, examining, if not actually promoting, a particular internal structure for the community rather than attempting to find a place for the community among others. Guillaume's comments about the shift in tone are confirmed by the document's overall demeanor in relation to its unredacted predecessor: the text reveals an internal political struggle on a grand scale, addressing the communal features without regard to its "fit" within the other monotheistic religions. What was relevant to the community—or at least to the authors who were articulating their vision for it—shifted dramatically in much less than a century.

From this distanced perspective, ibn Ishaq's original *Sira* does what hagiographies everywhere tend to do: it demonstrates how the saint, or in this case, the Prophet, exemplified a preexisting religious ideal, adapting it to a new world, a new circumstance, through personal action and teachings, looking to the past to valorize the present. However, the later edited text of ibn Hisham functions more as a "sacred biography," again to utilize Reynolds and Capps's distinction.[16] Sacred biography concerns itself with the creation of a new tradition and its organization, asserting independence from prior religious modalities, looking to the present or more immediate past to valorize the future. And there is, of course, a fine line between modifying a preexisting tradition and creating something new; they are hardly separable in many instances and can, just by some measured editing, turn a text completely from one into the other. The two versions of the *Sira* neatly capture this tension between exemplifying a preexisting religious ideal, either by a new embodiment or a shift in emphasis, and founding something arguably altogether different (figure 1). And this is the tension that prevails in Sufi hagiographies, a tension that may help to explain why certain figures, such as Nizam al-Din Awliya (d. 1325), emerge within the tradition as more powerful and popular creators of a "new" Sufi tradition rather than simply embodying the old, even though acknowledged to be faithful to that earlier piety.

FIGURE 1.

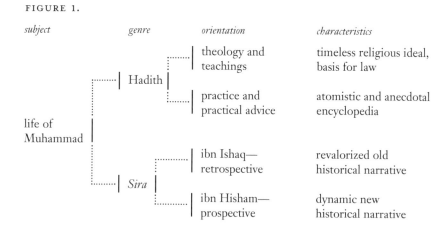

subject	genre	orientation	characteristics

subject | *genre* | *orientation* | *characteristics*

life of Muhammad

Hadith — theology and teachings — timeless religious ideal, basis for law

practice and practical advice — atomistic and anecdotal encyclopedia

Sira — ibn Ishaq— retrospective — revalorized old historical narrative

ibn Hisham— prospective — dynamic new historical narrative

The Dialectic in the Biographical Images of Sufi Hagiography

In my study of religious biography over the last twenty-five years, I have observed that the dynamic nature of the hagiographical dialectic is often lost in generalities that do little more than articulate some vague connection between the biographical image of the present and those of the past. One of the most common forms is the appeal to the concept of "influence," a general term that posits a connection but does not specify its nature, primarily because it is used to disguise the lack of clarity in precisely how the two or more participants actually relate.[17] This dynamic was explicitly invoked when Lawrence argued that later saints in the *silsila* do not simply look to prior exemplars for inspiration but are defined by and define themselves in their light, starting of course with Muhammad and certainly including those following, an act that follows a trajectory not unlike that played out in writing and circulation of the *Sira*. No saintly image can be articulated without taking into account those who came before, each adding to the definition of the *pir* or *shaykh* as institution. This addition, as we might now expect, is either one of *emphasis*, wherein the preexisting ideal is highlighted, leading to some kind of reordering of priorities for those who follow, or one of *creation*, where new images of piety are established and linked to the old. As previously noted, in the naive version of this interaction within the Chishti order, every *shaykh* would be expected to carry the image of all previous *shaykhs*. Thus arguably the most famous *shaykh*, Nizam al-Din, would of necessity emulate—or at least his followers would be expected to construe his biography to demonstrate (which is a somewhat different proposition)—in some fundamental way the actions of his predecessors, going back to the first Chishti *shaykh* in South Asia, Mu'in al-Din Chishti (d. 1236). Yet as Lawrence recognized that nearly all of the histories of Sufism in South Asia attest, Nizam al-Din has been and still is much more celebrated in South Asia, his spiritual image more widely circulated than Mu'in al-Din and considerably more than the two intervening *shaykhs* of the lineage, Qutb al-Din (d. 1235) and Farid al-Din (d. 1265). He eclipses those before and after.

Nizam al-Din's popularity and scope—indeed even within the tradition itself, he is singled out with 'Abd al-Qadir Jilani (d. 1166), who preceded him in Baghdad[18]—suggest that the process is not cumulative. Nor is the process the opposite, an ever-diminishing embodiment of a golden, bygone era of virtue, where the ability of the *shaykh* to capture that original inspiration weakens in every generation, as has been argued for at least one other lineage.[19] The image of a saint is dictated to a certain extent by the *shaykhs* before him and can, in that discursive arena, only emerge in interaction with previous parameters. But the process also works retrospectively, for as Lawrence reasons: "Each major saint becomes a crucial, indispensable link extending the spiritual charisma—and hence the organizational longevity—of his order (*tariqa/silsila*). *Inevitably the* shaykh *as a* shaykh *reshapes the way in which his followers think about all antecedent—and also all subsequent—saints.*"[20]

This process is dialectical, but it is of a curious sort because the images from the past, while providing a standard for the present, are incapable of resisting the change wrought by their present interpretation. The older images can help shape the present images but cannot counter any changes the present makes about their own past. Each *shaykh* will remake the entire hagiographical tradition, but some do so more dramatically than others. A later historical figure, such as Nizam al-Din, redefines what it means to be *shaykh* for all those who preceded him, in large part, we suspect, because of a greater personal charisma and, just as importantly, the efforts of his followers to perpetuate his image. Part of that charisma, which is always so difficult to identify, is actually the result of his action in revalorizing the religious ideal held dear by the tradition. One might argue that it is the further job of the saint to revalorize older images of piety, but because historical circumstances change, revalorizing is always a redefining, not a simple revival or continuation of the past. This activity combines the same tension we saw illustrated in the *Sira* of ibn Ishaq and its redaction by ibn Hisham. Remembering Dilthey, revalorizing is a function of the present (both subject and author), making the tradition relevant for the audience, both for those who immediately surrounded the master and those who would follow the image perpetuated in the hagiography.[21]

While there is clearly a cumulative feature to the inheritance, certain *shaykhs* stand out, in part, because they have redefined the tradition, but also because they have their images better perpetuated by their followers, magnifying the impact. Innovative *shaykhs* cross the line from exemplifying the previously articulated religious ideals to creating new ones. Less visible *shaykhs*, we might then deduce, do not tend to be as creative, serving to emulate the older ideals but not forging new ones. No doubt, in some cases, the originality may be present but insufficiently recognized or articulated to inspire followers to capture them through hagiography.[22] This dual activity—the portrayal of exemplifying the old and creating a new religious ideal—gives rise to the recognition of greater or lesser *shaykhs*.

Because the standard for the *shaykh* is fluid and has to be remade for every generation, it would appear that part of what sets some *shaykhs* apart from others is their response to previous images of religiosity. The impact of the biographical image would seem to be directly proportional to the adaptation of the religious ideal to contemporary issues of everyday life and spirituality, that is, its relevance to the *shaykh*'s community.[23] Those prominent figures can be easily identified by the extent of the following centered on the cult of the shrine with which they are affiliated, which inevitably includes the propagation of the saint's particular teachings, by example in hagiography and by direct instruction in personal writings, practical instructions, and miscellaneous notes taken by followers.

The corpus of hagiographical materials that preserve and perpetuate this image of piety are diverse, including the sayings and records of observed spirituality, *malfuzat* and *tazkirah*, specific instructions in *maktubat* (letters of clarification and guidance), and *isharat* (thematic treatises by the master or his disciples).[24] Not all *shaykhs* intervene directly in the perpetuation of their own image, but notably Nizam al-Din personally approved at least one set of collected conversations and sayings (*malfuzat*), a compilation in five fascicles recorded by Amir Hasan Sijzi, who subsequently submitted it to the master, who then corrected it and filled in some of the gaps. The text, initially collected in A.H. 707 (1308 C.E.), was titled *Fawa'id al-Fu'ad*, or *Morals for the Heart*.[25] The narrative of Nizam al-Din's life, however, was perhaps best conveyed by Amir Khurd's *Siyar al-awliya*, which, although characterized as an "untidy amalgam of *malfuzat* and *tazkirah*," integrated a trove of biographical detail about the great master.[26] The volume of this literature serves as an indirect measure of impact. Yet in each succeeding generation's treatment of Nizam al-Din's life and teachings, the relevance gradually shifted, and the image of religiosity was once again revalorized, this time by the authors perhaps as much by the subject himself.

In keeping with Lawrence's observation that Nizam al-Din is somehow more important than others, it is notable that a few generations later a compilation of *malfuzat* of Sayyid Gisu Daraz, Muhammad Akbar Husayni's *Jawami' al-Kalim*, contains more direct references to Nizam al-Din that to Gisu Daraz's own *pir*. This text is an example of how a later *shaykh* interacted with and reshaped the prior image, which could not resist the change but in this case apparently refused to be overpowered by a lesser, later inspiration. The record of these biographical images and their shifting memories has produced and continues to produce a gradually changing history for the Chishti tradition, as Lawrence and colleague Carl W. Ernst have outlined in their recent survey of the order. In telling that history, they found it necessary to do what many hagiographers do: they had to choose Chishti masters who revalorized and reformulated the tradition in the light of those who had gone before. Five are singled out for special treatment, precisely for the reformulating or revalorizing tendency noted above: Khwaja Mu'in al-Din Chishti, Shaykh Qutb al-Din Bakhtiyar Khaki, Shaykh Farid al-Din Ganj-i Shakar, Shaykh Nizam al-Din Awliya, and Shaykh Nasir al-Din Chiragh-i Dihli (147–71).[27] Nizam al-Din Awliya is featured as the "standard bearer for Chishti spirituality" and the "foremost of all masters."[28]

The Subject and Ostensible Subject in Hagiography

If enduring relevance of teaching and action is what has made for greatness among Sufi *shaykhs*, then relevance must be the result of creating a new religious ideal that has adapted or transformed the old to a new era. This ideal in turn has been embodied by—or perhaps, more accurately, has been portrayed by the hagiography to be inherent within—the *shaykh*, such as Nizam al-Din. If the memory of such *shaykhs* is never free from the religious ideals so embodied, we can predict that the historical dimensions of the saint's life will eventually yield to the dominance of the religious ideal. That is to say, the *bios* in the two-part biographical image inevitably becomes little more than a vehicle for the teachings, the religious ideal articulated and embodied. Without that religious ideal, the life itself is of little significance to the religious follower; yet the teachings have the capacity to stand independently, to be extracted from the life. The individual life, then, can only continue in service of the religious ideal, and that makes the religious ideal and its transcendent truth the "real subject" of the hagiography. The individual *shaykh* is, in some basic way, only the "ostensible subject," providing the opportunity to articulate the religious ideal.

While the historical life may serve as inspiration for subsequent followers, lay and professional alike, and in many cases provide a model for emulation (when it can be emulated), aspiration, or meditation (when it can only be admired), it is ultimately the religious ideal that shapes the appropriation of the *shaykh* by those who come later. In retrospective biography this has been especially evident, for apart from occasional acknowledgments of particular actions of previous *shaykhs* germane to the current figure, it has always been the teachings that were appropriated and transformed. There are two very closely related effects of this appropriation. First, the more completely the religious ideals are transformed by the creative *shaykh*, the greater the change he will have worked on the memory of those who preceded him. That newly constructed image modifies all subsequent memory of earlier figures, who can no longer resist the new direction—the change in emphasis. Second, and undoubtedly to a certain extent as the result of the first, the more distant the remove in time, the more stylized the earlier *bios* becomes. The reasons for the latter are straightforward enough. Because it is the religious ideal that controls the biographical image, any hagiography or sacred biography will reflect the ideals embraced by the immediate author, even if it is during the lifetime of or immediately after the saint. Actions that do not explicitly support that religious ideal tend not to be portrayed; actions that do will be the ones remembered, will be the ones to make up the primary record. These facts, of course, change over time.[29] Years later, when the religious ideal is revalorized, even slightly, the biographical detail needed to support this new interpretation may no longer be part of the group's recorded history, so the historical *bios* will succumb to the stylizing effects of highlighting, creating contours that over time will heavily elide the historical *bios* and render the image more and more consistent with the driving theological or doctrinal perspective. Any of a saint's actions that fails to support or otherwise illuminate the religious ideal will tend over time to be forgotten or misremembered, and this is a place where hagiography often departs dramatically from other forms of biography because of the overt function of hagiography to establish religious doctrine. Where biography may be ideologically driven, ideology is not automatically the primary objective. Subsequently when the religious ideal is itself revalorized by later figures, the basic materials for reconstructing the *bios* of earlier *shaykhs* are simply no longer available, and in order to illustrate the new ideal, new actions must be invented or ascribed to the older historical figure.

This ascription of action is, of course, the point at which we see the individual life succumb completely to the service of the religious ideal, the worldwide tendency for the narrative of the saint's life to accumulate all manner of legendary and miraculous tales and detailed stories completely unknown to the original community in which the figure lived and worked. Following this line, we can observe that the older the image of the *shaykh*, the more likely the accretion of legendary and miraculous stories. Tradition writes a new kind of history, but it is one that often has a stylizing and generalizing effect. To return once again to Nizam al-Din, one need only look at the hagiographical profile created in the *Afzal al-Fawa'id* by the poet Amir Khusro (d. 1325). Khusro was affiliated with the lineage but not central to it. As a poet and eulogizer of his not-so-intimate master, his biographical image contained numerous examples of Nizam al-Din's otherwise undocumented displays of *karamat* and other miraculous activities. Notably this text was composed while Nizam al-Din was still alive, for they died the same year.[30] Later authors, however, picked up and extended the legends.

It would seem to be self-evident that the more complete the hagiographical treatment, especially including the personal instruction of the *shaykh*, the more likely the *shaykh* to withstand the subsequent revalorizing, appearing in each generation to speak cogently with relevance, because sufficient material, biographical and instructional, would be available to construct a seamless new image. Yet even Nizam al-Din was subjected to this stylizing process before he died. It is even easier, later, to stylize images of older figures and manipulate them to support new religious ideals. In this process distinct figures often begin to blur into the standardized or formulaic profiles generated by the expected characteristics, such as those enumerated by Schimmel and Digby noted above. But the standard for this stylization is the more recent *shaykh*, who, if he is powerful enough, will provide a profile to which all previous masters will be made to conform. Not surprisingly this impulse to impose uniform characteristics wreaks havoc on the historical *bios* in any kind of positivist sense and becomes itself a litmus test for measuring the saintliness of different *shaykhs*. Examples of this abound in the Sufi traditions of greater South Asia. We see, for example, early evidence of this in 'Abd Allah Ansari (d. 1089), who first expanded Sulami's *Tabaqat al-Sufiya* (Generations of the Sufis) to embrace the Persian lineages, which four centuries later was dramatically expanded by Jami, whose *Nafahat al-uns* (Breezes of Intimacy) stretches to include 567 figures.[31] There is a multitude of such writings, and each one seeks to shape the lineages and highlight the religious ideals held dear to the point of rewriting the histories in favor of a particular *shaykh*. In another significant instance, Dara Shikuh composed the *Safinat al-Awliya'* (The Ship of Saints), an encyclopedic hagiography that depends heavily on Jami but truncates entries in such a way that the presentation is pitched to "affirm 'Abd al-Qadir Jilani as the foremost Sufi exemplar and the Qadiriyya as the paramount Sufi brotherhood, but also to undergird his own spiritual authority vis-à-vis rival claims to Qadiri spirituality."[32] Just as ibn Hisham reoriented ibn Ishaq's *Sira*, many of the later hagiographical compilers have altered their predecessors parallel to how later saints alter images of figures in their own lineages.

We can conclude then that the subject of Sufi hagiography subtly shifts over time, from the individual who embodies a religious ideal to the religious ideal embodied by, or made to embody, the individual. The original subject (individual) gradually becomes the "ostensible subject," and this would seem to be a generalizable feature for all hagiography and religious biography, not just Sufi. Indeed the ability of the tradition to dehistoricize its most important leaders may well be indexical to the power of the religious ideal within the biographical image. So why then do some figures seem to dominate others in the memory of the tradition, as Lawrence was led to ask in his initial essay? The secret does indeed rest with the community, and the community that manages to perpetuate most successfully a stable memory. So an individual, such as Nizam al-Din, who retains a persona inspiring followers through the centuries, whose personal works continue to expand in circulation, can only be one whose religious ideal is so rich that it can withstand the periodic revalorizations of his hagiographers. His biographical image must be founded on a religious ideal that has remained or can be adjusted in relevance to his followers, certainly sufficient to preserve his memory above all others. The source of this continuing inspiration is more, however, than simply the life turned into a hagiographical narrative; it will include the primary material that mirrors the combined effect of the *Sira* and the Hadith. The former provides the framework within which to understand the latter, while the latter inscribes the importance of the former. By analogy it may well be that the successful hagiographies within the Sufi tradition, the narratives of *tazkirah* with their stories of exemplary behavior and extraordinary action, connected to the sayings found in *malfuzat,* are made more enduring by the isolable teachings found in the practical guides of *maktubat* and the more theologically pointed *isharat* (figure 2).

FIGURE 2.

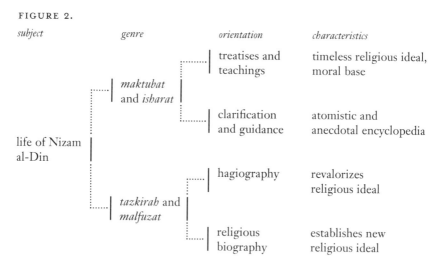

subject	genre	orientation	characteristics
		treatises and teachings	timeless religious ideal, moral base
	maktubat and *isharat*		
		clarification and guidance	atomistic and anecdotal encyclopedia
life of Nizam al-Din			
		hagiography	revalorizes religious ideal
	tazkirah and *malfuzat*		
		religious biography	establishes new religious ideal

It is no coincidence that Nizam al-Din's popularity is in direct proportion to the quantity and quality of this additional material beyond the narratives of his life. This material serves as a trove of primary sources to shape and perpetuate his and other *shaykhs'* images according to the needs of the time, making him perpetually relevant. The power of the hagiography depends on the substance of the supporting theological reflection and practical instruction, the moral base of the *shaykh's* importance. The textual base is necessary but insufficient by itself to perpetuate that memory; it is the shrine, of course, that serves as the physical anchor for this memory, the focal point of his continuing physical presence, the basis for the community to perpetuate the image. The structure of these documents makes clear that they are symbiotically bound, and it is the religious ideal that endures as the real subject of the tradition, while the ostensible subject in the person of the *shaykh*—or more importantly, his memory—remains as a historical reminder and example for the following.

NOTES

1. Bruce B. Lawrence, "The Chishtiya of Sultanate India: A Case Study of Biographical Complexities in South Asian Islam" in *Charisma and Sacred Biography*, ed. Michael A. Williams (Chico, Calif.: Scholars, 1982), 47–67, esp. 49 and 65; hereafter cited as "Biographical Complexities." The reference is to Clifford Geertz, *Islam Observed: Religious Development in Morocco and Indonesia* (New Haven, Conn.: Yale University Press, 1968), see esp. pp. 25–35.

2. Annemarie Schimmel has elaborated the *imitatio Muhammadi* in *And Muhammad Is His Messenger: The Veneration of the Prophet in Islamic Piety* (Chapel Hill: University of North Carolina Press, 1985).

3. Annemarie Schimmel's and Simon Digby's lists of characteristics are summarized in Lawrence, "Biographical Complexities," 51; the combined list can be found on the following page. These characteristics become the focal point of a more sophisticated treatment in Ernst and Lawrence's survey of the Chishti movement in South Asia; see Carl W. Ernst and Bruce B. Lawrence, *Sufi Martyrs of Love: The Chishti Order in South Asia and Beyond* (New York: Palgrave Macmillan, 2002), esp. chap. 4.

4. It is notable that the essay in question here is in a volume titled *Charisma and Sacred Biography*. While many accept a Weberian notion of charisma as the operational standard, perhaps Dabashi's treatment of charisma in the life of Muhammad pushes the paradigm about as far as possible, arguing that it was Muhammad's charisma that overthrew the old order and then became institutionalized to make Islam what it is today (with predictable chapters on routinization [chap. 5], perpetuation [chap. 6], and dissemination [chap. 7]); see Hamid Dabashi, *Authority in Islam: From the Rise of Muhammad to the Establishment of the Umayyads* (New Brunswick, N.J.: Transaction, 1993).

5. Frank E. Reynolds and Donald Capps, eds., *The Biographical Process: Studies in the History and Psychology of Religion* (The Hague: Mouton, 1976), introduction.

6. Talal Asad, *The Idea of an Anthropology of Islam* (Washington, D.C.: Georgetown University Center for Contemporary Arab Studies, 1988); see also his *Genealogies of Religion: Discipline and Reasons of Power in Christianity and Islam* (Baltimore: Johns Hopkins University Press, 1993).

7. Wilhelm Dilthey, *Pattern and Meaning in History: Thoughts on History and Society* (New York: Harper, 1962); see especially the two essays "The Historical Relevance of Biography and Autobiography" (83–95) and "The Individual Life and Its Meaning" (95–112). In a very useful way of conceptualizing the problem, Dilthey argues in these essays for the orientation of the historian to the subject by seeing the past in terms of meaning (patterns), the present in terms of relevance (value inscribed by interpreting immediate experience in the light of the past), and the future in terms of purpose or, at least, intention (that leads to actions, thereby shaping the world). For a good summary

of these positions, see H. P. Rickman, *Wilhelm Dilthey: Pioneer of the Human Studies* (Berkeley: University of California Press, 1979), especially the sections dealing with *Bedeutung* and *Erlebnis*.

8. The construction of this discursive arena has been outlined elsewhere; see Tony K. Stewart, "Surprising Bedfellows: Vaisnava and Shi'i Alliance in Kavi Aripha's 'Tale of Lalamon,'" *International Journal of Hindu Studies* 3, no. 3 (1999): 265–98. The concept is heavily dependent on that articulated by Jonathan Culler, "Presupposition and Intertextuality," *Modern Language Notes* 91, no. 6 (1976): 1380–96.

9. *The Life of Muhammad: A Translation of Ishaq's "Sirat Rasul Allah,"* ed. 'Abdu'l-Malik b. Hisham, trans. Alfred Guillaume (London: Oxford University Press, 1955; repr., Karachi: Oxford University Press, 1987). Background materials are taken from the introduction to this text. I am indebted to Gordon Newby, who first pointed out some of the unique features of the *Sira* when we taught a class in the late 1980s on religious biography.

10. See M. M. Bakhtin, "Epic and Novel" and "Forms of Time and of the Chronotope in the Novel," in *The Dialogic Imagination: Four Essays*, ed. Michael Holquist, trans. Caryl Emerson and Michael Holquist (Austin: University of Texas Press, 1981), 3–40 and 84–258, respectively.

11. Alfred Guillaume, introduction to *Life of Muhammad*, xxvii.

12. As John Kitchen has pointedly observed, "The attraction historians have for hagiography leads to one of the most mis-matched unions perhaps ever encountered in humanistic scholarship," for hagiography is not about factual portrayal. In the next breath Kitchen's profound indictment moves to the other most commonly adopted disciplined approach to interpretation, when he observes, "If historians in general do not deal adequately with the religiosity of the texts, those who treat hagiography as literature generally show little concern with how the religious dimension may relate to the way in which the stories are told." John Kitchen, *Saints' Lives and the Rhetoric of Gender: Male and Female in Merovingian Hagiography* (New York: Oxford University Press, 1998), 11. Kitchen has rightly indicted both industries, curiously enough, both represented by Guillaume's approach; but Guillaume narrowly sidesteps the critique when he sees the organization of the community as the motivating factor in the edited text. For a very sophisticated treatment of Sufi hagiography that does not fall prey to these tendencies, see Vincent J. Cornell, *Realm of the Saint: Power and Authority in Moroccan Sufism* (Austin: University of Texas Press, 1998).

13. Hayden White's treatment of historical narratives is particularly germane here. See Hayden White, *Metahistory: The Historical Imagination in Nineteenth-Century Europe* (Baltimore: Johns Hopkins University Press, 1973), and *The Content of the Form: Narrative Discourse and Historical Representation* (Baltimore: Johns Hopkins University Press, 1987).

14. I am indebted to the work of Barbara Herrnstein Smith, which first alerted me to the complex and necessary role of value in the canon-making process; see her *Contingencies of Value: Alternative Perspectives for Critical Theory* (Cambridge, Mass.: Harvard University Press, 1988).

15. Gordon Darnell Newby, *The Making of the Last Prophet: A Reconstruction of the Earliest Biography of Muhammad* (Columbia: University of South Carolina Press, 1989).

16. Reynolds and Capps, eds., introduction to *Biographical Process*, esp. 2–8.

17. For more on this, see Tony K. Stewart and Carl W. Ernst, "Syncretism," in *South Asian Folklore: An Encyclopedia*, ed. Margaret A. Mills, Peter J. Claus, and Sarah Diamond (London: Routledge, 2003), 586–88. *Relate*, likewise, is a term that disguises the specifics of connection and causality.

18. Lawrence, "Biographical Complexities," 54–55.

19. This observation about the dynamic nature of the biographical image runs completely counter to the argument made by Art Buehler regarding what he calls the "mediating *shaykh*" in the Naqshbandiyya, an argument that proposes that the saintliness of the *shaykh* dwindles through time and that has an unacknowledged teleological dimension to it; see Arthur F. Buehler, *Sufi Heirs of the Prophet: The Indian Naqshbandiyya and the Rise of the Mediating Sufi Shaykh* (Columbia: University of South Carolina Press, 1998).

20. Lawrence, "Biographical Complexities," 53–54; emphasis in original.

21. I am reminded of Frank Kermode's essay on the literary classic, in which he argues that what makes a classic is the text's ability to revalorize its message in each generation, an inherently political act connected to dominant forms of power. The analogy with the role of the *shaykh* is not superficial. See Frank Kermode, *The Classic: Literary Images of Permanence and Change*, T. S. Eliot Memorial Lectures 1973 (New York : Viking, 1975).

22. This important observation is consistent with Lawrence's argument that it is the community perpetuating the biographical legacy that is responsible for the greater (or lesser) popularity.

23. There is an additional element that affects the prominence of a particular *shaykh* (or any other subject of religious hagiography): the prominence of followers. On the surface it would appear that the presence of industrious, socially well-connected, or intellectually brilliant followers who actively promote and perpetuate the life and teachings of a particular religious figure is ultimately one of serendipity, completely accidental. But I am inclined now to see the attraction of such figures as an index itself to the power of the *shaykh* or other religious leader to make the teachings relevant to the contemporary world. The greater the relevance, the more likely the teacher to enjoy this following; the more prominent the following, the more historically prominent the teacher in a mutually reinforcing symbiosis.

24. Lawrence, "Biographical Complexities," 56.

25. Bruce B. Lawrence, trans., *Nizam al-Din Awliya: Morals for the Heart; Conversations of Shaykh Nizam ad-din Awliya Recorded by Amira Hasan Sijzi*, annotated by Lawrence, introduction by Khaliq Ahmad Nizami, Classics of Western Spirituality 74 (New York: Paulist Press, 1992).

26. Bruce B. Lawrence, *Notes from a Distant Flute: The Extant Literature of Pre-Mughal Indian Sufism* (Tehran: Imperial Iranian Academy of Philosophy, 1978), 28–32.

27. Ernst and Lawrence, *Sufi Martyrs of Love*, esp. chaps. 3–4.

28. Ibid., 70.

29. See, for instance, the complex case of construing martyrdom, as described in Carl W. Ernst, "From Hagiography to Martyrology: Conflicting Testimonies to a Sufi Martyr of the Delhi Sultanate," *History of Religions* 24, no. 4 (1985): 308–27.

30. Lawrence, *Notes from a Distant Flute*, 24, 36, 45. Robin Rinehart's study of the Punjabi god-man Swami Ram Tirath is the best documentation of this tendency I have encountered. See Robin Rinehart, *One Lifetime, Many Lives: The Experience of Modern Hindu Hagiography*, AAR The Religions Series, no. 6 (Atlanta: Scholars Press, 1999).

31. Ernst and Lawrence, *Sufi Martyrs of Love*, 48–49.

32. Ibid., 51.

꙳

Dancing with Khusro

Gender Ambiguities and Poetic Performance in a Delhi Dargah

_____

SCOTT KUGLE

The candle's life is sweet so don't fear this burning
    for delightful blazes moths' religion is yearning
On passionate heads enemies' curses are a crown
    in love-struck lanes ruined reputation is true learning
It's not so manly to scatter infidel corpses
    in the corps of lovers real men die by self-spurning
Bring an open flask, Khusro, you king of love don't ask permission
    surprise assault brings patience's submission and reason's overturning[1]

This poem's author is Amir Khusro, one of the most illustrious figures of medieval South Asia. He was a great poet and also an exemplary Sufi disciple. The intimate relationship between disciple and spiritual guide was a crucial field for embodying sacred power and Islamic ideals in premodern South Asia. Up until his death in 1325 C.E., Khusro created Persian *ghazals* or love lyrics of great depth, Hindi poems in praise of his spiritual guide, Nizam al-Din Awliya, and musical settings of Islamic prayers and praise that defined the tradition of *qawwali* singing. His personality, poems and the performances they inspire are very fruitful places for us to focus the resources of contemporary critical theory for a greater understanding of Islam, which is the goal of this essay.

    Qawwali singing at the tomb of saints brings together the "high culture" of literature or theology and the "popular culture" of folk performances or public religiosity. It is a very dynamic example of folk practice of Islam in South Asia, though it has roots in performance arts and poetry that were considered classical in premodern times, before modern reform movements marginalized them as "unorthodox" or "lower-class" phenomena. Just as *qawwali* brings together classical and popular—or high and low culture—so also contemporary critical theory brings together intellectual and popular cultures in its analysis. It seeks to unify macroanalysis that highlights social structures and discursive tropes with microanalysis that affirms the importance of psychological states, embodied emotions, and ethical imperatives that drive personal agency. It tries to elucidate how social categories and political boundaries are enforced through a variety of dispersed practices, sites, and disciplines that are not ordinarily associated with "politics" in order to reveal both the possibilities for resistance and limitations to freedom.

By applying methods of critical social theory to traditional themes and genres of Islamic studies, we hope to gain new perspectives on Islam and uncover new details and vistas that are truer—or if not truer in an ultimate sense, they might give us an image of what is true about Islam that is at least deeper, broader and clearer. This essay will touch on *qawwali* from many perspectives, from translating Persian poems and reflecting on the legacy of Chishti Sufis to debating the role of gender and explaining how fundamentalist movements that claim to defend for Islam actually threaten its rich intellectual and subtle spiritual legacy. To accomplish this, it will tack back and forth between the contemporary period and the fourteenth century when Amir Khusro composed poetry, devoted himself to Sufism, sang, and danced. It will focus upon the *khanqah*, or Sufi hospice, where Khusro kept company with his *pir*, his spiritual guide Nizam al-Din Awliya, a place that eventually housed the tombs of them both, becoming a vibrant place of Muslim pilgrimage and pluralistic religious devotion in Delhi.

Before we proceed, let us introduce Nizam al-Din for those not familiar with the Chishti Sufi heritage.[2] His teachings can be summarized in three statements. First, service to the needy is better than ritual worship: he used to teach that, although there are innumerable ways leading to God, the surest way to intimate knowledge of God is bringing happiness to others. Second, the presence of God is among the destitute and needy. Third, egoistic chauvinism is real idolatry to be combated by loving compassion, openhearted acceptance of others, and religious tolerance. To realize these teachings, one had to find a spiritual master and devote oneself to his loving service. One must embrace voluntary poverty by renouncing saving and hoarding. Finally one should revive the heart through listening to devotional music (singing poems, accompanied by drumming and occasionally stringed instruments) in gatherings that could erupt into ecstatic states and enraptured dance. Nizam al-Din left this institutional legacy along with the written record of his oral teachings as a spiritual legacy; yet in the person of Khusro, his most personable disciple, we have a very human portrait of these dual legacies at work in the imagination of an individual.

Recovering Nuances through Gender Studies

When critical theory is directed toward Islamic societies (or any society), the suppressed, ignored, and taken for granted appear in greater relief, drifting into focus in the center of critical analysis from their position on the margins of the normative order, between the lines of texts, or from under the surface of expected routines. Woman takes an equal place next to man in the analysis, even if in the social or religious situation analyzed she is obscured or disempowered. Through critical theory men can only be seen clearly through the lens of women, who are not usually seen at all. The feminist sector of critical theory has made these innovations possible, in dialogue with a rapidly changing reality on the ground as women organize, assert rights, work in public fields, and write/speak/chant with an articulateness formerly denied to them. Feminism created women's studies, and when that method of analysis is applied to Islamic sites such as the *dargah* of Nizam al-Din Awliya in Delhi, one gets a study such as Patricia Jeffery's *Frogs in a Well*.[3] There are dangers inherent in this method, especially when feminism is developed in Western societies and applied to Islamic ones without a critical recognition of complexity in the religious tradition, ambiguity in how Islam is lived out in local contexts, and reciprocity to allow Muslim women to shape the theoretical discussion itself. Sa'diyya Shaikh points out these dangers: "Some western feminists, who would otherwise be sensitized to questions of diversity, persist in making sweeping claims about Muslim women or Islam without engaging the necessary levels of complexity and specificity. . . . such western discourses on Muslim women are predicated on unquestioned cultural and social assumptions that do not allow for the engagement of specific Muslim societies on their own terms."[4]

In reaction to these dangers, many Muslim women have adapted feminist methods to Islamic sources of authority and claims about ultimate reality. This has given rise to a discourse of Islamic feminism, notes Shaikh (echoing miriam cooke).[5] Yet as Muslim women are taking possession of feminism on their own terms, the terms are changing in Western academies. Now gender studies seems to displace women's studies as critical social theory develops further. The object of analysis is not women as a distinct class affected by oppressive social orders and affecting social change with increasing creativity and assertiveness. The object of analysis has become gender as a concept, through which the status of women (like the status of men) is defined, enforced, policed, and made to seem natural, necessary, and even inevitable.

Many feminist scholars, Muslim and otherwise, are wary of these purported advances in the discipline of critical theory, which threaten to disperse the intellectual focus on woman before actual women can solidify the social gains in the real world that have slowly accrued to them through decades of struggle. Others are eager to question the binary division between women and men. The goal of gender studies is not just analysis of women and their social roles in order to further their emancipation and promote their fuller participation as equals. Its object is to understand how women are constituted (how the category of woman is defined, created, and reinforced by social norms) as different from men. Men no less than women are the objects of its analysis, suggesting that women and men are contingent, with the boundary between them flexible, the roles situation specific, culturally relative, and constantly under renegotiation. A good example of feminist analysis that takes a male persona as its subject is Bruce Lawrence's small study of how Nizam al-Din Awliya as a male Muslim saint was shaped by the women around him and how his masculinity developed through a vow of celibacy.[6] Gender studies highlights the intrinsic connection between gender and sexuality, dispersing its analysis from women as a class to all the variations (lesbians, homosexual men, those who occupy a hermaphrodite position or defy classification, as well as celibate persons and prostitutes) whose gender identity and sexual persona create problems for any hegemonic social order.

Many feminist scholars look upon these developments with alarm. Gender studies seems to embrace a postmodern method, like that of Michel Foucault and his advocates, that disperses subjectivity and dissolves the agency of social actors. If taken to extremes, it seriously compromises critical theory's ethical goal to promote social change. However, gender studies, with its de-essentializing imperative, offers some useful advantages. The critical emphasis on gender rather than on women allowed gay and lesbian studies to join in the dialogue as a distinct but complementary set of voices. Yet gay and lesbian studies has also been decentered by a critical leap forward into queer theory, which sometimes seems to erase the actual agency of nonheterosexual persons or of gay and lesbian movements for social change. Gilbert Herdt clarifies the border between gay and lesbian studies and queer theory when he writes,

> Where gay and lesbian literature discovered itself by narrating the lived experience of being on the margin or growing up closeted then coming out, queers shun these attributes in favor of studying and interpreting texts, especially literature and popular culture. Queer theory seeks to find the cracks and cleavages between things rather than the things themselves. . . . By use of the "deconstruction" or reinterpretation of texts, queer theorists worry over linkages among epistemology, theory, literature, philosophy and popular culture. In lesbian and gay writing, the person/subject—however marginalized—was regarded as whole and unitary, and the struggle of the scholar was to investigate and regain the wholeness of the experience shattered by the secrecy and marginalization of same-gender desires in the past. . . . Queer theory, however, argues that history and culture descriptions are never distinguishable from the authors and assumptions of normality through which subjects or objects are described.[7]

The de-essentializing pressures within newer currents of critical theory may advance the feminist project of emancipation rather than threaten it if they are applied with flexibility, insight, and wise balance. Its insights could help free women from the limitations of patriarchal norms while also freeing men from the same norms that give them overt power, but at the expense of limiting their potential for fulfillment and happiness. In other words "masculinity" is a critical topic of analysis, a social construction that is "fragile, provisional, something to be won and then defended, something under a constant threat of loss."[8] Gender studies uncovers the fragility of empowered masculinity while recovering the multiplicity of masculine roles within a given social milieu, emphasizing their plurality, flexibility, and interchangeability while acknowledging how patriarchal power structures limit men's performance of masculine possibilities.[9]

More simply stated, not all men prosper under a patriarchal order, even if some do. Young men are under the authority of elders, whom they obey or imitate in order eventually to replace or displace. Working men are under the control of property owners, upon whom they depend even as their interests conflict. Slaves are under the ownership of masters, who deny a slave's masculinity even as his male body is used for labor, skill, or pleasure. Homosexual men are under the threat of heterosexual men, whom they must imitate, even though it makes impossible their emotional fulfillment. And finally asexual or celibate men are under the demands of a procreative order that thwarts their aspiration to direct their energies toward other goals, whether worldly or otherworldly. Gender studies encourages us to denaturalize "the man" to articulate the varieties of masculine types, roles, and behaviors that are defined against women and also against other men.

Gender studies asks the simple question, "What makes a person into a man?" The answer is contingent upon "what makes a person into a woman," and that distinction is a matter of intense conflict. This conflict generates tension that is expressed in oppressive routines, intermittent violence, and threatening playfulness. In Islamic societies an analysis of gender that focuses upon masculinity is applicable well beyond the apparent arenas of mosque, market, and battlefield. It also applied to the circumcision ceremony, the barbershop, the conjugal bed, the courtroom, and the throne room.

Ethics and Music at the Khanqah in Delhi

In Islamic studies an especially productive place to apply this critical theory is the *khanqah*, or Sufi hospice, where social norms are temporarily or potentially eclipsed by the sacred power of direct contact with transcendent authority. Muslims go to the *khanqah* to do spiritual labor—to worship God (*'ibada*) through serving others (*khidma*) and humbling oneself within a communal gathering in hopes of receiving the blessing (*baraka*) of well-being in the outer world, spiritual ascension in the inner world, and salvation in the next world. The *khanqah* is a place of transformation, a liminal space, in Victor Turner's theoretical scheme, one tightly woven into the fabric of social routine.[10] It is a theater where masculine norms are questioned and reaffirmed, abandoned and reinforced, inverted and tempered. As devotees (*murid*) interact with a spiritual master (*pir*), they not only gain spiritual teachings of a living person, but also visit the graves of his ancestors who localize the Prophet Muhammad's character, and ultimately encounter God's presence in ways both subtle and overt. The rituals at the *khanqah* help devotees, mainly adult men, to suspend (or shed) the values of autonomy, independence, mastery, and assertiveness that the patriarchal social order demands of them, giving them space to perform alternate values of dependence, reciprocity, servitude, and humble deference. The goal is to ease anxiety and abandon self-preoccupation so that one can gain insight into one's egoistic limitations, withdraw one's rational grasping at wealth, status, and security, and ultimately open up space in the heart and mind for love.

In *khanqahs* where the musical and meditative ritual of *sama'* is performed, the quest for love can become quite heated, vivid, and loud. One can, through the vehicle of poetry and music, leave aside (or perhaps transcend) parts of one's routine, egoistic consciousness or even leave oneself entirely in rapture, literally standing outside the self. This is the experience of *wajd*, or ecstatic abandon, that Bruce Lawrence has written about and translated directly from the oral teachings of Nizam al-Din's delicate discussions of the topic.[11] If one leaves one's egoistic routine, for a moment or an evening or longer, one also leaves aside gender roles that structure that routine. One thereby opens oneself to attitudes, gestures, and behaviors that are normally forbidden to men in patriarchal regimes. As Khusro said in the poem that opens this essay, "On passionate heads enemies' curses are a crown / in love-struck lanes a ruined reputation is true learning / It's not so manly to scatter infidel corpses / in the corps of lovers real men die by self-spurning."

Chishti Sufis in South Asia cultivate the arts of *sama'*, providing examples whose vividness comes to startling clarity under the lens of gender studies. The interactions between a spiritual master and his disciple are most clearly modeled by Nizam al-Din Awliya and his beloved follower, Amir Khusro. Khusro is an important figure in Indo-Muslim culture far beyond his role as a Sufi disciple. He is an archetypal Indian Muslim, a soldier and poet, who was eloquent in Persian and learned in Sanskrit, the son of a Turkic father and an Indian mother. He is the "parrot of India" through whose sweet speech the contradictions and possibilities of Indian Muslims in the medieval period come alive (both for his contemporaries in fourteenth-century Delhi and for us in the present who read his reflections or hear his poems sung in *sama'* performances). In coediting *Beyond Hindu and Turk* with David Gilmartin, Bruce Lawrence promoted the creative dismantling of this enduring binary in the city of religion in South Asia. Upon the dividing line between Hindu and Turk stands Khusro—who does not simply straddle the divide or synthesize the apparent opposition but actually dances on the fence to show its artificiality.

In addition to being beyond Hindu and Turk and "diffusing Hindu/Muslim boundaries," did Khusro play with other contested divides?[12] Critical theory encourages us to look at whether he also pointed beyond male and female, as do the performances of traditional music in South Asia, about which musicologist Bonnie Wade has observed, "What might seem a woman's song text may in *khyal* be sung by a man or a woman. Likewise, what seems a specifically Hindu text is just as likely to be sung by a Muslim artist."[13] Khusro's playful poetics and avid devotion to his spiritual guide provide evidence that the gender divide was not as impermeable as we might assume of a medieval society and that sexuality roles based upon binary gender division may not have been as inflexible as most scholars take for granted.

Masculine Ambiguities and Contact with the Sacred

Anthropologists engaged in critical social theory describe how the inversion of social norms is a form of supplication or a way of requesting closeness to a source of power. As one approached the ruler in Indo-Muslim courts, one approached in prostration: one's habitual bodily comportment was radically altered. Abdellah Hammoudi has very adroitly shown how such inversion of norms in deference to royal authority was even more complexly applied in Sufi communities. One approached a powerful saint by suspending or abdicating one's routine comportment as a patriarchal male.[14] A male disciple could only approach a male spiritual guide in one of two ways: as seducer in a homoerotic social role that inverts sexual norms or as subservient effeminate in a feminine social role that inverts gender norms.

In order to express sanctity, Sufi Muslims often cross the socially defined boundary of gender. Here *sanctity* connotes perceptible markers of self-surrender, abandoning worldly ambition, devotion, and love of God. And gender crossing signifies that a man takes up the social markers of woman: to wear women's clothing; to adopt women's speech, song, and gesture; to take on a woman's role in erotic interactions or even in sexual interactions. In a complementary but distinct way, male Sufis may shed many of the signs of social status, including the patriarchal status of masculinity, as a sign of surrender without performing these signs of surrender in the outer form of feminine gender. They might do this by wearing outlandishly colored clothes, wearing no clothes, shaving the beard and mustache, leaving family and ascribed status, or inviting condemnation and blame. Such performances focus male passion toward another man, transforming the subject into a passionate lover, so that love transgresses social and religious boundaries as a metaphor for transcending them. In this way transgender behavior and homoerotic behavior are closely linked but are not reducible to each other. Sufis in South Asia inverted gender roles or cultivated homoerotic attraction in order to show supplication. In situations of deference to the authority of a Sufi master, and to make the self vulnerable to receive mystical insight, men's bodies were placed in positions that contradicted patriarchal norms, a position we can observe in Khusro.

Even as he worked as a royal poet and military noble in the court of the sultan of Delhi, Khusro dedicated his life to the humble and impoverished Sufi Nizam al-Din Awliya. Their relationship can only be described as a romantic friendship of love. To express his intimacy with Nizam al-Din, Khusro sang verses in Hindi, in which he takes on the voice and persona of a woman. He transgresses gender norms by portraying Nizam al-Din as the beloved groom, while he sings in the voice of the bride swooning with love and expectation. "On the first night of meeting [the groom] I stayed awake the whole night // My body, the mind of the lover, the two in one color."[15] Here the term *color (rang)* also means an essence or a spiritual quality that permeates the matter of an object and animates it, just as dye might saturate fabric.

Such Hindi poems continue to be sung as the core repertoire of *qawwali* music. The poetic speaker addresses her beloved as *sajan*, an endearment for a male beloved. "My lover is going away in the morning / my eyes will die with weeping // Make the night so long / so there will be no morning."[16] Not all these examples are confined to literary productions. There is anecdotal evidence that Khusro sang his poetry in supplication to Nizam al-Din. Total abandon in love could only be expressed through such transgressive performances.

A popular anecdote illustrates this dynamic. Nizam al-Din was unusual for a Sufi master in that he never married. Yet he was fond of children and held his nephew dear. When the young boy died, Nizam al-Din was inconsolable; he stoically continued serving others but could not manage to smile for many months. Khusro returned to Delhi from his frequent trips with the army and court and found his spiritual guide still mourning. To cheer him Khusro dressed up as a female courtesan with bangles on his arms and bells on his ankles and danced before his spiritual guide. His transvestite performance had the comic and erotic power to break his master's long sadness, and Nizam al-Din could not help but smile.[17]

Another story explains how Khusro's poetry acquired its special eloquence and simple sweetness. Khusro met Khidr, the semiprophetic figure who represents constant inspiration and is associated with the color green, the revival of life through wisdom, and rejuvenation through the water of life.[18] In the dream, Khusro "asked him for a drop of his saliva that could impart wonderful sweetness and eloquence to his poetry and warrant him an eternal fame. 'That gift,' replied Khidr, 'I have already bestowed upon Saʿdi [the first poet to excel in the Persian *ghazal*].' The poet much dejected went to his teacher and related the occurrence, whereupon the saint [Nizam al-Din] dropped into his mouth his own saliva which turned out to be as efficacious and potent as that of the old man, Khidr."[19] He later sang the praise of this potent wine from the mouth of his spiritual teacher: "From his lips I found the saliva / that gives life and luster to my speech," he versifies, making a resonant rhyme between the word for lustrous, life-giving moisture (*ab*) and saliva (*lu'ab*), which also sounds like playful dalliance (*la'b*). In many *ghazals* he boasts of the ferment of ecstasy that love engendered within him, love in his relationship with his spiritual teacher who acted as his *Saqi*, or wine pourer of dazzling beauty.

> Saqi, bring me wine, for today begins my ecstasy
> > Keep the cup full, for an empty cup heralds my mortality
> For passion I gave my life that over my corpse you might linger
> > Can lovers living in alienation expect any other intimacy?
> It's my fate to recite alone all night tales of love's exquisite pain
> > The sleeplessness you note in me is from this epic's immensity
> Enough of these words snared in insanity-evoking beauties' chains
> > The spirit of every *ghazal* I compose ferments with original ecstasy![20]

Through his poetic and musical legacy, Khusro became the paradigmatic Sufi disciple for later generations of Sufis in South Asia, especially in his Chishti community.

Khusro rarely donned women's clothes to dance before his spiritual master but often adopted a woman's voice to express his devotion. This is especially the case when he writes poems in old Hindi, in the folk idiom of which the lover who speaks is a young woman pining for her beloved, sneaking from home and family to see him, and braving the destructive gossip of the village to follow her passion.[21] In one poem he sings, "Let the village housewife say what she likes, I have stolen a glance from the eye of Nizam. Khusro, tonight's the wedding night—I stayed awake with my lover, the body is mine but the heart is my lover's, both suffused in one color. His darling face and charming form I've hidden deep in my heart—Khusro sacrificed at the feet of Nizam, I've been sold a priceless maid!"[22] The "maid" that is sold in marriage to Nizam al-Din is Khusro himself, offered as a selfless sacrifice to his Sufi master. The feminine voice and masculine name coexist in shimmering tension in these verses, a favorite for *qawwali* performances.

Another Hindi poem of Khusro reveals that his gender transformation is a trope rather than a personal idiosyncrasy. It is the most dramatic way for a male Sufi to display surrender and devotion to a spiritual authority who is seen as both a powerful and empowering male. Just as Nizam al-Din loved his own spiritual guide, Farid al-Din "Ganj-i Shakar," or "the Sugar Treasure," so Khusro sees himself as a young woman excited into frenzy at her own approaching wedding.

"Ganj-i Shakar's little darling, Nizam, is the bridegroom today—come everyone, join in greeting him, for Nizam's the bridegroom today. Pearls, diamonds,
and rubies in his robe, the saints stand for his procession—ask whatever you
wish, for Nizam is the bridegroom today. His nickname is God's Beloved, for
his sake give up life, limb, and riches—come everyone, join in to tease him, for
Nizam's the bridegroom today. Khusro is ready to sacrifice both body and soul
for Nizam—come everybody, join in the celebrating, for Nizam's the bridegroom today."[23] The tone of these poems is sweet with the joy of expectation
and charged with erotic energy. The wedding night is a metaphor for the meeting of hearts in a spiritual bond, expressed through the sensual energy of a
meeting of bodies in an erotic embrace. *Wisal* (union) is the term to describe
this experience, which is both rapture and death.

In folk imagery of village Hindi, the experience of *wisal* is like being dyed in
the color of one's beloved, the way an old garment is drowned in a dye vat to be
pulled out renewed with vibrant color and revived with vibrant life. To achieve
it, one has to risk everything: one's pride, one's ego, one's reputation, and one's
very life. In another Hindi poem, Khusro sings, "Enchant me with your color,
give me color, O vibrant one—You are my master, God's Beloved. My veil and
my lover's turban, give them both a springtime hue—You are my master, God's
Beloved. If you ask a price for this vibrant color, keep my youth as a pledge—
You are my master, God's Beloved. I fell down at the door of your court, so keep
safe my modesty and shame—You are my master, God's Beloved. Nizam al-Din
Awliya, my spiritual guide, give me love with vibrant passion—You are my master, God's Beloved."[24]

The enduring legacy of Khusro's gender-bending is in his Hindi poems.
They play against the Hindu folk idiom of female lovers, which made his single
episode of dancing in courtesan's dress before Nizam al-Din so joyful, hilarious,
and effective. Yet this single transvestite performance episode inspired later imi-
tations that were even bolder, such as that of the Chishti Sufi from Gujarat
named Musa Sada Sohag (died 1449 C.E.), whose transgender identity was more
deeply challenging to patriarchal presumptions. His story has been preserved in
local hagiographies commemorating the rich Sufi legacy of Ahmadabad, where
he is buried.[25]

Transgender and Homoerotic Possibilities: Trope or Experience?

Musa Sada Sohag was an ascetic and scholarly minded Sufi who went to pay
respects to the tomb of a respected Sufi master, as is the custom of Chishti Sufis,
before departing for the hajj pilgrimage. He visited the tomb of Nizam al-Din
Awliya in Delhi. While he was meditating at the tomb, female courtesans and
prostitutes were singing songs of praise and dancing out of devotion in the
courtyard before the tomb. Musa denounced the practice of allowing such

undignified women to perform at the saint's tomb and condemned it in the light of Islamic law. He then proceeded to Mecca and made the obligatory pilgrimage, before turning to Medina to visit the Prophet Muhammad's tomb. However, at the outskirts of Medina, as his story is told in hagiographic records, he became stuck. A voice from beyond spoke to him, asking him how he could dare to visit the Prophet when his Sufi patron in Delhi remained annoyed. Musa realized that his stray thought—criticizing the courtesans and prostitutes who danced before Nizam al-Din's tomb—had angered the long-dead Sufi master. He abandoned his intent to visit the Prophet in Medina and hurried back to Delhi.

The closer he got to Delhi, the more agitated Musa became. An affront to one's Sufi master was the worst form of presumptuousness and arrogance—how could he draw close enough to Nizam al-Din's presence to beg forgiveness? At the threshold Musa remembered the story of Khusro. Since he had sinned by thinking evil of the courtesans, he must approach the tomb dressed as a courtesan. Since he harbored suspicion against the good intent of the dancers, he must beg forgiveness by dancing like a woman in the courtyard before the saint's tomb. In a fit of profound empathy and self-abnegation, Musa took on the persona of those he had despised.

As he danced before Nizam al-Din's tomb in women's clothes and bangles, Musa became enraptured and fell in a swoon. In this state he experienced the dawning of inner, intuitive light. Upon awakening, he said, "Since I experienced such enlightenment only while dancing in women's clothes, I will never take them off!" What began as a play act of supplication became a permanent state of gender transgression, as he took on the persona of a woman, donned the red clothes of a bride awaiting her groom, and adopted the nickname Sada Sohag, "the Eternal Bride." Thereafter Musa insisted on being treated as a woman and not a man; he had become she, at least in her own eyes. At Musa Sada Sohag's death, fellow Sufis rallied to honor her memory and protect her from the legal minded who might strip her, as a corpse, of her adopted femininity, especially the bangles that were squeezed up over her wrists to adorn her masculine forearms.

Musa is the clearest example of transgression of gender boundaries as an expression of this distinctively Islamic saintliness. He performed gender transgression self-consciously, to display his status of sainthood. However, the reverse dynamic could also prevail: gender transgression may prompt the response of sanctification by the surrounding Muslim society without itself being self-consciously performed as a claim of sainthood. There are many people (unlike Musa Sada Sohag) who cross the boundary of gender and take on the role of women for reasons other than compulsion of being a saint. Men might identify as "hermaphrodites" because of anatomical ambiguity, social alienation, or sublimation of homoerotic desire or because of the psychological self-perception that they are actually women in men's bodies. This is the case of the *hijras* who made up the dedicated following of Musa Sada Sohag. The *hijras* are granted a holy status by premodern Islamic society in South Asia due to the awe and fear that surrounds any social object that does not succumb to the dichotomies that structure society: dichotomies such as masculine/feminine, dominant/submissive, and earning/nurturing. In the *hijras'* case, desire is transgressive because it must switch genders before finding its object: a man must act as a woman before he can desire intimacy with a masculine object of desire. What is queer is the gender of the desiring subject rather than the sexual orientation as defined by the object of desire. In contrast with Musa Sada Sohag, Khusro did not consistently invert gender roles, but rather inverted sexuality roles through same-sex eroticism. He exhibits with great vividness another whole range of "homoerotic" phenomena in which the male gaze eroticizes the beauty of a masculine figure.

In Sufi hagiography there are many examples of this dynamic, of male Sufis who look upon other men with erotic desire. Often these are Muslim males who look with desire upon men of a distinctly different class: either younger men or non-Muslim men. Such a practice is called, in Persian and Urdu, *shahid-bazi*, or "playing the witness game." In Iranian and South Asian Sufism, this practice is a sign of surrender and renunciation and is sometimes an active pursuit of beauty and devotion to the ideal of comradely intimacy. Khusro, who provided us with early and vivid examples of gender-bending homoeroticism, also provides us with charming examples of gaze-centered homoeroticism. In a Persian poem, he wrote: "Ah, Delhi and its young beauties with turbans placed roguishly awry. The path on which they stroll blooms with swaying roses. As they stroll, in their wake follow lovers, tears of blood flowing. These saucy young Hindus have made the Muslims into sun worshipers."[26] The turban or cap awry (*kaj kulahi*) is the masculine sign of youthful beauty and rakish good looks. It appears many times in Khusro's more secular love poetry, as he praises with evident relish the beauty of younger men, especially Hindus. In the male Muslim gaze, a Hindu youth could be unattainably beloved, and in that role they can slay the Muslim lover in a titillating inversion of military prowess. We must remember that Khusro was not just a Muslim poet and Sufi but also a Turkish knight and courtier of an Islamic empire, the Delhi Sultanate, that conquered most of South Asia by force of arms. "It's not friends or relatives who knock me senseless / but youths in the streets with hair disheveled and caps awry // They ask, "Why give your heart to such handsome riffraff?" / By God, I don't give them my heart—they just steal it away!"[27]

Can we read such examples of Khusro's poetry as an expression of his sexual orientation? Scholars of Persian and Urdu poetry have long argued this point, not just about Khusro but about many great poets in the South Asian Muslim literary canon. In this literature metaphors for the beloved, when they are gendered at all, are usually inflected toward identifying the beloved as a younger man who inspires love, longing, and even lust in a older male poet admirer. Descriptions of beauty focus intently on the subtle grace of wisps of hair: the down on a beloved's cheek could denote either a masculine or feminine beloved, while the new growth of a mustache that frames the lips unambiguously denotes a masculine beloved. Rarely do poets indicate that expressing such admiration for homoerotic male beauty is shameful, though equally rarely do the poems express physical consummation in any erotic union or sexual act.

Khusro is unusual in that he, for a moment, acknowledges that his poetic expression crosses a boundary of social restraint. One of his delightful Persian *ghazals* contains this couplet, which boldly describes a beautiful lip until it balks at the suggestion of consummation: "That new sprout of hair on your cheek, that simple innocent lip—it's as if . . . / No, isn't the subject more beautiful if it remains unnamed?" This couplet seems to suggest a love that dare not say its name, and indeed at least one medieval biographical collection of famous Persianate poets and Sufis insists that Khusro and his fellow poet and disciple of Nizam al-Din, Amir Hasan Sijzi (1254–1336), were not just best friends but also lovers. He writes that "the bird of Amir Khusro's heart fell into the snare of the beauty of Hasan, who was a courtier in the service of Sultan ʿAlaʾ al-Din Firoz . . . and composed many *ghazals* in honor of Hasan, such as this one":[28]

> Along the road of passion, free of disaster one just can't live
> Until the chest is charred, in happiness one just can't live
> Though I endure hardships, even this cruelty must have an end
> Since you know, don't you, that in such injustice one just can't live
> My soul is like a trapped bird, but people say, why suffer so?
> Safely within the enchanting hunter's cord one just can't live
> You are the nourishment of my life, so at least give the breeze a message
> After all, this simple man's a man, on air alone one just can't live
> Endure this injustice, Khusro, don't breath a word of lovers' cruelty
> Day and night with complaints and sighs one just can't live

Admittedly this source is biased and may not reflect factual information. Its author, Husayn Gazargahi, a sixteenth-century Iranian Sufi and poet, argues that all great male Sufis had male lovers and that this was the cause of their greatness. Yet the narrative Gazargahi reports is vivid and does resonate with many of Khusro's poems, even if it takes them literally, even miraculously.

> Amir Khusro's relationship with him [Hasan Sijzi] stepped out the corner of secrecy into the wilderness of publicity. Self-seeking courtiers alerted the king, who asked Khusro, "Poet! Have you recited no verses [about this affair]?" He answered, "No, I have recited nothing." The King demanded,

"Then speak now in verse!" So Khusro recited: "I possess the quality of love as a gift by my God's generosity—Sorrow's sackcloth on my bare back is my raiment of royalty." After this, he reached such a level of passion that he became one of those holy people shrouded in blame (*malamat*), and all tongues were speaking about him. [He recited . . .] "This willful heart dragged my affairs down to ruined repute—Khusro, obeying commands of the heart has born heavy fruit!"

The King turned his ear to the blame people poured upon Khusro and sought a solution. At first the King forbade him from keeping company with Amir Hasan, but the cord of his love was such that it could not be severed. The King heard that Khusro was now mixing with Hasan and was going under cover of secrecy to his house. He demanded Hasan and in anger gave him a few lashes. From there Hasan went to Khusro's house. When the King heard this, that his [Khusro's] metaphorical love became bedecked with the jewels of real love, he summoned both Khusro and Hasan and inquired about their love to see if there was any taint of selfishness and lust between them. In the crucible of trial the gold of their love appeared, and they came out true in the balance. Despite thus knowing that their love was not selfish, the King demanded that two just persons be brought into the courtroom of love to bear witnesses to the sincerity of their claim. Khusro said, "From between him and me the duality of two has bitten the dust!" He drew his arm out of his shirt, saying, "Maybe a truthful lover has something up his sleeve . . . ," and revealed that his body displayed the scars of the lashes that they had inflicted upon Hasan! He recited this quatrain of Shaykh [Fakhr al-Din] 'Iraqi: "Love came, like my life-blood in artery and vein till I emptied of blood and with my friend filled to the brim. Every part of my existence embraces my friend's essence—perhaps the name is mine, but otherwise everything is him."[29]

Gazargahi may have fictionalized the events of this story, yet the intimate friendship they depict was real. Both Khusro and Hasan were literati in the court, and both were spiritual brothers—fellow disciples of Nizam al-Din Awliya, whose oral teachings they preserved in separate writings.[30] It is impossible to tell whether their friendship was romantic or sexual. However, there is something "queer" about Khusro that comes across in his poetry.

Khusro's poetry takes refuge in the boundaries of ambiguity, both to hide his "real" intent that might be sexual and also, as an expert poet, to heighten the tension he inspires in his listeners. He composed erotic verses that crossed and recrossed the boundary between Persian and Hindi, with lines that alternated in each language or lines that started in one language and ended in the next. This compositional technique allowed him to express erotic admiration for males hidden with a humorous shift to a new language that allowed for a double reading.[31] Khusro treats a provocative male-to-male kiss in a different style in Persian—a style that is less directly erotic and more metaphysical, with its sexual energy not wrapped in a riddle but rather infused into the subtle allusions to symbols of the *ghazal*, like the message-bearing breeze, the wine tavern among ruins, and the blues-singing masochist of a narrating poetic voice. In this *ghazal* he writes, "Don't give his lip, oh reckless imagination, leave to meet my lip. Don't give pistachios and dates to a bird that feeds on dried husks. If you should pass him, morning breeze, then bring dust from his feet—with its darkness decorate my eyes but please don't give his feet my kiss. The heart and soul of Khusro is spent only to acquire you—Weigh their worth however you wish, but don't give anything in exchange!"[32] Khusro's poetry, whether in Persian, Hindi, or a clever blending of both, can deal with flirtation and eros in a purely secular voice. It invites us to speculate about the author's actual sexual orientation and whether the budding mustache above the lip might be, in his imagination, more than just a stock poetic metaphor for emerging yet ephemeral beauty.

Mutual Reinforcement of Erotic and Spiritual Love

However, before reducing eros to sexual desire, we should observe how Khusro employs erotic energy for devotional love for his spiritual guide and ultimately toward God. A famous anecdote can illustrate this for us, as we bear in mind his homoerotic verses about youths in Delhi with the caps awry. Once Khusro was sitting by the river Jamuna with his Sufi guide, Nizam al-Din Awliya. When they observed some Hindus bathing and offering prayers to the dawn sun, the Sufi master noted their style of worship with approval (paraphrasing Qur'an 22:66): "To every community there is a religious way and a direction for prayer" (*har qawm ra-st rahi dini o qiblah gahi*). Khusro spontaneously added, "man qiblah rast kardam janib-i kaj kulahi," making this line into a rhyming couplet that is sung to this day in *qawwali* performances: "Every community has a right way and a direction to pray / and I turn in prayer to face the captivating one whose cap's awry." Some tell this story while noting that Nizam al-Din used to wear his cap or turban awry in a jaunty style, turning Khusro's lyric into a note of devoted love of his spiritual teacher. However, the "cap awry" could denote "The Beloved" in all its universality and ambivalence. It could denote a living person with a beautiful form or a spiritual guide whose beautiful qualities live on after death, or it could denote God as the epitome of beauty beyond life and death or refer simply to beauty as an abstract idea that comes to the eye of the beholder in any guise.

Nizam al-Din's offhand comment about the rightness of the Hindus' worship (which was actually a disguised citation of the Qur'an) invoked the religious dimension of *rasti*, or right conduct in ethical and ritual spheres. Khusro took his comment from the level of rational discourse to poetic inference by crafting it into a couplet, noting that his own right conduct is devoted love toward an object of beauty; thus Khusro slipped from *rasti* to the religious dimension of *masti*, passionate love characterized by devotional fervor, intoxicated abandon, and ecstatic experience. The real enjoyment of the verse is knowing there is a third dimension indicated by the movement from *rasti* to *masti*, and that is the religious dimension of *nisti*, the extinction or passing away from self-consciousness that is the goal of mystical currents within religious traditions (whether this experience is actualized, idealized, or theorized). When this couplet is sung in Chishti gatherings of *sama'*, slipped into another poem to intensify a moment of climax, it has the potential to spark such an experience of springing out of self-concern, a moment of selflessness (*nisti* in Persian or *fana'* in Arabic) in listeners attuned to its subtleties.

Khusro, in this verse and many others, celebrates the Sufi practice of *shahid-bazi*, playing the witness game: worshiping to the beauty of God as it might manifest in any created form. Most medieval Sufis in the Persian-speaking realm found such manifestations of divine beauty most clearly and consistently in the form of young men. Such homoerotic gazing contemplation (whether combined with actual romantic attachment, physical intimacy or sexual desire, or left "chaste") was an important though controversial feature of Sufism in South Asia, as well as Iran and Arab lands. Hagiographic and poetic evidence attests to its presence in the lives of eminent mystics, such as Shams-i Tabrezi who inspired Mawlana Rumi; Ahmad Ghazali, the master of Persian love poetry; and Fakhr al-Din 'Iraqi, the interpreter of Ibn 'Arabi in poetry (whose poetry Khusro quotes in the fictional account of his love for Amir Hasan). This is true despite the reticence of modern scholars to acknowledge it, and Western scholars seem more reticent than Iranian or South Asian scholars.[33] It is refreshing that a younger generation of scholars such as Bruce Lawrence and Carl Ernst (who each have one foot planted in the Western academy and the other in South Asian spaces) are more open and honest about these nuances: they write that of *sama'* that "for the genuine seeker, music was intended to optimize the dyadic relationship between human love and a Divine Beloved. Because of the subtlety of verse as well as the waywardness of human emotion, however, the dyad could be (and sometimes was) construed as the love of two human beings for one another, whether that of a man for a woman or a man for a boy or occasionally a man for another man."[34]

What is "queer" about Amir Khusro, as someone who not only participated in *sama'* but also wrote verse that now makes up its classic repertoire? It is not simply that he wrote erotic verses and love poems directed toward other men, for the thrust of his poetic work goes far beyond the label "homosexual." Rather he wrote love poetry for his Sufi master, who was clearly beyond a merely sexual desire or purely romantic attachment. His metaphors of same-sex love extended even to God, whose divinity was not just transcendently other but also fascinatingly present in beauty, no matter where it might be found. In this way Khusro's poetry is completely informed by *wahdat al-wujud*, the "oneness of being." This Sufi concept, which elevates all loves to act as pathways toward love of God, was popularized in South Asia through *sama*, listening to love poetry in a devotional setting that might erupt into ecstatic gesture or rapturous dance. One of Khusro's *ghazals*, often sung in *sama* sessions, leaves it entirely unclear whether the beloved, whose glance throws him into raptures that teeter on obliteration, is an amorous friend, a spiritual guide, or some manifestation of God's merciful presence perceived through the translucent veil of human imagination in partly sensual forms.

> Intoxicating eye, O bewildering—Dangling locks, O bewildering
>   Adoring wine, O bewildering—Weaving seduction, O bewildering!
> Drawn up for my execution, beneath the sword I prostrate my head
>   Your proud dalliance, O bewildering—My abject longing, O bewildering!
> The wonder of beauty and splendor, of downy cheek, black mole, and
>   curling hair
>   The cypress stature, O bewildering—The haughty height, O bewildering
> Not in standing nor in kneeling, not in bowing or laying forehead to the
>   ground
>   Remember the beloved and pass away—That's prayer, O bewildering![35]

Another of Khusro's *ghazals* even specifies that the Prophet Muhammad can become the polymorphous beloved, whose beauty leaves the gazer stricken:[36]

> I don't know where it was, that place I passed last night
>   On every side the dance of the stricken, that place I passed last night
> I saw one with angel's form, with cypress stature and cheeks like tulips
>   From head to toe the image plagued my heart, that place I passed last night
> Rivals, listen carefully to his voice, you fear he might seduce me
>   What difficulty for intimate conversation, that place I passed last night
> The master of that gathering was God alone in a place beyond all place
>   Muhammad was its glowing candle, that place I spent last night[37]

These two poems are often woven together in actual *qawwali* performance, because they share many of the same images of seduction, bewilderment, sacrifice, and transcendence. Such performances, in which ritual actions, devotional environments, poetic images, musical melodies, and syncopated rhythms fuse into a synesthetic religious experience, make Sufism effective as a mode of contemplation and personal transformation for those who are open to it and sensitive to its ways. And it is in Sufi shrines built over or around the tombs of saintly figures, such as that of Nizam al-Din Awliya in Delhi where Amir Khusro himself is buried, that the most effective of these performances are held.

We conclude this essay citing the power of performance. Over the past three decades, as feminist theory has become more integrated into critical social theory, it has focused on the idea that gender is "performative." Gender is not an essential given that is beyond culture to shape, nor is it a social construction that is beyond individual agency to effect. Rather it is a performance, in which individual and social audiences are caught up in a mutually reinforcing interaction of background assumptions, asserted roles, and articulated interpretations that allow for variation, reversal, and even inversion of expected norms. Premodern Islamic society in South Asia allowed such nuances, as we have seen in the life and words of Khusro, even as it enforced a patriarchal social order.

That premodern Islamic social order is now gone. The Persian-speaking Turkic rulers who governed it and patronized its religious institutions were overthrown in 1857. The Sufi communities who cultivated a religious system that centered on passionate love and existential transformation as the highest expression of Islam still exist but no longer occupy a central position in the society, not even in the Muslim minority, let alone in the wider pluralistic democracy that is the new nation of India.

Sufi shrines in Delhi, including that of Nizam al-Din Awliya where Khusro is buried, face mounting challenges as they struggle to persist as sacred sites.[38] The gender-bending subtleties of the stories of Khusro are largely lost, for custodians of his tomb recently told me that the story of his cross-dressing dance was replaced by a monkey-imitating dance. Indian society among Muslims as well as Hindus has become less accepting of gender ambiguity and sexuality diversity over the course of the twentieth century.[39]

It remains to be seen whether in the future the rising forces of religious communalism can be tempered by the contrasting discourse of human rights, civil society, and religious pluralism. If the champions of human rights and civil virtue can reach back into the past of premodern religious experience, they might bolster their cause to support the rights of women and other vulnerable minorities (like homosexuals or *hijras*). The contemporary rights of these groups must be rooted in premodern cultural legacies if they are to gain traction against the forces of religious communalism. Critical theory in the study of Islam and other religious traditions can help engineer a balance between political effectiveness and cultural authenticity. The welfare of many depends upon the success of this delicate project.

NOTES

1. Wazir al-Hazan Abidi, ed., *Intikhabat-i Ghazaliyat-i Khusro* (Lahore: Majlis-i Taraqqi-yi Urdu, n.d.), ghazal 22; my translation.

2. For the teachings of Nizam al-Din, see the translation by Bruce B. Lawrence, *Nizam al-Din Awliya: Morals for the Heart; Conversations of Shaykh Nizam ad-din Awliya Recorded by Amira Hasan Sijzi*, annotated by Lawrence, introduction by Khaliq Ahmad Nizami, Classics of Western Spirituality 74 (New York: Paulist Press, 1992).

3. Patricia Jeffery, *Frogs in a Well: Indian Women in Purdah* (London: Zed, 1979).

4. Saʿdiyya Shaikh, "Spiritual Cartographies of Gender: Ibn Arabi and Sufi Discourses of Gender, Sexuality and Marriage" (Ph.D. diss., Temple University, 2004), 17.

5. Saʿdiyya Shaikh, "Gender Justice: Muslim Women's Approaches to Feminist Activism" in *Progressive Muslims: On Justice, Gender, and Pluralism*, ed. Omid Safi (Oxford: Oneworld, 2003), 147–62; miriam cooke, *Women Claim Islam* (New York: Routledge, 2000). Many others have contributed to this debate, including Azza Karam, Ziba Mir Hosseini, Amina Wadud, and Asma Barlas.

6. Bruce B. Lawrence, "Honoring Women through Sexual Abstinence: Lessons from the Spiritual Practice of a Pre-Modern South Asian Sufi Master, Shaykh Nizam al-Din Awliya," in "Festschrift für Annemarie Schimmel," ed. Maria Subtelny, special issue of the *Journal of Turkish Studies* 18 (1994): 149–61.

7. Gilbert Herdt, *Same Sex, Different Cultures: Gays and Lesbians across Cultures* (Boulder, Colo.: Westview, 1997), 9.

8. Kate Wood and Rachel Jewkes, "Violence, Rape and Sexual Coercion: Everyday Love in a South African Township," *Gender and Development* 5, no. 2 (1997): 42.

9. See, for example, recent scholarship: R. W. Connell, *The Men and the Boys* (Cambridge: Polity, 2000); Victor Jeleniewski Seidler, *Man Enough—Embodying Masculinities* (London: Sage, 1997); John MacInnes, *The End of Masculinity: The Confusion of Sexual Genesis and Sexual Difference in Modern Society* (Buckingham: Open University Press, 1998); and Rachel Adams and David Savran, eds., *The Masculinity Studies Reader* (London: Blackwell, 2002).

10. Victor W. Turner, *The Ritual Process: Structure and Anti-structure* (London: Routledge & Kegan Paul, 1969).

11. See Nizam al-Din Awliya's discussion of *wajd* in Lawrence, *Morals for the Heart*; Bruce B. Lawrence, "The Early Chishti Approach to Samaʿ," in *Islamic Society and Culture: Essays in Honour of Professor Aziz Ahmad*, ed. Milton Israel and N. K. Wagle (Delhi: Manohar, 1983), 69–93; and Carl W. Ernst and Bruce B. Lawrence, *Sufi Martyrs of Love: The Chishti Order in South Asia and Beyond* (New York: Palgrave Macmillan, 2002), 37.

12. Bruce B. Lawrence, "The Diffusion of Hindu/Muslim Boundaries in South Asia: Contrasting Evidence from the Literature and the Tomb Cults of Selected Indo-Muslim Shaykhs," in *Identity and Division in Cults and Sects in South Asia*, ed. Peter Gaeffke and David Utz (Philadelphia: Proceedings of the South Asia Seminar, 1984), 125–32.

13. Bonnie Wade, *Khyal: Creativity within North India's Classical Music Tradition* (New York: Cambridge University Press, 1984), 22. Other scholars transliterate this genre of classical Hindustani vocal music as *khayal*.

14. Abdellah Hammoudi, *Master and Disciple: The Cultural Foundations of Moroccan Authoritarianism* (Chicago: University of Chicago Press, 1997), 89.

15. Zoe Ansari, ed., *Life, Times and Works of Amir Khusrau* (Delhi: National Amir Khusrau Society), 158. In Hindi: *Khusro rain suhag ki, jaagi pi ke sang / tan meraa, man piu kaa, do bhaey ek rang.*

16. In Hindi: *Saajan sakare jaaenge main marenge roey / badhya aisi rain kar bhor kadi na hoey.*

17. The story was recounted to me by a contemporary custodian of Nizam al-Din's tomb and shrine in Delhi, who deemphasized the erotic nature of the performance and reemphasized the comic nature, commenting that Khusro "even leapt about like a monkey."

18. Khidr is identified as the servant of Moses (who baffles the Prophet with his intuitive wisdom) and the servant of Alexander (who searches for the font of the water of life); these stories are told in the Qur'an, but Khidr is not mentioned by name.

19. Mohammad Wahid Mirza, *Life and Times of Amir Khusrau* (Delhi: Idarah-i Adabiyat-i Delhi, 1974), 117.

20. *Intikhabat-i Ghazaliyat-i Khusro,* ghazal 23; my translation.

21. "Old Hindi," or Hindavi, refers to the medieval vernacular of Delhi and its environs, also called Khari-Boli, or the vernacular of Mathura and Brindaban called Braj.

22. The Hindi poem "Ghar nari ganwari chahe so kahe," my adaptation of the translation by I. A. Adni in Khalid Ahmad and Kamran Anwar, *Rung: A Tribute to Sufi Poets and Musicians,* music recording (Pakistan: Citibank, 2003).

23. In Hindi: *Ganj-i Shakar kaa laal, Nizaam, aaj dulhaa bano hai*; my adaptation of the translation by S. R. Faruqi, in Ahmad and Anwar, *Rung.*

24. In Hindi: *Mohai apni hi rang mein rang de rangile*; my adaptation of the translation by David Mathews, in Ahmad and Anwar, *Rung.*

25. Muhammad Yusuf Mutala, *Mashayikh-i Ahmadabad,* 2 vols. (Ahmadabad: Maktaba Mahmudiyya, 1993), 1:209–11.

26. S. A. H. Abidi, "A Persian Poet Par Excellence," in *Amir Khusrau: Memorial Volume* (Delhi: Government of India Press, 1975), 64–65.

27. Ansari, *Life, Times and Works of Amir Khusrau,* 158.

28. Amir Kamal al-Din Hussayn Gazargahi, *Majalis al-ʿUshshaq* (Tehran: Intisharat-i Zarın, 1996), 184. The *ghazal* of Khusro that follows, quoted by Gazargahi, is number 1615 in Iqbal Salah al-Din and Sayyid Wazir al-Hasan Abidi, eds., *Kulliyat-i Ghazaliyat-i Khusro* (Lahore: Packages Limited, 1972), 3:751-2. Translation of all text and poetry from Gazargahi is mine.

29. Gazargahi, *Majalis al-ʿUshshaq,* 187–88.

30. Amir Hasan Sijzi wrote *Fawaʾid al-Fuʾad,* or *Morals of the Heart,* and while Amir Khusro is reputed to have written a companion piece, *Afzal al-Fawaʾid,* which Lawrence and Ernst assert is not an authentic composition by Khusro about Nizam al-Din Awliya; see Ernst and Lawrence, *Sufi Martyrs of Love,* 229.

31. *Amir Khusrau: Memorial Volume,* 18. For example in Gujarat he once met a beautiful Brahmin youth who was chewing pan with such abandon that bright red spittle was oozing onto his lip. In reaction to such allure, Khusro composed this verse, partly in Persian with the second half in old Hindi: "I saw a Hindu youth, possessed of wondrous beauty / As I approached to speak, his face was like a red rose // I said, 'Come

close that I might steal a kiss from your lip . . .' / He replied, 'My God, and act against religious duty?'" Other examples of Khusro's homoerotic verse in Hindi can be found in Ansari, *Life, Times and Works of Amir Khusrau*, 289.

32. *Intikhabat-i Ghazaliyat-i Khusro*, ghazal 331; my translation.

33. Nasrollah Pourjawadi, "The Witness Play of Ahmad Ghazali in Tabriz," trans. Scott Kugle, in *Reason and Inspiration in Islam: Essays in Honour of Hermann Landolt*, ed. Leonard Lewison (London: Tauris, 2005), 200–220.

34. Ernst and Lawrence, *Sufi Martyrs of Love*, 35.

35. In Persian: *chashm-i maste 'ajabe, zulf-i daraze 'ajabe*; my translation.

36. *Raqs-i bismil* (dance of the stricken) refers to the wild gyrations of an animal when its throat has been half severed for sacrifice, with *bismil* referring to the phrase "in the name of God," which is pronounced before slaughtering any animal.

37. Translation by Scott Kugle and Iqbal Ghani Khan (may Allah be merciful with him), martyred professor of history at Aligarh Muslim University.

38. Bruce B. Lawrence and Scott Kugle, "Competing for Loyalty: Strategies for Survival at Chishti *Dargahs* of Delhi in the 21st Century," *Journal of the Henry Martyn Institute* 27 (2008): 110–26.

39. For a detailed discussion of changing view of gender and sexuality under British colonial occupation and subsequent modernity, see Scott Kugle, "Sultan Mahmud's Make-Over: Colonial Homophobia and Persian-Urdu Poetics," in *Queering India: Same-Sex Love and Eroticism in Indian Culture and Society*, ed. Ruth Vanita (New York: Routledge, 2001), 30–46.

✥

The Perils of
Civilizational Islam
in Malaysia

CARL W. ERNST

Whenever I asked my Malaysian friends what they thought about civilizational Islam (*Islam hadhari*), they always smiled.[1] The meaning of that smile was challenging. Was it a sign of approval? Was it simply a characteristic of the famous Malaysian politeness? Or was it a way of questioning this formulation, which has become a major slogan echoing in the public life of Malaysia? I never was quite sure, but it seems to me that in this response there was an ambivalence combined with a rueful respect for the power of public relations. The fate of this phrase—"civilizational Islam"—is tied up with the public role of religion in Malaysia, with all its paradoxes and contradictions. The concept of civilizational Islam is an example of the way in which Islam is defined in the context of the nation-state, a topic of immense importance, to which Bruce Lawrence has drawn attention in his book *Shattering the Myth*. As Lawrence points out, "Islam is also a modern ideology subordinated to the dominant ideology of this century, nationalism, and it is the relationship of Islam to nationalism that is at once pivotal and understudied."[2] Whatever else it may be, civilizational Islam is a program promoted by the government of Malaysia, and it is inseparable from the nationalist agenda. The deeper question is whether civilizational Islam is merely a slogan aimed at satisfying multiple audiences, or whether it actually offers the prospect of infusing the Malaysian government with the principles of Islamic ethics, in a way that will advance the fortunes of the nation, reassure non-Muslim minorities in Malaysia, and persuade America and Europe that Malaysia is indeed a progressive Muslim state. Accomplishing all of that is a tall order, and the apparent irony of those Malaysian smiles may be recognition of the magnitude, or perhaps the impossibility, of that task.

Civilizational Islam (Islam Hadhari)

The formulation of Islam Hadhari is recent. Prime Minister Abdullah Badawi, the successor to former prime minister Mahathir since October 2003, has promoted this phrase as the key to Malaysia's role in the world today. Although Badawi seems to have first mentioned the phrase in September 2003, while he was still deputy prime minister, the most important speech he gave on this topic was delivered to the United Malay National Organization (UMNO) on September 23, 2004.[3]

The subject of civilizational Islam is promoted by a number of Web sites sponsored by the Malaysian government.[4] They tend to gloss the concept of Islam with English adjectives such as *flexible* and *universal*, and Malay words such as *maju* (progressive) and *berakhlak* (productive). The phrase "Islam Hadhari" evidently takes its key term from the adjectival form of the Arabic word *hadara*, meaning civilization, discussed below; the spelling reflects a local Malay convention in Roman transliteration of Arabic script. The minister has not technically defined civilizational Islam in clear and specific terms, but he frequently describes it atmospherically in terms of a number of convergent goals for the ideal society: "Islam Hadhari is an approach that emphasises development, consistent with the tenets of Islam and focused on enhancing the quality of life. It aims to achieve this via the mastery of knowledge and the development of the individual and the nation; the implementation of a dynamic economic, trading and financial system; an integrated and balanced development that creates a knowledgeable and pious people who hold to noble values and are honest, trustworthy, and prepared to take on global challenges" (speech of September 23, 2004). Civilizational Islam is said to be synonymous with the quest to achieve the following ten goals:

I. Faith and piety in Allah
II. A just and trustworthy government
III. A free and independent people
IV. Mastery of knowledge
V. Balanced and comprehensive economic development
VI. A good quality of life
VII. Protection of the rights of minority groups and women
VIII. Cultural and moral integrity
IX. Safeguarding the environment
X. Strong defenses

The overall emphasis of Prime Minister Badawi's formulations is the joining of ethics with development and national success.

Aside from the first of the ten goals of civilizational Islam, however, it is not immediately clear why an agenda of national development is being associated with Islam. The other nine goals might well be part of the program of any government that announces a program of progress and development. Yet a considerable number of Islamic reference points are displayed in all official discussions of the subject. Repeatedly one finds on Islam Hadhari Web sites the following verse from the Qur'an (al-Qasas, 28:77): "But seek, with that (wealth) which Allah has bestowed upon you, the home of the Hereafter; and forget not your portion of lawful enjoyment in this world; and do good as Allah has been good to you, and seek not mischief in the land. Verily, Allah likes not the *Mufsidun* (those who commit great crimes and sins, oppressors, tyrants, mischief makers, corrupters)." Such a scriptural citation emphasizes simultaneous pursuit of salvation in the next world and success in this world as concomitant and complementary activities. To give a more specific grounding to this Islamic ethic, Prime Minister Badawi invokes the rational principle of "the objectives of religious law" (*maqasid al-shariʿa*) as formulated by such classical scholars as al-Ghazali; the prime minister characterizes these objectives as "life, intellect, faith, property and progeny"; to this list he is willing to add as further goals "justice, human dignity and even economic development" (January 10, 2004; paragraph 36). In his view adoption of these principles means practicality and rationality rather than legalism and literalism. He places himself on the side of reformers in the style of Muhammad ʿAbduh and advocates the application of independent legal reasoning (*ijtihad*). At the same time, he distances himself from Islamists and fundamentalists, whom he dismisses as representatives of a less than credible form of political Islam. In this way he aligns himself with those who seek to carve out a moderate path for Islam today.

There are definitely political contexts for the program of civilizational Islam, both national and international. Within Malaysia UMNO has from its founding articulated Islam as one of the key factors in Malay identity, yet in recent years it has been challenged by an Islamist party, PAS, which in the 1990s made significant strides and captured some provincial governments. PAS leadership has ridiculed the concept of civilizational Islam, making the pun that it really means Islam *hadd hari* ("Islam limited to a day" in Malay) and condemning it as a heresy alongside the Mughal emperor Akbar's "divine faith" (*din-i ilahi*). There is definitely a sense in Malaysia that the government's slogan of civilizational Islam is an attempt to claim Islamic legitimacy and deny it to the fundamentalist opposition. In addition there is the extremely important fact that Malay Muslims are barely a 50 percent majority in the country, and so negotiations with the large Chinese and Indian communities must be part of any government strategy. It is not accidental that "rights of minority groups and women" figures as the seventh point in the Islam Hadhari program. Efforts have been made by the Institute of Islamic Understanding (IKIM), the chief government think tank on Islam, to reassure non-Muslim Malaysians that their rights and welfare are assured by civilizational Islam. Moreover Prime Minister Badawi is clearly concerned by the failures of the Malays to take full advantage of the preferences they have received for the past two decades under the New Economic Policy of Mahathir (September 23, 2004; paras. 46–64), and he wants to inspire the creation of "towering personalities" among the Malays. On the international level, the promulgation of Islam Hadhari coincided with Malaysia's chairmanship of the Organization of Islamic Conference (OIC), which became in effect a bully pulpit for Badawi to claim a leading role for Malaysia in international conflict resolution, increased trade with majority Muslim countries, and promotion of a more open and diverse Islamic discourse. Finally with respect to "Western" countries, Malaysia is presented as a moderate and progressive Muslim nation and a partner in the war against terrorism, but at the same time a resolute critic of injustices committed against Muslim countries (Palestine, Iraq) and a vigorous defender of Islam against negative stereotypes. All of these factors form the political parameters surrounding the formulation of Islam Hadhari. But these political factors in themselves do not explain the ideological impact of this concept in which *Islam* is the basic subject and *civilization* is the modifier. What is the added value conferred by civilization?

Brief History of "Civilization"

The English word *civilization* is barely two centuries old, but it does have a certain prehistory. Aristotle in his *Politics* established the tradition of reflecting on the development of small kin groups into the larger urban organization of the city. Later philosophers in Islamicate milieus continued in this vein, including most notably Al-Farabi (d. 950) in his interpretation of Platonic and Aristotelian political thought; he employed the Arabic word for city (*madina*), in the sense of an advanced urban society equivalent to the Greek *polis*.[5] Likewise the great North African historian Ibn Khaldun (d. 1382) developed a sociological analysis of the interplay between urban, sedentary life (*hadara*) and the nomadic life of the desert (*badawa*) as the two main forms of human society ('*umran*).[6]

But a radical shift took place during the eighteenth century, as European colonial control over the rest of the world brought about new mental attitudes. Samuel Johnson rejected the term *civilization* in his English dictionary of 1755, remarking that there was already a perfectly good word with that meaning: *civility*. Toward the end of the eighteenth century, however, *civilization* had caught on firmly (both in French and English), with a very special meaning having little to do with civility. Science and rationality furnished the new basis for empire. Military technology, in which Europe had definitely seized the advantage, permitted forcible conquest of the rest of the world. The scientific doctrine of race, in particular, provided a rationalization for Europe's domination of the world. Thinkers such as Auguste Comte proclaimed that five advanced European nations (England, France, Italy, Spain, and Germany) constituted the vanguard of humanity. Charles Darwin's theory of evolution was applied in ways indicating that white Europeans were more highly evolved than the rest of humanity and hence were obliged to rule. For the British it was the "white man's burden," while for the French it was the "civilizing mission." Karl Marx and Friedrich

Engels formulated the theory of the "Oriental mode of production," and it was commonly accepted that peoples of the East were by nature suited to "Oriental despotism." Civilization was restricted to Europe; the rest of the world was restricted to barbarism. European colonial rule was therefore the gift of civilization.[7]

The ideological response from the Middle East and other regions of the world initially paralleled the realization that Europeans were more advanced in technology and weapons; many accepted at face value the confident proclamation that Europe alone possessed civilization. Ottoman intellectuals of the early nineteenth century borrowed the term *civilization* in this sense and spelled it in Arabic script, later replacing it with Ottoman term *medeniyet*.[8] Modern Arabic seems to have adopted Ibn Khaldun's term *hadara* as the equivalent of the European concept of civilization.[9] In modern Persian the preferred term (derived from Arabic *madina*) is *tamaddun*, which again has the sense of both living in cities and possessing culture.[10] The novelty of this terminology is clear when we see formulations such as Arabic civilization (*al-hadara al-ʿarabiyya*) or Islamic civilization (Arabic, *al-hadara al-islamiyya*; Persian, *tamaddun-i islami*) as deliberate alternatives to the European norm. The choice of Islam Hadhari as the Malay phrase for civilizational Islam indicates, by its adoption of this Arabic root, that it takes an oppositional position contesting exclusive European ownership of civilization. The more common Malay term for civilization, *peradaban*, is derived instead from the Arabic word *adab*, and it highlights the meaning of culture and civility rather than the ideological notion of successful scientific civilization, but that nuance seems not to have been desired here. Thus Badawi's formulation of civilizational Islam stands in a lineage of anticolonial critique.

The justification of this anticolonial rhetoric is evidently the persistence of prejudicial views of Islamic civilization, years after official decolonization. The chief spokesman for this viewpoint in recent years has been Samuel Huntington, whose provocative article "The Clash of Civilizations" was expanded into a widely read book.[11] His thesis, based on a superficial and tendentious reading of history, claimed that there are a given number of civilizations (up to eight in theory) that will inevitably clash until one emerges triumphant. After eliminating the least important of these civilizations, he concludes by postulating an eventual death struggle between the progressive West and the retrograde Islamic world.

This argument was met with dismay and concern among intellectuals and political leaders in majority-Muslim countries. It was only a few years ago that most of these countries lay under European colonial domination, the result of aggressive European military expansion in Africa, the Middle East, and Asia since the days of Napoleon. Would this argument be used to unleash new military adventures against the enemies of "the West"? Significant voices were raised to refute this confrontational position. President Mohammad Khatami of Iran responded by proposing an alternate view, which he called the "dialogue of civilizations." The foundation of the Center for Civilizational Dialogue at the University of Malaya that same year (1996), under the leadership of Anwar Ibrahim, clearly belongs to the same historical moment. The United Nations optimistically adopted the formula of "dialogue of civilizations" as a theme for worldwide discussions in 2001. "Civilizational Islam" therefore is a phrase that carries considerable ideological momentum from long-standing debates from the colonial and postcolonial eras.

There are several arenas where the implications of Islam Hadhari are played out, but perhaps the most significant one is the realm of science. The prime minister makes frequent linkages between Islamic beliefs and scientific development: "Islam demands the mastery of science and technology and the enhancement of skills and expertise. Many verses in the Qur'an that touch on the need to master science and technology should be studied. All Muslim students should be aware of Islam's contribution to science and technology that brought about the birth of the Renaissance in Europe. Initiatives to produce more Malay scientists who are capable of making new discoveries must be intensified" (September 23, 2004). The argument for the essential connection between Islam and science is one that emerged from anticolonial rhetoric in resistance to the hegemonic Euro-American claims over science. Some official formulations of civilizational Islam also portray it not merely as an ethical basis for Malaysian government but also as "a noble and universal approach to correct the negative impact of Western philosophies that plague the present society."[12] This observation falls into the category of the Occidentalism that has been such a characteristic feature of the rhetoric of former prime minister Mahathir as well as neotraditional intellectuals such as Syed Naquib al-Attas, who is discussed below.[13] In this respect it is striking to see how difficult it is to escape ideologies such as "the Islamization of knowledge" whenever the subject of Islam is mentioned in Malaysia.

A Defense of Prime Minister Badawi

As mentioned previously the concept of civilizational Islam has come in for some criticism, particularly from fundamentalist quarters, but even those Malaysians disposed to be favorable to the prime minister might be excused for scratching their heads in some bewilderment as to the meaning of this slogan. Aside from government press releases of speeches by Badawi, there has not been much of a documentary trail to indicate the precise implications of Islam Hadhari. During my residence in Malaysia in 2005, I was invited to give a lecture in March at the IKIM think tank that I called "Rethinking Islam in the Contemporary World, and Reinforcing Civilizational Islam in Contemporary Muslim Society." I had the distinct impression that my audience was nearly as clueless about the topic as I was, yet as a senior visiting scholar I was evidently expected to clarify the subject. I did so briefly and delicately, couching all of my observations in the subjunctive mood; for example I remarked that Islam Hadhari may be success- ful if it actually achieves the goal of ethical government in a pluralistic society but that it faces charges of failure and insincerity if it is simply instrumental to the attainment of material goals or ends up as a knee-jerk response to colonial- ism. Evidently my remarks were received with some approval, since I was invited back the following month to give a keynote lecture for a conference on ethics. The following year IKIM held an extensive series of conferences dedicated to each of the ten principal goals of civilizational Islam.

In the meantime it was interesting to consider a widely advertised publication, which appeared in April 2005, devoted to clarifying the philosophical views of Badawi. This book, *Abdullah Ahmad Badawi: Revivalist of an Intellectual Tradition*, which filled the windows of Kuala Lumpur bookstores on publication, deserves to be described in detail. It is prefaced with photographs of the prime minister, his wife, both his parents, and his grandfather. It begins with a brief Malay poem by the prime minister, composed in 2003, titled "In Search of Everlasting Peace," in which he declares that he seeks not material wealth but spirituality. This poem calls upon key references from the Islamic tradition, including the schol- ars al-Ghazali and al-Shafi'i, the Qur'an, and the Prophet, and it concludes with an intimate evocation of the divine presence. After these atmospheric touches, the first chapter concerns Badawi's political career. This was chiefly written by Ng Tieh Chuan, a publisher who previously (1981) had written a laudatory biog- raphy of Prime Minister Mahathir; it was Ng who conceived this book project. The chapter is a straightforward and informative account of the path taken by this successful politician, who, it should be noted, majored in Islamic studies at the University of Malaya. The rest of the book has been written by Syed Ali Tawfik al-Attas, who obtained his doctorate in 2002 from the International Institute of Islamic Thought and Civilization (ISTAC) in Kuala Lumpur, with a dissertation on medieval Islamic philosophy; he is also a son of Syed Naquib al-Attas, the eminent scholar (and founding director of ISTAC), whose name has already been mentioned.

Al-Attas takes over in chapter 2 with a rather different tone of unabashed hagiography, going back to the prime minister's grandfather, Abdallah Fahim, and tracing his ancestry to Muslim missionaries from the Arab world. There is a distinct suggestion that this was a family connected to a Sufi order. The grand- father, born in Mecca in 1869, is praised not only for his religious knowledge but also for his scientific interest in astronomy. He is credited with saintly, miracu- lous qualities and with the use of astronomy to declare the most propitious hour for the declaration of Malaya's independence in 1957. This combination of religious and scientific expertise sets the tone for the understanding of civilizational Islam.

Chapter 3, "The Predicament," launches us back into the consideration of Islam Hadhari itself, noting that it was initially understood as a way of "undermining the Muslim opposition" and "trying to introduce an idea or way of thinking geared towards improving the economic opportunities of the Malays" (52). The author considers the problem of the politics of UMNO and Islam as the unifying element of Malay identity, and he questions the disunity caused by the Muslim opposition (PAS), concluding that they have taken to using Islam as a "mere slogan in the political arena" (57). At this point the author brings in philosophical anthropology, relying heavily on the writings of his father, to diagnose the moral shortcomings of the Malay people. In doing so al-Attas displays a remarkably bold ability to praise his subject, Badawi, while simultaneously editing out the latter's "erroneous" phrases, which he nevertheless records in the footnotes (67n28). At the same time, he makes highly critical comments about the lack of religious knowledge among current authorities in Malaysia in universities.

Now the stage has been cleared for two lengthy chapters on medieval Islamic philosophy, which constitute fully one-third of the book. This tactic is justified not only by the author's predilection for philosophy, but also as a way of unraveling the esoteric reference to al-Ghazali in the prime minister's prefatory poem. The exposition begins with a sharp cleavage between "the worldview of Islam juxtaposed against the Greek and Western worldviews" extracted without much alteration from the author's dissertation (74n3). Despite the prominence in this argument of categories from the European Enlightenment (worldview, system), al-Attas (again quoting liberally from his father) sees the Western worldview as based on nature, reason, and historical development, while the Islamic worldview is an unchanging revelation based on certainty. Syed Naquib al-Attas is also quoted to the effect that, unlike other languages, the Arabic language "is not subject to change and development nor governed by the vicissitudes of social change as in the case of all other languages which derive from culture and tradition."[14] After giving a rapid account of the development of early Islamic philosophy, al-Attas presents al-Ghazali as the culmination of this tradition and the rescuer of Islamic revelation from the excesses of rationalist philosophers (Ibn Sina) and Shiʿite fanatics.

At last we are ready for chapter 6, "'Islam Hadhari' Explained." It will not be surprising, in the light of al-Attas's liking for pedantic rehearsals of philosophical method, that he begins this chapter with a review of the procedures of classical logic. This leads into the description of the scholastic notion of quiddity according to medieval Arab logicians. The point here is that Islam has already been determined to be perfect. This means that there are no varieties of Islam,

nor is there any way of classifying it into genus and species. Therefore, according to al-Attas, one cannot define Islam or qualify the term with an adjective
such as *hadhari*.[15] With regard to Islam Hadhari, this leads to the surprising conclusion that "it is *not* possible to describe the phrase in a manner which will lead
to intelligibility. . . . We must conclude, therefore, that the phrase 'Islam Hadhari' is *not* a concept" (133; emphasis original). Al-Attas goes to some trouble to
reject the spelling *hadhari*, which he argues should rather be transliterated as
hadārī.[16] While noting the presumed meaning of *hadārī* as pertaining to urban
life, he rejects the notion that there may be "another kind of Islam practiced by
those not living in cities." In short Islam Hadhari in the sense of civilizational
Islam "is unacceptable to Islam." Why is this the case? "Unlike western civilizations, it is the worldview of Islam that determines and gives rise to culture, and
consequently civilization." Syed Naquib al-Attas, in fact, derives one of the Arabic words for civilization, *tamaddun*, from *din*, ordinarily translated as "religion"
but in his view "meaning civilization and refinement in social culture."[17] In
other words the concept of civilization that has been claimed by "the West" is
really derived from Islam in its religious essence, and there is no reason to com-
pete with this derivative notion by proposing a civilizational Islam. In a book
that purports to be a defense of the prime minister and his philosophy, this
abrupt dismissal of any significance to the program of Islam Hadhari seems at
first sight contradictory. But al-Attas seems to regard the proposal as one that
has at least some strategic applicability. "One may only conclude that this modern term has been offered in apology for the backwardness suffered by the Muslims of today" (136). Therefore Islam Hadhari does not mean civilizational
Islam, but instead should be described as "understanding the present age in the
framework of Islam" (140).

The book then closes with an epilogue proposing that the true solution to
Muslim identity lies in the philosophy of al-Ghazali, which embraces revelation
as well as reason. Al-Attas takes this opportunity to condemn "the age of activism
and feeble-mindedness" that he associates with the fundamentalist and anti-
rational descendants of Ibn Taymiyyah, such as Mawdudi, Abu Hasan al-Nadwi,
and Hasan al-Banna. The revival of the Muslim intellectual tradition is then left
to the care of UMNO, for "the establishment of authority and an intelligent
society. This is true democracy in Islam" (147).

A number of questions may be raised about this presentation of the philosophy of Prime Minister Badawi, but for the moment, one will suffice. At first
glance it seems counterproductive for the defenders of the prime minister to
describe his program of civilizational Islam as nonsensical, and further to denounce the Malays for their moral and intellectual shortcomings. Nevertheless
it seems that the prime minister did not find fault with the way his views were
defended. Shortly after the publication of the book, Syed Ali Tawfik al-Attas was

appointed to the position of director general of IKIM, the number-two position under Chairman Tan Sri Ahmad Sarji. In that capacity he has delivered pronouncements on matters such as the legality of condoms as a health issue from an Islamic perspective.[18] So did the book deliver an effective argument in support of Islam Hadhari as an ethical approach to governance? Or was it an opportunistic endorsement of the government's pronouncements in ideological terms?[19]

Concluding Reflections

Evaluating the ethical content of civilizational Islam is a challenging task. One way forward has been proposed by cyberanthropologist David Hakken, who has examined the implications of Islam Hadhari in the realm of culture and technology, with specific reference to open-source software.[20] Hakken points out that the position of Badawi is certainly ethical, but he observes that its ethical proposals are stated in contradictory terms: some are modernist, embracing the universal values of the Enlightenment, others are developmental and progressive ("Knowledge Society by 2020"), while others illustrate a postmodern ethics to be evaluated in terms of achievement. There are also models grounded in the Malay experience, as well as appeals to pluralism and cosmopolitanism. Hakken argues that a coherent ethical expression of civilizational Islam with respect to open-source software requires the identification of one of these ethical positions as dominant, and he considers the postmodern form of Islam Hadhari ethics to be suitable for this application. Hakken further points out one of the key unspoken backgrounds for Islam Hadhari, which is Anwar Ibrahim's parallel proposal of "civil society" (*masyarakat madani*), a very similar social vision that Badawi is competing with and co-opting. (Anwar Ibrahim, former deputy prime minister under Mahathir, has reemerged as a political factor since his controversial prison sentence on charges of sodomy was overturned).

In terms of practical ethical applications, Hakken is correct in highlighting postmodern ethics, where achievement may be measured. Here one may compare the ten criteria of ethical behavior that Malaysian activist Chandra Muzaffar has proposed to evaluate the morality of governance in contemporary Islamic states.[21] Muzaffar wants to know exactly what progress has been made in dealing with poverty, curbing ostentation, reducing economic disparities, eliminating corruption, exposing sexual misdemeanors among elites, upholding the rule of law, observing accountability, consulting citizens, preserving individual responsibility, and preserving rights of non-Muslims. It is not clear whether the formulation of Islam Hadhari is amenable to being focused exclusively in such practical directions, despite the clear presence of such targets of ethical achievement in the prime minister's formulation. The rhetorical and ideological turn given to Islam Hadhari by his defender, Syed Tawfik al-Attas, seems destined to be in the ascendant, to judge from the latter's elevation to a primary position of articulating the Malaysian regime's Islamic policies.

Al-Attas, as a spokesman for an ideological and Occidentalist notion of Islam, sees himself as an ardent opponent of the European Enlightenment, but the intellectual weapons that he uses against it are a very much derived from the Enlightenment itself. This is true of a number of other neotraditionalist philosophies, which had been adapted from ultramontane Catholic thinkers by anticolonial European traditionalists and perennialists who embraced Islam.[22] There is probably a postmodern element present as well in the entire "Islamization of knowledge" movement, according to which authentic identity consists only in categories that are defined and labeled as Islamic. The problem is that it is very tempting to allow the rhetorical assertion of Islamic legitimacy to substitute for any genuine ethical substance. As Chandra Muzaffar remarks of Islamic elites and the issues of poverty, corruption, and accountability, "Women's attire and other preoccupations of theirs, such as gender interaction, sexual norms, prohibition of liquor, hudud (Islamic criminal law) and the status of the murtad (apostate) are far more important to them in defining Islamic morality and identity."[23]

Al-Attas himself sees the universalism of Islamic ethics as antithetical to the UN-based human rights concept that permits people to reject the religion of their birth, which he sees as allowing the free expression of apostasy from Islam.[24] This allergy to apostasy appears to have animated the Malaysian government's suppression in August 2005 of the "Sky Kingdom" movement, a multireligion community in Terengganu known as the "teapot sect" because of its colorful monuments symbolizing different religions. State Islam Hadhari Development Committee deputy chairman Muhammad Ramli Nuh, in announcing the arrest of the sect members and the demolition of their monuments, stated that leader Ayah Pin would be charged (under a state fatwa) with humiliating Islamic teachings and with promoting deviant teachings.[25] In this respect the Sky Kingdom movement has shared the fate of Darul Arqam, a Sufi-inspired messianic movement that was banned by the Malaysian government in 1994 for deviant teachings.[26] The Malaysian government, through its Department of Islamic Development Malaysia (JAKIM) and its enforcement wing (JAWI), does not hesitate to clamp down on unauthorized religious movements by using the colonial-era Internal Security Act, which has not been repealed following Malaysian independence in 1957. Farish Noor argues that UMNO policies in reality continue to promote the supremacy of the Malay Muslim community while systematically repressing religious pluralism through crackdowns on conversion and heedless destruction of non-Muslim religious sites. "Here lies the trap that the UMNO leadership has dug for itself: While promoting a vision of Islam that is plural, modern and liberal, it has also cultivated a community that is narrow, reactionary and conservative."[27]

Ultimately one cannot escape the fact that religion in Malaysia is a state monopoly. This too is a legacy of the colonial period, when British administrators ceded the then-unimportant areas of religion and custom to the control of the Malay sultans. Since the early twentieth century, it has been illegal in Malaysia to publish anything on Islam without permission from the state authorities. This rigorous state control of religion stands in contrast with the situation in neighboring Indonesia, where a different colonial experience and secular nation-state articulation allows an enormous nongovernmental public space for the expression of religion. As Lawrence has remarked, "Yet fifty years after the founding of the United Nations and the near elimination of European control over much of Asia and Africa, one must remain wary of how postcolonial independence has been shaped by the immediate past. The British may have gone home, and the French mission to civilize (*la mission civilisatrice*) declared a failure, but British and French, as also Dutch and Russian, legacies persist in the Muslim world."[28] Both the expression and the regulation of Islam in Malaysia emerge from the modern history of colonialism as well as the politics of the postcolonial nation-state. So when PAS gained control of Selangor province in the March 2008 elections, it quickly seized the opportunity to ban the promulgation of Islam Hadhari in mosques and Islamic institutes, on the grounds that it constituted a distortion of Islam.[29]

Thus the formula of Islam Hadhari still leaves many questions unanswered. By its expression as a government decree, Prime Minister Badawi's formulation of civilizational Islam as a project of the nation-state has more in common with Baruch Spinoza's concept of devotion to the state[30] or Jean-Jacques Rousseau's civil religion[31] than it does with either traditional Islamic statecraft or contemporary concepts of nongovernmental civil society. Recent electoral setbacks for UMNO and increasing gains by opposition parties (including Anwar Ibrahim's People's Justice Party) may indicate that the prime minister's program has a limited shelf life. Here we can recall the observation of Pierre Bourdieu regarding slogans: "The power of the ideas that he [the spokesperson] proposes is measured not, as in the domain of science, by their truth-value . . . but by the power of mobilization that they contain, in other words, by the power of the group that recognizes them."[32] In any case Islam Hadhari, despite its remarkably broad claims, remains very much a child of the particular political experience of Malaysia. And the gap between its rhetoric and its political context is undoubtedly what makes people smile.

NOTES

1. I was Fulbright lecturing and research scholar in Islamic studies at the University of Malaya in Kuala Lumpur from January to May 2005.

2. Bruce B. Lawrence, *Shattering the Myth: Islam beyond Violence* (Princeton, N.J.: Princeton University Press, 2000), 9.

3. Prior to the election of Mohd Najib bin Tun Abdul Razak as the new prime minister in April 2009, Badawi's speeches on civilizational Islam could be tracked on his official Web site (http://www.pmo.gov.my/ [accessed December 27, 2008]) through the link "Islam Hadhari," and then through the link "Speeches"; reference to the prime minister's speeches here is by date. Many of the same links can still be found on this site by searching for "hadhari" on this page.

4. These government Web sites include http://www.islamhadhari.net/ (Malay, English, and Arabic) and http://www.islam.gov.my/islamhadhari/ (the Malaysian Ministry of Islamic Affairs, Malay and English, with extensive video animation). Accessed August 10, 2009.

5. Soheil Muhsin Afnan, *Philosophical Terminology in Arabic and Persian* (Leiden: Brill, 1964), 278–79.

6. The term *hadara* occurs six times in Ibn Khaldun's *Muqaddima*, and five times in his *Ta'rikh* (citations available at http://www.alwaraq.net/ [accessed June 27, 2009]).

7. Charles H. Long, "Primitive/Civilized: The Locus of a Problem," *History of Religions* 20, no. 1/2 (1980): 43–61

8. Niyazi Berkes, "Medeniyyet," in *Encyclopaedia of Islam*, 2nd ed., ed. P. Bearman, Th. Bianquis, C. E. Bosworth, E. van Donzel, and W. P. Heinrichs, available online by subscription at http://www.brillonline.nl/ (accessed July 17, 2009).

9. Modern sources for the use of *hadara* in Arabic include a number of references to Arabic translations from European publications, listed in Zirikli's *A'lam* (1927), Edward A. Van Dyck's *Iktafa'* (1896), and Louis Cheiko's (d. 1927) *Ta'rikh al-adab al-'arabiyya* (citations available on http://www.alwaraq.net/ [accessed June 27, 2009]).

10. 'Ali Akbar Dikhuda, *Lughat nama*, s.v. "*tamaddun*," http://www.loghatnaameh .com/ (accessed July 17, 2009). The term is listed in standard premodern dictionaries but does not have much of a history of use.

11. Samuel P. Huntington, "The Clash of Civilizations," *Foreign Affairs* 72, no. 3 (1993): 22–28; Samuel P. Huntington, *The Clash of Civilizations and the Remaking of World Order* (New York: Simon & Schuster, 1996). This book, in November 2001, was the number 18 best seller on Amazon.com.

12. Mohd. Roslan bin Mohd Saludin, "Islam Hadhari a Way Forward," *Star*, September 8, 2005, http://www.ikim.gov.my/v5/index.php?lg=1&opt=com_article&grp =2&sec=&key=821&cmd=resetallhttp://www.ikim.gov.my/bm/paparmedia.php?key= 821 (accessed July 17, 2009).

13. See the review article by Alexander Horstmann, "Mapping the Terrain: Politics and Cultures of Islamization of Knowledge in Malaysia," *Kyoto Review of Southeast Asia* 5 (March 2004), http://kyotoreview.cseas.kyoto-u.ac.jp/issue/issue4/article_339.html (accessed July 8, 2009).

14. Syed Ali Tawfik al-Attas and Ng Tieh Chuan, *Abdullah Ahmad Badawi: Revivalist of an Intellectual Tradition* (Subang Jaya: Pelanduk, 2005), 86n20, citing Syed Muhammad Naquib al-Attas, *Islam and Secularism* (Kuala Lumpur: International Institute of Islamic Thought & Civilisation, 1978), 46.

15. A slightly similar Aristotelian argument was adopted by Wilfred Cantwell Smith with regard to the term religion, but in that case he denied that religion could be

defined, because it has no essence, and therefore does not exist as a separate and definable entity.

16. While *hadārī* is certainly a common transliteration of the original Arabic word, the chaotic situation of multiple transliteration systems for rendering Arabic script into Roman is by no means easy to reduce to a single answer.

17. Al-Attas and Ng, *Abdullah Ahmad Badawi*, 136, quoting Syed Naquib al-Attas, "Muslim World Needs a Meeting of Minds," *New Straits Times*, October 5, 2004. For a historical discussion of the etymology of *madīna*, see Jaroslav Stetkevych, "Toward an Arabic Elegiac Lexicon: The Seven Words of the *Nasîb*," in *Reorientations: Arabic and Persian Poetry*, ed. Suzanne Pinckney Stetkevych (Bloomington: Indiana University Press, 1994), 58–129, esp. 87.

18. "Distribution of Free Condoms a Health Issue, Not Syariah-Related," available online (item 6) at http://www.ahrn.net/index2.php?option=content&task=view&id =2359&pop=1&page=0 (accessed July 17, 2009).

19. A similar question was posed by Peter Hardy, "Abul Fazl's Portrait of the Perfect Padshah: A Political Philosophy for Mughal India—or a Personal Puff for a Pal?" in *Islam in India, Studies and Commentaries*, vol. 2, *Religion and Religious Education*, ed. Christian W. Troll (New Delhi: Vikas, 1985), 114–37.

20. David Hakken, "Free/Libre and Open Source Software: A Good Way to 'Hadharize' Technology?" paper presented at the Third Workshop on Transdisciplinary Research, "ICT and Islam Hadhari," Universiti Sains Malaysia, April 2005.

21. Chandra Muzaffar, "Morality in Public Life: A Challenge Facing Muslims," in *Muslims-Dialogue-Terror* (Petaling Jaya: International Movement for a Just World, 2003), 1–21.

22. See my review article, "Traditionalism, the Perennial Philosophy, and Islamic Studies," *Middle East Studies Association Bulletin* 28 (December 1994): 176–81, available online at http://www.unc.edu/%7Ecernst/Traditionalism.htm (accessed July 8, 2009).

23. Muzaffar, "Morality in Public Life," 10.

24. Al-Attas and Ng, *Abdullah Ahmad Badawi*, 145–46. Al-Attas remains open, however, to revisionism with regard to received opinions on the subject of interest (*riba'*) in Islamic law.

25. For details, see "Malaysia 'Teapot Cult' Attacked," BBC News, July 18, 2005, http://news.bbc.co.uk/2/hi/asia-pacific/4692039.stm (accessed July 8, 2009); "Sky Kingdom/Ayah Pin," Apologetics Index, available online at http://www.apologeticsindex .org/s/s53.html (accessed June 30, 2009).

26. Ahmad Fauzi Abdul Hamid, "The Futuristic Thought of Ustaz Ashaari Muhammad of Malaysia," in *The Blackwell Companion to Contemporary Islamic Thought*, ed. Ibrahim Abu-Rabi (Oxford: Blackwell, 2006). In the 1980s Darul Arqam was seen as one of the three most important independent Islamic organizations in Malaysia, along with ABIM and the Tablighi Jama'at; see Judith Nagata, *The Reflowering of Malaysian Islam: Modern Religious Radicals and Their Roots* (Vancouver: University of British Columbia Press, 1984), esp. 104–16.

27. Farish Noor, "Islam Hadhari Can't Save Malaysia," available online at http:// jedyoong.wordpress.com/2008/02/28/farish-noor-islam-hadhari-cant-save-malaysia/ (accessed December 18, 2008).

28. Lawrence, *Shattering the Myth*, 10.

29. Sean Yoong, "Malaysia Opposition Stages Showdown with PM over His 'Civilizational Islam' Concept," Associated Press, May 28, 2008, http://sg.news.yahoo.com/ap/20080528/tap-as-gen-malaysia-islamic-dispute-b3c65ae.html (accessed December 18, 2008).

30. "We can now clearly understand how the sovereign is the interpreter of religion, and further, that no one can obey God rightly, if the practices of his piety do not conform to the public welfare; or, consequently, if he does not implicitly obey all the commands of the sovereign." Baruch Spinoza, *A Theologico-Political Treatise*, trans. R. H. M. Elwes (Charleston, S.C.: Bibliobazaar, 2008), 296 (19:45).

31. "There is therefore a purely civil profession of faith of which the Sovereign should fix the articles, not exactly as religious dogmas, but as social sentiments without which a man cannot be a good citizen or a faithful subject." Jean-Jacques Rousseau, *The Social Contract, or Principles of Political Right*, trans. G. D. H. Cole (Lawrence, Kans.: Digireads .com Publishing, 2006), 65 (IV.8).

32. Pierre Bourdieu, *Language and Symbolic Power*, ed. John B. Thompson, trans. Gino Raymond and Matthew Adamson (Cambridge, Mass.: Harvard University Press, 1991), 190.

☞

History and Normativity in Traditional Indian Muslim Thought

*Reading Shari'a in the Hermeneutics of
Qari Muhammad Tayyab (d. 1983)*

EBRAHIM MOOSA

. . . There used to be a time, we believe, when we could say who we were. Now we
are just performers speaking our parts.

J. M. Coetzee, *Elizabeth Costello*

The distant past is one of those things that can enrich ignorance. It is infinitely
malleable and agreeable, far more obliging than the future and far less demanding
of our efforts. It is the famous season favored by all mythologies.

Jorge Luis Borges, "I, a Jew," in *Selected Non-Fictions*

Introduction

For the better part of the past two centuries, if not longer, Muslim thinkers have
endlessly bruited about the phenomenon of *ijtihad*, the right to personal intellectual commitment and interpretation in juridical, moral, and theological
thought.[1] It is difficult to provide a simple translation of the term *ijtihad* since it
had become a catachresis: a perversion of a word or trope that no longer adheres
to its literal referent.[2] For as much as one may wish to show the philological
meaning of *ijtihad* to be self-explanatory as "intellectual effort," the concept dis-
seminates a multiplicity of meanings in terms of its history. *Ijtihad* is one of
those words in the Muslim vocabulary that reflects social and political struggles
within the body politic of Muslim societies over centuries.

Ijtihad has a meaning of informed opinion in the preformative usage of Islam.
When asked how he would govern if he did not find directive teachings in the
Qur'an or the Sunna, Mu'adh bin Jabal, a companion of the Prophet, uttered a
phrase later immortalized in the annals of Islamic law: "I will exert myself to
reach an informed opinion (*ajtahid ra'yi*)," he is reported to have said.[3] Then in

the formative period, with the rise of the legal schools, the term underwent a change. *Ijtihad* came to signify the actions of a jurist formulating a juridico-moral opinion by resorting to analogy in the absence of explicit guidance from any authoritative source.[4] Later on, among Sunni practitioners, *ijtihad* sanctioned the binding nature of interpretative authority reached by a hierarchy of master jurists (*mujtahidun*) in the multiple discursive schools (*madhahib*, sing. *madhhab*) of Muslim jurisprudence. Settled and authoritative juridico-moral opinions, together with their interpretative principles, became hierarchically structured in terms of a protocodification of the opinions of the early generations of the respective schools.[5] Ironically *ijtihad*-based moral formulations within discrete discursive traditions in early Muslim history contributed to a moral consensus of sorts that tied practitioners to a set of practices and decisions by way of binding precedent (*taqlid*). Beyond precedent personal intellectual commitment and effort (*ijtihad*) on the part of scholars was only permitted in limited instances and was policed by a host of conditions, terms, and qualifications.[6]

In the hands of modern Muslim reformers of various hues, whether traditionalist, modernist, revivalist, or maximalist in orientation, the term *ijtihad* signified several things. Some with guileless ferocity advocated *ijtihad* to serve as a proverbial silver bullet that would remedy all Muslim ills. By invoking the necessity to *do ijtihad*, a scholar or ideologue staked a certain claim not to adhere blindly to past practice or tradition. Nevertheless the desiccated algebra of pro-*ijtihad* rhetoric semaphored a range of intellectual attitudes. These attitudes ranged from favoring an intellectual and cultural renaissance and a yearning for free thinking, if not disavowing tradition, to a plea for intellectual egalitarianism in juridical and moral thought. Often one would find that those who lamented the absence of *ijtihad* in modern Muslim intellectual practice often flashed a pervasive "scapegoat historiography," one that represented myriads of pillbox theories of catastrophic Muslim political decline and intellectual lag and how *ijtihad* would miraculously reverse such setbacks.[7] Surely any *ijtihad* without a commitment or search for new knowledge can be guaranteed to be a stillborn enterprise.

In his work on modern Islam, Bruce Lawrence has pointed out that certain strands of modern Islam wanted to jettison the juridico-moral tradition of Islam instead of pursuing critical engagement. Some varieties of Islamic fundamentalism, Lawrence wrote, wanted to rescue the Shariʿa "from the obfuscation with which the medieval jurists overlaid it."[8] Some modern Muslim revivalists, he continued, refused to expand legal authority allowed by *ijtihad* and instead sought to craft a streamlined version of the Shariʿa.[9] By translating the meaning of the Shariʿa into policy goals, many revivalists gave currency to the rhetoric of the "purposes of Shariʿa" (*maqasid al-Shariʿa*) as panacea. This meant that the Shariʿa preserved five conditions: life, mind or mental health, the species through procreation, property, and religion. Yet it would not be incorrect to say that the strongest voices in favor of *ijtihad*, even *ijtihad* manqué, came from a cross section of revivalist groups, from moderate ones such as the Muslim Brotherhood in Egypt and the Middle East and the Jamat-i Islami in South Asia to radical groups such as al Qaeda.

Sunni traditionalists, whose mystical writings Lawrence had explored in greater detail than their juridical writings, maintained that certain limited forms of *ijtihad* were still eminently desirable. However, their view of *ijtihad* differed substantially from the unbounded *ijtihad* advocated by modern reformers and revivalists that would in the end deliver a streamlined version of the Shari'a that sounded more like a policy document than a discursive tradition concerned with the formation of the self. Lawrence together with Carl Ernst has explored the genealogy of Chishti thought in South Asia.[10] While they examine Chishti spirituality with punctilious detail, there still remains a rich web of Sufi metaphysics in relation to discourses on the Shari'a that have yet to be mined. Islamic mysticism for some South Asian Chishtis deepens the meaning and purpose of the juridico-moral discourse, while the legal or ethical discourse restrains mystical exuberance. What I further hope to suggest is that debates for or against *ijtihad* shroud particular notions of history, temporality, self, and society that underpin the social imaginary of its authors and the communities they represent.

Qari Muhammad Tayyab

In an essay titled *Ijtihad aur taqlid* (Independent Reasoning and Authority), written sometime in the late 1960s or early 1970s, Qari Muhammad Tayyab (d. 1403/1983), former principal of the Dar al-'Ulum Deoband in India, offered a rather different take on the issue of *ijtihad* compared to the dominant narrative advocated by Muslim modernists, reformers, and revivalists. Unless one were in the thicket of the madrassa world of the Indo-Pakistan subcontinent, Tayyab's name would not mean much. Yet by all accounts he was a paragon of traditional piety and learning of the Indian Hanafi-Deobandi tradition. In postpartition India he assumed a role of pontifical solemnity during a five-decade stewardship as principal (*mohtamim*) of the famous Deoband seminary.

Apart from his stature as a *bien-pensant*, he also enjoyed a distinguished ancestral pedigree.[11] He was the grandson of Muhammad Qasim Nanautvi (d. 1297/1880), the highly revered founding figure of the Dar al-'Ulum at Deoband, in Uttar Pradesh. Tayyab's father, Hafiz Muhammad Ahmad (d.1347/1928), was also a principal of the Dar al-'Ulum for four decades. After the latter's death, his youthful, but reluctant, son Tayyab, after much cajoling from Deoband's venerable hierarchy, assumed the deputy principal's job and later became principal in 1929.[12]

Under Tayyab's leadership the Deoband seminary increased in national and international visibility as it grew in terms of student numbers, faculty, and campus

expansion. But there were also spells marked by faculty feuds and the resigna-
tion of senior figures. He remained in his post till 1981, when he faced the most
severe test of leadership in a bitter administrative showdown with a rival group
within the seminary that culminated in his removal.[13]

Irrespective of Tayyab's success or failure as an administrator, there was little
doubt among his peers—friend and foe alike—that his predisposition toward
theology, philosophy, and mysticism gave unique shape to his insights in Muslim thought. His razor-sharp intellect and philosophical insights impressed his
peers, who conferred on him the sobriquet "Savant of Islam" (*Hakim al-Islam*).
With Ashraf 'Ali Thanawi, the doyen and most prolific of the Deoband scholars and a preeminent Sufi *shaykh*, as his spiritual director (*murshid/shaykh*) who
also ordained him as his validated spiritual successor (*khilafa-e majaz*), Tayyab
rose rapidly in the Deoband hierarchy.[14] With this investiture he also inducted
novices from all over India to the Chishti spiritual order.

Ijtihad *and* Taqlid

In his treatment of Islamic law and moral philosophy, Tayyab followed in the
footsteps of the acclaimed Shah Wali Allah (d. 1762) by mingling metaphysics
and discourses of law with traditionalist Muslim narratives of what might
approximate a philosophy of history-cum-sociology of moral philosophy and
law. Treatments of Islamic law or moral philosophy in Western languages, with
notable exceptions, rarely gave attention to the nonpositivistic elements encoded
in legal writings. Often juridical writings that are mingled with the grammar of
metaphysics and mysticism are shunted off as studies in spirituality and rele-
gated to the study of religion and unrelated to Islamic law. In fact as Baber
Johansen so accurately pointed out, legal positivism had become the new orthodoxy and normative grounds for the study of Islamic law at the hands of some
prominent Arab or Muslim legal figures.[15]

In *Ijtihad aur taqlid* Tayyab sheds light on independent reasoning (*ijtihad*) and
its use in the postformative juridical tradition; coupled to this is his take on how
one dealt with canonical authority in law (*taqlid*).[16] Tayyab showed an awareness
that many jurists adhered to a despotically normative consensus, one that
judged adherence to a canonical law school to be tantamount to obedience to
the revealed law (*shari'a*) itself.[17] Canonical law schools, in his view, were the
fruits of intellectual struggle—*ijtihad*—and should be viewed as paths to traditions of practice. Or to put it differently, they were ethical paths or traditions
that were intergenerationally transmitted. In a refreshing push for moral and
juridical pluralism, Tayyab pleaded with the confessional community (*ummah*)
of Muslims to view these *ijtihadi* paths as merely many ways of protecting the
integrity of religion (*din*).[18] Here he gently cautioned South Asian Hanafis, often

criticized for their rigidity, to view other law schools as legitimate expressions of adherence to normativity.

Tayyab's views are best assessed when compared to nineteenth- and twentieth-century debates on *ijtihad* in different parts of the Muslim world. By the end of the nineteenth century in the Middle East there were vociferous calls to embrace *ijtihad*. Hewing the Qur'an tightly to a prophetic tradition-driven hermeneutic in India was the Ahl-i Hadith movement that in principle subscribed to *ijtihad* as an obligation on Muslims to mine the scriptural sources continuously for truth.[19] The Ahl-i Hadith constituted the reform-minded lobby that energetically resisted the discursive schools' (*madhahib*) approach to moral and ethical guidance; but it was also a conservative type of reform focused on rituals instead of issues of nation-building and social transformation. Rather the Indian Ahl-i Hadith were closer in spirit to the ideas of the Salafi *ulama* of the Arab countries whom they loyally followed. Indian Muslim modernists too made fervent petitions in favor of *ijtihad*. They also invoked Shah Wali Allah as their intellectual beacon and later claimed the philosopher Muhammad Iqbal as a ventriloquist for their reformist and modernist cause.

Meanwhile the traditional Hanafi authorities were certainly not disenchanted with their school tradition. In fact they tenaciously defended its validity as a normative expression of tradition. And despite their vocal, if not at times explosive, internecine hostility over theological matters, the *ulama* of both the Barelvi and Deobandi schisms thought their scholastic Hanafi legal tradition to be eminently suited to meet their needs and the challenges posed by British colonialism.[20] This indefatigable Hanafi orthodoxy continued into postpartition India and Pakistan.

A complex set of reasons account for the lack of receptivity among Indian Hanafis for the protestant and modernizing zeal that readily gripped their *ulama* counterparts in the Middle East. One chief reason was the resistance the Indian Hanafi scholars gave to the unfettered license to engage in juridical *ijtihad*. It was not only their robust faith in the superiority of Hanafi jurisprudence and moral philosophy as an alternative to Western norms that explained their resilience. Rather their resolve was nourished by what they observed to be the unintended consequences of pro-*ijtihad* voices in the Arab world. Indian Hanafis noted that those Arab *ulama* who espoused *ijtihad* were also gradually and unconsciously capitulating to a process of secularization that involved moral compromises with modern modes of living.[21] For traditional Hanafis the latter was the most threatening aspect of the pro-*ijtihad* camp. Moreover the pro-*ijtihad* rhetoric in the Arab world overlapped with a more ambitious desire to engineer a cultural renaissance (*nahda*). Of course hand in glove with the rhetoric of renaissance were the calls for *ijtihad* that were often streaked with strains of Arab nationalism and socialist tendencies. While many traditionalist scholars (*ulama*) in the Arab Middle East joined this pro-*ijtihad* cultural and political chorus, such commitments were anathema to their South Asian counterparts.

Perhaps there was another psychological reason why South Asian Hanafi *ulama* resisted *ijtihad*. Were they to accept *ijtihad*, it would signal a singular ideological capitulation on their part to their long-standing and bitter rivals, the Indian Ahl-i Hadith scholars, who were not awed by modernity, either. In fact one of the reasons for the existence of Tayyab's institution, the seminary at Deoband, was to confront the challenge of Ahl-i Hadith Salafism. The latter leveled trenchant criticisms against the Hanafis for elevating the voice of tradition above what they claimed was the fresh and continuously accessible inspiration of revelation.

Revelatory authority in the Deobandi incarnation of the Indo-Persian intellectual tradition, Tayyab pointed out, was not antithetical to reason and metaphysical concerns. Any norm, he argued, had to relate to a sense of wholeness and rationalism, and metaphysics cemented that relation.[22] This attitude stood in contrast to an almost dominant contemporary trend in Muslim epistemology that gave the final and absolute authority to unalloyed and unmediated commands derived from fairly commonsensical renderings of the Qur'anic revelation and prophetic dicta while eschewing a coherent hermeneutic. Tayyab clearly favored the rationalist-cum-metaphysical hermeneutic. "Every legal particular," he confidently wrote, "embodies a universal. Universals embody wisdom and a universal interest. Therefore, every interest is connected to an instant of perfection; every perfection is linked to one or another divine attribute."[23]

Tayyab's language unsuspectingly draws one's attention to metaphysics by invoking universals and wisdom, relating such concerns to juridical concerns, ethics, and questions of public interest. At the same time he also inflects the discourse of mysticism and piety by invoking terms such as *perfection* and the fullness of divine attributes on the human psyche. This more complex and multilayered approach to law still has some cachet in certain strands of South Asian Islam. Traditional Hanafi scholarship in South Asia unapologetically converses about juridical norms in relation to cosmology. In South Asian Hanafi intellectual circles legal discourse effortlessly communes with a heady mix of metaphysics, dialectical theology (*kalam*), and mysticism (*tasawwuf*).

Transcendence, Narrative, and Temporality

Secreted in Tayyab's narrative on extraordinary effort and interpretative commitment (*ijtihad*) is his concept of history, a notion perhaps more captivating and deserving of closer attention. Tayyab's notion of history in many ways resembles a form of *historia*, where narrative frames the key questions of his interpretative paradigm. It was akin to narrative history as opposed to a chronicled history. Narrative history, as Hayden White points out, dramatizes historical events and novelizes certain historical processes in order to demonstrate that the "truths in which narrative history deals are of an order different from those of its social scientific counterpart."[24]

Both poetic and noetic aspects of narrative history inform Tayyab's philosophy of jurisprudence. In his discourse two terms worked in tandem: *takwin* and *tashri*ʿ. *Takwin* denoted creation or cosmogony, and *tashri*ʿ denoted the process of norm production. Muslim theologians theorized *takwin* as "the creation of form out of matter."[25] In other words it was the existence of something material that came into being or was preceded by a sovereign act of divine willing and knowing.[26] Just as *takwin* was realized through a gradual process, the normative order, *tashri*ʿ, was also linked to divine attributes that foreshadowed the onset of gradualism in history as an ideal.

Features of gradualism, *taʾanni* or *tadrij*, emanated from the divine attribute of *rububiyyat*, a Creator who nourished gradually.[27] In other words the normative order was something that formed over time and became known within a temporal sphere. Thus both the cosmic and normative orders were related to time. The emphasis on the generation of the universe was of course to mark a moment in the cosmological development of an ordered universe, rather than the restricted idea of creation.

Tayyab developed his ideas through a series of homologies. A homology, Raymond Williams reminds us, is where there is a correspondence in origin and development, which is different from analogy, for the latter emphasizes a correspondence in appearance and function.[28] In Tayyab's view there is a homology between the process of temporal creation (*takwin*) and the process of norm making (*tashri*ʿ). The alliteration and play between *takwin* and *tashri*ʿ—cosmos and nomos—signified a homological relation. Then Tayyab reverts to analogy. In nature one is a witness, he notes, to both the "work of God" and the "word of God." How? By apprehending God's "work" one is a witness to the *act of creation*, and in attesting to God's "word" one is a witness to an *act of revelation*. The parallels he draws here between the book of nature and the book of God could not be more obvious.[29] Temporal creation in nature and norm making via revelation coalesced and shared a singular ontological horizon in Tayyab's view.

Temporal creation (*takwin*) on the one hand and nomothetic production (*tashri*ʿ) on the other both, argued Tayyab, had a single beginning. They mirrored the two cosmic universes: the universe of creation and the universe of command (ʿ*alam al-khalq wa al-amr*). The latter reference was intuited from Qurʾanic terminology, invoking a realm where the cosmic and normative coexisted. For Tayyab beginnings were located in a narrative. He put the Qurʾanic narrative to work in which a cosmic day was equal to a thousand earthly years. The well-known cosmological myth of creation in the Abrahamic tradition claimed that the world was created in a period of six days. However, in the view of many commentators, the process of creation always remained inscrutable.[30] One of Tayyab's pratfalls was an egregious display of literalism that propounded a fuzzy theory of Islamic evolution, claiming the world was created over a period of six thousand years! In doing so he also departed from the practice of traditional exegetes, many of whom had refrained from speculating on the empirical nature of cosmological references in the revelation.[31] Traces of a now-discredited eighteenth- and early-nineteenth-century version of creationism based on Genesis also seemed to have made its way into Tayyab's account. Biblical genealogies about two centuries ago suggested that the earth was six thousand years old, whereas Tayyab asserted, drawing on Islamic sources, that the advent of the Prophet Muhammad occurred exactly six thousand years after the first human, Adam, had made his appearance.[32] These serious factual lapses aside, I think the Tayyab's larger point remained valid.

Just as the cosmological order unfolded within chronological or natural time, the normative order, too, unfolded in natural time. The homology was perfect: the unfolding of the cosmos over time paralleled the uncoiling of normative practices in the long duration of human experiences. The latter culminated in the moral order brought by the Arabian Prophet. There was also some correspondence between cosmic and earthly times. "Within a period of 6,000 years," Tayyab pointed out, "the perfection (*takmil*) of matters related to cosmology and norms occurred." From his subsequent explanation one could read him as saying that the relationship of cosmos to nomos paralleled certain discrete features of physical evolution and social evolution, respectively, even though one had to discount his hazardous enthusiasm to calculate the exact amount of time involved.[33]

What both the cosmic and nomothetic spheres shared was their rootedness in certain unalterable and universal premises and principles. Tayyab's cosmology consisted of several interlocking universals (*kulliyat*). Thriving on the classics from Aristotle to Ibn Sina, he recalled the four principles or primary elements of water, earth, fire, and air as universals. These in turn generated other universals such as minerals, animals, and vegetation in a hierarchical order.[34] Similarly in the nomothetic sphere, the foundations and universals of religion were premised on rules, regulations, doctrines, and values. How did the cosmological and normative narratives square in Tayyab's homology? Actually they harmonized via unchanging and stable universals. Not only is the emphasis on the universal a key element in Tayyab's interpretative framework, but even the particulars carried the imprint of the universal when they were expressed in a coherent fashion. He writes, "Every particular [in law or *fiqh*] embodies a universal knowledge. Hidden in this universal knowledge [are two things]: a wisdom and a universal interest. Hence, every interest is connected to an instant of perfection, which in turn is attached to one or another divine attribute."[35]

But universality did not mean that a static order prevailed. When one investigates both nature and the cosmos, Tayyab says, it becomes possible to discover new wonders and mysteries. Tapping into the potential of nature produces an unending number of inventions for civilization. Familiarity with the normative process enables one to penetrate the hidden knowledge and secrets underlying the universal norms, the order of values and rules. By deploying these discursive tools, he claims, one can "produce new secondary questions, subtleties and nuances; realities and insights for religiosity (*tadayyun*)."[36] Just as scientific discovery (*iktishaf*) deepens our knowledge of the cosmological realm (*takwin*), similarly continuous intellectual labor (*ijtihad*) deepens our appreciation of the normative order (*tashriʿ*).[37]

Tayyab's sonorous rhetoric of inherent dynamism in nature and norms did not mean that he was sanguine on the lawfulness of developing new principles of interpretation (*ijtihad*) in law or moral philosophy. In his view both *ijtihad* and adhering to authority (*taqlid*) functioned as a pair—a role required and deemed desirable in the revealed law (Shariʿa).[38] Both terms—*ijtihad* and *taqlid*—metonymically related to a whole spectrum of meanings of creativity and authority. In order to be effective, both ideas had to be activated within an ordered realm (*nizam*), irrespective of whether such an order was of a religious or secular nature. The *character* of the order was more important than its *form*: it should neither be repressive and static, in Tayyab's view, nor be so fragmented and dispersed as to be ineffective.

Hermeneutics of Ijtihad

Three threads were interwoven in Tayyab's overall interpretative frame (hermeneutic): piety, epistemology, and history. Overlooking these dimensions can result in a serious misreading of his project and simultaneously distort his unique perspective on things. In contemporary discussions of de novo and autonomous interpretation of Muslim law, ethics, and moral philosophy, one will seldom find the project of norm making, or norm discovery, as some prefer to call it, to be tied to questions of piety, the subjectivity of the jurist, and the personal ethics of the scholar. Tayyab, however, not only gave considerable attention to the subjectivity of the religious intellectual or scholar but made it the centerpiece of his discussion on the interpretation of the religious teachings.

In the discussion thus far, his story has centered on the discovery of new possibilities (*ijad*) in the cosmic realm (*takwin*) similar to the "book of nature" and the discovery of norms (*ijtihad*) in the normative realm (*tashriʿ*) as the equivalent of the "book of God." Now a third dimension, completing the triad, discusses how the divine imprint became manifest on every human heart and soul, or what mystics would call the "tablet of the heart."[39]

Piety

Starting with prophets, Tayyab points out, revelation (*wahy*) encodes the subjectivities of divinely deputed emissaries; the big picture of the moral order is transmitted via their subjectivities to the rest of humanity. Prophets adopted various means in order to achieve the larger goals and objectives of their missions by way of rules and practices only after their subjectivities were purified and perfected. There were clear advantages to prophets whose souls were spiritually elevated: for one it made it easier to provide role models in moral rectitude, and communities did not have to reinvent the wheel in certain issues. Since prophets were endowed with a level of moral and spiritual perfection beyond that of ordinary mortals, it was easy for them to construe the content of moral practices for their followers.[40]

On the other hand, lesser mortals, such as scholars, first had to discover the secondary rules of the moral and legal order through knowledge acquired from tradition via study and inquiry. As this class advanced in spiritual blessing (Urdu, *barkat*; Arabic, *baraka*) and piety (*tazkiya-e nafs* and *tasfiya-e qulub*) and all of these internal conditions were acquired by way of extensive exercises in meditation and introspection, they gradually grasped the larger moral picture of universal norms and moral reasons behind ethical practices. Spiritual preparation enabled scholars to perfect their grasp in extrapolating norms, to apply the correct types of analogical reasoning to their work, and to reach advanced levels of commitment and ability in the discovery of norms and values (*ijtihad*) embedded in the teachings. Faithful adherence to learning, as well as practice (*'ilm va 'amal*), not only enhanced the integrity of scholars, but also facilitated divine wisdom being vouchsafed to them.[41] Tayyab approvingly cited a fragment of a prophetic tradition that stated: "Whoever acts on the learning they had acquired, God then discloses to them [special] knowledge they did not acquire [discursively]."[42]

A key word for ethical formation frequently used in the mysticism-friendly juristic discourses is *dhawq*. While the word literally means "to taste" or "sapience," it is suggestive of connoisseurship in spiritual wisdom and knowledge of divine things. It presupposed that the subject was exposed to ethical and spiritual training in order to appreciate esoteric knowledge by developing an aesthetically sensitive ethical sensibility. Endowed with this capacity, the jurist was now further equipped to give coherence to all exoteric learning in terms of the overall purpose of religion, which was salvation. Master jurists (*mujtahidun*) who were endowed with a pious predisposition and subjectivity or those who had self-consciously cultivated such a capacity, said Tayyab, were permitted to rely on privileged saintly knowledge or gnosis (*'ilm ladunni*) granted to them. This disposition was a resource they could rely on when they exercised ethical and juridical discretion in discursive practices.

Those who criticized jurists for resorting to rational discourse failed to realize, Tayyab remonstrates, that the ideal jurist was one who combined scriptural learning with gnostic piety. Rebutting charges leveled against jurists who combined rationalism with piety, Tayyab possibly had puritan and scripturalist (*salafis*) trends in mind when he unapologetically stated that

> in fact these [juristic] opinions are neither based on opinion or analogy, nor are they exclusively the yield of the capacities of the mind to be discounted as mere deeds of gross subjective discretion (*tasarruf-e dhati*). In fact, these learned opinions are the product of the ethical/spiritual temperament (*dhawqi quwwat*) of a jurist, one premised on the application of the *Shari'a* dictum to "combine learning with practice." As observations of such genuine spiritual experiences reveal, God transmits special knowledge into the heart of the master-jurist. In fact, the discretion in question is part of the *Shari'a* and located in the essence of *Shari'a*. . . . Like all heavenly revelations (*Shara'i' samawiyya*) that are exclusively from God, they finally become manifest by way of the tongues and hearts of prophets. . . . A non-prophet to whom inspiration (*ilham*) is vouchsafed through divine unveilings (*kushuf ilahi*) and knowledge of norms (*'ulum tashri'i*) is in the terminology of the Shari'a called "the inspired one or the one who was addressed [by God]" (*muhaddath*).[43]

In this pietistic version of Shari'a, the sanctified subjectivity or knowledge of the heart illumined by divine light (gnosis) became part of the revealed norm. If on occasion gnosis torqued the norm against the obvious meaning of a text, then Tayyab obviously found justification to exercise such hermeneutical discretion. He drew on the authority of a prophetic report that purported that the Qur'an was revealed in seven dialects (*sab'a ahruf*) and that each verse contained both "an exterior" sense (*zahar*) and "an interior" sense (*batan*). And the boundary of each verse, the report clarified, had an anagogic dimension, namely a mystical and spiritual sense (*muttala'*).[44] Here the hermeneutical observation point transmuted into a virtual panopticon from where everything could be observed with clarity and sensitivity.[45] One should note that a peculiar quality of understanding (*fahm*) associated with the autonomous intellectual or master jurist (*mujtahid*) recurred in Tayyab's treatment of this topic. Discursive understanding here was mingled with divine afflatus: the one who wished to qualify as a master jurist was also simultaneously someone whose subjectivity was molested by divine inspiration; he was a *muhaddath* with whom Providence shared the larger plan for the moral and salvific education of humanity.[46]

This perspective of a master jurist being someone who had a special spiritual disposition and a sanctified subjectivity was not unique to the Deobandi scholars, although they were among the few contemporary schools to articulate explicitly their juridical deliberations within a paradigm of piety. The fourteenth-century jurist-theologian Taqi al-Din Ahmad Ibn Taymiyyah extolled the clarity of intellectual vision if it was linked to spiritual merit.[47] Spiritual clarity was like a luminescent lamp and a dwindling lamp on a dark night: each would disclose its surrounding space according to the strength of its light. Similarly believers who were guided by, in his words, the "heart's inspiration" (*al-ilham al-qalbi*) could in the absence of directive guidance make intuitive judgments that were in accord with the truth and the "light of the Qur'an." These intuitive verdicts in refuting something to be false and flawed were in epistemic status parallel to the authority of the types of textual statements (*al-qawl, al-ʿilm,* and *al-zann*) that jurists used in their work. Ibn Taymiyyah then goes on to cite the prophetic report on the virtues of persons known to enjoy the status of a *muhaddath*, counting the companion ʿUmar to be among this category of persons. A *muhaddath* was someone to whom divine inspiration was vouchsafed and whose heart the Divine addressed: *al-mulham al-mukhatab fi sirrihi.*[48]

Epistemology

Tayyab had a clear-eyed view of the link between the piety and inner self-perfection of the jurist, on the one hand, and matters of epistemology and discursive knowledge, on the other. In fact he proposed a dialectical relationship between the gnosis of the jurist and the discursive knowledge of the tradition. Anyone left pondering about discursive knowledge for the purposes of intellectual autonomy (*ijtihad*) should first pay attention to "tradition" or "modes of religious knowledge that was transmitted" (*riwayat*) and, second, not ignore the importance of "comprehending" (*dirayat*) such transmitted knowledge in all its hermeneutical complexity.[49]

Instrumental learning, such as the verification of reports and authenticity of texts, as well as their different modes of transmission and preservation over time and, finally, the interpretation and understanding of such teachings, was all in Tayyab's view part of a larger providential scheme. If the persons associated with the transmission of knowledge, learning, and the hermeneutical processes were bereft of saintly virtues, then such a deficit will prove to be damaging to the integrity of revealed knowledge. Personal piety was an index of integrity and was assumed to serve as a deterrent against any degradation of the sources of information.

The gravity and enormity attached to the exercise of intellectual autonomy can be attributed to several things. For one the master jurist had an intimate role in shaping as well as disclosing the knowledge of revelation as contained in the

Qur'an and in the practice of the Prophet Muhammad. Then it further required that such learning be meticulously relayed to the community. In other words the task at hand lent an aura of sanctity to the person and office of the jurist (*faqih*). So what matched the responsibility shouldered by the jurist was the extraordinary authority that such persons wielded in the transmission and production of the tradition.

Tayyab placed the role of the *mujtahid* in a larger historicist frame. He acknowledged human diversity in the understanding of phenomena. This could well result in some people being smarter than others. However, not every smart person, he observed, could qualify to be an autonomous intellectual authority. "Only trustworthy understanding (*fahm*) is credible and by an act of divine love, divinely gifted knowledge (*'ilm ladunni*) reaches the heart of the *mujtahid*. In other words, it is a realm parallel to the realm of creation: any person of greater or lesser understanding cannot become an inventor (*mujid* [active participle of *ijad*]). In every age there is a surplus of inventors. But when the wisdom of God, the Sublime, wishes to see the advance and progress (*taraqqi*) of certain aspects of a civilization (*tamaddun*) above others, then It [Divine Wisdom] over time identifies a few distinguished persons [literally, 'minds'] and delegates them to undertake the creative work."[50] Tayyab left little doubt in the mind of his reader that he subscribed to a providential understanding of history. To reinforce the point, he continued: "Similarly, in matters concerning the realm of moral commands (*kai'nat-e 'amr*) not every intelligent and smart person can become one who wielded authority to attain intellectual autonomy (*mujtahid*). Nor are *mujtahids* born in every age. Whenever Divine Wisdom wishes to disclose certain concealed aspects of religiosity then individuals of extraordinary talent are made to arise and in their hearts is placed a temperament for intellectual autonomy (*dhawq-e ijtihad*). With their divinely endowed sensibility (*wahbi dhawq*) these persons elucidate specific dimensions [of religion] with clarity . . . and present it to the community (*ummah*)."[51]

Tayyab makes two distinct hermeneutic moves. In the first move, the invisible hand of Providence plays a crucial role in human affairs. Apart from the uncanny echoes of Adam Smith, in Tayyab's words the invisible hand of Providence promoted and regulated the public interest and distributed what was necessary in every age of life.[52] The second move signals the importance of a division of labor.

History

Temporality was the centerpiece of Tayyab's narrative on the production of moral knowledge in Islam. A unique conception of time also framed his philosophy of history. Indeed time in Tayyab's model was sliced like gourmet sandwiches in a hamper with no two blandishments having identical garnishings. Tayyab imagined each epoch in time as having unique features. It was as if he visualized each with its own DNA while providing something akin to a map of sequenced time. In the scenario he sketched, he assumed that in each given community and at specific times in history, people had unique abilities, talents, and potential. With these talents they performed and fulfilled a variety of functions. But after some time—and here Tayyab did not clarify whether this happened over decades or centuries—these abilities disappeared and were supplanted by other talents and capacities more suitable to the newer epoch.

For example Tayyab believed that the labor invested in transmitting knowledge (*riwayat*) of the Shari'a was perfected by the early communities of Muslim scholars. Prodigious memories in oral cultures came to good use in order to secure for posterity a record of the activities of the nascent Muslim community in Arabia. If the period of the oral tradition of Islam was not paired with an epoch in which people had prodigious memories, the interdependent readings of the primary sources of Islam might in all likelihood have vanished. But by providential fiat these talents peaked within several generations and then flattened; such distinctive features only remained relevant at particular moments in history. Without using the term *evolution*, Tayyab was unequivocal as to what he meant: when certain capacities and talents were not needed, then social evolution ensured that these capacities gradually disappeared. A similar pattern was discernable in the transmission, recording, and dissemination of prophetic reports (*hadith*). Hadith historiography that verified chains of transmissions and their innumerable narrators had been perfected, Tayyab argued, in the early centuries of Islam. The bulk of that intellectual edifice was already established. Today, in his view, there was very little need to continue with elaborate critiques of Hadith transmitters. Why? Because the talents, learning, and predispositions required for such tasks were no longer regnant.

Similarly the comprehension (*dirayat*) of the broad outlines of the Shari'a too had been perfected by earlier generations. Therefore it would be redundant to reinvent the same tasks in the present without a genuine and justifiable need. In fact he invoked a naturalistic argument, saying that humans had evolved and no longer exhibited capacities and talents to understand the original narratives of the faith. For example the early jurists established the universal principles (*kulliyat*) of the juridical-moral order followed by linking an innumerable number of real-life cases and particulars (*juz'iyat*) to the logic of a universal. In what might be Tayyab's least satisfactory point, he claimed without explaining that the talents to undertake such foundational tasks were no longer with us. And in terms of the abstract genetics of temporality that Tayyab fostered, one suspected that, like dinosaurs, certain types of work and talent were just no longer around.

Seeking to pursue *ijtihad* by way of discerning the *ratio legis* of rules, practices, and doctrines in the same manner the early generations of scholars had was in his view a futile pursuit. The early scholars had elegantly perfected this task by elaborating the taxonomies of legal reasons. Reinventing such tasks, in his view, would amount to engaging in a redundant activity. It was a natural rule, he said, that when a certain goal was reached and saturated then the potential required to fulfill such tasks also naturally became extinct.[53] One wonders what Tayyab would have made of the information age, in which scientific invention had opened an infinite number of possibilities for the computation and processing of information in literate cultures where new conceptions of memories (social imaginaries as well as conceptions of the past), society, and normativity supplanted previous ones. Would not the information age have something to contribute to the construction of Islamic thought in a radically different way from what classical Muslim scholars had imagined?

Tayyab's theory was not free from ideological commitments that lead to a specific set of beliefs overriding the gathering of facts and information of the past. Historical studies, Hayden White points out, were also caught on the horns of a dilemma.[54] In order to be a science, history had to have a theory; but to have an interest in theory meant to foreclose on the disinterested gathering of information. The resolution of this dilemma was called the historicist vision of historical reality. Historicity advanced a social mode of being in the world marked by a particular experience of temporality, not unlike Tayyab's reflections about time.

Drawing on the work of Reinhart Koselleck helped White to make a crucial distinction between historical time and natural time. Thus the content of history, he writes, "could be grasped as social reality undergoing changes quite unlike those that nature underwent."[55] "Historical change could be seen to differ from natural change," White continues, "by its heterogeneity, multileveledness, and variability of rate of acceleration. With the discovery that the time of history was different from the time of nature, men also came to believe that historical time could be affected by human action and purposiveness in ways that natural time could not, that history could be 'made' as well as 'suffered,' and that a historical knowledge true to its 'concept' provided the prospects for a science of society that balanced the claims of experience with the insistencies of expectation, hope, and faith in the future."[56]

In Tayyab's view propositional attitudes from perceptual sensations to spiritual orientations differed in major ways from one time period to another. While there is little reason or evidence to suspect that Tayyab was familiar with the thoughts of Johann Gottfried von Herder, there are uncanny parallels between the eighteenth-century German thinker and this twentieth-century Indian thinker. One reason for the coincidence in thought could be that both men valued tradition. One passage from Herder is more than suggestive and captures the parallels. In words directed at Kant, Herder writes: "In reality, every mutable thing has within itself the measure of its time; this persists even in the absence of any other; no two worldly things have the same measure of time. . . . There are therefore (one can state it properly and boldly) at any one time in the universe innumerably many times."[57] While Herder's point is to stake out the multiple nature of time and its atomism, he does undoubtedly link all mutable things to time. Tayyab's point, too, is to connect every thing to the measure of its time, and hence no two moments and things were the same: each was unique.

Canonical traditions in Tayyab's view were certainly vulnerable to radical criticism and revision. Radical revision could effectively disable the groundwork laid by the founders. Tayyab chafed at the pretentiousness of certain modern Muslim thinkers who wished to throw open the doors to intellectual autonomy and de novo interpretation of the tradition. In his broadsides he caricatured Muslim modernist claims with a warning: trying to engage in *ijtihad* would not only undo the intellectual labors of past scholars; even worse, he predicted, it would uncoil the canon and produce a totally distorted and unrecognizable Islam.

With his moral solicitude evident, one can begin to understand, without endorsing his position, why Tayyab's elaborate theory tried to naturalize the temporal order of the tradition into unique units, each with its own peculiarities. After explicating his view of natural temporality, he superimposed or used the same template for historical temporality. The uniqueness of time and the things produced in time, as part of a concept of history, allowed Tayyab to paint the self-authenticating scholars—the founders and master jurists of the major law schools—in radiant and exceptional colors. In his account the world of the master jurists was a peerless one, a state of exception orchestrated by providence and never to be repeated. Here Tayyab was clearly engaged in a "naturalistic fallacy" of deriving an *ought* from an *is*. He concluded that how one perceives things *are* is also how they *ought* to be. This is no surprise, since he did not distinguish between natural and historical time and thought both to be identical. The upshot of his meditations was that certain intellectual practices and questions ought not to be entertained. And if there were precedents in the past for such methods of inquiry, then in his view they should remain one-off occurrences. Why these modes of inquiry and practices should remain inimitable, Tayyab did not explain. A skeptic could also conclude that his hermeneutic favored the interests of the learned classes, the *ulama*, whose role would be indispensable as interpreters and authorities of the tradition. A less skeptical explanation could be that he attempted to safeguard the operation of the canonical tradition, masking his fears that aggressive and foundation-shaking questions could undo its coherence.

The only form of intellectual autonomy (*ijtihad*) that Tayyab tolerated was what he called "a general investigation and inquiry related to the Qur'an and Sunna that facilitated reflections that would make visible the subtleties and realities [of these two sources]."⁵⁸ Ijtihad here meant to generate normative teachings in order to establish standards for practices in every age and to give appropriate moral-juridical responses (fatwas). Another form of *ijtihad* that he condoned was labors to refute attacks on Islam. Defenders of Islam were urged to draw new inspiration from the authoritative "source texts" (*nusus*), which in addition to the Qur'an and prophetic reports also implied the invocation of other authoritative scholarly writings, especially those that had been canonized in the tradition. Here Tayyab did view adjustments as well as innovation in dogmatic theology favorably, in order to advance the possibility of individual *ijtihad*, and came very close to Muslim modernist positions like those advanced by Shibli Nu'mani and Muhammad Iqbal, both prominent intellectual figures in prepartition India.⁵⁹

Conclusion

Tayyab explained every epoch with providence's hand directing the moral compass of Muslim society through different modes of learning and knowledge. Despite some resemblance to Herder, one cannot help thinking that his narrative was also a kind of apologetic. One required more than just persuasion to accept some of his propositions unless one had a purchase on his concept of history that rested at the center of his project: natural time the way he understood it had a homology in historical time. For Tayyab history occurred *in* time, namely, natural time, as well as *through* time, namely, historical time, since both were identical in his framing. The way he repeatedly paired historical time to nature left one in no doubt that he conflated the two. If so, then he imagined history to occur *through* time, which in itself was a very modern move. There were strong overtones of salvation history in Tayyab's writings. The need to control and construct the past had to do with the way the present and future were construed both in terms of eschatology and also in terms of the velocity of change brought on by modernity. It remains to be seen if Tayyab's understanding of *ijtihad* will go with him and his generation to their graves or whether his followers will set the agenda for the future like votive pillars to the glory of the tradition in the next hundred years.

Writing about Ibn Khaldun, Bruce Lawrence shows that what was different about the fifteenth-century North African scholar was his "ability to travel in the imagination of his own world, to create another perspective that at once linked him to his contemporaries yet set him apart from them."⁶⁰ The key word here is *difference* in all its deconstructionist glory, where it means "to differ" as well as "to defer" (as in to postpone or delay). In many ways Tayyab and his Deobandi cohorts cherished their unique social imagination, which I hope I have succeeded in demonstrating, and how it set them apart from some but also related them to others both contemporaneously as well as over time. This raises the questions: Do Tayyab and his colleagues represent a distinct trend in South Asian traditionalism with a vision of *ijtihad* and *taqlid* and thus of Islamic reform that was different in its modus operandi compared to trends that enjoyed currency in the Middle East? Or was this a form of apologetics and traditionalist dogmatic theology whose relevance might be seriously questioned? I am reluctant to make hasty judgments. Whether we perceive this as traditionalist "quirkiness or eccentricity, narcissism or genius," to cite Lawrence once again, does not detract from the profound merits of the arguments.[61] This specific Indian tradition of law mingled with spirituality, as Lawrence points out elsewhere, was not only under threat from revivalists, but they would also be challenged by a whole new global constituency, previously unthinkable, namely, Muslim cybernauts.[62] In the age of the Internet, he writes, "authority is more diffuse now than it was two hundred, or even ten, years ago," and *ijtihad*, once the purview of the *ulama*, now belongs to the World Wide Web and even includes women, whose voices and opinions can be distinctly heard in cyberspace. While it is difficult to pronounce what the impact of e-*ijtihad* will be, one can with some certainty predict that *ijtihad* conceived and conducted in this new medium will ontologically change the age-old Muslim practice, similar to the way it underwent change because of modernist pressures. This possibility, needless to say, was one that Tayyab did not even imagine, let alone countenance when he somberly meditated on this issue in the previous century.

It is clear that the discursive tradition of at least one strand of Islamic traditionalism in South Asia viewed "Islamic law" or juridical theology to be related to more than just material conditions and contingencies; it was also intimately related to fundamental questions of subjectivity and ontology. South Asian and Iranian traditional scholars, to my knowledge, remained the last vestiges of tradition where the theological and spiritual aspects of religiosity were scrupulously adhered to as an integral part of juridical discourse. In the discussions above, I provided some glimpses as to how the practice of norm making was deeply implicated in the practices of spirituality. A jurist, from this perspective, was not only a practitioner of discursivity; he was also the purveyor of piety. Talking about the role of the spiritual master, the *pir*, in medieval Indian Islam, Lawrence succinctly captured the role of the pious jurist along the lines Tayyab contemplated this individual: "Living at a point in time within a community . . . the pir mediates the will of God; he makes alive the sanctity of the Qur'an and the reverence for Tradition; he transmits stories and recites poetry that reflect a right outlook and correct behavior, or sometimes merely provide relief from the tedium of spiritual discipline. He becomes the embodiment of piety, learning and hope. He prays and he teaches; he teaches and prays."[63] In short, spiritual and ethical formation was part of the habitus of the jurist-theologian, whose being was intimately related to the process of norm making or the discovery of the ethical and moral norm for everyday behavior that is equally part of the pursuit of the Divine. Actually it might be more accurate to say that in Tayyab's view, the jurist was the instrument of Providence. The jurist fulfilled a minor prophetic role as heir to the knowledge of the prophets (*waratha-t al anbiya'*) and thus was also the addressee of divine afflatus (*muhaddath*).

NOTES

1. In this article the polysemous term *ijtihad* will approximate the following senses in translation: independent thinking, independent juridical reasoning, self-authenticating principles, and juridical discretion.

2. See Gayatri Chakravorty Spivak, *A Critique of Postcolonial Reason* (Cambridge, Mass.: Harvard University Press, 1999), 331. Also see the *Oxford English Dictionary*, s.v. "catachresis."

3. Abu Hamid Muhammad b. Muhammad al-Ghazali, *Al-mustasfa min 'ilm al-usul*, ed. Sulayman al-Ashqar, 2 vols. (Beirut: Mu'assasat al-Risala, 1417/1997), 2:164.

4. Muhammad b. Idris al-Shaf'i, *Al-risala*, ed. Ahmad Muhammad Shakir (Beirut: al-Maktaba al-'Ilmiyya, n.d.), 507–14.

5. See Muhammad 'Abd al-Hayy al-Laknawi, "Al-nafi' al-kabir li man yutali' al-jami' al-saghir," in *Majmu'a sab'a rasa'il* (Karachi: Saeed, 1418/1997), 173–215.

6. See Wael B. Hallaq, ed., "Issues and Problems," special issue of *Islamic Law and Society* 3, no. 2 (1996); also Mohammad Fadel, "The Social Logic of Taqlid and the Rise of the Mukhatasar," *Islamic Law and Society* 3, no. 2 (1996): 193–233, and Sherman A. Jackson, "Taqlid, Legal Scaffolding and the Scope of Legal Injunctions in Post-Formative Theory Mutlaq and 'amm in the Jurisprudence of Shihab Al-Din Al-Qarafi," *Islamic Law and Society* 3, no. 2 (1996): 165–92.

7. Abul Hasan Ali Nadwi, *Islam and the World* (Lucknow: Islamic Research Academy, 1980); Muhammad 'Abid al-Jabiri, *Nahnu wa al-turath* (Beirut: al-Markaz al-Thaqafi al-'Arabi, 1993), esp. 11–72.

8. Bruce B. Lawrence, *Defenders of God: The Fundamentalist Revolt against the Modern Age* (San Francisco: Harper & Row, 1989; repr., Columbia: University of South Carolina Press, 1995), 214.

9. Ibid., 215.

10. Carl W. Ernst and Bruce B. Lawrence, *Sufi Martyrs of Love: The Chishti Order in South Asia and Beyond* (New York: Palgrave Macmillan, 2002), 118–25.

11. 'Abd al-Hayy b. Fakhr al-Din al-Hasani, *Nuzhat al-khawatir*, 8 vols. (Multan: Tayyab Akademi, 1413/1992), 7:420–22.

12. Mawlana Habib Allah, ed., *Majalis hakim al-umma ma' sawaneh-e hayat hakim al-islam hazrat mawlana qari Muhammad*, 2 vols. (Multan: Idara Ta'lifat-e Ashrafiya, 1417 A.H.), 1:65–67.

13. On this conflict, see Muhammad Manzoor Nu'mani, *Dar al-ulum Deoband ka qadiya 'awam ki 'adalat main* (Deoband: Daftar-e Ihtimam Dar al-'Ulum Deoband, c. 1403/1982).

14. For more on Thanawi, see Muhammad Qasim Zaman, *Ashraf 'Ali Thanawi* (Oxford: Oneworld, 2008), and Habib Allah, *Majalis*, 1:42–45.

15. Johansen Baber, *Contingency in a Sacred Law: Legal and Ethical Norms in the Muslim Fiqh*, ed. Ruud Peters and Bernard Weiss, Studies in Islamic Law and Society, vol. 7 (Leiden: Brill, 1999), 58.

16. I am aware that many scholars translate *taqlid* as *imitation*, but observing or following is merely metonymy for adherence to authority.

17. Qari Muhammad Tayyab, *Ijtihad aur taqlid* (Lahore: Idara-e Islamiyat, 1978), 6.

18. Ibid.

19. See Claudia Preckel, "Ahl-i Hadith," in *Encyclopaedia of Islam*, ed. Gudrun Krämer et al. (Leiden: Brill, 2008), available online at http://www.encislam.brill.nl/subscriber/entry?entry=ei33_COM-0107 (accessed July 15, 2009).

20. Muneer Goolam Fareed, *Legal Reform in the Muslim World: The Anatomy of a Scholarly Dispute in the Nineteenth and Early Twentieth Centuries on the Usage of Ijtihad as a Legal Tool* (San Francisco: Austin & Winfield, 1996), 145.

21. Muhammad Yasin Akhtar al-A'zami Misbahi, "Note of the Academy-Kalimat al-Majma'," in Ahmad Rida al-Qadiri al-Barelwi, *Jadd al-mumtar 'ala radd al-muhtar*, vol. 1 (Hyderabad: al-Matba'a al-'Aziziyya, 1982), 6.

22. Tayyab, *Ijtihad aur taqlid*, 39–44.

23. Ibid., 18.

24. Hayden White, *The Content of the Form: Narrative Discourse and Historical Representation* (Baltimore: Johns Hopkins University Press, 1987), 44.

25. Samih Dughaym, ed., *Mawsu'a mustalahat 'ilm al-kalam al-islami*, 2 vols. (Beirut: Maktaba Lubnan, 1998), 1:379; Sa'd al-Din Mas'ud b. 'Umar al-Taftazani, *Sharh al-'aqa'id al-nasafiya: Fi usul al-din wa 'ilm al-kalam*, ed. Claude Salama (Damascus: Wazara li'l-Thaqafa wa 'l-Irshad al-Qawmi, 1973), 62; Muhammad 'Abd al-'Aziz Parharwi, *Al-nibras sharh sharh al-'aqa'id* (Bindyal Sharif, Sargoda: Shah 'Abd al-Haqq Academy, 1397/1977), 234.

26. Muhammad A'la al-Tahanawi, *Mawsu'a kashshaf istilahat al-funun wa al-'ulum*, ed. Rafiq al-'Ajam, 2 vols. (Beirut: Maktaba Lubnan, 1996), 1:85, 505; Parharwi, *Al-nibras sharh sharh al-'aqa'id*, 235.

27. Tayyab, *Ijtihad aur taqlid*, 9.

28. Raymond Williams, *Marxism and Literature* (Oxford: Oxford University Press, 1986), 105.

29. Tayyab, *Ijtihad aur taqlid*, 7.

30. Muhammad Rashid Rida, *Tafsir al-qur'an al-hakim al-shahir bi tafsir al-manar*, 12 vols. (Beirut: Dar al-Ma'rifa, n.d.), 8:444–54.

31. Al-Hafiz 'Imad al-Din Abu al-Fida' Isma'il Ibn Kathir and Muhammad 'Ali al-Sabuni, ed., *Mukhtasar tafsir Ibn Kathir*, 3 vols. (Beirut: Dar al-Qur'an al-Karim, 1402/1981), 2:25.

32. See H. Allen Orr, "A Religion for Darwinians?" *New York Review of Books*, August 16, 2007, 33.

33. Tayyab, *Ijtihad aur taqlid*, 12.

34. Ibid. Also see Aristotle, "Metaphysica," in *The Basic Works of Aristotle*, ed. Richard McKeon (New York: Modern Library, 2001), 697, and Seyyed Hossein Nasr, *An Introduction to Islamic Cosmological Doctrines* (Bath: Thames & Hudson, 1978).

35. Tayyab, *Ijtihad aur taqlid*, 18.

36. Ibid., 13.

37. Ibid.

38. Ibid., 56.

39. Abu Hamid Muhammad b. Muhammad al-Ghazali, "Kitab al-tawhid wa al-tawakkul," in *Ihya 'ulum al-din* (Beirut: Dar al-Kutub al-'Ilmiyya, 1421/2001), 4:219.

40. Tayyab, *Ijtihad aur taqlid*, 25.

41. For similar views of the role of esoteric knowledge in moral thought, see Muhibb Allah Ibn'Abd al-Shakur, *Musallam al-thubut fi usul al-fiqh*, 2 vols. (Beirut: Dar al-Kutub al-'Ilmiya, 1403/1983), 2:401–2.

42. Tayyab, *Ijtihad aur taqlid*, 26.

43. Ibid., 27.

44. For more on the anagogic or *muttala'*, see Louis Massignon, *Essay on the Origins of the Technical Language of Islamic Mysticism*, trans. Benjamin Clark (Notre Dame, Ind.: University of Notre Dame Press, 1997), 95.

45. The reference to the panopticon is borrowed from Michel Foucault, who puts to use Jeremy Bentham's tower from where all inmates in a prison can be effectively viewed and monitored; see Michel Foucault, *Discipline and Punish: The Birth of the Prison*, trans. Alan Sheridan (New York: Vintage, 1995), 200.

46. Tayyab, *Ijtihad aur taqlid*, 27.

47. Taqi al-Din Ahmad Ibn Taymiyyah, *Majmu'a al-fatawa*, 2nd ed., ed. 'Amir al-Jazzar and Anwar al-Baz, 32 vols. (Mansura, Egypt: Dar al-Wafa', 1419/1998), 19:29.

48. Ibid.

49. Tayyab, *Ijtihad aur taqlid*, 60.

50. Ibid., 40.

51. Ibid.

53. See Adam Smith, *The Theory of Moral Sentiments*, ed. D. D. Rapahel and A. L. Macfie (Indianapolis: Liberty Fund / Oxford University Press, 1984), 184, esp. n. 7.

53. Tayyab, *Ijtihad aur taqlid*, 60.

54. Hayden White, foreword to *The Practice of Conceptual History: Timing History, Spacing Concepts*, by Reinhart Koselleck (Stanford, Calif.: Stanford University Press, 2002), x.

55. Ibid., xi.

56. Ibid.

57. Cited in Reinhart Koselleck, *Futures Past: On the Semantics of Historical Time*, trans. Keith Tribe (Cambridge, Mass.: MIT Press, 1985), xxii.

58. Tayyab, *Ijtihad aur taqlid*, 64.

59. See Mehr Afroz Murad, *Intellectual Modernism of Shibli Nu'mani* (Lahore: Institute of Islamic Culture, 1976); Muhammad Khalid Mas'ud, *Iqbal's Reconstruction of Ijtihad* (Lahore: Iqbal Academy Pakistan, 2003).

60. Bruce B. Lawrence, "Introduction to the 2005 Edition," in *The Muqaddimah*, ed. Franz Rosenthal and N. J. Dawood (Princeton, N.J.: Princeton University Press, 2005), viii.

61. Ibid.

62. miriam cooke and Bruce B. Lawrence, introduction to *Muslim Networks from Hajj to Hip Hop*, ed. miriam cooke and Bruce B. Lawrence (Chapel Hill: University of North Carolina Press, 2005), 23–25.

63. Bruce B. Lawrence, *Notes from a Distant Flute: The Extant Literature of Pre-Mughal Indian Sufism* (Tehran: Imperial Iranian Academy of Philosophy, 1978), 91.

⚜

Afterword

Competing Genealogies of Muslim Cosmopolitanism

BRUCE B. LAWRENCE

Among the transformative shifts in the American academy during the past quarter of a century is the emergence of Islam not as an outsider but as an insider to debates about religion and culture, history and society. No volume had signaled the beginning of this shift more emphatically than *Approaches to Islam in Religious Studies*, edited by Richard C. Martin, in 1985. Divided into five parts, it examines the categories of scripture and prophecy, ritual and community, religion and society, scholarship and interpretation before addressing the crucial issue pervading all categories and all inquiries into Islam: to what extent does Islam evoke a transcendent otherness beyond the skein of scholarly examination, and so faulted by some scholars, no matter how lofty the intent of the examiner, whether Muslim or non-Muslim? In divergent essays two Muslim authors pen the final thoughts for the Martin volume. Muhammad Abdul-Rauf projects his vision as a scholarly imam who wants to build bridges between Muslims and others. It is a matter of constant reflection and conscious commitment for him. But for Fazlur Rahman one cannot imagine the "other" without intensive awareness of one's own location. In effect Rahman takes up the delicate issue posed by another Chicago Islamicist, Marshall Hodgson: to what extent do scholars have to declare their precommitments, not just religious ones but also scholarly?

Hodgson's challenge has been etched in his magnum opus, still the gold standard of academic inquiry into Islam: *The Venture of Islam: Conscience and History in a World Civilization* (1974). The challenge is explicit, if complex, at once intimate and infinite: "only by a conscious and well-examined understanding of the limits of scholarly precommitments and of what is possible within and beyond them can we hope to take advantage of our immediate humaneness to reach any direct appreciation of major cultural traditions we do not share—and perhaps even of traditions we do share." In addressing the interplay of Islam and Christianity, Hodgson offers the danger of opposite valuations: "Muslims have historically seen Christianity as a truncated or perverted Islam," while many

Western scholars—whether Christian, Jewish, or secular—have viewed Islam "as a Christianity manqué."[1]

The study of Islam cannot escape recognition of the pitfalls of prejudgments. Added to them is the divergence of two variant approaches, roughly schematized as Orientalist, with a view to the past and defining texts, and social scientist, with a gaze on the present and understanding communities. Neither suffices to meet the challenge that the study of Islam poses to the human mind, and above all to the mind engaged in academic labor. For the self-aware and resilient scholar, Rahman etches the paramount need: to embrace "an inter-disciplinary approach, encompassing several disciplines with defined methods of research."[2]

In the decades since Rahman made his plea, the challenge to be aware of prejudgments has persisted, even as the number of disciplines that impinge on the study of Islam has mushroomed; yet there has not emerged a consensus on what are best practices for studying lived Islam. Disciplinary labor without defined methods of research, warns Rahman, "remains myopic, resulting in dangerous generalizations," while elaborate methods of research not grounded in disciplinary details "become abstract, in fact, chimerical."[3]

It is to conjoin method with description, or theory with practice, that the current volume of essays was conceived. It is titled *Rethinking Islamic Studies* because its editors, as also its contributors, pursue a related set of queries. Before revisiting their several arguments and insights, let me first note three of the most evident queries that inform their individual and collective labor. The first and broadest is about academic labor itself: *Are the roots of religious studies still so firmly situated within Judeo-Christian prejudgments, categories, and expectations that there is no room for Islam, or at least for an Islam recognizable to Muslims, in this same matrix?* However one addresses that query, one cannot escape the central preoccupation with boundary drawing, that is, the effort to find the core of what is deemed to be authentic and Muslim, which leads to the second question: *What are the distinctions between orthodox, normative, and "folk" Islam? Where is the center? What are the peripheries? Why and how does Shari'a recur in all discussions?* Ironically, those who ask these questions today are no longer best identified as either Muslim or non-Muslim, but rather as citizens of the world. They are like-minded utopians, contingently related to one space but virtually connected to multiple spaces. They spend much time—perhaps too much time—on the World Wide Web.

Hence one must ask a third question, not imaginable during the 1970s when Hodgson wrote or the mid-1980s when the Martin volume was published: *How do Muslim immigrants engage the media, and how has the communications revolution affected not just their outlook but also the way that Islam is approached in the academy via the public square, with impact in Asia and Africa as well as Euro-America?*

These queries begin with the notion that religion itself remains a topic that can be discretely framed within a discipline, and that it must be marked by recognizable, recurrent traits that generate a method of research at once accessible and acceptable to all. In what follows I want to argue that one can no longer make sense of religion by itself; instead it must be linked to kindred concepts, paramount among them "cosmopolitanism." Religion qua cosmopolitanism confers a special benefit for the study of Islam. It no longer focuses exclusively on Islam or Muslims. Instead of privileging or deriding one religious tradition vis-à-vis others, it shows the boundedness of religious communities within a larger complex of commercial exchange and social comity best etched by the term *oikoumene* or, in Hodgson's apt phrase, the "Afro-Eurasian oikoumene."[4]

Two books shackle method to the study of religion: Jonathan Z. Smith, *Imagining Religion* (1982), and Talal Asad, *Genealogies of Religion* (1993). Echoing their labor but also amplifying it is a third: Thomas A. Tweed, *Crossing and Dwelling: A Theory of Religion* (2006). What Smith, Asad, and especially Tweed foreground is the need to make choices about what are "constitutive disciplinary terms," and that quest relates to boundaries: how do specialized terms "constitute or mark the boundaries of a field of study?"[5] Each term, after all, carries within itself the echoes of other terms, reflecting what Smith calls "the unconscious syntactics of intellectual thought." Hence one needs to bridge syntactics with semantics, that is, "a self-conscious lexicon," and apply both to pragmatics in order to reach the holy grail of intellectual inquiry, namely, "an individual expression reflecting, both consciously and unconsciously, the conjunction of syntax and semantics within a personal and historical environment." If that sounds complex, it is, and Smith is unabashed in lauding complexity as part and parcel of the process of sustained self-reflection: what each individual expression will do, or should do, he argues, is to integrate "a complex notion of pattern (world view) and system (culture) with an equally complex notion of history (context)."[6]

Talal Asad would agree but with a variant emphasis. Too much scholarship, in his view, settles for semantics while ignoring syntactics (rival terms) and also pragmatics (the location, most often the privileged, postcolonial, residual Protestant location of the researcher). As a corrective Asad proposes looking at constitutive disciplinary terms over time and across cultures. He then proposes a revisionist approach that traces the genealogy of major terms, such as *belief, ritual, discipline,* and *orthodoxy.* He places them all in a public domain of inquiry, argument, and testability that another notable theorist, José Casanova, argues is the major defining characteristic of modern, secular inquiry. In sum we must welcome "the process whereby religion abandons its assigned place in the private sphere and enters the undifferentiated public sphere of civil society to take part in the ongoing process of contestation, discursive legitimation, and redrawing of the boundaries."[7]

One term above all others invites contestation, skirts legitimation, and yet seeks to redraw boundaries: *cosmopolitanism.* Though it appears in none of the above books, it looms larger and larger within contemporary studies of religion. Its prominence may be traced back at least to 1994 and to the Martha Nussbaum essay "Patriotism and Cosmopolitanism."[8] In that essay Nussbaum draws on a variety of Greek sources to argue that cosmopolitanism boosts universal citizenship, the rights of all over the privileges of few. It contrasts with patriotism, which can, and too easily does, become a narrowly parochial, self-serving, nationalist ideology. Lou Ruprecht lauds Nussbaum for her advocacy of "the Aristotelian way" but goes beyond her in describing as "primarily *cosmopolitan*" the "ethos implicit in meeting persons whom we do not yet know, especially when the meeting takes place in a culture, or a language, not our own." For Ruprecht "the fundamental ethos of the great Mediterranean city" is first and foremost *cosmopolitanism.*[9]

In *Postethnic America* (1995), Hollinger links cosmopolitanism to religion, making it the decisive term for analyzing the limits of both pluralism and multiculturalism. He invokes an elusive triad of competing constitutive terms: *pluralism, multiculturalism,* and *cosmopolitanism.* The later two rival each other for public acceptance and policy advocacy. Both relate to diversity but with variant emphases: while "multi-culturalism is rent by an increasingly acute but rarely acknowledged tension between cosmopolitan and pluralist programs for the defense of cultural diversity . . . , cosmopolitanism promotes multiple identities, emphasizes the dynamic and changing character of many groups, and is responsive to the potential for creating new cultural combinations."[10]

Since the tragedy of 9/11, cosmopolitanism has received less attention than negative categories, such as "fundamentalism" or "Islamism." Muslims and non-Muslims alike invoke such terms in response to the challenge of rethinking Islam, or reimagining an Islamic reformation, at the outset of the twenty-first century and in the shadow of the "war on terror." The major problem is dyadic logic: reasoning bracketed by, and limited to, sets of two that are not complementary but competitive, not providing an exit from, but a burrowing into, perpetual conflict. As soon as you frame a category, whether Islamism or fundamentalism or extremism, you ascribe to it a negative valence vis-à-vis positive categories, whether they be modernity, citizenship, pluralism, and/or human rights. The rhetorical dice are preloaded. The outcome will always redound against the first and in favor of the second. You engage in what the Sudanese activist and Emory legal scholar Abdullahi Ahmed An-Naʿim has called "false dichotomies and unnecessary dilemmas."[11]

Contrasts are always multiple and layered, not singular and exclusive. To avoid the premature judgments that false dichotomies invariably produce, one must first step outside the narrow choice of linguistic convention or popular usage; one must look instead at language in relation to both values and institutions.[12] Abdullahi An-Naʿim has done this powerfully in his most recent book. The state, he argues, neither can nor should have anything to do with Islam qua religion, since "the state is by definition a secular political institution, especially in the context of Islamic societies."[13] Islamic law or the Shariʿa should be pursued, but it should be by instruments and agents outside the governing group or party in power; to the extent that juridical norms pertain, they are channeled through civil society, asserted in public space, and sustained through civic reason. An-Naʿim pleads for a universal ban on the convergence of religion and politics in Muslim nation-states, yet all modern-day Muslim polities are premised on this convergence; what pertains is centralized authority exercised by the state on behalf of whichever form of Islam best suits its rulers. Not only does the state define Islam, each such definition competes with the definition of other Muslim nation-states, since the majority of Muslims, though sharing ideals of collective solidarity, continue to live within borders and boundaries marked by surveillance and censorship that pit one Muslim nation-state against another.

And so the issue is not so much external as internal. There may be an abstract canvas of Islam or Islamism vs. the West or modernity, but what matters, both practically and analytically, are the local, the immediate, and the contingent aspects of each polity and society that determine its modus vivendi within the current world order.

The essays of this volume have taken up precisely the challenge to redefine Islam apart from both fundamentalists/Islamists and their statist/nationalist opponents. Collectively they try to project a larger, cosmopolitan canopy for Islam beyond the iterations, at once local and ideological, of several Muslim actors. With these central themes of the volume in mind, I will now discuss how they are integral to each part and each essay of *Rethinking Islamic Studies*.

Part 1

Part 1 attempts to rethink modernity, especially modern intellectual discourse, from Islamic perspectives. The authors share a concern with fundamentalism; they view it instrumentally, as a template for gauging one dimension of contemporary Muslim thought and experience.

Vincent Cornell is concerned to identify and curtail Muslim exceptionalism. Pleas for Muslim exceptionalism, in his view, cloud a higher vision of universal comity; they ill serve Muslims and non-Muslims alike. To buttress his case, Cornell summons a broad, if disparate, quorum of political commentators, from John Locke and Thomas Jefferson to Sayyid Qutb and Sherman Jackson. Especially the perspective of Jackson exemplifies for Cornell what is most pervasive and dangerous about Shariʿa fundamentalism: it becomes a reflex preserving but also highlighting Muslims as not quite Americans. They aspire to American citizenry yet pledge allegiance to the Shariʿa above the U.S. Constitution. "By not 'conferring upon [the Constitution] the status of law (or even a source of law) that is binding on the Muslim moral/religious conscience on a par with the *shariʿah*, [Jackson] depicts the American Muslim community as a de facto *milla*[14] with its own religiously based laws."

Cornell contrasts Jackson's stance with that of another American Muslim leader, Imam Feisal Abdul Rauf.[15] The United States is already a Shariʿa-compliant state, argues Abdul Rauf, since the values of the Declaration of Independence are equivalent to those of Islamic law. In effect while "Jackson seeks a modus vivendi between the Shariʿa and the U.S. Constitution, . . . Abdul Rauf seeks what John Rawls called an 'overlapping consensus' of political rights and values." Implicit in Cornell's comparison/contrast is both an affirmation of Islamic precedence and a preference for political liberalism, itself the carrier of cosmopolitan values. While "traditional Islamic political theory could only tolerate difference[,] it could not incorporate a theory of difference into its conception of justice and rights." In other words it could not be fully and persuasively cosmopolitan.

In a cosmopolitan order, justice and rights must be articulated in the contemporary public square. They must be subjected to what Rawls calls public reason, and Abdullahi An-Naʿim civic reason. That very invocation of reason, in turn, depends on a consensus or appeal to a higher authority, whether it be the Constitution or the Islamic Shariʿa. And the litmus test for the proper exercise of public reason, with the adequate provision of justice and rights, becomes the status of minorities. How are minorities defined? How are they protected, individually and collectively? These questions, though not answered by Cornell, are raised in a compelling manner by his flexible, multitiered inquiry into the foundational elements of the epistemological crisis of Islam.

For Katherine Ewing, too, the status of minorities looms large. How do we make sense of public/civic reason, she asks, within the limits of Western rationality but also with reference to the challenge that minorities pose to modern democracies? Her key term is not *pluralist*, as with Cornell, or *progressive*, as with Omid Safi (see below), but rather *cosmopolitan*. In this choice she is influenced by Kwame Anthony Appiah, who issued a manifesto for cosmopolitanism in 2006, staging "his vision of a harmonious, globalized social order based on pluralism and tolerance" as the both antithesis and the antidote to neofundamentalists.[16] Ewing selects a diasporic Turkish Islamic organization as the test case for exploring how one might expand the meaning of modern, a.k.a cosmopolitan, subjectivity to include her Turkish Islamic subjects, even though the latter do not fit the familiar cultural labels of "nation" and "citizenry" common to Western theorists.

Ewing reaches for a different, more defensible notion of universals and universalism. Human rights, freedom, and democracy—all are claimed as values that the modern German state arrogates to itself both to define and to defend, to legislate and to enforce. Her Turkish Islamic subjects retain practices of modest dress for women and abstinence from alcohol and pork that differ from their non-Muslim neighbors in modern-day Germany. They also have similar differences with their former compatriots, Turkish secularists, over the same issues. Yet diasporic Turkish Muslim residents of Germany affirm public debate, support the welfare of children and women and protection of their rights, advocate freedom of worship, uphold the right not only to vote but also to buy and sell, build and trade in competitive markets—in short they are pluralist libertarians and capitalist democrats with one difference, a Muslim/Turkish difference that favors private practices and codes for public dress sanctioned by Islam. Trying to understand the very concept of God "in a fully modern way," Ewing hopes that "people who have been labeled fundamentalist may be a site for new, as yet unimagined visions of a future that transcends today's dichotomies and even our historically contingent modernism." In other words they can embody, even as they project, cosmopolitan values.

Yet what about those societies that are linked not to Turkish but to Iranian origins, perspectives, and opportunities as well as quandaries? Omid Safi provides several insights. Above all he raises the issue of women's voices as a primary step for descriptive balance and analytic yield. Women are absent from Cornell, though presumably are implicit in his arguments, to wit, that gender rights, like minority rights, would be the hallmark of public/civic reason properly exercised. They are occluded in Ewing, because her Muslim women had their choices mediated through male family members. Safi is intent to demonstrate that Islamic reform Iranian-style, unlike its Euro-American profile in Cornell's essay or its Turkish parallel in Ewing's essay, includes women not just as subjects but also as voices. Men, of course, dominate in the public square of Iran as elsewhere. There is the former Iranian president Mohammad Khatami, the renowned philosophical giant Abdalkarim Soroush, and more recent figures such as Mohsen Kadivar, Mujtahid Shabestari, Hasem Aghajari, and Akbar Ganji. They are all men, many of them related to the clerical establishment, albeit at odds with its prevalent ideology. Yet there are also notable, influential women such as the conservative women's rights advocate Mehrangiz Kar, her liberal counterpart, Ziba Mir-Hosseini, and, of course, the best-known Iranian woman reformer, the 2003 Noble Peace Prize laureate, Shirin Ebadi. Better than any other observer of the current Iranian intellectual scene—itself a dizzying tapestry of opinions and perspectives, ideologies and agendas—Safi has positioned Ebadi as a reformer who eschews the language of reform. "Whereas Soroush, Shabestari, and Kadivar [her male counterparts] operate in familiar Islamic discourses (philosophy, theology, and law, respectively), Ebadi operates more fluidly outside," notes Safi, so much so that "it remains to be seen *what legacy her work will have for religious reform, as is indeed the case for all the Iranian reformers.*"

I have italicized the last phrase of Safi's lucid exposé of Ebadi because it raises the question that pervades all the other essays in this volume: beyond correcting narrowly dyadic, male-dominant, logocentric interpretations of Islam, interpretations that privilege top-down Muslim norms and values over the lived, everyday experience of Afro-Asian as well as Euro-American Muslims, where is the there there? Where do we find real change in the self-perception and the practice of Muslims? Iranian reformers have signaled some accommodation to women's rights, but it is also in cyberspace that we begin to see references to women's rights, including their rights to lead prayer in public worship. No less an "authority" than Wikipedia has documented this change. Cross-pollination—within Islamic circles as well as between Muslims and non-Muslims—has to be measured on the World Wide Web and through the formation of new Muslim networks. It is a fragile, new labor. It is at once contingent and reversible, yet it circulates in public space and empowers, even as it emboldens, minorities. It is, in short, the leading edge of a new form of Muslim cosmopolitanism. Safi ends his essay with the plea for an Iranian derived cross-pollination within the Muslim arc, one that works because Iranian intellectuals "are fluent in English, German, and French in addition to the expected Arabic. One can only hope," he adds, "that at least some portion of the global Muslim reform audience will learn Persian to engage their imaginative and daring project."

Part of what makes "our historically contingent modernism" contingent, according to Kevin Reinhart, is Arabocentrism. It isn't merely that Arabs have been thrust onto center stage due to the vagaries of the contemporary market, with its cyclical yet ever-expanding demand for energy resources that derive from Middle East / majority-Muslim locations. It is rather that Arabs are now reclaiming a notion of the pure Islamic past, one measured solely by the criterion of Arab authenticity. Yet if Reinhart's analysis is correct, not only will there be few Arabophones, or Anglo- or Franco- or Deutschophones, who venture to learn Persian, but the accent on Arabic will be increasingly theological as well as cultural, driving a deeper wedge between Salafi Arabophones and the rest of the Muslim community worldwide.

Reinhart stages his argument with a set of escalating assumptions that appear commonsensical to his Arab triumphalist subjects: (1) native Arabic speakers who are Muslim have prestige over all other, non-Arabic-speaking Muslims; (2) the original Arabic Qur'an has a transparent, singular, and incontestable meaning; (3) "leading advocates of this putatively naive reading of the Qur'an have been the adherents of the movement called Salafiyyah"; (4) the need to understand Salafiyyah or Salafism as a two-pronged movement, one that was initially characterized by a modernizing liberalism but has now been replaced by a scripturalist, purist, and literalist ethos, identified first with Arab nationalism and more recently with the global jihadi movement.

The consistent thread in all phases of the Salafi movement is an unreconstructed Arabism, promoting Arabs as central to all major historical developments in the Muslim world and also the Qur'an as the centerpiece of Arab genius. The flip side of foregrounding the Qur'an as an Arabic document is to downgrade all non-Arabic religious scholarship, whether Muslim or non-Muslim. "Scholarship not produced in Arabic, whether Islamic or non-Islamic, cannot be authentic, cannot be significant," observes Reinhart, with more than a touch of sarcasm, "because it lacks the single qualifying characteristic of important religious scholarship," namely, Arabic, canonical Arabic, classical Arabic. The consequence of brute Arabism, as Reinhart goes on to note, is a lack of engagement not just with the rich, diverse complexity of the Islamic past but also with other intra-Muslim perspectives in the contemporary period. In short it is anticosmopolitan rather than hypercosmopolitan, as was the vision of Islamic civilization proposed by the fourteenth-century Muslim historian and social theorist Ibn Khaldun. If there is a thinness and hollow echo to much contemporary Arabic Islamic scholarship, it is made all the more notable, and regrettable, because, as Reinhart comments, what "one reads on the Web from Pakistani journals or Indonesian sources, and certainly a good deal of (often critical) religious thought from Iran as well as from Turkey, has a degree of subtlety and engagement. This simply seems not to be found in Arabic Islamic-world discussions of Islam." It is non-Arabs, in his view, who herald a cosmopolitan future for the Muslim world as a whole.

What then is the level of discourse in American Islam? How is Islam understood and practiced by Muslims in the continental United States? Are they too under the shadow of Arabocentrism, or do they partake of a latent, and subtly emergent, Muslim cosmopolitanism? They are incipient cosmopolitans, according to Jamillah Karim. Her essay is sharply attuned to the gender, racial, and locational markings that affect her Muslim subjects who are neither Arab nor Middle Eastern. She addresses the challenges of citizenship that beset urban African American Muslim women in ways that test their spiritual bonding with urban South Asian Muslim women. Women's mosque attendance, women's dress, women's work—all relate to the underlying resistance of African American Muslim women to immigrant norms, or what one called "cultural Islam or hearsay Islam." Far from privileging Arabic as the necessary instrument for Islamic knowledge, they perceive the Sunna, or example of the Prophet Muhammad, as their criterion of authenticity. African American Muslim women critique their South Asian sisters to the extent that the latter seem to conform—in dress code, mosque prayer, and general deportment—to Arab, specifically Saudi, norms, but at the same time they welcome, as an extension of their own grounding in black feminist consciousness, the opportunity for work choice, which at least some South Asian Muslim women seem to enjoy, that is whether to have day-time public jobs or to remain at home as mothers and caregivers.

The consistent, overriding issue for Karim's subjects is recognition of difference and change as simultaneous, double-edged aspects of American Muslim identity. While Sherman Jackson had identified two major cultural trajectories for American Islam, to wit, *Black Religion* and *Immigrant Islam*, both marked in the subtitle of his book, these women, unlike their male counterparts, are not concerned with the issue that had occupied Jackson: compliance or noncompliance with the Shariʿa and/or constitutional norms.[17] India, in cultural norms, expectations, and practices, is as remote from Arabia as it is from Africa. Women are cultural custodians, and so Karim's non-Arab subjects perceive transnational Muslim formations as constantly in flux: immigrants and indigenous Muslim women learn from each other, respect each other, disagree with each other, and at the same time provide a way forward for themselves and their families in twenty-first-century urban America. They project themselves as patriotic Americans who are also Muslim cosmopolitans.

Part 2

Part 2 broaches big ideas, tracing their emergence, their consequence, and also their limits. Its authors are self-conscious about their methodological assumptions and also about the limits of their academic labor within and beyond the fold of Islamic studies.

How does empirical analysis illumine the social origins of Islamist movements? That is the big question that motivates the survey by Charles Kurzman and Ijlal Naqvi. There are three categories of Islamists whom they identify in trying to answer their central query, which is also the title of their essay: "Who are the Islamists?" The three categories of Islamists are leaders, activists, and supporters.[18] To understand and evaluate these groups, Kurzman and Naqvi rely on a wide range of social scientific data, especially but not solely the European and World Values Surveys. Hence we find that the question that occupied Cornell recurs here; yet it is traced with reference not to intellectual or epistemological assertions but rather to survey data. Instead of asking whether liberal democratic or Islam-specific norms prevail, one should ask: who believes in implementing only the laws of the Shariʿa or who supports democracy? The two options were not seen as contradictory by the respondents since the percentage of agreement on adherence to the Shariʿa in seven majority-Muslim nations ranged from as low as 44 percent in Bangladesh to 80 percent in Egypt, while in these same seven countries 79 percent of all those surveyed also supported democracy!

In one of my early publications, *Defenders of God* (1989), I had challenged the value of social scientific labor, especially the lack of self-awareness of limits, that is, self-criticism. Kurzman rises to the challenge. He notes, in conclusion, that sociologists do admit to self-criticism, and in his case he admits to the short-comings of "the objectivist approach to the study of Islam." Lacking a single set of socioeconomic determinants of Islamism, he calls for "further humanistic research into the self-understandings of Islamists—so long as the findings of this research are subjected to the checks and balances of all available evidence, including 'hard' data." While applauding the intent of this conclusion, one must never cease to try to identify what is "hard" about the "hard" data found through surveys. I continue to affirm, with Kurzman, that in-depth interviews are a supe-rior mechanism for culling "hard" data. Consider the in-depth interviews of Saad Eddin Ibrahim into Egyptian Islamist groups, results first published in 1980 and then, fifteen years later, in 1995. Kurzman has done a better job than any other social scientist in framing, exploring, and trying to expand the data base provided by Ibrahim. "To what extent are Ibrahim's foundational studies," asks Kurzman, "confirmed by other research on the social bases of Islamist activism?" He explores a range of data to attempt to answer that query, specifi-cally, "biographical encyclopedia entries, quantitative case studies, and survey data." Yet his rigorous, extensive research produces a disappointing result: "The short answer to the question in our paper's title, 'Who are the Islamists?,' is any-body. We find no strong demographic predictors of Islamist leadership, activism, or sympathy."

As disheartening as is that outcome, it provides a cautionary tale for those who rely too narrowly on social scientific methods or data when examining con-temporary Islam. It is a tale yet to be told in Pakistan, at least in the major gov-ernment ministries. Looking at relationships of center-periphery in South Asia, David Gilmartin compares them with those in the late Roman Empire and notes that one of the common features in both societies was the role of the holy man or saint. The saint was said to be an exemplar, but beyond the narration and memory of his life was the embodiment of his power—his transcendent or charismatic power—in the place of his burial. Saints' tombs, as much as their saintly denizens, come to project the tensions of political power, with local authority residing in the periphery yet claimed by those who represent the cen-ter. This tug-of-war continued under British colonial rule in India. Sufis, or Mus-lim saints, became contested. The British lauded the memory of the dead saint more than the activities of his living successors. Those who opposed the British were drawn to the local sources of power that Sufi exemplars represented, so much so that it was not the *ulama* but Sufis who helped, as Gilmartin states, in "mobilizing the support necessary in the elections of 1946 to give victory to the Muslim League and make the creation of Pakistan a reality."

This implication of Sufi exemplars and Sufi shrine custodians in the Pakistan nationalist project did not end with independence in 1948. It continues today.

One of its most interesting sidelights, explored here for the first time by Gil-martin, is the challenge of relating Sufism to Pakistani national identity. Two branches of the central government have devised competing strategies for co-opting the power of local Sufis and their shrines for the Pakistani state. Their divergence is of interest, but of even greater interest is the heavy reliance of one branch—the Institute of Folk Heritage (IFH)—in their research methodology on the universal language of social science. The traditions of folk studies were not indigenous to the Mughal Empire or Islamic civilization; instead, like social science itself, they had deep roots in European nationalism and were adapted to the Pakistani nationalist project. In dealing with popular customs at a major Pakistani shrine—one that produced malformed children as part of the saint's "legacy"—IFH researchers relied on social "scientific" explanations to give meaning to such customs as part of the underlying, universal fabric of folk practices in Pakistan.

Is the science therefore prejudicial, its results contaminated, and its further use to be restricted? No, argues Gilmartin; it is part of the effort of this branch of the Pakistani state to be recognizably modern, which is to be scientific, em-bracing popular culture but reimagining its elements through the prism of social science. In sum they try to use social science both to underscore their own authority and to promote a form of Muslim cosmopolitanism. The outcome of this process continues to evolve, but always under the supervision, and with the intervention, of the state. Can bad science lead to good politics and cosmopol-itan glimmerings, at least in the short run? This might be the takeaway message from Gilmartin's forensic inquiry into the contingency and creation of popular culture in modern-day Pakistan.

Yet it is the accent on popular culture from his essay that provides the vital link to the essay, "Formations of Orthodoxy: Authority, Power, and Networks in Muslim Societies," by Richard C. Martin and Abbas Barzegar. The key term here is *orthodoxy*, or the institutions and practices deemed to be orthodox by given groups, in this case within the expansive period of Islamic history. The big idea is also the crucial argument, to wit, how do popular religious ideas and movements become seedbeds fostering later notions of orthodoxy?

The general portrait of orthodox-heterodox in Islam has been etched by Hamid Dabashi: "'Orthodox' and 'heterodox' are polemical, not hermeneutic terms; they conceal a web of intricate relationships—social and doctrinal. . . . It is the political success of a given interpretative reading that renders a religious position 'orthodox.' 'Heresies' and 'heterodoxies' are partially defeated 'ortho-doxies'; and all these are concealing terms."[19] Yet Dabashi does not provide a social explanation for the emergence of competing "orthodoxies," and it is fit-ting in the part of this volume dedicated to rethinking religion in both social scientific and humanistic perspectives that Martin and Barzegar have tried to do just that. Like Gilmartin they find value in comparing what happened in Islamic civilization with the profile of the Roman Empire.[20] In both cases "popular religious movements can be the source of orthodoxy in religion and are not necessarily the result of corruption of and straying from orthodoxy."

Martin, along with Barzegar, then moves in two directions to explore and defend this thesis. On the one hand, he examines the classic instance of a war over dogma within Islamic circles. It occurred in the ninth and tenth centuries. It was inspired by the rational speculation that the Muʿtazilites spearheaded and led to the theory that the Qurʾan was in fact "created," rather than inspired as revelation, then written down by scribes who heard the utterances of the Prophet Muhammad, which were "exactly" the words of God. The debate over the created Qurʾan mirrored a social problem: how to accommodate the masses, those who are the vulgar common folk, to the demands of abstract logical thought—whether framed as philosophy or theology—only capable of comprehension by the educated, the elite? Again with reference to Latin Christendom, that question suggests too strict a notion of class warfare and conceals the more likely explanation: "that orthodox religion at any given moment in history is the result of the historical evolution of competing popular religious ideas and practices." In other words the elite and the masses are not walled off from each other; they constantly interact, and it may often be that popular religious ideas come from the margins rather than the center and that orthodoxy is commingled with heresy, even as both are subject to the contingencies of social change and political power.

This thesis is alternatively illustrated not from premodern, tenth-century Islam but from modern-day, late-twentieth- and now twenty-first-century Islamic sources. Is it not also the case that there is a spectrum of possibilities that link margins to center, popular to official notions of religion, and does not this spectrum embrace Muslim experiences of globalization, as also "the new forms of religious expression appearing in cyber-Islam and in transnational Islamic social movements"? Without being New Age triumphalists, Martin and Barzegar go so far as to postulate Muslim networks as a framework for newly emergent formations of "orthodox" Islam. They espy hopeful signs for this social scientific chrysalis in the lapidary synthesis of world history produced by two generations of McNeills,[21] as well as in the collaborative publications that have marked labor on Muslim networks in the Research Triangle Park of North Carolina partnering with Emory University in Atlanta. Martin and Barzegar conclude that of all the structures persistent over time that define Islam, networks loom large: "An important dimension of the larger context of Islamic history has been the many educational, social, and economic networks that have made adaptation to the Internet a natural move, even for the most traditional Muslim groups and movements." The information age portends a new era for Muslim cosmopolitanism: a virtual dream, it might yet become a sociopolitical reality.

Part 2 ends, however, on a note of demurral from social scientific or even humanistic–social scientific plateaus of insight, synergy, and new vision. "Caught between Enlightenment and Romanticism: On the Complex Relation of Religions, Ethnic, and Civic Identity in a Modern 'Museum Culture'" is important for its suggestive, almost playful intervention in the debate between social scientists and humanists. The nature of labor, argues Louis Ruprecht, is much less important than the outcome of the debate in part 1, between pluralist, inclusive, and cosmopolitan moderns on the one hand and culture-specific, exclusive wannabe moderns on the other. Ruprecht embraces the Hodgsonian trajectory of world history, moving from Old World to New not through religious caricatures but with an accent on the critical roles of language and culture over time. Correctly Ruprecht perceives Hodgson to be unhinging the standard "orthodox" formulation of world history. Hodgson devotes volume 1 of *The Venture of Islam* to the formative period or "the Ancients," volume 3 to the present period or "the Moderns," but in between he sees the nexus joining Ancients to Moderns as the work of multiple languages and cultures that collectively stage what becomes Islamic, or Islamicate, civilization. The middle period is not "medieval" but transitional: to see the modern only in terms of technological or material concerns is to ignore the genius, as also the courage, of those individuals who embraced their own autonomy yet always on behalf of the collective good. For cosmopolitanism to prevail, there must be not only a social framework but also individuals who inherit, then expand, premodern ideals for their generation.

Ruprecht, with David Hollinger, embraces the cosmopolitan ideal. Yet he is skeptical about the prospect of its near-term realization. The "many "—whether groups, languages, or cultures—cannot be labeled as multicultural; they must also be marshaled toward some common goal, a new vision of the collective good, one even beyond Hodgson's imagining. That utopian—albeit never Romantic—future is the cosmos itself, and the people who strive for it, populate it, and even die for it are cosmopolitans. How then do these cosmopolitans relate to religious networks? By moving beyond what Ruprecht terms "that eminently Romantic conception—the modern nation-state, as defined by a national identity grounded in an ethnic history"—but also by moving beyond what he then terms "that preeminently Enlightenment body of internationalism, the United Nations." Cosmopolitans, in effect, are defined by what they leave behind: first the nation-state, and then the super body of states, that is, all structures that mask myriad self-interests even while pretending to provide a global framework on behalf of the common good.

What lies ahead? Could there be a cosmopolitan world citizenship? Perhaps, but that vision lies beyond the myopic fantasia conjured by and through modern museums. Cosmopolitans honor no showcases, rejecting them all as reflective of territorial or spatial or culture-specific interests. Cosmopolitans are neither local nor global but both simultaneously; one presumes they invoke the arc of "civic reason," such as advocated by Rawls and An-Naʿim, though the instruments for affecting such a citizenship are omitted from Ruprecht's otherwise evocative essay.

Part 3

If Part 3 is about pivotal performers, spiritual élans, literary dalliance, and juridical norms, it also reinforces the notion of cosmopolitan identity as inflected in several Asian Muslim settings. Its authors are unabashed in charting new paths to consider the evidence of the past and to project bold trajectories for the future.

Tony Stewart's lead essay in part 3 is boldly revisionist. He sees biography as collective urgings writ large. "It may not be the individual as much as the model of piety itself that takes hold," he argues. He scans genres, their creation, their perpetuation, and also their transformation. He analyzes both the charismatic subject, as gleaned from sacred biography, and the ostensible subject, as projected in hagiography. Above all he concerns himself with the dialectical nature of biographical images generated through Sufi hagiography. Chief among South Asian cases are the Chishtiya in particular, and central to the Chishtiya is the figure of Shaykh Nizam al-Din Badaʾuni, a.k.a. Shaykh Nizam al-Din Awliya (d. 1325). Stewart is intent to lay bare the process of biographical writing. Memory is the crucial vehicle for adducing a model of piety, highlighting selected virtues and actions deemed of value to the individual or community, at a given moment in time. It is the temporality, or presentist motives, of biographical and hagiographical authors that Stewart strives to underscore. The most "generalizable feature of all Islamic religious hagiography," in his view, is the cumulative layering of interests and perspectives that shape, then reshape first the biography of the Prophet Muhammad and then the biographies of subsequent heroes, including those spiritual heroes known as Sufi masters or *mashaʾikh*. The lines between religion and politics become blurred since "intentionally or not, religious biographies are political. They are political because the genre itself is not designed to reflect the ruminations of the author for his private consumption, but for community." In other words Stewart defines as political whatever is produced for a broad, public audience, whether a reading or, in the case of much Sufi literature, a listening public.

Yet this process is further complicated by the distinction between major and minor saints. How are they so identified? Stewart downplays the impact of the shrine. (Only on the final page does he acknowledge that "the shrine, of course, . . . serves as the physical anchor for this memory, the focal point of his [the saint's] continuing physical presence, the basis for the community to perpetuate the image.") Instead he defines a process where later saints are related to earlier exemplars in a dialectical rather than a linear fashion. They combine both emphasis on a preexisting ideal and also creation, albeit disguised, of new images of piety. Especially in South Asian Sufism, the observer confronts a spectrum of biographical/hagiographical material, from observational literature (*malfuzat* and *tazkirat*), letters of instruction written by the saint (*maktubat*), and treatises for spiritual guidance (*isharat*). There is no objective core of data against which one can separate the "true" from the spurious, but rather a ebb and flow between the historical life (more or less accurate) and the religious ideal (always open to reinterpretation). It is here that one can, and should, make a distinction between hagiography and biography. In promoting a particular religious ideal, "hagiography often departs dramatically from other forms of biography because of the overt function of hagiography to establish religious doctrine. Where biography may be ideologically driven, ideology is not automatically the primary objective." Citing numerous examples of this process, Stewart then concludes that "the subject of Sufi hagiography subtly shifts over time, from the individual who embodies a religious ideal to the religious ideal embodied by, or made to embody, the individual." It is here that community aspirations play a major role, accenting some pious subjects over others, giving them a historical role as major successors or even founders of a particular Sufi brotherhood.

Stewart's deep analysis of literary sources, genres, and motives is admirable. It advances our understanding of a process too often occluded or dichotomized by less theoretically adroit scholars. What needs to be added, however, is the impact of nonliterary sources, such as the tomb cult and political patrons identifying with that cult. Sometimes cultic activities and liminal associations are little more than spurious—that is, apocryphal or at least unverifiable—literary sources that reimagine, and also exaggerate, both the tomb cult and its political patronage. Yet it is this other, seldom examined feature of institutional Sufism in general and the Chishti tomb cult of Shaykh Nizam al-Din Awliya in Delhi that forms the basis for Scott Kugle's essay.

"Dancing with Khusro: Gender Ambiguities and Poetic Performance in a Delhi *Dargah*" acknowledges that contemporary critical theory must be brought to bear on the understanding of these ancient shrines and their lofty denizens. Just as Stewart foregrounded a range of literary critics (Dilthey, Bakhtin, and White) to examine the dialectic of Sufi hagiography, so Kugle resorts to scholarship on Muslim women (Jeffery, Shaikh, and cooke) and also on gender identity (Herdt, Seidler and MacInnes) to understand (a) how women are constituted as different from men, yet (b) how both "women and men are contingent, with the boundary between them flexible, the roles situation specific, culturally relative, and constantly under renegotiation."

The move to define male-female, men-women in a broader, more nuanced frame of analytic reference is itself valuable, but it becomes merely the first step toward a powerful new hermeneutic that Kugle advances for the bracketing of

high culture (literature, theology, philosophy) with popular culture (folk performances, everyday lyrics, musical repertoires), and the use of both to understand the subject of his essay, Amir Khusro. If Ruprecht invokes an image of the
cosmopolitan world citizen as an antimuseum globalist, Kugle projects Khusro
as a microcosm of all that cosmopolitanism could ever be. Khusro was at once
a court poet, paid to write and perform by the sultan, and a Sufi devotee, committed to respect and obey his spiritual master above all others, including the
sultan. It is in that dual, conflictive loyalty that Khusro emerges as a truly liminal figure in the history of premodern Muslim India, especially during the high
period of the Delhi Sultanate, itself the major polity and staging ground for
what later became Mughal India, the regional model for medieval cosmopolitanism writ large.

To uncover and project Khusro in a fuller light, Kugle resorts to *qawwali*, a
form of musical improvisation at Sufi saint tombs or *dargahs*, in this case the
dargah of Shaykh Nizam al-Din. The same Nizam al-Din who figures promi-
nently in Stewart's essay becomes here not the subject but the object of Khusro's
frolicsome verse. Their relationship tests several boundaries, beyond the obvious
one of religion and politics, between the apolitical *shaykh* and the hyperpolitical
sultan. Instead, as Kugle argues, the performance of Khusro at the *dargah* of
Nizam al-Din also reveals how "rituals at the *khanqah* [*dargah*] help devotees,
mainly adult men, to suspend (or shed) the values of autonomy, independence,
mastery, and assertiveness . . . , giving them space to perform alternate values of
dependence, reciprocity, servitude, and humble deference." In short real men
can also act like women, at least within the confines of the Sufi *khanqah/dargah*.

But even this flirtation with what Kugle calls "masculine ambiguities and contact with the sacred" does not exhaust the multiple roles that Khusro plays, or
performs, at the shrine of Nizam al-Din. On the one hand, he comports with
an ideal of devotion that is announced and repeated ad infinitum in Sufi hagiography, to wit, male Sufis look upon other men, chiefly men of a different class,
with erotic desire. And so are we to presume that Khusro and Nizam al-Din,
himself a celibate or unmarried saint, shared more than spiritual camaraderie,
bolstered by musical zest and lyrical indulgence? Kugle, like Khusro, dances on
the edge of respectability or at least conventional explanations of male-male intimacy. Instead of proposing a love that cannot speak its name between the Sufi
master and the court poet, Kugle cites a similar love between Khusro and his
contemporary, who was also his rival both in the court and in the *dargah*, Amir
Hasan Sijzi. Quoting a sixteen-century Iranian Sufi poet, Hussayn Gazargahi,
who openly argued that "all great male Sufis had male lovers and that this was
the cause of their greatness," Kugle asserts that the "apocryphal" narrative attributed to Khusro by Gazargahi "is vivid and does resonate with many of Khusro's
poems, even if it takes them literally, even miraculously."

At the same time that his reading of verses and narratives constructed around verses are exploratory, even suggestive, Kugle is careful to pull back from making factual claims. Instead he wants to make clear that ambiguity—about status and gender, place and faith—are all relative to the perspective of the performer and also the audience. The deepest of all ambiguities surrounds the divine beloved: Is he or she the object or the subject of desire, or both? Does not the cultus of Sufi shrines, including and especially that of Nizam al-Din in Delhi, honor that ambiguity more fully than the buttoned-down, flattened metaphysic of fundamentalist opponents of Sufi dalliance? Kugle answers in the affirmative. He argues that performance is an undervalued, yet critically central, feature of Sufi vitality, that it includes a complex relationship between individual and social audience where both "are caught up in a mutually reinforcing interaction of background assumptions, asserted roles, and articulated interpretations that allow for variation, reversal, and even inversion of expected norms." At the same time, Kugle acknowledges, with more than a twinge of sadness, the disappearance of the kind of premodern Islamic social order that made possible these performances, these outcomes, and these dazzling narratives of ambiguity, intrigue, and ecstasy. Not only is Persian literature marginalized, but also Sufi communities, the custodians and transmitters of this legacy in both its high and popular forms, "no longer occupy a central position in the society, not even in the Muslim minority, let alone in the wider pluralistic democracy that is the new nation of India." Cosmoplitanism, to survive, needs institutional structures, an expanded public space, without which local tastes, restrictive norms, and punitive codes can, and will, prevail.

What has replaced that lost cosmopolitan world is an effort to come to terms with the Shariʿa or Islamic juridical comportment as the heart and soul of the Indo-Persian tradition in modern South Asia. That is the story taken up by Ebrahim Moosa in the third essay of part 3, "History and Normativity in Traditional Indian Muslim Thought: Reading Shariʿa in the Hermeneutics of Qari Muhammad Tayyab." There are few key terms more value laden than *ijtihad*, and those who resort to it often link it to reformist logic but without investigating its juridical, or as Hodgson would say, its Shariʿa-minded undercurrent. Jurists are also moralists, or at least moral authorities, and what Moosa does is to uncover and lay bare how *ijtihad*, like its dyadic opposite, *taqlid*, are both invested with meanings that come from a variety of perspectives—traditionalist, modernist, revivalist, and maximalist—yet none of them exhaust the surfeit of meaning intrinsic to the juridical-moral discourse that is embedded within the twin categories of *ijtihad* and *taqlid*. Moosa's subject is a major North Indian juridical authority, Qari Muhammad Tayyab, himself the leader of the major madrassa, or Muslim seminary, in Uttar Pradesh, Dar al-ʿUlum at Deoband. Moosa provides a dazzling exposé of the several complex levels of reasoning in one tract by Qari

Muhammad. Titled *Ijtihad aur taqlid*, it reveals how Indian scholars differentiated not only their jurisprudence but also their moral philosophy from that of
their Arab contemporaries and coreligionists as well as the Indian followers of
these same Arab revivalists (the Ahl-i Hadith).

The positive outcome of this debate for the kernel of Muslim authenticity in
a colonially defined political era was to embrace both *ijtihad* and *taqlid;* hence
the title of *Ijtihad aur taqlid* presents not a choice but a synergy, one reflex with
its alternate, and it is their alteration and continuous interaction that can and
does produce an inherent dynamism. Tayyab advocated not merely a juridical
but a sociopolitical ideal. The larger purpose of the Shariʿa was to embrace both
independent reasoning and reliance on canonical authority for the public good.
"In order to be effective," explains Moosa, "both ideas had to be activated within
an ordered realm (*nizam*), irrespective of whether such an order was of a religious or secular nature. The *character* of the order was more important than its
form: it should neither be repressive and static, in Tayyab's view, nor be so fragmented and dispersed as to be ineffective." Far from being a premodern perception of language and authority, Tayyab's theory, which also reflected his
ideological precommitments, echoes Hayden White's distinction between natural time and historical time, even as it resonates with Herder's notion of multiple times coexisting at one moment. (Ernst Bloch refers to this same phenomenon
as the contemporaneity of the noncontemporaneous.)[22]

Moosa concludes this creative vignette of one of the most seminal yet understudied figures of the Deoband movement by noting that it was Tayyab's social
imaginary that set him apart from others. He projected the extraordinary habitus of the jurist-theologian, who was also the moral compass for his extended
community, yet even he may not have been prepared for the new echoes of
authority that the information revolution has unleashed. "While it is difficult to
pronounce what the impact of e-*ijtihad* will be," concludes Moosa, "one can
with some certainty predict that *ijtihad* conceived and conducted in this new
medium will ontologically change the age-old Muslim practice, similar to the
way it underwent change because of modernist pressures."

It is this same defiance of change while embodying it that also infuses the
essay by Carl Ernst. Ernst used his experience as a visiting American scholar in
Malaysia during 2005 to inquire into the layered meaning of the slogan that
became the hallmark of the most recent Malay prime minister.

For Abdullah Badawi, Islam Hadhari, or civilizational Islam, represented the
way in which Islam remained in the modern commercial world of global capitalism, but with its own brand name: Islam as above all equivalent to development,
defined in market terms that conjoin ethics to economic prowess to regional
success to global renown. The Islam Hadhari slogan relates to the familiar slogan that has marked Malaysia's larger neighbor, Indonesia, and one suspects that

Badawi hoped to achieve as much traction with Islam Hadhari as Indonesian politicians have with *pancasila*, or the five principles. Both have the double virtue of simplicity and ambiguity, and while the Indonesian model continues to be debated, above all because its first postulate does not specify Islam as its referent,[23] the Malay motto suggests the historical origin as well as contemporary relevance of Islam. It projects Islam as, above all, an inclusive civilizational construct. Ibn Khaldun, the fourteenth-century Maghribi jurist-cum-historian, becomes the counterpart to Samuel Huntington, the contemporary American advocate of civilizations as inherent units of competition. Unlike Huntington, Ibn Khaldun embraces opposites within his deployment of *ʿumran* or civilization as the umbrella category for urbane, civil units connected to one another within the cosmos or oikoumene.

All this may seem progressive, irenic, and laudable, except it too has an ideological edge. Badawi projects himself, and by extension Malaysia, as the flag bearer in Southeast Asia for the Muslim past and also the carrier of Muslim potential for the near- and long-term future in the global economy. Yet beyond the seeming benevolence of this project is a war within Islam for the heart and soul of its core values. Badawi wants to arrogate to the Malay state the primary role of guiding Islam worldwide toward what has been described as "Knowledge Society by 2020." The cyberanthropologist David Hakken, quoted at length by Ernst, has demonstrated that this developmental view of Islam Hadhari conflicts with other views that might be more naturally expressive of pluralism (all linked to a common source) or cosmopolitanism (all related to a common ethos). For Hakken it is the postmodern form of Islam Hadhari ethics that dominates, all the more so since it implicitly competes with another slogan/national aspiration, *masyarakat madani* or (Muslim) civil society, linked to a prior deputy prime minister, Anwar Ibrahim.

Beyond these debates what has become clear, and what Ernst illustrates from numerous sources and with cumulative insight, is the political control of civil society by the Malay state. Religion, in Malaysia as in Turkey and also in Pakistan, is packaged as a state monopoly. Even more than in Turkey or Pakistan, "since the early twentieth century, it has been illegal in Malaysia to publish anything on Islam without permission from the state authorities. This rigorous state control of religion stands in contrast with the situation in neighboring Indonesia, where a different colonial experience and secular nation-state articulation allows an enormous nongovernmental public space [that is, civil society] for the expression of religion."

Though there may be no single route to a cosmopolitan future, the several routes offered by these essays provide a road map through numerous trajectories of the modern Muslim world. They leave little doubt that Muslims will be as well represented in the global future as they have been in the historic past of world civilizations. Hodgson rather than Huntington will have the final word, and Muslims as well as non-Muslims will be the beneficiaries of that colloquy.

NOTES

1. Marshall G. S. Hodgson, *The Venture of Islam: Conscience and History in a World Civilization*, 3 vols. (Chicago: University of Chicago Press, 1974), 1:28–29.

2. Fazlur Rahman, "Approaches to Islam in Religious Studies: Review Essay" in *Approaches to Islam in Religious Studies*, ed. Richard C. Martin (Tucson: University of Arizona Press, 1985), 202.

3. Ibid.

4. Hodgson, *Venture of Islam*, 1:30–45, introduces this revisionist term as part of a larger effort to both define civilization studies beyond the Oriental studies grid and also to link civilization in its broadest trajectory to Islamic studies beyond the Arab / Middle East geopolitical time frame. Thirty-five years later, his is a vision yet to be implemented, either within Islamic studies or related disciplines.

5. Thomas A. Tweed, *Crossing and Dwelling: A Theory of Religion* (Cambridge, Mass.: Harvard University Press, 2006), 30.

6. Jonathan Z. Smith, *Imagining Religion: From Babylon to Jonestown* (Chicago: University of Chicago Press, 1982), 28–29.

7. José Casanova, *Public Religions in the Modern World* (Chicago: University of Chicago Press, 1994), 65–66.

8. First published in *Boston Review* 19, no 5 (1994): 1–8, it was reprinted in Nussbaum's *For Love of Country?* ed. Joshua Cohen (Boston: Beacon, 2002), 3–20.

9. Louis A. Ruprecht Jr., *Symposia: Plato, the Erotic, and Moral Value* (Albany: State University of New York Press, 1999), 14.

10. David A. Hollinger, *Postethnic America: Beyond Multiculturalism* (New York: Basic Books, 1995), 3–4.

11. See Abdullahi Ahmed An-Naʿim, *Islam and the Secular State: Negotiating the Future of Shariʿa* (Cambridge, Mass.: Harvard University Press, 2008), 260. He invoked this phrase in discussing the relationship between Islam, the state, and society in contemporary Indonesia, but it also applies to the dyadic categories under review in this essay.

12. The argument I am advancing here evokes in summary form the distinction elaborated by Bruce Lincoln in *Holy Terrors: Thinking about Religion after September 11* (Chicago: University of Chicago Press, 2003), 6–7. There Lincoln demurs from Clifford Geertz, Asad, and others in offering his own "polythetic and flexible" definition of religion, to wit, that it comprises discourse, practices, community, and institutions. I prefer to use but three tangents and terms to discuss religion, namely, language, values, and institutions, though my crucial agreement with Lincoln, and indebtedness to him, is to accent the critical role of institutions in any assessment of what is meant by religion and how it functions cross-culturally.

13. An-Naʿim, *Islam and the Secular State*, 261.

14. A *milla* is self-governing religious community, existing under the authority and protection of the Ottoman Turkish state.

15. Abdul Rauf, in turn, is indebted to Muhammad Asad, the quintessential Muslim cosmopolitan of the twentieth century.

16. Appiah unreflexively echoes Olivier Roy's use of the term *neofundamentalists*, and that choice, at least, must be revisited, if not revised, by reference to Peter Mandaville, to wit, that neither neofundamentalism nor post-Islamism, another Roy neologism, have analytic utility unless one presumes that fundamentalism, as also Islamism, were coherent, homogeneous ideologies, which, as numerous case studies have shone, they were not. See Peter Mandaville, *Global Political Islam* (London: Routledge, 2007), 348, and Asaf Bayat, "What Is Post-Islamism?" *ISIM Review* 16 (2005): 5.

17. It is this aspect of Jackson's work that Vincent J. Cornell has extensively and productively examined in the initial essay of this volume.

18. Islamist leaders are further split into two subcategories according to their educational background: one subset is trained in secular schools, the other in religious seminaries or madrassas.

19. Hamid Dabashi, *Authority in Islam* (Rutgers, N.J.: Transaction, 1992), 71.

20. And also like Gilmartin, Martin and Barzegar cite the lucid, evocative scholarship of Peter Brown, in particular his study *The Cult of the Saints: Its Rise and Function in Latin Christianity* (Chicago: University of Chicago Press, 1981).

21. See J. R. McNeill and William H. McNeill, *The Human Web: A Bird's-Eye View of World History* (New York: Norton, 2003).

22. Ernst Bloch, *Heritage of Our Times*, trans. Neville and Stephen Plaice (Cambridge: Polity, 1991), 97. "Not all people exist in the same Now. They do so only externally, through the fact that they can be seen today. But they are thereby not yet living at the same with others."

23. For the discussion of the political and religious complexities of *pancasila*, within a broad framework that analyzes also the tension between diversity and pluralism in contemporary Indonesia, see An-Na'im, *Islam and the Secular State*, 223–66.

Contributors

ABBAS BARZEGAR is an assistant professor of Islam in the Department of Religious Studies at Georgia State University. His research focuses on competing historical narratives through the lens of Sunni-Shi'ite polemics in the early 'Abbasid period. With Richard Martin, he coauthored the volume *Islamism: Contested Perspectives on Political Islam* (2009).

VINCENT J. CORNELL is Asa Griggs Candler Professor of Middle East and Islamic Studies at Emory University. His major works are *The Way of Abu Madyan* (1996), *Realm of the Saint: Power and Authority in Moroccan Sufism* (1998), and the five-volume set *Voices of Islam* (2007). He is currently working in Islamic theology and moral philosophy and is a key participant in the Building Bridges Seminars hosted by the archbishop of Canterbury.

CARL W. ERNST is the William R. Kenan Jr. Distinguished Professor of Religious Studies and director of the Carolina Center for the Study of the Middle East and Muslim Civilizations at the University of North Carolina at Chapel Hill. His published research, based on the study of Arabic, Persian, and Urdu, has been mainly devoted to the study of Islam and Sufism.

KATHERINE PRATT EWING is an associate professor of cultural anthropology and religion at Duke University. She has done field research in Pakistan and Turkey and among Muslims in Germany and the United States. Her most recent books are *Stolen Honor: Stigmatizing Muslim Men in Berlin* (2008) and the edited volume *Being and Belonging: Muslims in the United States since 9/11* (2008).

DAVID GILMARTIN is a professor of history at North Carolina State University. He is a specialist in the modern history of the Indian subcontinent and European imperialism. His publications include *Empire and Islam: Punjab and the Making of Pakistan* (1988) and *Beyond Turk and Hindu* (2000, coedited with Bruce B. Lawrence).

JAMILLAH KARIM is an assistant professor of religious studies at Spelman College in Atlanta. She received her Ph.D. in religious studies from Duke University in 2004. Her research interests include Islam and Muslims (African American, South Asian, and Arab) in the United States, Islamic feminism, race and ethnicity, and immigration and transnational identity. She is the author of *American Muslim Women: Negotiating Race, Class, and Gender within the Ummah* (2009).

SCOTT KUGLE is a research scholar in comparative religious and Islamic studies. His research focuses on Sufi communities in North Africa and South Asia. His book *Sufis and Saints' Bodies* (2007) addresses how the human body is imagined in Islamic culture. His recent book *Homosexuality in Islam* (2010) examines how Isalamic theology deals with sexuality and gender diversity.

CHARLES KURZMAN is a professor of sociology at the University of North Carolina at Chapel Hill. He is author of *The Unthinkable Revolution in Iran* (2004) and *Democracy Denied, 1905–1915* (2008) and editor of *Liberal Islam: A Source Book* (1998) and *Modernist Islam, 1840–1940: A Sourcebook* (2002).

BRUCE B. LAWRENCE is the Nancy and Jeffrey Marcus Humanities Professor of Religion at Duke University. From South Asian Sufism to American Islam, his research and writings have spanned a wide range of the Islamic tradition. As a comparativist of religion, he is also interested in issues of religious violence and fundamentalism. Most recently he is the author of *The Qur'an: A Biography* (2006) and an editor of *On Violence: A Reader* (2007, with Aisha Karim).

RICHARD C. MARTIN is a professor of Islamic studies and history of religions at Emory University and past president of the American Research Center in Egypt. He writes and lectures on Islamic religious thought; religion, social conflict, and violence; and Islam and secularism. With Mark R. Woodward and Dwi Atmaja, he is the author of *Defenders of Reason in Islam: Mu'tazilism from Medieval School to Modern Symbol* (1997). He is editor in chief of the *Encyclopedia of Islam and the Muslim World* (2004).

EBRAHIM MOOSA is an associate professor of Islamic studies in the Department of Religion at Duke University. His research focuses on moral philosophy, studies in al-Ghazali, and comparative Muslim ethics. He is the author of the award-winning book *Ghazali and the Poetics of Imagination* (2005) and edited *Revival and Reform in Islam: A Study of Islamic Fundamentalism* (2000), by Fazlur Rahman. Moosa was named a 2005 Carnegie Scholar for research on the madrassas of the Indo-Pakistan subcontinent.

IJLAL NAQVI is a Ph.D. candidate in sociology at the University of North Carolina at Chapel Hill. He studies questions of democracy in Muslim-majority countries and is currently working on his dissertation, titled "Access to Power: Development, Culture, and Democracy in Pakistan."

A. KEVIN REINHART teaches in the religion department at Dartmouth College. His research interests include Islamic theology, ritual, and Late Ottoman intellectual history. He is author of *Before Revelation: The Boundaries of Muslim Moral Thought* (1995). His essay "Legitimacy and Authority in Islamic Discussions of

'Martyrdom Operations' / 'Suicide Bombings'" appeared in *Enemy Combatants, Terrorism, and Armed Conflict Law* (2008).

Louis A. Ruprecht Jr. holds the William M. Suttles Chair as Professor of Religions of the Ancient Mediterranean in the Department of Religious Studies at Georgia State University. Most recently he is author of *God Gardened East* (2008) and *This Tragic Gospel* (2008). He is currently working in the Secret Archives of the Vatican Library in order to complete two book projects on the origins and subsequent history of the Vatican Museums.

Omid Safi is a professor of Islamic studies at University of North Carolina at Chapel Hill and the chair of the Study of Islam at the American Academy of Religion. He is the editor of the volume *Progressive Muslims: On Justice, Gender, and Pluralism* (2003) and *Voices of Islam: Voices of Change* (2007). His *Memories of Muhammad* was published by HarperCollins in 2009.

Tony K. Stewart is a professor of South Asian religions and literatures at North Carolina State University and the director of the Bangla Language Institute on the campus of Independent University, Bangladesh in Dhaka. His research and teaching focus on the early modern religious communities of the Bangla-speaking world. He is the author *The Final Word: The Caitanya Caritamrta and the Grammar of Religious Tradition* (2010). His *Fabulous Females and Peerless Pirs: Tales of Mad Adventure in Old Bengal* (2004) began a sustained examination of Hindu-Muslim interaction in Bengali folk hagiographies. He is currently working on a book with the working title *The Romance of the Pirs: Muslims and Hindus in the Mythic Literatures of Early Bengal*, which will be accompanied by an anthology of translated works.

Index

38334633R00205

Made in the USA
Middletown, DE
07 March 2019